lonely pl

USA

TOP SIGHTS, AUTHENTIC EXPERIENCES

THIS EDITION WRITTEN AND RESEARCHED BY

Karla Zimmerman, Amy C Balfour, Sandra Bao,
Sara Benson, Adam Karlin, Becky Ohlsen, Zora O'Neill,
Kevin Raub, Brendan Sainsbury, Regis St Louis,
Ryan Ver Berkmoes, Mara Vorhees, Greg Ward

Lonely Planet's
Ultimate USA Itinerary

This is Lonely Planet's ultimate USA itinerary, which ensures you'll see the best of everything the country has to offer.

For other recommended paths to travel, check out our itineraries section (p18). For inspiration on themed travel, see If You Like... (p24).

From left: Lincoln Memorial (p131), Washington, DC; Art Deco Historic District (p186), Miami; Mule deer, Yosemite National Park (p321)

ROZANNE HAKALA / GETTY IMAGES ©; PAUL GIAMOU / GETTY IMAGES ©; DAVID COURTENAY / GETTY IMAGES ©

Week 1

Washington, DC, to Boston

❶ Begin in **Washington, DC**, the nation's capital. Spend two days taking in the memorials, monuments and free Smithsonian museums. At night, eat and drink with the cool cats in Shaw or Logan Circle.

🚗 3½ hours or 🚌 4 to 5 hours

❷ Next up: **New York City**, America's largest metropolis. With three days you can ramble in Central Park, see the Statue of Liberty, detour across the Brooklyn Bridge and catch a Broadway show.

🚗 4 hours or 🚌 4½ hours

❸ Onward to **Boston** for a few days. Spend one day exploring the Freedom Trail's historic sites and North End's atmospheric eateries. Spend the next taking a boat trip to Provincetown on Cape Cod.

✈ 3½ hours or 🚌 34 hours

Hudson Bay

Gulf of St. Lawrence

Minnesota

Lake Superior

OTTAWA

Maine

Augusta

Montpelier

St. Paul

Michigan

Lake Huron

NH

NEW ENGLAND p87

Wisconsin

Lake Michigan

VT

Concord

Mississippi

Lansing

Madison

New York

Albany

MA

Boston

RI

Hartford

Providence

Des Moines

Iowa

Pennsylvania

CT

NEW YORK p35

Illinois

CHICAGO p155

Harrisburg

NJ

Columbus

Trenton

Springfield

Indianapolis

Annapolis

MD

Dover

Missouri

Ohio

WV

DE

Jefferson City

Indiana

Charleston

WASHINGTON, DC p127

eka

Frankfort

Virginia

Richmond

Arkansas

Kentucky

Raleigh

Nashville

Tennessee

North Carolina

APPALACHIAN MOUNTAINS

South Carolina

Little Rock

Atlanta

Columbia

Alabama

Georgia

Mississippi

Louisiana

Jackson

Montgomery

NORTH ATLANTIC OCEAN

Baton Rouge

Mississippi

Tallahassee

WALT DISNEY WORLD p201

NEW ORLEANS p213

Orlando

Florida

MIAMI p179

NASSAU

BAHAMAS

Gulf of Mexico

HAVANA

CUBA

Welcome to the USA

America is home to such diverse cities as Los Angeles, Las Vegas, Chicago, Miami, Boston and New York City – each a brimming metropolis whose name alone conjures a million different notions of culture, cuisine and entertainment.

This is a country of road trips and great open skies, where four million miles of highways lead past red-rock deserts, below towering mountain peaks, and across fertile wheat fields that roll off toward the horizon. The scenic country lanes of New England are a fine starting point for the great American road trip.

On one evening in the US, thick barbecue ribs and smoked brisket come piping hot at a Southern roadhouse, while talented chefs blend organic produce with Asian accents at award-winning West Coast restaurants. Steaming plates of fresh lobster served off a Maine pier, oysters and champagne in a fashion-forward wine bar in California, a decadent slice of deep-dish pizza in Chicago – these are just a few ways to dine à la Americana.

The USA has made tremendous contributions to the arts. Georgia O'Keeffe's wild landscapes, Robert Rauschenberg's surreal collages, Alexander Calder's elegant mobiles and Jackson Pollock's drip paintings have entered the vernacular of 20th-century art, while Chicago and New York have become veritable drawing boards for the great architects of the modern era.

> *a country of road trips and great open skies*

Golden Gate Bridge (p292), San Francisco
FRANCISCO MARTINEZ / ALAMY STOCK PHOTO ©

CANADA

Washington

Olympia

Columbia

Montana *Missouri* North Dakota

Helena **Bismarck**

Salem

Oregon Idaho South Dakota

Boise **Pierre**

Wyoming

Nevada R O C K Y Cheyenne Nebraska

Carson Salt Lake City

City **Denver** Lin

Sacramento **YOSEMITE NATIONAL** Utah M O U N T A I N S

PARK p321

SAN FRANCISCO *Colorado* Colorado Kansas

p289

LAS VEGAS p235

California **GRAND CANYON** Santa Fe Oklahoma

NATIONAL PARK p247 City

LOS ANGELES p261 Okl

Phoenix New

Rio Grande Mexico

Arizona

Texas

N O R T H

P A C I F I C

O C E A N

MEXICO

N

0   1,000 km

0   500 miles

Week 2

Miami to Chicago

❹ Start in **Miami**. Check out the Art Deco Historic District, lively Little Havana, splashy Miami Beach and nightlife-rich South Beach during a two-day stint.

✈ 1 hour or 🚗 4 hours

❺ Head north to Walt Disney World. Spend one day in the Magic Kingdom, seeing Cinderella's Castle and the evening fireworks. The next day go on safari at Animal Kingdom.

✈ 1½ hours or 🚗 9 hours

❻ Drive or fly to New Orleans. Take two days to soak up the French Quarter manors, the Tremé's history, the spicy Creole food and jazzy clubs.

✈ 2½ hours or 🚃 19 hours

❼ Head to Chicago for a day of sky-high architecture, vast museums and hefty pizza.

✈ 3¾ hours or 🚗 26 hours

Staying Longer

Las Vegas to Yosemite National Park

❽ Fly or drive to **Las Vegas** for a few days of flashing neon, lavish casinos and eye-popping curiosities on the Strip.

🚗 5 hours

❾ Drive to the Grand Canyon, America's most mesmerizing abyss, for a couple of days of hiking.

🚗 7½ hours

❿ Motor on to Los Angeles and bask for three days amid Hollywood's movie stars and on Santa Monica's beaches.

✈ 1½ hours or 🚗 6 to 7 hours

⓫ Go to San Francisco for two days, where the Golden Gate Bridge, Alcatraz and foodie-packed Ferry Building await.

🚗 4 hours

⓬ Drive to Yosemite National Park and immerse yourself in the jaw-dropping, granite-peaked beauty.

Contents

Plan Your Trip

USA's Top 12 6
Itineraries 18
If You Like................ 24
Month by Month..... 26
Get Inspired............ 29
Family Travel........... 30
Need to Know......... 32

New York City 35

Central Park..............38
Statue of Liberty...... 44
Brooklyn Bridge........ 46
MoMA..........................48
The High Line............ 50
Broadway 52
Walking Tour:
Urban Icons................ 54
Walking Tour:
SoHo Shops 56
Sights............................58
Tours 69
Shopping 69
Entertainment..............72
Eating..............................75
Drinking & Nightlife...... 81
Where to Stay...............85

New England 87

Fall Foliage 90
Acadia National
Park...............................92
Freedom Trail 96
Walking Tour:
Freedom Trail 98
Boston 100
Sights............................100
Tours 106
Shopping 106
Entertainment............ 107

Eating............................108
Drinking & Nightlife.....110
Salem............................112
Cape Cod & the
Islands 112
Nantucket.....................115
Martha's Vineyard........117
Vermont........................118
New Hampshire 120
Coastal Maine 121

Washington, DC 127

National Mall 130
Capitol Hill 136
Walking Tour:
Capitol Hill 138
Sights............................140
Activities 144
Tours 145
Entertainment............ 145
Eating............................ 146
Drinking & Nightlife....150

Chicago 155

Millenium Park..........158
Art Institute of
Chicago 160
Walking Tour:
Art of the City..........162
Sights............................ 164
Activities 170
Tours 170
Shopping 171
Entertainment..............171
Eating............................ 173
Drinking & Nightlife ... 175

Miami 179

The Everglades 182
Art Deco Miami.........186
Walking Tour:
Art Deco Miami.........188

Sights............................193
Activities 196
Entertainment............196
Eating............................196
Drinking & Nightlife....198

Orlando & Walt
Disney World 201

Walt Disney World
Resort 204
Orlando 208

New Orleans 213

Mardi Gras................ 216
St Charles Avenue
Streetcar 220
Sights............................222
Tours 228
Entertainment............228
Eating............................ 229
Drinking & Nightlife ...232

Las Vegas 235

Cruising the Strip... 238
Sights & Activities 240
Entertainment............ 241
Eating............................242
Drinking & Nightlife....243

Grand Canyon
National Park 247

South Rim
Overlooks 250
South Rim.....................252
North Rim.....................255
Route 66 257
Flagstaff.......................257

Los Angeles 261

Santa Monica Pier..264
Hollywood 266
Griffith Park............. 268
Walking Tour:
Venice 272
Sights........................ 274
Activities................... 277
Shopping 279
Entertainment............279
Eating........................ 280
Drinking & Nightlife... 283

San Francisco 289

Golden Gate Bridge... 292
Cable Cars................ 294
Alcatraz 296
Ferry Building 300
Chinatown................ 302

Sights........................ 304
Tours 309
Shopping 310
Entertainment.............311
Eating........................ 313
Drinking & Nightlife.... 316
Where to Stay............. 319

Yosemite National Park 321

Glacier Point 324
Half Dome 326
**Yosemite Valley
Waterfalls................. 328**
Sights........................ 330
Activities....................332
Tours 332
Eating........................332

In Focus

USA Today 336
History 338
Food & Drink.........348
Sports 352
Arts & Culture 355

Survival Guide

Directory A–Z 359
Transport 369
Index 377
Symbols &
Map Key................386

Plan Your Trip
USA's Top 12

New York City

Home to striving artists, hedge-fund moguls and immigrants from every corner of the globe, New York City (p35) is constantly reinventing itself. It remains one of the world centers of fashion, theater, food, music, publishing, advertising and finance. A staggering number of museums, parks and ethnic neighborhoods are scattered through the five boroughs. Do as every New Yorker does: hit the streets. Every block reflects the character and history of this dizzying kaleidoscope, and on even a short walk you can cross continents. From left: Times Square (p63), Flatiron Building (p63)

New England

Petite New England (p87) packs in a lot between its rolling hills, rocky peaks and 5000 miles of coastline. Boston is arguably the USA's most historic city – site of the Boston Tea Party, Paul Revere's ride and the first battle of the Revolutionary War. Cape Cod is the perfect place to cool off on dune-backed beaches. Maine's Acadia National Park offers towering sea cliffs and surf-pounded shores. Meanwhile, covered bridges, steeple churches and seafood shacks pop up across the region. Top: New Hampshire (p120); Bottom: Portland (p121)

Washington, DC

No matter what your politics, it's hard to not fall for the nation's capital (p127). A buzz percolates among the city's grand boulevards, iconic monuments and power-broking buildings. There's no better place for exploring American history, whether tracing your hand along the Vietnam Veterans Memorial, checking out the Constitution at the National Archives, or gaping at Abe Lincoln's hat at the Smithsonian museums. Cobblestoned neighborhoods, groovy markets and jazzy bohemian quarters add to the vibe. White House (p140)

Chicago

The Windy City will blow you away with its cloud-scraping architecture, lakefront beaches and world-class museums. But its true mojo is its blend of high culture and earthy pleasures. Is there another city that dresses its Picasso sculpture in local sports-team gear? Where residents queue for hot dogs in equal measure to some of North America's top restaurants? Sure, the winters are brutal, but come summer, Chicago (p155) fetes the warm days with food and music festivals. Jay Pritzker Pavilion (p159), designed by Frank Gehry

Miami

How does one city get so lucky? Most content themselves with one or two highlights, but Miami (p179) seems to have it all. Beyond the stunning beaches and Art Deco Historic District, there's culture at every turn. In cigar-filled dance halls, Havana expats dance to *son* and boleros; in exclusive nightclubs stiletto-heeled, fiery-eyed Brazilian models shake to Latin hip-hop; and in the park old men clack dominoes. To top it off, street vendors and restaurants dish out diverse flavors from the Caribbean, Cuba, Argentina and Spain.

TRAVELSTOCK.CA / GETTY IMAGES ©

Walt Disney World

Want to set the bar high? Call yourself 'the happiest place on earth.' Walt Disney World (p201) does, and then pulls out all the stops to deliver the exhilarating sensation that you are the most important character in the show. Despite all the frantic rides, entertainment and nostalgia, the magic is watching your own child swell with belief after they have made Goofy laugh, been curtsied to by Cinderella, guarded the galaxy with Buzz Lightyear and battled Darth Maul like your very own Jedi knight.

New Orleans

Reborn after Hurricane Katrina in 2005, New Orleans (p213) is back. Caribbean-colonial architecture, Creole cuisine and a riotous air of celebration seem more alluring than ever in the Big Easy. Nights are spent catching Dixieland jazz, blues and rock in bouncing live-music joints, and the city's annual festivals are famous the world over. 'Nola' is also a food-loving town; feast on lip-smacking jambalaya, soft-shelled crab and Louisiana *cochon* (pulled pork) before hitting the bar scene on Frenchman St.

8

Las Vegas

Sin City is a neon-fueled ride through the nerve center of American strike-it-rich fantasies. See billionaires' names gleam from the marquees of luxury hotels. Hear a raucous soundscape of slot machines, clinking martini glasses and the hypnotic beats of DJs spinning till dawn. Sip cocktails under palm trees and play blackjack by the pool. Visit Paris, the Wild West and a tropical island, all in one night. It's all here in Las Vegas (p235) and it's open 24 hours, for the mere price of a poker chip (and a little luck). Bellagio (p239)

GAVIN HELLIER / ROBERTHARDING / GETTY IMAGES ©

PETERSCODE / GETTY IMAGES ©

9

Grand Canyon National Park

You've seen it on film and heard about it from all and sundry who've made the trip. Is it worth the hype? The answer is a resounding 'yes'. The Grand Canyon (p247) is vast and nearly incomprehensible in age – it took 6 million years for the canyon to form, and some rocks exposed along its walls are 2 billion years old. Peer over the edge and you'll confront the great power and mystery of this earth we live on. Once you see it, no other natural phenomenon quite compares. From left: South Rim (p252); Mule deer

ANDREW KENNELLY / GETTY IMAGES ©

RICHARD CUMMINS / GETTY IMAGES ©

MATTHEW MICAH WRIGHT / GETTY IMAGES ©

Los Angeles

Although it's the entertainment capital of the world, there's more to Los Angeles (p261) than silver-screen stars. This is the city of quirky Venice Beach, carnivals in Santa Monica and rugged Griffith Park. Dig deeper and you'll find museums displaying every kind of ephemera and vibrant multiethnic 'hoods where great food lies just around the corner. And yes, the movie studios and celebrities are here, too, in a little place called Hollywood. Clockwise from top: Griffith Observatory (p270); Huntington Beach (p286); Venice Beach (p272)

JEAN-PIERRE LESCOURRET / GETTY IMAGES ©

San Francisco

Amid the clatter of trams and the thick fog that sweeps in by night, the diverse hill and valley neighborhoods of San Francisco (p289) invite long days of wandering, with colorful Victorian architecture, great indie shops and gorgeous waterfront views. Cycle across the Golden Gate Bridge, commune with poets in the Haight and immerse in the Castro's mighty gay scene. You'll eat well wherever you go, from tiny dim-sum spots in Chinatown to Michelin-starred bistros to mural-clad taquerias in the Mission District. Cable cars (p294)

KAORI TANABE / GETTY IMAGES ©

Yosemite National Park

Yosemite's iconic glacier-carved valley never fails to get the heart racing, even when it's loved bumper-to-bumper in summer. In springtime, get drenched by the spray of its thundering snowmelt waterfalls, and twirl singing to the *Sound of Music* in high-country meadows awash with wildflowers. The scenery of Yosemite (p321) is intoxicating, with dizzying rock walls and formations, and ancient giant sequoia trees. If you look for it, you'll find solitude and space in the 1169 sq miles of development-free wilderness.

Plan Your Trip
Five-Day Itinerary

S. GREG PANOSIAN / GETTY IMAGES ©

East Coast Exploration

This trip takes in three cities with distinct personalities – politically charged Washington, DC, cosmopolitan New York City and historic and heady Boston. Cap it off with a jaunt out to Provincetown for a look at Cape Cod's lovely seaside.

❶ Washington, DC (p127)

Spend the day taking in the grandeur of the **Mall**. Admire the mighty-domed **Capitol**, then head to the nearby **National Gallery of Art** for a look at the staggering collection. Stroll past the **Washington Monument** and somber **Vietnam Veterans Memorial**, before ending at the **Lincoln Memorial**. Come evening, have dinner and drinks in one of the lively spots off Dupont Circle or Logan Circle.

○ **Washington, DC to New York City**

🚆 **3½ hrs** Amtrak Northeast Regional train to Penn Station

❷ New York City (p35)

After arriving, promenade in lovely **Central Park**, browse the galleries of the vast **Metropolitan Museum of Art**, and end the day with ethnic eats and bar-hopping in the East Village. On day two, catch an early-morning subway to Lower Manhattan and walk across the **Brooklyn Bridge**.

DENISTANGNEYJR / GETTY IMAGES ©

Afterward, wander through Chinatown, then go up to SoHo for lunch. In the evening, dine in a cozy, candlelit spot in the West Village, followed by live jazz at the **Village Vanguard**.

○ **New York City to Boston**

🚌 **4hrs** Amtrak Northeast Regional train to South Station

❸ Boston (p100)

Start the day on **Boston Common** and set off on the brick-lined Freedom Trail, wandering past historic homes and fabled meeting houses. Have lunch at the venerable Union Oyster House. In the evening feast on old-world cuisine at a charming local haunt in the North End, Boston's 'Little Italy'. End the night at the Warren Tavern, one of the city's most atmospheric old pubs.

○ **Boston to Provincetown**

🚢 **1½ hrs** Departs from the World Trade Center Pier

❹ Provincetown (p113)

Hire a bike and ride through forest and along dunes on the Cape Cod Rail Trail. After the ride, refuel on juicy crustaceans at the Lobster Pot. Take a quick stroll through town then head out to Race Point Beach, dramatically set at the northern tip of the Cape. For dinner, feast on yet more seafood, then grab a cocktail at a waterfront bar and watch the night unfold.

Left: Public Garden, Boston (p104)
Right: Race Point Beach (p113), Provincetown

Plan Your Trip
Ten-Day Itinerary

Big Apple to the Big Easy

Delve into two of the USA's most fascinating cities – New York City and Washington, DC – for their world-class museums, iconic buildings, and top-notch food and entertainment options. Then head south for sparkling beaches, Disney magic and Cajun cooking on a ramble through Miami, Orlando and New Orleans.

❶ New York City (p35)

Spend two days exploring the metropolis, visiting memorable people-watching 'hoods such as Chinatown, the West and East Villages, SoHo, Nolita and the Upper West Side. Museum-hop down the Upper East Side. Wander in **Central Park**, along the **High Line** and across the **Brooklyn Bridge**. Prioritize iconic sights, including the **Statue of Liberty** and **MoMA**. In the evenings, catch a Broadway show or a concert at legendary **Carnegie Hall** or the **Lincoln Center**.

○ **New York City to Washington, DC**

🚃 **3½ hrs** Amtrak Northeast Regional train

❷ Washington, DC (p127)

Take two days to see the nation's capital. Spend one day on the **National Mall**, exploring the monuments, memorials and Smithsonian museums. On the next day, head to Georgetown for shopping, café-hopping and ambling along atmospheric tree-lined streets. At night, seek out eating and drinking hot spots in Logan Circle, Shaw and Capitol Hill.

○ **Washington, DC to Miami**

✈ **2½ hrs**

❸ Miami (p179)

Get ready for two days in body-beautiful Miami. Stroll the Technicolor backdrop of the **Art Deco Historic District**, delve into

New York City ①
3½ hrs 🚌
Washington, DC ②

2½ hrs ✈

✈ 1½ hrs

⑤
New
Orleans

④
Walt Disney
World ③ Miami
🚗 4 hrs

JOHN ELK / GETTY IMAGES ©

the contemporary art scene in Wynwood and connect with Miami's Latin roots in Little Havana. Set aside plenty of downtime for playing in the waves, and for long walks on **Miami Beach**, and plan at least one night out in South Beach.

◆ Miami to Walt Disney World

🚗 **4hrs** Head north along Florida's Turnpike toll road

④ Walt Disney World (p201)

So many theme parks, so little time. You'll have to make some tough choices for your two-day stay. The safe bet: spend day one in the **Magic Kingdom**, seeing Cinderella's Castle, Pirates of the Caribbean and nightly fireworks; on day two go on safari at **Animal Kingdom** and see a show in the Tree of Life. Epcot is another top option.

◆ Walt Disney World to New Orleans

🚗 **9hrs** West via I-75 and I-10

✈ **1½ hrs** From Orlando

⑤ New Orleans (p213)

By day explore the French Quarter and **Jackson Square**, or head to the Tremé to learn about New Orleans' deep African American roots. Ride the **St Charles Avenue Streetcar** and ogle the mansions. In the evenings, have a Cajun feast at **Cochon** or **Coop's**, and then go to hear live jazz at a club on Frenchman St.

Left: Art deco buildings, Miami (p179)
Right: St Louis Cathedral (p222), New Orleans

Plan Your Trip
Two-Week Itinerary

PHOTOGRAPH BY ASIM BHARWANI / GETTY IMAGES ©

Cross-Country Icons

This journey starts in the heartland, with Chicago, and then swoops west, road-tripping through neon-lit Las Vegas, movie-star-rich Los Angeles and freewheeling San Francisco. A national park with an awe-inspiring canyon pops up, as does another with mammoth mountains and raging waterfalls.

❶ Chicago (p155)

It has been said that Chicago is the most American of cities, so begin here for a few days. Visit the venerable **Art Institute**, eat deep-dish pizza, gape at the sky-high architecture, meander through the sculptural wonderland of **Millennium Park**, and hit a few of the city's legendary blues clubs.

Chicago to Las Vegas

3¾ hrs (by plane)

❷ Las Vegas (p235)

Spend two days in Sin City, aka Las Vegas, checking out the surreal and over-the-top design of this casino kingdom, where you can travel from ancient Rome to the South Pacific without leaving the Strip. At night, see top-notch shows and take in the city's riotous nightlife.

Las Vegas to Grand Canyon National Park

5hrs Via Hwy 93, I-40 and Hwy 180 to the South Rim.

❸ Grand Canyon (p247)

The Grand Canyon's age and vast size boggle the mind. Allocate a couple of days in the park to hike, jaw-drop at the sunsets and revel in the experience of standing atop one of Earth's great wonders. The South Rim has the easiest access; the North Rim is more remote.

Grand Canyon National Park to Los Angeles

7½ hrs West via I-40

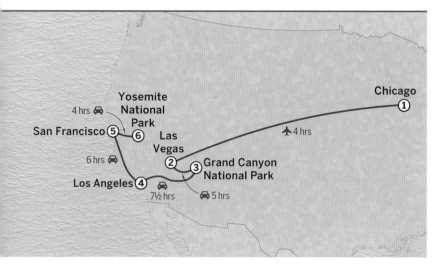

➍ Los Angeles (p261)

Hang out for three days in Los Angeles. Take in the beachside neighborhoods of tony Santa Monica and eccentric Venice. Spend a day wandering around Hollywood and ever-evolving Downtown, and eat your way around the globe in Little Tokyo. Snap the Hollywood sign from the **Griffith Observatory**, and celebrity-spot (or play in the waves) in Malibu.

➲ Los Angeles to San Francisco

🚗 **6hrs** North on I-5

🚗 **10hrs** Via Pacific Coast Hwy

➎ San Francisco (p289)

Spend two or three days in the gorgeous City by the Bay. There's loads to do: walk across the fog-clad **Golden Gate Bridge**, sail to the former prison island of **Alcatraz**, eat chowhound-style at the **Ferry Building**, explore evocative Chinatown and visit great museums. You'll drink and sup like a rock star wherever you go.

➲ San Francisco to Yosemite National Park

🚗 **4hrs** Via Hwy 120 or Hwy 140

➏ Yosemite National Park (p321)

End your trip with a few days in this dreamy landscape of dizzying granite peaks, thunderous waterfalls and gemstone lakes.

Left: Griffith Observatory (p270), Los Angeles

Plan Your Trip
If You Like...

Local Delicacies

Union Oyster House
Guess what gets shucked
and sucked in this Boston
restaurant? (p108)

Coop's Place Prime New
Orleans spot to sample
jambalaya and other Cajun
dishes. (p230)

Lobster Dock You just
can't beat a Maine seaside
shack for cracking into a
crustacean. (p124)

Giordano's Chicago's
deep-dish pizza behemoth.
(p174)

Exquisito Restaurant
Roast pork and plantains
in Miami's Little Havana.
(p197)

Architecture

Chicago Birthplace of the
skyscraper, Chicago has
magnificent works by many
of the great 20th-century
architects. (p155)

New York City The much-
photographed classics
include the art-deco Chrysler Building, the majestic
Brooklyn Bridge and the
spiraling Guggenheim. (p35)

Miami Miami's art-deco
district is a Technicolor
dream come to life. (p186)

San Francisco See elegant
Victorians, cutting-edge
21st-century masterpiec-
es and possibly the most
beautiful bridge in the
world. (p289)

New Orleans A gorgeous
French colonial center, plus
grand mansions reached via
a historic streetcar. (p213)

Historic Sights

Freedom Trail, Boston
Visit Paul Revere's home,
an 18th-century graveyard
and 14 other Revolutionary
War sites along the 2.5-mile
path. (p96)

Washington, DC See
where Lincoln was assassinated, Martin Luther King
Jr gave his famed speech
and Nixon's presidency was
undone. (p127)

Alcatraz Catch a ferry to
the notorious island prison
where D-block solitary cells
raise goosebumps. (p296)

**John F Kennedy National
Historic Site** Immerse
yourself in the Kennedy
lifestyle in the house where
Jack and various siblings
were born. (p106)

JOHN ELK / GETTY IMAGES ©

Museums

Smithsonian Institution
USA's premier treasure
chest is this group of 19
museums. (p141)

**Metropolitan Museum of
Art** Boasts a trove of two
million artworks. (p68)

Art Institute of Chicago
The nation's second-largest
art museum (after the Met)
has masterpieces aplenty.
(p160)

National WWII Museum
Powerful photos of D-Day
and gripping oral histories
bring it to life. (p225)

Mob Museum Learn about
Al Capone, Lucky Luciano
and other practitioners of
organized crime. (p240)

Beat Museum Artifacts
and literary ephemera pay
homage to Kerouac and
pals. (p304)

Parks

Acadia National Park
Maine's unspoiled wilder-
ness offers surging coastal
mountains, towering sea
cliffs and surf-pounded
beaches. (p92)

Everglades National Park
Florida's watery wonder-
land is home to crocodiles,
stealthy panthers and
mellow manatees. (p182)

Barataria Preserve Gators,
tree frogs and fluttering
birds hang in the swamp-
lands around New Orleans.
(p229)

Central Park Rich and
wild green wonderland in
the heart of New York City.
(p38)

Millennium Park Chicago's
downtown centerpiece
shines with whimsical public artworks. (p158)

Nightlife

New Orleans Go beyond
Bourbon St into the
neighborhoods where jazz,
Dixieland and zydeco spill
from clubs. (p232)

New York City As Sinatra
sang, it's the city that
doesn't sleep, with bars and
clubs staying open until
4am nightly. (p81)

Los Angeles Don't miss the
legendary Sunset Strip for
A-list artists. (p283)

Las Vegas Swish nightclubs galore and sexy, acrobatic live shows. (p243)

Chicago Cool little clubs
slouch on every corner and
blues, jazz and indie rock
spill out. (p175)

Left: Pritzker Pavilion (p159), Chicago
Right: Barataria Preserve (p229)

Plan Your Trip
Month by Month

TRISH MAYO / GETTY IMAGES ©

January

Snowfall blankets large swaths of the country. Ski resorts kick into high gear, while sun lovers go to warmer spots such as Florida.

✤ Chinese New Year

In late January or early February, you'll find colorful celebrations and feasting anywhere there's a Chinatown. NYC throws a festive parade, though San Francisco's is the best, with floats, firecrackers and bands.

February

Aside from mountain getaways, many Americans dread February with its long dark nights and frozen days. For foreign visitors, this can be the cheapest time to travel, with discount rates for flights and hotels.

✤ Mardi Gras

Held in late February or early March, on the day before Ash Wednesday, Mardi Gras (Fat Tuesday) is the finale of Carnival. New Orleans' celebrations (www.mardigrasnew orleans.com) are legendary as colorful parades, masquerade balls, feasting and plenty of hedonism rule the day.

March

The first blossoms of spring arrive in the south. In the mountains, it's still high season for skiing. Meanwhile, drunken spring-breakers descend on Florida.

✤ St Patrick's Day

On the 17th, the patron saint of Ireland is honored with brass bands and ever-flowing pints of Guinness; huge parades occur in New York, Boston and Chicago (which goes all-out by dyeing the Chicago River green).

✤ National Cherry Blossom Festival

The brilliant blooms of Japanese cherry blossoms around DC's Tidal Basin are celebrated with concerts, parades, taiko drumming, kite-flying and 90 other events during the five-week fest (www.national cherryblossomfestival.org). More than one million people go each year, so book ahead.

SEAN PAVONE / GETTY IMAGES ©

April

The weather is warming up, but April can still be unpredictable with chilly weather mixed with a few, teasingly warm days up north. Down south, it's a fine time to travel.

☆ Jazz Fest

On the last weekend in April, New Orleans hosts the country's best jazz jam (www. nojazzfest.com), with top-notch acts, great food and crafts.

🎊 Patriot's Day

Massachusetts' big day out falls on the third Monday in April and features Revolutionary War re-enactments and parades in Lexington and Concord, plus the Boston Marathon and a much-watched Red Sox game.

May

May is true spring and one of the loveliest times to travel, with blooming wildflowers and generally mild sunny weather.

🎊 Cinco de Mayo

Celebrate Mexico's victory over the French with salsa music and pitchers of margaritas across the country. LA and San Francisco throw some of the biggest bashes.

June

Summer is here; Americans head to the shore or to national parks and vacationers fill resorts, bringing higher prices.

🎊 Gay Pride

In some cities, gay pride celebrations last a week, but in San Francisco, it's a month-long party.

☆ Chicago Blues Festival

It's the globe's biggest free blues fest (www. chicagobluesfestival.us), with three days of the music that made Chicago famous. More than 500,000 people head to Grant Park's multiple stages in early June.

Left: Chinese New Year celebrations in New York City
Right: National Cherry Blossom Festival

🏊 Mermaid Parade

In Brooklyn, NYC, Coney Island celebrates summer's steamy arrival with a kitsch-loving parade (www.coneyisland.com), complete with skimpily attired mermaids and horn-blowing mermen.

☆ Tanglewood Musical Festival

Open-air concerts run all summer long (late June to early September) in an enchanting setting in western Massachusetts

July

Summer is in full swing. The prices are high and the crowds can be fierce, but it's one of the liveliest times to visit.

🏊 Independence Day

The nation celebrates its birthday with a bang, as nearly every town and city stages a massive fireworks show. Washington, DC, New York and Boston are all great spots.

☆ Pageant of the Masters

This eight-week-long arts fest (www.lagunafestivalofarts.org) brings a touch of the surreal to Laguna Beach, CA. On stage, costumed actors create living pictures – imitations of famous works of art – accompanied by narration and an orchestra.

August

Expect blasting heat, with temperatures and humidity less bearable the further south you go. You'll find packed beaches, high prices and empty cities on weekends, when residents escape to the nearest waterfront.

☆ Lollapalooza

This mondo rock fest (www.lollapalooza.com) sees more than 100 bands spilling off eight stages in Chicago's Grant Park on the first Friday-to-Sunday in August.

September

Cooler days arrive. Concert halls, gallery spaces and performing arts venues kick off a new season.

☆ New York Film Festival

Just one of many big film fests (www.filmlinc.com) in NYC; this one features world premieres from across the globe.

October

Temperatures fall as autumn brings fiery colors to northern climes. It's high season where the leaves are most brilliant (New England); elsewhere expect lower prices and fewer crowds.

🏊 Halloween

In NYC, you can don a costume and join the Halloween parade up Sixth Ave. West Hollywood in Los Angeles and San Francisco's Castro district are great places to see outrageous outfits. Salem, MA, also hosts spirited events throughout October.

November

No matter where you go, this is generally low season, with cold winds discouraging visitors despite lower prices (although airfares skyrocket around Thanksgiving).

🏊 Thanksgiving

On the fourth Thursday of November, Americans gather with family and friends over day-long feasts. NYC hosts a huge parade, and there's pro football on TV.

December

Winter arrives as ski season kicks off in the Rockies (out east conditions aren't usually ideal until January).

🏊 Art Basel

This massive arts fest (www.artbaselmiamibeach.com) is four days of cutting-edge art, film, architecture and design, plus much hobnobbing with a glitterati crowd on Miami Beach.

🏊 New Year's Eve

Join festive crowds to celebrate or plot a getaway to escape the mayhem. Whichever you choose, plan well in advance. Expect high prices (especially in NYC).

Plan Your Trip
Get Inspired

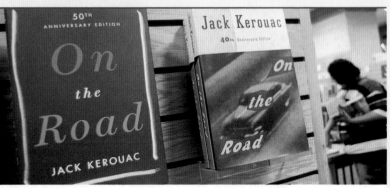

Read

Motherless Brooklyn (Jonathan Lethem, 1999) Darkly humorous novel with a cast of wild characters.

The Amazing Adventures of Kavalier & Clay (Michael Chabon, 2000) A brilliant Pulitzer Prize–winning novel of art, adventure, escapism and comic books.

Song of Solomon (Toni Morrison, 1977) Powerful coming-of-age story full of magic, mystery and folklore by one of America's finest novelists (and a Nobel Prize winner).

On the Road (Jack Kerouac, 1957) A Beat Generation classic of post-WWII America.

Watch

The Hangover (Todd Phillips, 2009) Hilarious tale of things gone horribly wrong at a bachelor party in Vegas.

Annie Hall (Woody Allen, 1977) Funny and poignant tale of love and loss – one of Allen's best.

Philadelphia Story (George Cukor, 1940) Brilliantly written romantic comedy starring Cary Grant, Katherine Hepburn and James Stewart.

Easy Rider (Dennis Hopper, 1969) Bikers on a journey through a nation in turmoil.

Listen

Mothership Connection (Parliament, 1975) One of the finest funk albums of all time.

Kind of Blue (Miles Davis, 1959) Beautifully conceived jazz album.

Highway 61 Revisited (Bob Dylan, 1965) The finest of road music by a folk-singing legend.

What's Going On (Marvin Gaye, 1971) Groundbreaking work by one of Motown's native sons.

Off the Wall (Michael Jackson, 1979) MJ's grooviest album still rocks after all these years.

Nevermind (Nirvana, 1991) Launched the fist-pumping grunge movement.

Plan Your Trip
Family Travel

The USA offers superb attractions for all ages: theme parks, zoos, eye-popping aquariums, hikes in wilderness reserves, natural-history exhibits, beaches and hands-on science museums.

Need to Know

Change facilities Found in most public buildings and restaurants.

Cribs (cots) Available at most hotels.

High chairs Available at most restaurants, as are booster seats.

Diapers (nappies) Widely available.

Health Pack basic medicines; standard of hospital care is excellent.

Children's menus Often available, and many restaurants are willing to improvise to make a kid-friendly meal. Chinese, Mexican or Italian restaurants are the best bet for finicky young eaters.

Strollers Bring an umbrella stroller.

Transport Major car-rental firms can supply car seats; request them when booking.

Planning

Weather and crowds are all-important considerations when planning a US family getaway. The peak travel season across the country is June to August, when schools are out and the weather is warmest. Expect high prices and abundant crowds; you'll need to reserve well in advance for popular destinations. The same holds true for winter resorts during January to March.

Be conservative when planning road trips. Keep distances short, don't string driving days together, and try to arrive an hour before mealtime, so everyone can unwind.

Lodging

Motels and hotels typically have rooms with two beds, which are ideal for families. Some also have roll-away beds or cribs that can be brought into the room for an extra charge. Some hotels offer 'kids stay free' programs for children up to 12 or sometimes 18 years old. Be wary of B&Bs, as most don't allow children; ask when booking.

PHILIPPE LISSAC / GODONG / GETTY IMAGES ©

Planes & Trains

Domestic airlines don't charge for children under two. Those aged two and over must have a seat. Very rarely, some resort areas (like Disneyland) offer a 'kids fly free' promotion. Amtrak and other train operators occasionally run similar deals, with kids up to 15 years old riding free.

Discounts

Child concessions often apply for tours and admission fees, with some discounts as high as 50% off the adult rate. However, the definition of 'child' can vary from under six to under 16 years. Some popular sights also have discount rates for families. Most sights offer free admission to children under two years.

Helpful Resources

Family Travel Files (www.thefamilytravelfiles. com) Ready-made vacation ideas, destination profiles and travel tips.

The Best Theme Parks & Animal Spotting

Walt Disney World, Florida (p204)

Universal Orlando, Florida (p208)

Animal Kingdom, Florida (p204)

Disneyland, California (p276)

National Zoo, Washington DC (p144)

Aquarium of the Americas, New Orleans (p226)

Kids.gov (www.kids.gov) Eclectic, enormous national resource; download songs and activities, or even link to the CIA Kids' Page.

Travel with Children For all-around information and advice, check out Lonely Planet's *Travel with Children*. Get kids involved and excited with a copy of the *Not for Parents USA* book.

Left: Children's Creativity Museum (p305), San Francisco
Right: Universal Orlando Resort (p208)

Plan Your Trip
Need to Know

When to Go

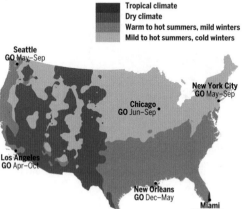

Tropical climate
Dry climate
Warm to hot summers, mild winters
Mild to hot summers, cold winters

Seattle
GO May–Sep

New York City
GO May–Sep

Chicago
GO Jun–Sep

Los Angeles
GO Apr–Oct

New Orleans
GO Dec–May

Miami
GO Dec–Apr

High Season (Jun–Aug)

o Warm days across the country, with generally high temperatures.

o Busiest season, with big crowds and higher prices.

o In ski resort areas, January to March is high season.

Shoulder Season (Oct & Apr–May)

o Milder temperatures, fewer crowds.

o Spring flowers (April); fiery autumn colors (October) in many parts.

Low Season (Nov–Mar)

o Wintry days, with snowfall in the north, and heavier rains in some regions.

o Lowest prices for accommodations (aside from ski resorts and warmer getaway destinations).

Currency

US dollar ($)

Language

English

Visas

Visitors from Canada, the UK, Australia, New Zealand, Japan and many EU countries don't need visas for less than 90-day stays. Other nations see http://travel.state.gov.

Money

ATMs widely available. Credit cards accepted at most hotels, restaurants and shops.

Cell Phones

Foreign phones that operate on tri- or quad-band frequencies will work in the USA. Or purchase inexpensive cell phones with a pay-as-you-go plan once you're there.

Driving

Drive on the right; the steering wheel is on the left side of the car.

Daily Costs

Budget: Less than $100

- Dorm beds: $25–40; campgrounds: $15–30; budget motels: $60–80
- Travel on buses, subways and other mass transit: $2–3
- Lunch from a café or food truck: $5–9

Midrange: $150–250

- Double room in midrange hotel: $100–250
- Popular restaurant dinner: $50–80 for two
- Car hire: from $30 per day

Top End: More than $250

- Lodging in a resort: from $250
- Dining in top restaurants: $60–100 per person
- Big nights out (plays, concerts, nightclubs): $60–200

Useful Websites

Lonely Planet (www.lonelyplanet.com/usa) Destination information, hotel bookings, travel forum and photos.

Exchange Rates (www.xe.com) Current exchange rates.

National Park Service (NPS; www.nps.gov) Gateway to America's greatest natural treasures, its national parks.

Eater (www.eater.com) Foodie insight into two dozen American cities.

New York Times Travel (http://travel.nytimes.com) Travel news, practical advice and engaging features.

Roadside America (www.roadsideamerica.com) For all things weird and wacky.

Opening Hours

Opening hours vary; the following is a general guide.

Bars 5pm to midnight Sunday to Thursday, to 2am Friday & Saturday

Banks 8:30am to 4:30pm Monday to Friday

Nightclubs 10pm to 4am Thursday to Saturday

Post offices 9am to 5pm Monday to Friday

Shopping malls 9am to 9pm

Stores 9am to 6pm Monday to Saturday, noon to 5pm Sunday

Supermarkets 8am to 8pm; some open 24 hours

Important Numbers

Emergency 🕿 911

USA country code 🕿 1

Directory assistance 🕿 411

International directory assistance 🕿 00

International access code from the USA 🕿 011

Arriving in the USA

John F Kennedy International Airport, New York (p369)

From JFK take the AirTrain to Jamaica Station and then LIRR to Penn Station, which costs $12 to $15 (45 minutes). A taxi to Manhattan costs $52, plus toll and tip (45 to 90 minutes).

Los Angeles International Airport (LAX) (p369)

LAX Flyaway Bus to Union Station costs $8 (30 to 50 minutes); door-to-door Prime Time & SuperShuttle costs $16 to $30 (35 to 90 minutes); and a taxi to Downtown costs $51 (25 to 50 minutes).

Miami International Airport (MIA) (p369)

SuperShuttle to South Beach for $21 (50 to 90 minutes); taxi to Miami Beach for $35 (40 to 60 minutes); or take the Metrorail to downtown (Government Center) for $2.25 (15 minutes).

For more, see the **Survival Guide** (p358) ➡

NEW YORK CITY

New York City

Epicenter of the arts. Dining and shopping capital. Trendsetter. New York City wears many crowns, and spreads an irresistible feast for all.

With its compact size and streets packed with eye-candy of all sorts – architectural treasures, old-world cafés, atmospheric booksellers and curiosity shops – NYC is an urban wanderer's delight. Crossing continents is as easy as walking over a few avenues in this jumbled city of 200-plus nationalities.

You'll find sprawling galleries and museums devoted to everything from fin de siècle Vienna to immigrant life in the Lower East Side. Then, when the sun sinks and luminous skyscrapers light up the night, New York transforms into one grand stage. Whether high culture or low, New York embraces it all.

☑ In This Section

Central Park	38
Statue of Liberty	44
Brooklyn Bridge	46
MoMA	48
The High Line	50
Broadway	52
Sights	58
Tours	69
Shopping	69
Entertainment	72
Eating	75
Drinking & Nightlife	81

✿ What's On

Tribeca Film Festival (www.tribecafilm.com) Robert De Niro co-organizes this prestigious local downtown film fest; held in April.

Fleet Week (www.fleetweeknewyork.com) Dressed in their formal whites, an annual convocation of sailors and naval ships descend on the city in May.

Village Halloween Parade (www.halloween-nyc.com) Features wildly costume-clad marchers and cheering onlookers. Anyone can join.

★ Top Tip

To escape the crowds, try the North Meadow (north of 97th St) or the Harlem Meer.

Like the city's subway system, the vast and majestic Central Park, an 843-acre rectangle of open space in the middle of Manhattan, is a great class leveler – which is exactly what it was envisioned to be. Created in the 1860s and '70s by Frederick Law Olmsted and Calvert Vaux on the marshy northern fringe of the city, the immense park was designed as a leisure space for all New Yorkers, regardless of color, class or creed.

Olmsted and Vaux (who also created Prospect Park in Brooklyn) were determined to keep foot and road traffic separate and designed the crosstown transverses under elevated roads to do so. That such a large expanse of prime real estate has survived intact for so long proves that nothing eclipses the heart, soul and pride that forms the foundation of New York City's greatness.

Throughout the year, visitors find free outdoor concerts at the **Great Lawn**, precious animals at the **Central Park Wildlife Center** and top-notch drama at the annual Shakespeare in the Park productions, held each summer at the open-air **Delacorte Theater**. Some other recommended stops include the ornate Bethesda Fountain, which edges the Lake; the **Shakespeare Garden** (west side, btwn 79th & 80th Sts), which has lush plantings and excellent skyline views; and the **Ramble** (mid-park from 73rd to 79th Sts), a wooded thicket that's popular with bird-watchers.

While parts of the park swarm with joggers, in-line skaters, musicians and tourists on warm weekends, it's quieter on weekday afternoons – but especially in less well-trodden spots above 72nd St such as

Bethesda Terrace and Mall

the Harlem Meer and the **North Meadow** (north of 97th St).

People flock to the park even in winter, when snowstorms can inspire cross-country skiing and sledding or a simple stroll through the white wonderland, and crowds turn out every New Year's Eve for a midnight run. The **Central Park Conservancy** (☎212-310-6600; www.centralparknyc. org/tours; 14 E 60th St; ⓢN/Q/R to 5th Ave-59th St) offers ever-changing guided tours of the park, including those that focus on public art, wildlife and places of interest to kids.

☑ **Don't Miss**

Tours with the Central Park Conservancy (www.centralparknyc.org/walkingtours); many are free, others cost $15.

BRUCE YUANYUE BI / GETTY IMAGES ©

Strawberry Fields

This tear-shaped garden serves as a memorial to former Beatle John Lennon. It is composed of a grove of stately elms and a tiled mosaic that reads, 'Imagine.' Find it at the level of 72nd St on the park's west side.

Bethesda Terrace & Mall

The arched walkways of Bethesda Terrace, crowned by the magnificent Bethesda Fountain, have long been a gathering area for New Yorkers. To the south is the Mall, a promenade shrouded in North American elms. The southern stretch, known as **Literary Walk**, is flanked by statues of famous authors.

Conservatory Water & Around

North of the zoo at the level of 74th St is the Conservatory Water, where model sailboats drift lazily and kids scramble about on a statue of Alice in Wonderland. There are Saturday story hours at the **Hans Christian Andersen statue** to the west of the water (at 11am from June to September).

Great Lawn & Around

The Great Lawn is at the center of the park – between 79th and 86th Sts – and is surrounded by ball fields and London plane trees. Immediately to the southeast is the **Delacorte Theater**, as well as **Belvedere Castle**, a lookout. Further south, between 72nd and 79th Sts, is the leafy **Ramble**, a popular birding destination. On the southeastern end is the Loeb Boathouse, home to a waterside restaurant that offers rowboat and bicycle rentals.

✗ **Take a Break**

Have a martini at the **Loeb Boathouse** (Map p74; ☎212-517-2233; www.thecentral parkboathouse.com; Central Park Lake, Central Park, at 74th St; mains $25-36; ⊗ hours vary; ⓢA/C, B to 72nd St, 6 to 77th St).

Central Park

THE LUNGS OF NEW YORK

The rectangular patch of green that occupies Manhattan's heart began life in the mid-19th century as a swampy piece of land that was carefully bulldozed into the idyllic nature-scape you see today. Since officially becoming Central Park, it has brought New Yorkers of all stripes together in interesting and unexpected ways. The park has served as a place for the rich to show off their fancy carriages (1860s), for the poor to enjoy free Sunday concerts (1880s) and for activists to hold be-ins against the Vietnam War (1960s).

Since then, legions of locals – not to mention travelers from all kinds of faraway places – have poured in to stroll, picnic, sunbathe, play ball and catch free concerts and performances of works by Shakespeare.

Loeb Boathouse
Perched on the shores of the Lake, the historic Loeb Boathouse is one of the city's best settings for an idyllic meal. You can also rent rowboats and bicycles and ride on a Venetian gondola.

Duke Ellington Circle

Harlem Meer

The Blockhouse

North Woods

97th St Transverse

Fifth Ave

86th St Transverse

The Great Lawn

Central Park West

Conservatory Garden
The only formal garden in Central Park is perhaps the most tranquil. On the northern end, chrysanthemums bloom in late October. To the south, the park's largest crab apple tree grows by the Burnett Fountain.

STEVEN GREAVES / GETTY IMAGES ©

Jacqueline Kennedy Onassis Reservoir
This 106-acre body of water covers roughly an eighth of the park's territory. Its original purpose was to provide clean water for the city. Now it's a good spot to catch a glimpse of waterbirds.

ANGUS OSBORN / GETTY IMAGES ©

Belvedere Castle
A so-called 'Victorian folly,' this Gothic-Romanesque castle serves no other purpose than to be a very dramatic lookout point. It was built by Central Park co-designer Calvert Vaux in 1869.

The park's varied terrain offers a wonderland of experiences. There are quiet, woodsy knolls in the north. To the south is the reservoir, crowded with joggers. There are European gardens, a zoo and various bodies of water. For maximum flamboyance, hit the Sheep Meadow on a sunny day, when all of New York shows up to lounge.

Central Park is more than just a green space. It is New York City's backyard.

FACTS & FIGURES

» **Landscape architects** Frederick Law Olmsted and Calvert Vaux

» **Year that construction began** 1858

» **Acres** 843

» **On film** Hundreds of movies have been shot on location, from Depression-era blockbusters such as *Gold Diggers* (1933) to the monster-attack flick *Cloverfield* (2008).

Conservatory Water
This pond is popular in the warmer months, when children sail their model boats across its surface. Conservatory Water was inspired by 19th-century Parisian model-boat ponds and figured prominently in EB White's classic book, *Stuart Little*.

Bethesda Fountain
This neoclassical fountain is one of New York's largest. It's capped by the *Angel of the Waters*, which is supported by four cherubim. The fountain was created by bohemian-feminist sculptor Emma Stebbins in 1868.

Metropolitan Museum of Art

Alice in Wonderland Statue

79th St Transverse

The Ramble

Delacorte Theater

The Lake

Fifth Ave

Central Park Zoo

65th St Transverse

Sheep Meadow

Strawberry Fields
A simple mosaic memorial pays tribute to musician John Lennon, who was killed across the street outside the Dakota Building. Funded by Yoko Ono, its name is inspired by the Beatles song 'Strawberry Fields Forever.'

The Mall / Literary Walk
A Parisian-style promenade – the only straight line in the park – is flanked by statues of literati on the southern end, including Robert Burns and Shakespeare. It is lined with rare North American elms.

Columbus Center

CHRIS MELLOR / GETTY IMAGES ©

Statue of Liberty

In a city full of American icons, the Statue of Liberty is perhaps the most famous. Despite featuring on a thousand postcards, up close it still has the power to inspire.

Great For...

☑ **Don't Miss**

The views from Lady Liberty's crown – they are breathtaking (but remember to reserve tickets well in advance).

History

Conceived as early as 1865 by French intellectual Edouard Laboulaye as a monument to the republican principles shared by France and the USA, the Statue of Liberty is still generally recognized as a symbol for at least the ideals of opportunity and freedom to many. French sculptor Frédéric-Auguste Bartholdi traveled to New York in 1871 to select the site, then spent more than 10 years in Paris designing and making the 151ft-tall figure **Liberty Enlightening the World**. It was then shipped to New York, erected on a small island in the harbor and unveiled in 1886. Structurally, it consists of an iron skeleton (designed by Gustave Eiffel) with a copper skin attached to it by stiff but flexible metal bars.

Ferry to Liberty Island

CHARLES KNOX / ALAMY STOCK PHOTO ©

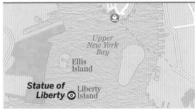

❶ Need to Know

📞212-363-3200, tickets 877-523-9849; www.nps.gov/stli; Liberty Island; adult/child incl Ellis Island $18/9, incl crown $21/12; ⏰8:30am-5:30pm, check website for seasonal changes; Ⓢ1 to South Ferry, 4/5 to Bowling Green, then 🚢to Liberty Island

✕ Take a Break

Pack a picnic for the trip, or chow beforehand at Battery Park's **Shake Shack** (Map p60; www.shakeshack.com; 215 Murray St, btwn West St & North End Ave; burgers $5.19-9.50; ⏰11am-11pm; Ⓢ A/C, 1/2/3 to Chambers St).

★ Top Tip

Pick up a free audio guide when you reach Liberty Island; there's even a kid's version.

Visiting the Statue of Liberty

Access to the crown is limited, so reservations are required. Book as far in advance as possible (additional $3 admission). Pedestal access is also limited, so reserve in advance (no additional fee). Keep in mind, there's no elevator and the climb from the base is equal to a 22-story building. Otherwise, a visit means you can wander the grounds, take in the small museum and enjoy the view from the 16-story observation deck in the pedestal.

The trip to Liberty Island, via ferry, is usually made in conjunction with nearby Ellis Island. Ferries leave from Battery Park and tickets include admission to both sights. Reserve in advance to cut down on long wait times.

Ellis Island

An icon of mythical proportions for the descendants of those who passed through here, Ellis Island and its hulking building served as New York's main immigration station from 1892 until 1954, processing an astounding 12 million arrivals. The process involved getting the once-over by doctors, being assigned new names if their own were deemed too difficult to spell or pronounce, and basically getting the green light to start new lives in America.

The three-level Ellis Island Immigration Museum features narratives from historians, architects and the immigrants themselves. The tour brings to life the museum's hefty collection of personal objects, official documents, photographs and film footage.

RASPU / GETTY IMAGES ©

Brooklyn Bridge

Marianne Moore's description of the world's first suspension bridge – which inspired poets from Walt Whitman to Jack Kerouac even before its completion – as a 'climactic ornament, a double rainbow' is perhaps most evocative.

Great For...

☑ Don't Miss

Empire Fulton Ferry, part of Brooklyn Bridge Park located just past the span, for its dramatic bridge and skyscraper views.

A New York icon, the **Brooklyn Bridge** (Map p60; S 4/5/6 to Brooklyn Bridge-City Hall, J to Chambers St) was the world's first steel suspension bridge. Indeed, when it opened in 1883, the 1596ft span between its two support towers was the longest in history. Although its construction was fraught with disaster, the bridge became a magnificent example of urban design, inspiring poets, writers and painters. Today, its pedestrian walkway – which begins just east of City Hall – delivers a soul-stirring view of lower Manhattan; you should reach Brooklyn after about a 20-minute walk.

Construction

Ironically, one man deprived of this view was the bridge's designer, John Roebling. The Prussian-born engineer was knocked off a pier in Fulton Landing in June 1869, dying

ⓘ Need to Know

The bridge walk is 1.3 miles (2km), but allow around an hour in either direction to stop and soak up the views.

✕ Take a Break

For drinks with a view, you can't beat **Brooklyn Bridge Park Garden Bar** (Map p60; brooklynbridgegardenbar.com; Pier 1, Brooklyn Bridge Park; ⏰noon-10pm Jun-Aug, to 6pm Apr, May, Sep & Oct; Ⓢ A/C to High St).

★ Top Tip

To beat the crowds, visit the bridge early in the morning.

of tetanus poisoning before construction of the bridge began. Consequently, his son, Washington Roebling, supervised its construction, which lasted 14 years and managed to survive budget overruns and the deaths of 20 workers. Washington suffered from the bends while helping to excavate the riverbed for the bridge's western tower and remained bedridden for much of the project; his wife Emily oversaw construction in his stead. There was one final tragedy to come in June 1883, when the bridge opened to pedestrian traffic. Someone in the crowd shouted, perhaps as a joke, that the bridge was collapsing into the river, setting off a mad rush in which 12 people were trampled to death.

Connecting Manhattan to Brooklyn, the bridge entered its second century as strong and beautiful as ever following an extensive renovation in the early 1980s.

Crossing the Bridge

Walking across the grand Brooklyn Bridge is a rite of passage for New Yorkers and visitors alike – with this in mind, walk no more than two abreast or else you're in danger of colliding with runners and cyclists. Take care to stay on the side of the walkway marked for folks on foot, and not in the bike lane.

The bridge and the smooth pedestrian/bicyclist path, beginning just east of City Hall, affords wonderful views of Lower Manhattan and Brooklyn.

Brooklyn Bridge Park

On the Brooklyn side, this ever-expanding park has revitalized a once-barren, 1.3-mile patch of shoreline and six abandoned piers. Highlights include free open-air summertime events such as film screenings (Pier 1); courts for basketball, handball and bocce, and a skating rink (Pier 2); and kayak and stand up paddleboard hire (Pier 4 beach).

DOSFOTOS / GETTY IMAGES ©

MoMA

Quite possibly the greatest hoarder of modern masterpieces on earth, the Museum of Modern Art (MoMA) is a cultural promised land. For art buffs, it's Valhalla. For the uninitiated, it's a thrilling crash course in the all that is beautiful and addictive about art.

Great For...

☑ Don't Miss

The outdoor sculpture garden; it's free to visit from 9:30am to 10:15am daily.

Since its founding in 1929, the museum has amassed over 150,000 artworks, documenting the emerging creative ideas and movements of the late 19th century through to those that dominate today.

Visiting MoMA

It's easy to get lost in MoMA's vast collection. To maximize your time and create a plan of attack, download the museum's free smartphone app from the website beforehand. MoMA's permanent collection spans four levels, with prints, illustrated books and the unmissable Contemporary Galleries on level two; architecture, design, drawings and photography on level three; and painting and sculpture on levels four and five. Many of the big hitters are on these last two levels, so tackle the museum from the top down before the fatigue sets

❶ Need to Know

Map p66; 📞212-708-9400; www.moma.org; 11
W 53rd St, btwn Fifth & Sixth Aves; adult/child
$25/free, 4-8pm Fri free; ⏱10:30am-5:30pm
Sat-Thu, to 8pm Fri, to 8pm Thu Jul-Aug; 📶♿;
Ⓢ E, M to 5th Ave-53rd St

✕ Take a Break

Nosh on Italian-inspired fare at MoMA's
Cafe 2 (Map p66; 📞212-333-1299; sandwiches & salads $12-14, mains $19; ⏱11am-
5pm, to 7:30pm Fri; 📶).

★ Top Tip

Keep your museum ticket handy,
as it also provides free entry to film
screenings and MoMA PS1.

---

in. Must-sees include Van Gogh's *Starry
Night,* Cézanne's *The Bather,* Picasso's *Les
Demoiselles d'Avignon,* and Henri Rous-
seau's *The Sleeping Gypsy,* not to mention
iconic American works like Warhol's *Camp-
bell's Soup Cans* and *Gold Marilyn Monroe,*
Lichtenstein's equally poptastic *Girl With
Ball* and Hopper's haunting *House by the
Railroad.*

Film Screenings

Not only a palace of visual art, MoMA
screens an incredibly well-rounded selection of celluloid gems from its collection of
over 22,000 films, including the works of
the Maysles Brothers and every Pixar ani-
mation film ever produced. Expect anything
from Hollywood classics to experimental
works. Your museum ticket will get you in
for free.

Lunchtime Talks

To delve a little deeper into MoMA's collection, join one of the museum's lunchtime
talks and readings (held daily at 11:30am
and 1:30pm), which offer expert insight into
specific works and exhibitions on view.

MoMA PS1

A smaller, hipper relative of MoMA, **MoMA
PS1** (📞718-784-2084; www.momaps1.org;
22-25 Jackson Ave, Long Island City; suggested
donation adult/child $10/free, admission free
with MoMA ticket; ⏱noon-6pm Thu-Mon; Ⓢ E/M
to 23rd St-Court Sq, G/7 Court Sq) is a master
at hunting down fresh, bold contemporary
art and serving it up in a Berlin-esque, ex-
school locale. Forget about pretty lily ponds
in gilded frames. Here you'll be peering at
videos through floorboards and debating
the meaning of nonstatic structures while
staring through a hole in the wall.

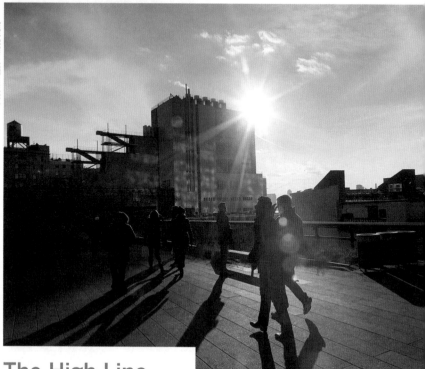

The High Line

A resounding triumph of urban renewal, the High Line is a remarkable linear public park built along a disused elevated rail line. This aerial greenway attracts millions of visitors each year.

Great For...

☑ Don't Miss

The third and final part of the High Line, which opened in 2014 and bends by the Hudson River at 34th St.

History

It's hard to believe that the High Line was once a disused railway that anchored a rather unsavory district of ramshackle domestic dwellings and slaughterhouses. The tracks were commissioned in the 1930s when the municipal government decided to raise the street-level tracks after years of deadly accidents.

By the 1980s, the rails became obsolete (thanks to a rise in truck transportation). Petitions were signed by local residents to remove the eyesores, but in 1999 a committee called the Friends of the High Line was formed to save the tracks and to transform them into a public open space. Community support grew and, on June 9, 2009, part one of the celebrated project – full of blooming flowers and broad-leaved trees – opened with much ado.

BRUCE YUANYUE BI / GETTY IMAGES ©

ⓘ Need to Know

Map p60; ☎212-206-9922; www.thehighline.org; Gansevoort St; ⊙7am-11pm Jun-Sep, to 10pm Apr, May, Oct & Nov, to 7pm Dec-Mar; 🚃M11 to Washington St, M11, M14 to 9th Ave, M23, M34 to 10th Ave, ⑤L, A/C/E to 14th St-8th Ave, C/E to 23rd St-8th Ave; FREE

✕ Take a Break

A cache of eateries, from sushi joints to creperies, is stashed within **Chelsea Market** (p78) at the 14th St exit.

★ Top Tip

Entrances are at Gansevoort, 14th, 16th, 18th, 20th and 30th Sts.

Along the Way

The main things to do on the High Line are stroll, sit and picnic in a park 30ft above the city. Along the park's length you'll encounter stunning vistas of the Hudson River, public art installations, fat lounge chairs for soaking up some sun, willowy stretches of native-inspired landscaping and a thoroughly unique perspective on the neighborhood streets below – especially at the cool Gansevoort Overlook, where bleacher-like seating faces a huge pane of glass that allows you to view the traffic, buildings and pedestrians beyond as living works of urban art.

Info, Tours, Events & Eats

As you walk along the High Line you'll find staffers wearing shirts with the signature double-H logo who can point you in the right direction or offer you additional information about the converted rails. Staffers also organize public art exhibitions and activity sessions, including warm-weather family events such as story time, science and craft projects, fun with food and more.

Free tours take place on Tuesday nights at 6:30pm in warmer months. Sign up near the 14th St entrance and arrive early to get a spot. Other special tours and events explore a variety of topics: history, horticulture, design, art and food. Check the event schedule on the website for the latest details.

The High Line also invites various gastronomic establishments to set up vending carts and stalls so that strollers can enjoy to-go items on the green. Expect coffee and ice cream during the warmer months.

New Amsterdam Theatre

Broadway

*Broadway is NYC's dream factory –
a place where romance, betrayal,
murder and triumph come with
dazzling costumes, toe-tapping tunes
and stirring scores.*

Great For...

☑ **Don't Miss**

The famed **Brill Building** (Map p66;
Broadway, at 49th St, Midtown West;
[S]N/Q/R to 49th St, 1, C/E to 50th St);
Carole King, Neil Diamond and Joni
Mitchell are among the musicians who
worked here.

Broadway Beginnings

The neighborhood's first playhouse was
the long-gone Empire, opened in 1893 on
Broadway between 40th and 41st Sts. Two
years later, cigar manufacturer and part-
time comedy scribe Oscar Hammerstein
opened the Olympia, also on Broadway,
before opening the Republic – now
children's theater **New Victory** (Map p66;
www.newvictory.org) – in 1900. This led to
a string of new venues, among them the
still-beating **New Amsterdam Theatre**
(Map p66; www.new-amsterdam-theatre.com)
and **Lyceum Theatre** (Map p66; www.shubert.
nyc/theatres/lyceum).

The Broadway of the 1920s was
well-known for its lighthearted musicals,
commonly fusing vaudeville and music
hall traditions, and producing classic tunes
like Cole Porter's *Let's Misbehave.* At the

Brill Building

PATTI MCCONVILLE / ALAMY STOCK PHOTO ©

W 54th St

50th St Ⓢ

Sixth Ave

Eighth Ave

◎ *Broadway*

42nd St-
Ⓢ Times Sq

W 40th St

❶ Need to Know

Theatermania (www.theatermania.com) provides listings, reviews and ticketing for any form of theater.

✕ Take a Break

Stiff drinks and a whiff of nostalgia await at **Jimmy's Corner** (p83) bar.

★ Top Tip

Many shows offer discounted, day-of 'rush' tickets, available when the box office opens; expect queues.

Getting a Ticket

Unless there's a specific show you're after, the best – and cheapest – way to score tickets in the area is at the **TKTS Booth** (Map p66; www.tdf.org/tkts; Broadway, at W 47th St, Midtown West; ◷3-8pm Mon, Wed-Sat, 2-8pm Tue, 3-7pm Sun, also 10am-2pm Tue-Sat & 11am-3pm Sun during matinee performances; Ⓢ N/Q/R, S, 1/2/3, 7 to Times Sq-42nd St), where you can line up and get same-day discounted tickets for top Broadway and off-Broadway shows. Download the free TKTS app for real-time updates of what's available. Always have a back-up choice in case your first preference sells out, and never buy from scalpers on the street.

The Longest-Running Shows

Following are the district's longest-running shows – the first three are still playing!

- ◉ *Phantom of the Opera*
- ◉ *Chicago*
- ◉ *The Lion King*
- ◉ *Cats*
- ◉ *Les Misérables*

same time, Midtown's theater district was evolving as a platform for new American dramatists. One of the greatest was Eugene O'Neill. Born in Times Square at the long-gone Barrett Hotel (1500 Broadway) in 1888, the playwright debuted many of his works here, including Pulitzer Prize winners *Beyond the Horizon* and *Anna Christie*. O'Neill's success on Broadway paved the way for other American greats like Tennessee Williams and Arthur Miller – a surge of talent that led to the establishment of the annual Tony Awards in 1947.

These days, New York's Theater District covers an area stretching roughly from 40th St to 54th St between Sixth and Eighth Aves, with dozens of Broadway and off-Broadway theaters spanning blockbuster musicals to new and classic drama.

Walking Tour: Urban Icons

Ah, the skyscraper – mankind's homage to human progress. New York City has plenty of 'em in every shape and size – and lots of other architectural icons, too.

Distance: 2 miles
Duration: 2 to 3 hours

✕ Take a Break

It's worth a detour to Artisanal (p80), a Parisian-style bistro that specialises in cheese.

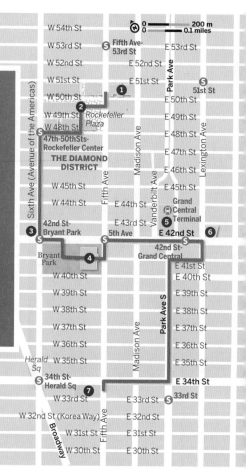

Start St Patrick's Cathedral;
Ⓢ B/D/F/M to Rockefeller Center

❶ St Patrick's Cathedral

The neo-Gothic **St Patrick's Cathedral** (www.saintpatricks cathedral.org; Fifth Ave, btwn 50th & 51st Sts; ⏰6:30am-8:45pm; Ⓢ B/D/F/M to 47th-50th Sts-Rockefeller Center) was built at a cost of nearly $2 million during the Civil War and is the largest Catholic cathedral in America.

❷ Rockefeller Center

Rockefeller Center (p64) is a magnificent complex of art-deco skyscrapers and sculptures. Enter between 49th and 50th Sts into the main plaza with its golden statue of Prometheus, then head up to the 70th floor of the GE Building just behind for an unforgettable view at the Top of the Rock observation deck.

❸ Bank of America Tower

The 366m **Bank of America Tower** (Sixth Ave, btwn 42nd & 43rd Sts) is New York City's third-tallest building and – perhaps surprisingly – one of the most ecofriendly.

❹ New York Public Library

At the corner of 42nd St and Fifth Ave stands the stately **New York Public Library** (Stephen A Schwarzman Building; www. nypl.org; Fifth Ave, at 42nd St; ⏰10am-6pm Mon

New York Public Library

BRUCE YUANYUE BI / GETTY IMAGES ©

& Thu-Sat, to 8pm Tue & Wed, 1-5pm Sun, guided tours 11am & 2pm Mon-Sat, 2pm Sun), guarded by a pair of regal lions called Patience and Fortitude. Step inside to peek at the spectacular Rose Main Reading Room.

❺ Grand Central Terminal

New York's beaux arts diva is **Grand Central Terminal** (www.grandcentralterminal.com; 42nd St, at Park Ave, Midtown East; ⊙5:30am-2am). Stargaze at the Main Concourse ceiling and share sweet nothings at the Whispering Gallery.

❻ Chrysler Building

Although William Van Alen's 1930 masterpiece, the **Chrysler Building** (405 Lexington Ave, at 42nd St, Midtown East; ⊙lobby 8am-6pm Mon-Fri), is best appreciated from afar, it's worth slipping into the sumptuous art-deco lobby, lavished with exotic inlaid wood, marble and purportedly the world's largest ceiling mural.

❼ Empire State Building

End your Midtown meander at the **Empire State Building** (p64), which provides a beautiful bird's-eye view of Manhattan and beyond. It's especially magical at sunset from the open-air observation deck on the 86th floor.

Finish Empire State Building; Ⓢ N/Q/R to Herald Sq

Walking Tour: SoHo Shops

Shopaholics across the world drool for SoHo and its sharp, trendy whirlwind of flagship stores, coveted labels and strutting fashionistas.

Distance: 0.8 miles
Duration: 30 minutes, not including shopping time

✕ **Take a Break**

Hang on until stop number 5, where you can try the delicious treats at Dean & DeLuca.

Start Café Integral

❶ A Shop with Single Origin

Charge up with a cup of single-origin coffee from **Café Integral** (www.cafeintegral.com; 135 Grand St, btwn Crosby & Lafayette Sts; ⏰8am-6pm Mon-Fri, 10am-6pm Sat, noon-5pm Sun; ⑤N/Q/R, J, 6 to Canal St), a teeny-tiny espresso bar inside kooky shop-cum-gallery American Two Shot. At the machine you'll probably find owner César Martin Vega, a 20-something obsessed with Nicaraguan coffee beans.

❷ Perfect Jeans

3x1 (www.3x1.us; 15 Mercer St, btwn Howard & Grand Sts; ⏰11am-7pm Mon-Sat, noon-6pm Sun; ⑤N/Q/R, J, 6 to Canal St) lets you design your perfect pair of jeans. Choose buttons and hems for ready-to-wear pairs (women's from $195, men's from $285), customize fabric and detailing on existing cuts ($525 to $750) or create a pair from scratch ($1200).

Dean & DeLuca

❸ Designer Kicks

Local craftsmanship also defines the footwear of emerging star **Alejandro Ingelmo** (www.alejandroingelmo.com; 51 Wooster St, btwn Broome & Grand Sts; ⏱11am-7pm Mon-Fri, noon-7pm Sat & Sun; Ⓢ1, A/C/E to Canal St), his imaginative kicks spanning sparkly basketball-style boots, to butterfly-inspired stilettos, to old-school American loafers sexed-up with a thick, downtown sole. Sneakers retail for around $600.

❹ Curbside Culture

The sidewalk engraving on the northwest corner of Prince St and Broadway is the work of Japanese-born sculptor Ken Hiratsuka, who has carved almost 40 sidewalks since moving to NYC in 1982. While this engraving took five or so hours of work, its actual completion took two years (1983–84), Hiratsuka's illegal nighttime chiseling often disrupted by police.

❺ A Gourmet Nibble

NYC loves its luxe grocers and **Dean & DeLuca** (☎212-226-6800; www.deananddeluca.com; 560 Broadway, at Prince St; ⏱7am-8pm Mon-Fri, 8am-8pm Sat & Sun; ⓈN/R to Prince St, 6 to Spring St) is one of the biggest names around town. If you're feeling peckish, ready-to-eat delectables include freshly baked cheese sticks, gourmet quesadillas and sugar-dusted almond croissants.

❻ Fragrance Flights

Drop into the library-like apothecary **MIN New York** (www.minnewyork.com; 117 Crosby St, btwn Jersey & Prince Sts; ⏱11am-7pm Mon-Sat, noon-6pm Sun; Ⓢ B/D/F/M to Broadway-Lafayette St, N/R to Prince St) and request a free 'fragrance flight,' a guided exploration of the store's extraordinary collection of rare, exclusive perfumes and grooming products. Look out for homegrown fragrances such as Brooklyn's MCMC and Detroit's Kerosene, as well as MIN's own coveted hair products. Prices span affordable to astronomical.

Finish MIN New York

◎ SIGHTS

◎ Lower Manhattan

National September 11 Memorial Museum Museum

Just beyond the reflective pools of the September 11 Memorial, you'll see an entrance pavilion that subtly, yet eerily, evokes a toppled tower. Inside, a gently sloping ramp leads to the subterranean exhibition galleries that evoke that horrific day on 2001. (Map p60; www.911memorial.org/museum; 180 Greenwich St, near Fulton St; adult/child $24/15, free 5-8pm Tue; ☺9am-8pm Sun-Thu, to 9pm Fri & Sat, last entry 2hr before close; ⛄; Ⓢ E to World Trade Center, R to Cortlandt St, 2/3 to Park Pl)

One World Observatory Viewpoint

Atop the highest building in the western hemisphere, One World Observatory, which opened in 2015, offers dazzling views from its 102-story perch. No other building in town rivals the jaw-dropping panorama of New York's urban landscape and its surrounding geography spread before you. (Map p60; ☏844-696-1776; www.oneworld observatory.com; cnr West & Vesey Sts; adult/child $32/26; ☺9am-8pm, last ticket sold at 7:15pm; Ⓢ E to World Trade Center, 2/3 to Park Pl, A/C, J/Z, 4/5 to Fulton St, R to Cortlandt St)

South Street Seaport Neighborhood

This 11-block enclave of shops, piers and sights combines the best and worst in historic preservation. It's not on the radar for most New Yorkers, but tourists are drawn to the sea air, the nautical feel, the frequent street performers and the mobbed restaurants. (Map p60; www.southstreetseaport.com; Ⓢ A/C, J/Z, 2/3, 4/5 to Fulton St)

◎ Wall Street & the Financial District

Battery Park & Around Neighborhood

The southwestern tip of Manhattan Island has been extended with landfill over the years to form **Battery Park** (Map p60; www.nycgovparks.org; Broadway, at Battery Pl; ☺sunrise-1am; Ⓢ4/5 to Bowling Green, 1 to South Ferry), so named for the gun batteries that used to be housed at the bulkheads.

Little Italy

MAREMAGNUM / GETTY IMAGES ©

Castle Clinton (Map p60; www.nps.gov/cacl; Battery Park; ⏰8am-5pm; 📷; ⑤1 to South Ferry, 4/5 to Bowling Green), a fortification built in 1811 to protect Manhattan from the British, was originally 900ft offshore but is now at the edge of Battery Park, with only its walls remaining.

◉ Tribeca & SoHo

The 'TRIangle BElow CAnal St,' bordered roughly by Broadway to the east and Chambers St to the south, is the more downtown of these two sister 'hoods. It has old warehouses, very expensive loft apartments and chichi restaurants.

SoHo, which takes its name from its geographical placement (SOuth of HOuston St) is filled with block upon block of cast-iron industrial buildings that date to the period just after the Civil War, when this was the city's leading commercial district. It had a bohemian/artsy heyday that had ended by the 1980s, and now this super-gentrified area is a major shopping destination, home to chain stores and boutiques alike.

Nearby are two small areas, NoHo ('north of Houston') and NoLita ('north of Little Italy'), respectively, are known for excellent shopping – lots of small, independent clothing boutiques – and dining.

◉ Chinatown & Little Italy

The best reason to visit Chinatown is to experience a feast for the senses – it's the only spot in the city where you can simultaneously see whole roasted pigs hanging in butcher-shop windows, get whiffs of fresh fish and hear the twangs of Cantonese and Vietnamese rise over the calls of knock-off-designer-bag hawkers on Canal St.

Little Italy, once a truly authentic pocket of Italian people, culture and eateries, is constantly shrinking (as Chinatown expands). Still, loyal Italian Americans, mostly from the suburbs, flock here to gather around red-and-white-checked tablecloths at one of a handful of longtime red-sauce

🏫 New York for Children

Contrary to popular belief, New York can be a pretty child-friendly city. Cutting-edge playgrounds abound, from Union Square to Battery Park, and there's lots of green space on the West Side. Other major attractions include the **Children's Museum of Manhattan** (Map p74; 📞212-721-1223; www.cmom. org; 212 W 83rd St, btwn Amsterdam Ave & Broadway; admission $12; ⏰10am-5pm Tue-Fri & Sun, to 7pm Sat; 👪; ⑤B, C to 81st St-Museum of Natural History, 1 to 86th St), the **Brooklyn Children's Museum** (📞718-735-4400; www.brooklynkids. org; 145 Brooklyn Ave, at St Marks Ave, Crown Heights; admission $11, free 2-6pm Thu; ⏰10am-5pm Tue-Sun; 👪; ⑤C to Kingston-Throop Aves, 3 to Kingston Ave), the Central Park and Bronx zoos and the Coney Island aquarium. A Circle Line cruise or the cheaper ferries (Staten Island or East River ferries) offer the opportunity to chug around New York Harbor. Governors Island is a great place for a picnic, free play and biking (with big four-wheel bikes for hire).

Coney Island Aquarium
BUENA VISTA IMAGES / GETTY IMAGES ©

◉ Lower East Side

First came the Jews, then the Latinos, followed by the hipsters and accompanying posers, frat-boy bros and the bridge-and-tunnel contingent. Today, this neighborhood, once the densest in the world, is

West & East Villages, Chinatown & Lower Manhattan

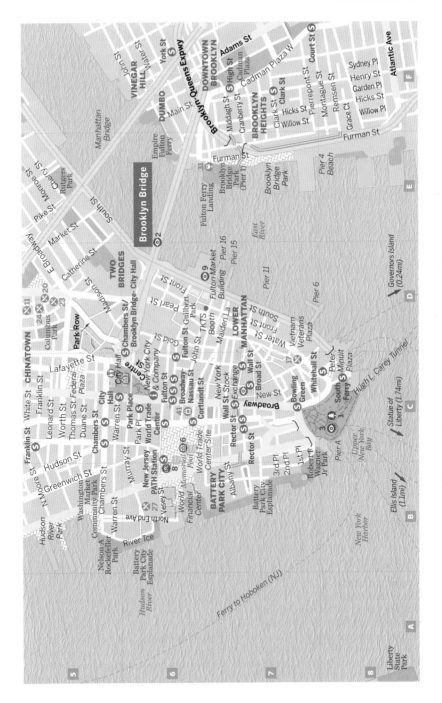

West & East Villages, Chinatown & Lower Manhattan

⊙ Sights
1	Battery Park	C8
2	Brooklyn Bridge	E6
3	Castle Clinton	C8
4	High Line	A2
5	Lower East Side Tenement Museum	D4
6	National September 11 Memorial Museum	C6
7	New Museum of Contemporary Art	D3
8	One World Observatory	B6
9	South Street Seaport	D6
10	St Patrick's Old Cathedral	D3

❸ Eating
11	Amazing 66	D5
12	Angelica Kitchen	D2
13	Balthazar	C4
14	Bánh Mi Saigon Bakery	D4
15	Boqueria Soho	C3
16	Cafe Mogador	D2
17	Fraunces Tavern	C7
18	Fung Tu	E4
19	Il Buco	D3
20	Joe's Shanghai	D5
21	Katz's Delicatessen	E3
22	Momofuku Noodle Bar	D2
23	Nom Wah Tea Parlor	D5
24	Original Chinatown Ice Cream Factory	D5
25	RedFarm	B2
26	Ruby's	D3
27	Shake Shack	B6
28	Spotted Pig	A2
29	Tacombi	D3
30	Vanessa's Dumpling House	D4
	Xi'an Famous Foods	(see 24)

❸ Drinking & Nightlife
	Apothéke	(see 23)
31	Brooklyn Bridge Park Garden Bar	E6
32	Buvette	B2
33	Employees Only	B2
34	Ten Bells	E4
35	Wayland	E2

❸ Entertainment
36	Joe's Pub	D2
37	Le Poisson Rouge	C3
38	Rockwood Music Hall	D3
39	Smalls	B2
40	Village Vanguard	B2

❸ Shopping
41	Century 21	C6
42	John Varvatos	D3
43	Obscura Antiques	E1
44	Other Music	C2
45	Strand Book Store	C1

focused on being cool, with low-lit lounges, live-music clubs and trendy bistros.

New Museum of Contemporary Art
Museum

Housed in an architecturally ambitious building, this is the city's sole museum dedicated to contemporary art, with often excellent shows (there's no permanent collection). (Map p60; ☏212-219-1222; www.newmuseum.org; 235 Bowery, btwn Stanton & Rivington Sts; adult/child $16/free, 7-9pm Thu by donation; ☺11am-6pm Wed-Sun, to 9pm Thu; ⑤N/R to Prince St, F to 2nd Ave, J/Z to Bowery, 6 to Spring St)

Lower East Side Tenement Museum
Museum

This museum puts the neighborhood's heartbreaking but inspiring heritage on full display in three recreations of turn-of-the-20th-century tenements, including the late-19th-century home and garment shop of the Levine family from Poland, and two immigrant dwellings from the Great Depressions of 1873 and 1929. Visits are by tour only, with knowledgeable guides bringing the past to life. Check the website for the full range of tours that operate throughout the day. Reserve ahead (tours fill up). (Map p60; ☏877-975-3786; www.tenement.org; 103 Orchard St, btwn Broome & Delancey Sts; adult/student from $25/20; ☺tours 10:15am-5pm Fri-Wed, to 6:30pm Thu; ⑤B/D to Grand St, J/M/Z to Essex St, F to Delancey St)

⊙ East Village

If you've been dreaming of those quintessential New York City moments – graffiti on crimson brick, punks and grannies walking side by side, and cute cafés with rickety tables spilling out onto the sidewalks – then the East Village is your Holy Grail. Stick to the area around Tompkins Square Park, and the lettered avenues (known as Alphabet City) to its east, for interesting little nooks in which to imbibe and ingest – as well as a collection of great little community gardens that provide leafy respites and sometimes even live performances.

West Village & Greenwich Village

Once a symbol for all things artistic, outlandish and bohemian, this storied and popular neighborhood – the birthplace of the gay-rights movement as well as former home of Beat poets and important artists – feels worlds away from busy Broadway, and in fact feels almost European. Known by most visitors as 'Greenwich Village,' although that term is not used by locals (West Village encompasses Greenwich Village, which is the area immediately around Washington Square Park), it has narrow streets lined with well-groomed real estate, as well as cafés and restaurants, making it an ideal place to wander.

Meatpacking District

The neighborhood was once home to 250 slaughterhouses and was best known for its groups of transsexual prostitutes, racy S&M sex clubs and, of course, its sides of beef. These days the hugely popular High Line park has only intensified an ever-increasing proliferation of trendy wine bars, eateries, nightclubs, designer clothing stores, chic hotels and high-rent condos.

Chelsea

This 'hood is popular for two main attractions: one, the parade of gorgeous gay men (known affectionately as 'Chelsea boys') who roam Eighth Ave, darting from gyms to happy hours; and two, it's one of the hubs of the city's art-gallery scene, with nearly 200 modern-art exhibition spaces, most of which are clustered west of Tenth Ave.

Flatiron District

The famous 1902 **Flatiron Building** (Map p66; Broadway, cnr Fifth Ave & 23rd St; **S** N/R,

F/M, 6 to 23rd St) has a distinctive triangular shape to match its site. Its surrounding district is a fashionable area of boutiques, loft apartments and a burgeoning high-tech corridor, the city's answer to Silicon Valley. Peaceful Madison Square Park, bordered by 23rd and 26th Sts and Fifth and Madison Aves, has an active dog run, rotating outdoor sculptures and a popular burger joint.

Union Square

Like the Noah's Ark of New York, **Union Square** (Map p66; www.unionsquarenyc.org; 17th St, btwn Broadway & Park Ave S; **S** 4/5/6, N/Q/R, L to 14th St-Union Sq) rescues at least two of every kind from the curling seas of concrete. Here, amid the tapestry of stone steps and fenced-in foliage, you'll find businessfolk, loiterers, skateboarders, college kids and throngs of protestors chanting fervently for various causes.

Union Square Greenmarket   Market

On most days, Union Square's north end hosts the most popular of the nearly 50 greenmarkets throughout the five boroughs, where even celebrity chefs come for just-picked rarities like fiddlehead ferns and fresh curry leaves. (Map p66; 212-788-7476; www.grownyc.org; 17th St, btwn Broadway & Park Ave S; 8am-6pm Mon, Wed, Fri & Sat; **S** 4/5/6, N/Q/R, L to 14th St-Union Sq)

Times Square

The intersection of Broadway and Seventh Ave – better known as Times Square – is New York City's hyperactive heart. Full of glittering lights and bombastic billboards, it's where the Centennial Ball, weighing in at nearly 6 tons, descends at midnight on New Year's Eve. (Map p66; www.timessquarenyc.org; Broadway, at Seventh Ave; **S** N/Q/R, S, 1/2/3, 7 to Times Sq-42nd St)

Midtown

The classic NYC fantasy – shiny skyscrapers, teeming mobs of worker bees, Fifth Ave store

 Queens

Of the city's five boroughs, Queens is top dog in size and runner-up in head count. Start your explorations in Long Island City (LIC). It's packed with contemporary art musts like **MoMA PS1** (p49) and the lesser-known **Fisher Landau Center for Art** (www.flcart. org). There's also the brilliant **Noguchi Museum** (www.noguchi.org). Watch the sun set over Manhattan from **Gantry Plaza State Park** (www.nysparks.com/parks/149), and dine in the locally loved restaurants lining Vernon Blvd.

You could also spend the day exploring neighboring Astoria, taste-testing its ethnic nosh spots; Greek restaurant **Taverna Kyclades** (www.tavernakyclades. com) is a favorite. Down Czech beers at the **Bohemian Hall & Beer Garden** (www.bohemianhall.com).

Further out, Flushing (home to NYC's biggest Chinatown) also merits a full-day adventure, with hawker-style food stands and restaurants – such as the superb **Hunan Kitchen of Grand Sichuan** (☏718-888-0553; 42-47 Main St, Flushing) – plus exotic grocery stores, kitschy malls and reflexology therapists.

Gantry Plaza State Park
CLARENCE HOLMES PHOTOGRAPHY / ALAMY STOCK PHOTO ©

windows, taxi traffic – and some of the city's most popular attractions can be found here.

Rockefeller Center   Historic Building
It was built during the height of the Great Depression in the 1930s, and construction of the 22-acre Rockefeller Center, including the landmark art-deco skyscraper, gave jobs to 70,000 workers over nine years and was the first project to combine retail, entertainment and office space in what is often referred to as a 'city within a city.' (Map p66; www.rockefellercenter.com; Fifth to Sixth Aves & 48th to 51st Sts; ⓈB/D/F/M to 47th-50th Sts-Rockefeller Center)

Empire State Building   Historic Building
Catapulted to Hollywood stardom both as the planned meeting spot for Cary Grant and Deborah Kerr in *An Affair to Remember*, and the vertical perch that helped to topple King Kong, the towering Empire State Building is one of the most famous members of New York's skyline. It's a limestone classic that was built in just 410 days during the depths of the Depression, at a cost of $41 million. (Map p66; www.esbnyc. com; 350 Fifth Ave, at 34th St; 86th-fl observation deck adult/child $32/26, incl 102nd-fl observation deck $52/46; ☺8am-2am, last elevators up 1:15am; ⓈB/D/F/M, N/Q/R to 34th St-Herald Sq)

Museum of Arts & Design   Museum
On the southern side of the circle, this museum exhibits a diverse international collection of modern, folk, craft and fine-art pieces. The plush and trippy design of **Robert** (Map p74; ☏212-299-7730; www.robertnyc. com; ☺11:30am-10pm Mon & Sun, to 11pm Tue, to midnight Wed-Sat), the 9th-floor restaurant, complements fantastic views of Central Park. (Map p74; MAD; www.madmuseum.org; 2 Columbus Circle, btwn Eighth Ave & Broadway; adult/child $16/free, by donation 6-9pm Thu; ☺10am-6pm Tue, Wed, Sat & Sun, to 9pm Thu & Fri; ☏♿; ⓈA/C, B/D, 1 to 59th St-Columbus Circle)

◉ **Upper West Side**

Shorthand for liberal, progressive and intellectual New York, this neighborhood comprises the west side of Manhattan from Central Park to the Hudson River, and from Columbus Circle to 110th St. Here you'll still find massive, ornate apartments and a diverse mix of stable, upwardly mobile folks (with many actors and classical musicians sprinkled throughout), and some lovely green spaces – Riverside Park stretches for 4 miles between W 72nd St and W 158th St along the Hudson River, and is a great place for strolling or simply gazing over the river.

Lincoln Center   Cultural Center

The billion-dollar-plus redevelopment of the world's largest performing-arts center includes the dramatically redesigned Alice Tully Hall and other stunning venues surrounding a massive fountain; public spaces, including the roof lawn of the North Plaza (an upscale restaurant is underneath), have been upgraded. The lavishly designed Metropolitan Opera House (MET), the largest opera house in the world, seats 3900 people. (212-875-5456, tours 212-875-5350; www.lincolncenter. org; Columbus Ave, btwn 62nd & 66th Sts; public plazas free, tours adult/student \$18/15; ; S 1 to 66th St-Lincoln Center)

American Museum of Natural History   Museum

Founded in 1869, this museum includes more than 30 million artifacts, interactive exhibits and loads of taxidermy. It's most famous for its three large dinosaur halls, an enormous (fake) blue whale that hangs from the ceiling above the Hall of Ocean Life and the elaborate Rose Center for Earth & Space – home to space-show theaters and the planetarium. (Map p74; 212-769-5100; www.amnh.org; Central Park West, at 79th St; suggested donation adult/child \$22/12.50; 10am-5:45pm, Rose Center to 8:45pm Fri, Butterfly Conservatory Oct-May; ; S B, C to 81st St-Museum of Natural History, 1 to 79th St)

Upper East Side

The Upper East Side (UES) is home to New York's greatest concentration of cultural centers, including the grand dame that is

watch the sun set over Manhattan from Gantry Plaza State Park

View of Manhattan from Gantry Plaza State Park

Times Square, Midtown Manhattan & Chelsea

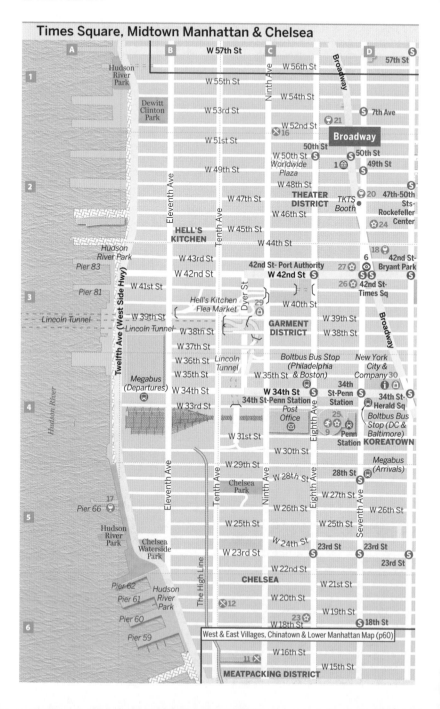

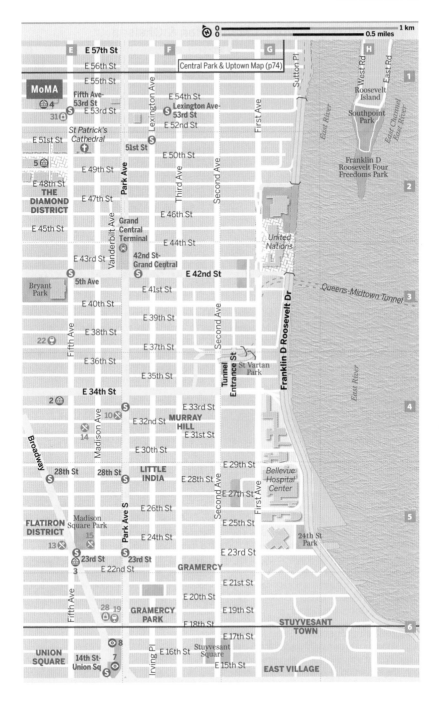

Times Square, Midtown Manhattan & Chelsea

◉ Sights
1	Brill Building	D2
2	Empire State Building	E4
3	Flatiron Building	E5
4	Museum of Modern Art	E1
5	Rockefeller Center	E2
6	Times Square	D3
7	Union Square	E6
8	Union Square Greenmarket	E6

⊕ Activities, Courses & Tours
9	New York Knicks	D4

⊗ Eating
10	Artisanal	E4
	Cafe 2	(see 4)
11	Chelsea Market	C6
12	Cookshop	C6
13	Eataly	E5
14	Hangawi	E4
15	Shake Shack	E5
16	Totto Ramen	C1

◉ Drinking & Nightlife
	Birreria	(see 13)
17	Frying Pan	A5
18	Jimmy's Corner	D3
19	Old Town Bar & Restaurant	E6
20	R Lounge	D2
21	Russian Vodka Room	D1
22	Top of the Strand	E3

⊕ Entertainment
23	Joyce Theater	C6
24	Lyceum Theatre	D2
25	Madison Square Garden	D4
26	New Amsterdam Theater	D3
27	New Victory Theater	D3

⊕ Shopping
28	ABC Carpet & Home	E6
29	Hell's Kitchen Flea Market	C3
30	Macy's	D4
	MoMA Design & Book Store	(see 4)
31	Uniqlo	E1

the Metropolitan Museum of Art, and many refer to Fifth Ave above 57th St as Museum Mile. Home to ladies who lunch as well as frat boys who drink, the neighborhood becomes decidedly less chichi the further east you go.

Metropolitan Museum of Art   Museum

With more than 2 million objects in its collections, the Met is simply dazzling. Its great works span the world, from the chiseled sculptures of ancient Greece to the evocative tribal carvings of Papua New Guinea. The renaissance galleries are packed with old world masters, while the relics of ancient Egypt fire the imagination – particularly the reconstructed Temple of Dendur, complete with 2000-year-old stone walls covered in hieroglyphics. (Map p74; ☏212-535-7710; www.metmuseum.org; 1000 Fifth Ave at 82nd St; suggested donation adult/child $25/free; ☺10am-5:30pm Sun-Thu, to 9pm Fri & Sat; ♿; Ⓢ4/5/6 to 86th St)

Guggenheim Museum   Museum

A sculpture in its own right, architect Frank Lloyd Wright's building almost overshadows the collection of 20th-century art that

it houses. Completed in 1959, the inverted ziggurat structure was derided by some critics, but it was hailed by others as an architectural icon. Stroll its sweeping spiral staircase to view masterpieces by Picasso, Pollock, Chagall, Kandinsky and others. (Map p74; ☏212-423-3500; www.guggenheim.org; 1071 Fifth Ave, at 89th St; adult/child $25/free, 5:45-7:45pm Sat by donation; ☺10am-5:45pm Sun-Wed & Fri, to 7:45pm Sat, closed Thu; ♿; Ⓢ4/5/6 to 86th St)

Frick Collection   Gallery

This spectacular art collection sits in a mansion built by Henry Clay Frick in 1914. The 12 richly furnished rooms on the ground floor display paintings by Titian, Vermeer, El Greco, Goya and other masters. It's rarely crowded, providing a welcome break from the swarms of gawkers at larger museums. (Map p74; ☏212-288-0700; www.frick.org; 1 E 70th St, at Fifth Ave; admission $20, by donation 11am-1pm Sun, children under 10 yr not admitted; ☺10am-6pm Tue-Sat, 11am-5pm Sun; Ⓢ6 to 68th St-Hunter College)

 TOURS

Big Onion
Walking Tours

Walking Tour

Popular, quirky guided tours specializing in ethnic and neighborhood tours. (☎888-606-9255; www.bigonion.com; tours $20)

🅰 SHOPPING

Home to myriad fashion boutiques, flea markets, booksellers, record stores, antique shops and gourmet grocers – New York City is quite simply one of the best shopping destinations on the planet.

🅰 Downtown

Strand Book Store

Books

The city's preeminent bibliophile warehouse, selling new and used books. (Map p60; ☎212-473-1452; www.strandbooks.com; 828 Broadway at 12th St; ⏱9:30am-10:30pm Mon-Sat, from 11am Sun; ⓢL, N/Q/R, 4/5/6 to 14th St-Union Sq)

Century 21

Fashion

A four-level department store loved by New Yorkers of every income. It's shorthand for designer bargains. (Map p60; ☎212-227-9092; www.c21stores.com; 22 Cortlandt St, btwn Church St & Broadway; ⏱7:45am-9pm Mon-Fri, 10am-9pm Sat, 11am-8pm Sun; ⓢA/C, J/Z, 2/3, 4/5 to Fulton St, R to Cortlandt St)

Other Music

Music

This indie-run CD store feeds its loyal fan base with a clued-in selection of offbeat lounge, psychedelic, electronica, indie rock etc, available new and used. There's also vinyl. (☎212-477-8150; www.othermusic.com; 15 E 4th St, btwn Lafayette St & Broadway; ⏱11am-8pm Mon-Wed, 11am-9pm Thu & Fri, noon-8pm Sat, noon-7pm Sun; ⓢ6 to Bleecker St, B/D/F/M to Broadway-Lafayette St)

Obscura Antiques

Antiques

This small cabinet of curiosities pleases both lovers of the macabre and inveterate antique hunters. Here you'll find taxidermic animal heads, tiny rodent skulls and skeletons, butterfly displays in glass boxes, photos of dead people, disturbing little (dental?) instruments, German landmine flags (stackable so tanks could see them),

old poison bottles and glass eyes. (Map p60; ☎212-505-9251; www.obscuraantiques.com; 207 Ave A, btwn 12th & 13th Sts; ⏱noon-8pm Mon-Sat, to 7pm Sun; ⓢL to 1st Ave)

ABC Carpet & Home

Homewares

A mecca for home designers and decorators brainstorming ideas, this beautifully curated, six-level store heaves with all sorts of furnishings, small and large. Shop for easy-to-pack knickknacks, designer jewelry, global gifts, as well as statement furniture, slinky lamps and antique carpets. Come Christmas season the shop is a joy to behold. (Map p66; ☎212-473-3000; www.abchome.com; 888 Broadway, at 19th St; ⏱10am-7pm Mon-Wed, Fri & Sat, to 8pm Thu, 11am-6:30pm Sun; ⓢ4/5/6, N/Q/R, L to 14th St-Union Sq)

John Varvatos

Fashion, Shoes

Set in the hallowed halls of former punk club CBGB, the John Varvatos Bowery store goes to great lengths to tie fashion with rock-and-roll, with records, '70s audio equipment and even electric guitars for sale alongside JV's denim, leather boots, belts and graphic tees. (Map p60; ☎212-358-0315; www.johnvarvatos.com; 315 Bowery, btwn 1st & 2nd Sts; ⏱noon-8pm Mon-Sat, to 6pm Sun; ⓢF to 2nd Ave, 6 to Bleecker St)

🅰 Midtown & Uptown

Macy's

Department Store

The grande dame of Midtown department stores sells everything from jeans to kitchen appliances. (Map p66; ☎212-695-4400; www.macys.com; 151 W 34th St, at Broadway; ⏱9:30am-10pm Mon & Wed-Fri, to 9:30pm Tue, 10am-10pm Sat, 11am-9pm Sun; ⓢB/D/F/M, N/Q/R to 34th St-Herald Sq)

Bloomingdale's

Department Store

Uptown, the sprawling, overwhelming Bloomingdale's is akin to the Metropolitan Museum of Art for shoppers. (Map p74; ☎212-705-2000; www.bloomingdales.com; 1000 Third Ave, at E 59th St, Midtown East; ⏱10am-8:30pm Mon & Tue, to 10pm Wed-Sat, to 9pm Sun; 📷; ⓢ4/5/6 to 59th St, N/Q/R to Lexington Ave-59th St)

Clockwise from above: Sunset over the Empire State Building (p64);
A meal at Katz's Delicatessen (p75); Red steps form the roof of the TKTS Booth in
Times Square (p63); Billboards in Times Square (p63); Manhattan Bridge

SIVAN ASKAYO / LONELY PLANET ©

KARSTEN BIDSTRUP / GETTY IMAGES ©

Uniqlo

*New York City is one of the
best shopping destinations
on the planet*

Uniqlo
Fashion

Uniqlo is Japan's answer to H&M and this is
its showstopping 89,000-sq-foot flagship
megastore. The forte here is affordable,
fashionable, quality basics, from tees and
undergarments, to Japanese denim, cash-
mere sweaters and high-tech parkas. (Map
p66; ☎877-486-4756; www.uniqlo.com; 666 Fifth
Ave, at 53rd St; ⊙10am-9pm Mon-Sat, 11am-8pm
Sun; ⒮E, M to Fifth Ave-53rd St)

MoMA Design &
Book Store
Gifts, Books

The flagship store at the Museum of
Modern Art is a fab spot to souvenir shop
in one fell swoop. Aside from stocking
gorgeous books (from art and architecture
tomes to pop culture readers and kids'
picture books), you'll find art prints and
posters, and one-of-a-kind knick-knacks.
For furniture, lighting, homewares, jewelry,
bags and MUJI merchandise, head to the

MoMA Design Store across the street. (Map
p66; ☎212-708-9700; www.momastore.org; 11
W 53rd St, btwn Fifth & Sixth Aves; ⊙9:30am-
6:30pm Sat-Thu, to 9pm Fri; ⒮E, M to 5th
Ave-53rd St)

Hell's Kitchen Flea Market
Market

Held on weekends, the market's many
stalls have furnishings, accessories, clothing and objects from past eras, courtesy of
170 choosy vendors. (Map p66; ☎212-243-
5343; 39th St, btwn Ninth & Tenth Aves; ⊙9am-
5pm Sat & Sun; ⒮A/C/E to 42nd St)

⊙ ENTERTAINMENT

New York magazine, *Time Out New York*
and the weekend editions of the *New York
Times* are great guides for what's on once
you arrive.

Choose from current theater shows by
checking print publications, or a website
such as **Theater Mania** (☎212-352-3101;
www.theatermania.com). You can purchase
tickets through **Telecharge** (☎212-239-
6200; www.telecharge.com) and **Ticketmas-
ter** (☎800-448-7849, 800-745-3000; www.
ticketmaster.com) for standard ticket sales,

or **TKTS ticket booths** (Map p60; www.tdf.
org; cnr Front & John Sts; ⏰11am-6pm Mon-Sat,
to 4pm Sun; **S**A/C, 2/3, 4/5, J/Z to Fulton St,
R to Cortlandt St) for same-day tickets to a
selection of Broadway and off-Broadway
musicals at up to 50% off regular prices.

Jazz lovers take note: there's a stunning
array of talent in NYC. **Smalls** (Map p60;
www.smallslive.com) is a subterranean jazz
dungeon that rivals the world-famous
Village Vanguard (Map p60; www.village
vanguard.com) in terms of sheer talent.

Heading uptown, Dizzy's Club Coca-
Cola, at **Jazz at Lincoln Center** (Map p74;
www.jazz.org) – one of Lincoln Center's three
jazz venues – has views overlooking Central Park and nightly shows featuring top
line-ups. Further north on the Upper West
Side, check out the **Smoke Jazz & Supper
Club-Lounge** (Map p74; www.smokejazz.com),
which gets crowded on weekends.

Joe's Pub   Live Music
Part cabaret theater, part rock and new-
indie venue, this small and lovely supper
club hosts a wonderful variety of styles,
voices and talent. (Map p60; ☏212-539-8500,
tickets 212-967-7555; www.joespub.com; Public
Theater, 425 Lafayette St, btwn Astor Pl & 4th St;
S6 to Astor Pl, R/W to 8th St-NYU)

Rockwood Music Hall   Live Music
This breadbox-sized concert space fea-
tures a rapid-fire flow of bands and singer/
songwriters on three different stages.
Many shows are free. (Map p60; ☏212-477-
4155; www.rockwoodmusichall.com; 196 Allen
St, btwn Houston & Stanton Sts; ⏰6pm-2am
Mon-Fri, from 3pm Sat & Sun; **S**F/V to Lower
East Side-Second Ave)

Le Poisson Rouge   Live Music
This basement club is one of the premier
venues for experimental contemporary,
from classical to indie rock to electro-
acoustic. (Map p60; ☏212-505-3474; www.
lepoissonrouge.com; 158 Bleecker St; **S**A/C/E,
B/D/F/M to W 4th St-Washington Sq)

Brooklyn Bowl   Live Music
This 23,000-sq-foot venue inside the former Hecla Iron Works Company combines

Performing Arts Venues

Brooklyn Academy of Music (BAM;
☏718-636-4100; www.bam.org; 30 Lafayette
Ave, at Ashland Pl, Fort Greene; **S**2/3, 4/5,
B, Q to Atlantic Ave) Sort of a Brooklyn
version of the Lincoln Center – in its
all-inclusiveness rather than its vibe,
which is much edgier – the spectacular
academy also hosts everything from
modern dance to opera, cutting-edge
theater and music concerts.

Carnegie Hall (Map p74; ☏212-247-7800;
www.carnegiehall.org; W 57th St at Seventh
Ave, Midtown West; ⏰tours 11:30am,
12:30pm, 2pm & 3pm Mon-Fri, 11:30am &
12:30pm Sat, 12:30pm Sun Oct-Jun; **S**N/Q/R
to 57th St-7th Ave) Since 1891, the historic
Carnegie Hall has hosted performances
by the likes of Tchaikovsky, Mahler and
Prokofiev, as well as Stevie Wonder,
Sting and João Gilberto. It's mostly
closed in July and August.

Joyce Theater (Map p66; ☏212-691-9740;
www.joyce.org; 175 Eighth Ave; **S**C/E to 23rd
St, A/C/E to Eighth Ave-14th St, 1 to 18th St) A
favorite among dance junkies because
of its excellent sight lines and offbeat
offerings, this intimate venue seats 472
in a renovated cinema.

Carnegie Hall
GRANT LAMOS IV / STRINGER / GETTY IMAGES ©

bowling, microbrews, food and groovy live
music. (☏718-963-3369; www.brooklyn
bowl.com; 61 Wythe Ave, btwn 11th & 12th Sts;
⏰6pm-2am Mon-Fri, from 11am Sat & Sun; **S**L
to Bedford Ave, G to Nassau Ave)

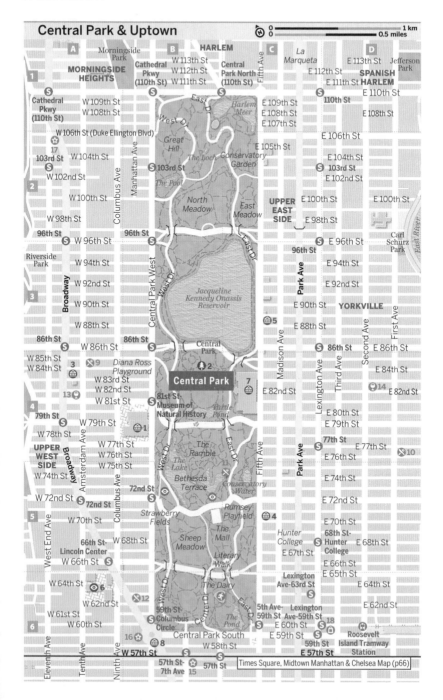

Central Park & Uptown

0 — 1 km
0 — 0.5 miles

Times Square, Midtown Manhattan & Chelsea Map (p66)

Central Park & Uptown

◎ **Sights**
1 American Museum of Natural
   History..B4
2 Central Park....................................B4
3 Children's Museum of Manhattan.............A4
4 Frick Collection.............................C5
5 Guggenheim Museum............................C3
6 Lincoln Center...............................A6
7 Metropolitan Museum of Art...................C4
8 Museum of Arts & Design......................B6

❽ **Eating**
9 Jacob's Pickles..............................A4
10 Jones Wood Foundry..........................D4
11 Loeb Boathouse..............................C5

12 PJ Clarke's.................................B6

◎ **Drinking & Nightlife**
13 Dead Poet...................................A4
14 Penrose.....................................D4
   Robert..................................(see 8)

◎ **Entertainment**
15 Carnegie Hall...............................B6
16 Jazz at Lincoln Center......................B6
17 Smoke Jazz & Supper Club-
   Lounge......................................A2

◎ **Shopping**
18 Bloomingdale's..............................D6

❽ EATING

❽ Lower Manhattan

Fraunces Tavern
American $$

Can you really pass up a chance to eat where George Washington supped in 1762? Expect heaped portions of beer-battered fish and chips, slow-roasted chicken pot pie and braised short ribs. Fraunces Tavern has great atmosphere – particularly on Sundays when there's traditional Irish music (3:30pm to 6:30pm). (Map p60; 🖉212-968-1776; www.frauncestavern.com; 54 Pearl St, at Broad St; mains lunch $14-38, dinner $20-38; ☺11am-10pm; ⓢN/R to Whitehall)

❽ Chinatown & Little Italy

Tacombi
Mexican $

Festively strung lights, foldaway chairs and Mexican men flipping tortillas in an old VW Kombie: if you can't make it to the Yucatan shore, here's your Plan B. Casual, convivial and ever-popular, Tacombi serves up delicious tacos, tender ceviche and creamy guacamole. Wash it all down with a pitcher of sangria, a glass of horchata or a mezcal margarita. (Map p60; 🖉917-727-0179; www.tacombi.com; 267 Elizabeth St, btwn E Houston & Prince Sts; tacos $4-6; ☺11am-midnight Mon-Wed, 11am-1am Thu & Fri, 10am-1am Sat, 10am-midnight Sun; ⓢF to 2nd Ave, 6 to Bleecker St)

Ruby's
Café $

All bases are covered at this inviting Aussie-inspired café. You'll find breakie-friendly avo toast (mashed avocado and fresh tomato on seven grain toast) and pancakes with caramelized apples and pears, and lunch-pleasers like pumpkin salad, pastas and juicy burgers (best ordered with truffle fries). Flat-white coffees and bottles of Bo-ag's complete your antipodean experience. (Map p60; 🖉212-925-5755; www.rubyscafe.com; 219 Mulberry St, btwn Spring & Prince Sts; mains $10-15; ☺9:30am-11pm; ⓢ6 to Spring St, N/R to Prince St)

❽ Lower East Side

Katz's Delicatessen
Deli $$

One of the few remaining Jewish delicatessens in the city, Katz's attracts locals, tourists and celebrities whose photos line the walls. Massive pastrami, corned beef, brisket and tongue sandwiches are throwbacks to another era, as is the payment system: hold on to the ticket you're handed when you walk in and pay cash only. (Map p60; 🖉212-254-2246; www.katzsdelicatessen.com; 205 E Houston St, at Ludlow St; sandwiches $15-22; ☺8am-10:45pm Mon-Wed & Sun, to 2:45am Thu, open all night Fri & Sat; ⓢF to 2nd Ave)

 Best Eating in Chinatown

With hundreds of restaurants, from holes-in-the-wall to banquet-sized dining rooms, Chinatown is wonderful for exploring cheap eats.

Xi'an Famous Foods (Map p60; xianfoods. com; 67 Bayard St, btwn Mott & Elizabeth Sts) Take-out counter serving delicious hand-pulled noodles and spicy cumin lamb 'burgers'; eat it in nearby Columbus Park.

Vanessa's Dumpling House (Map p60; www.vanessas.com; 118 Eldridge St, btwn Grand & Broome Sts) Great dumplings and sesame pancakes.

Amazing 66 (Map p60; www.amazing66. com; 66 Mott St, btwn Canal & Bayard Sts) Terrific Cantonese lunches.

Bánh Mì Saigon Bakery (Map p60; www. banhmisaigonnyc.com; 198 Grand St, btwn Mulberry & Mott Sts) Some of the best Vietnamese sandwiches in town.

Joe's Shanghai (Map p60; www. joeshanghairestaurants.com; 9 Pell St, btwn Bowery & Doyers St) Always busy and tourist-friendly. Does good noodle and soup dishes.

Nom Wah Tea Parlor (Map p60; nomwah. com; 13 Doyers St) Looks like a well-worn American diner, but is the oldest dim sum place in the city.

Original Chinatown Ice Cream Factory (Map p60; www.chinatownice creamfactory.com; 65 Bayard St) Flavorful scoops of green tea, ginger and lychee sorbets.

Nom Wah Tea Parlor

Fung Tu   Fusion $$
Celebrated chef Jonathan Wu brilliantly blends Chinese cooking with global accents at this elegant little eatery on the edge of Chinatown. The complex sharing plates are superb (try scallion pancakes with cashew salad and smoked chicken or crepe roll stuffed with braised beef, pickled cucumbers and watercress) and pair nicely with creative cocktails like the Fung Tu Gibson. (Map p60; 212-219-8785; www.fungtu.com; 22 Orchard St, btwn Hester & Canal Sts; small plates $13-18, mains $24-32; 6pm-midnight Tue-Sat, 4pm-10pm Sun; F to East Broadway)

SoHo & NoHo

Boqueria Soho   Tapas $$
This expansive, welcoming tapas joint features delectable classics, including *pulpo a la gallega* (Galician octopus), *gambas al ajillo* (garlic marinated shrimp) and creamy tortilla (Spanish omelet). You can watch the chefs in action as you sip a pink grapefruit sangria and peer into the open kitchen. (Map p60; 212-343-4255; www.boquerianyc. com; 171 Spring St, btwn West Broadway & Thompson St; tapas $6-18; noon-10:30pm Mon-Thu, noon-11:30pm Fri, noon-11:30pm Sat, noon-10:30pm Sun; C/E to Spring St)

Il Buco   Italian $$$
This charmingly rustic nook boasts hanging copper pots, kerosene lamps and antique furniture, plus a stunning menu and wine list. Sink your teeth into seasonal and ever-changing highlights like pan-roasted black bass with celery root puree or risotto with wild nettles, melted leeks and fresh goat cheese. (Map p60; 212-533-1932; www.ilbuco.com; 47 Bond St, btwn Bowery & Lafayette Sts; mains lunch $17-30, dinner $24-36; noon-midnight Tue-Sat, 6pm-midnight Sun & Mon; B/D/F/V to Broadway-Lafayette Sts; 6 to Bleecker St)

Balthazar   French $$$
Still the king of bistros, bustling Balthazar is never short of a discriminating mob. That's all thanks to its uplifting Paris-meets-NYC ambience and its stellar

Ramen at Momofuku Noodle Bar

something-for-everyone menu. Highlights include the outstanding raw bar, rich onion soup, steak frites and salade Niçoise. Weekend brunch here is a very crowded (and delicious) production. (Map p60; ☎212-965-1414; www.balthazarny.com; 80 Spring St, btwn Broadway & Crosby St; mains $19-45; ☺7:30am-midnight Mon-Thu, 7:30am-1am Fri, 8am-1am Sat, 7:30am-midnight Sun; ⑤6 to Spring St, N/R to Prince St)

🍽 East Village

Cafe Mogador   Moroccan $$

Family-run Mogador is a long-running NYC classic, serving fluffy piles of couscous, char-grilled lamb and merguez sausage over basmati rice and its famous tagines – traditionally spiced, long-simmered chicken or lamb dishes served up five different ways. A garrulous young crowd packs the space, spilling out onto the small café tables on warm days. Brunch is also first-rate. (Map p60; ☎212-677-2226; www.cafemogador. com; 101 St Marks Pl; mains lunch $8-14, dinner $17-21; ☺9am-midnight; ⑤6 to Astor Pl)

> *Chinatown is wonderful for exploring cheap eats*

Angelica Kitchen   Vegetarian $$

This enduring herbivore classic has a calming vibe and enough creative options to make your head spin. Some dishes get too-cute names, but all do wonders with seitan, spices and soy products, and sometimes an array of raw ingredients. Cash only. (Map p60; ☎212-228-2909; www.angelicakitchen.com; 300 E 12th St, btwn First & Second Aves; mains $17-21; ☺11:30am-10:30pm; 🖋; ⑤L to 1st Ave)

Momofuku Noodle Bar   Noodles $$

Ramen and steamed buns are the name of the game at this infinitely creative Japanese eatery, part of the growing David Chang empire. Seating is on stools at a long bar or at communal tables. The famous steamed chicken and pork buns are recommended. (Map p60; ☎212-777-7773; www.momofuku. com/noodle-bar/; 171 First Ave, btwn 10th & 11th Sts; mains $17-28; ☺noon-11pm Sun-Thu, to 1am Fri & Sat; ⑤L to 1st Ave, 6 to Astor Pl)

🍽 Chelsea, Meatpacking District & West (Greenwich) Village

Chelsea Market   Market $

This former cookie factory has been turned into an 800ft-long shopping concourse that caters to foodies with boutique bakeries, gelato shops, ethnic eats and a food court for gourmands. (Map p66; www.chelseamarket. com; 75 9th Ave, btwn 15th & 16th Sts; ⏰7am-9pm Mon-Sat, 8am-8pm Sun; ⑤A/C/E to 14th St)

Spotted Pig   Pub Food $$

This Michelin-starred gastropub is a favorite of Villagers, serving an upscale blend of hearty Italian and British dishes. Its two floors are bedecked with old-timey trinkets that give the whole place an air of relaxed elegance.It doesn't take reservations, so there is often a wait for a table. Lunch on weekdays is less crowded. (Map p60; ☎212-620-0393; www.thespottedpig.com; 314 W 11th St at Greenwich St; mains lunch $17-26, dinner $22-36; ⏰noon-2am Mon-Fri, from 11am Sat & Sun; ⑤A/C/E to 14th Sts; L to 8th Ave)

Cookshop   Modern American $$

A brilliant brunching pit stop before (or after) tackling the verdant High Line across the street, Cookshop is a lively spot for eye-opening cocktails, a perfectly baked breadbasket and a selection of inventive egg mains. Dinner is a sure-fire win as well. Ample outdoor seating on warm days. (Map p66; ☎212-924-4440; www.cookshopny. com; 156 Tenth Ave, btwn 19th & 20th Sts; mains brunch $14-20, lunch $16-24, dinner $22-38; ⏰8am-11:30pm Mon-Fri, from 10am Sat, 10am-10pm Sun; ⑤L to 8th Ave, A/C/E to 23rd St)

RedFarm   Fusion $$$

RedFarm transforms Chinese cooking into pure, delectable artistry at this small, buzzing space on Hudson St. Crispy duck and crab dumplings, sautéed black cod with black bean and Thai basil, and pastrami egg rolls are among the many creative dishes that brilliantly blend east with west. Waits can be long, so arrive early (no reservations). (Map p60; ☎212-792-9700; www.redfarmnyc.com; 529 Hudson St, btwn 10th & Charles Sts; mains $22-46, dim sum $10-16; ⏰5-11pm daily & 11am-2:30pm Sat & Sun;

S A/C/E, B/D/F/M to W 4th St, 1 to Christopher St-Sheridan Sq)

🍴 Union Square, Flatiron District & Gramercy Park

Shake Shack   Burgers $
Tourists line up in droves for the hamburgers and shakes at this Madison Square Park counter-window-serving institution. (Map p66; ☎646-747-2606; www.shakeshack.com; Madison Square Park, cnr 23rd St & Madison Ave; burgers $4.19-9.49; ☺11am-11pm; S N/R, F/M, 6 to 23rd St)

Eataly   Italian $$
The *pièce de résistance* here is a rooftop beer garden called **Birreria** (Map p66; ☎212-937-8910; www.eataly.com; 200 Fifth Ave, at 23rd St; mains $17-37; ☺11:30am-11pm Sun-Thu, to midnight Fri & Sat; S N/R, F/M, 6 to 23rd St). As for the rest of Eataly – it's the promised land for lovers of Italian food, a 50,000-sq-foot emporium with a countless array of tempting food counters. Think brick-oven pizza, creamy gelato, fresh-made pastas, pecorino-covered salads, perfectly pulled

espresso and much more. It's set amid a gourmet market, with plenty of picnic ideas. (Map p66; www.eataly.com; 200 Fifth Ave, at 23rd St; ☺8am-11pm; 🍴; S N/R, F/M, 6 to 23rd St)

🍴 Midtown

Totto Ramen   Japanese $
Write your name and number of guests on the clipboard by the door and wait for your (cash-only) ramen revelation. Skip the chicken; try the pork, which sings in dishes like miso ramen (with fermented soybean paste, egg, scallion, bean sprouts, onion and homemade chili paste). (Map p66; ☎212-582-0052; www.tottoramen.com; 366 W 52nd St, btwn Eighth & Ninth Aves, Midtown West; ramen from $10; ☺noon-4:30pm & 5:30-midnight Mon-Sat, 4-11pm Sun; S C/E to 50th St)

Hangawi   Korean $$
Sublime, flesh-free Korean is the draw at high-achieving Hangawi. Leave your shoes at the entrance and slip into a soothing, zen-like space of meditative music, soft low seating and clean, complexly flavored dishes. Show-stoppers include the leek pancakes and a seductively smooth tofu

★ Top Five Eateries
Il Buco (p76)

Momofuku Noodle Bar (p77)

Eataly (p79)

Xi'an Famous Foods (p76)

Katz's Delicatessen (p75)

From left: Shake Shack; Katz's Delicatessen (p75); Eataly

SIVAN ASKAYO / LONELY PLANET ©

BEN HIDER / GETTY IMAGES ©

 Explore Brooklyn

Brooklyn is a world in and of itself. In many people's minds, this borough has long succeeded Manhattan in the cool and livability factors. Here's a rundown of top neighborhoods for exploring:

Williamsburg Young alternative scene with loads of art galleries, record stores, bars and eateries.

Brooklyn Heights Gorgeous tree-lined streets and a promenade with stellar Lower Manhattan views (at the end of Montague St).

Dumbo Atmospheric brick streets on the waterfront; art galleries, shops, cafés and picture-postcard Manhattan views.

Fort Greene Pretty and racially diverse ''hood; home of famed Brooklyn Academy of Music (p73), a highly respected performing-arts complex and cinema.

Boerum Hill, Cobble Hill & Carroll Gardens Tree-lined streets, attractive brownstones, and restaurant-lined Smith and Court Sts.

Park Slope Classic brownstones, loads of great eateries and boutiques (along Fifth Ave and Seventh Ave), and lush 585-acre **Prospect Park** (www.prospect park.org) and the **Brooklyn Botanic Garden** (www.bbg.org).

Coney Island Old-fashioned boardwalk, amusement park and aquarium (www. nyaquarium.com).

Williamsburg
MAREMAGNUM / GETTY IMAGES ©

claypot in ginger sauce. (Map p66; ☏212-213-0077; www.hangawirestaurant.com; 12 E 32nd St, btwn Fifth & Madison Aves; mains lunch $11-30, dinner $19-30; ⊙noon-2:30pm & 5:30-10:15pm Mon-Fri, 1-10:30pm Sat, 5-9:30pm Sun; 🖉; Ⓢ B/D/F/M, N/Q/R to 34th St-Herald Sq)

Artisanal French $$$

For those who live, love and dream *fromage*, Artisanal is a must-eat. More than 250 varieties of cheese, from stinky to sweet, are found at this classic Parisian-style bistro. Creamy goodness aside, other favorite items include mussels, braised lamb shank and onion soup gratinée (with a three-cheese blend of course). (Map p66; ☏212-725-8585; www.arti sanalbistro.com; 2 Park Ave S, btwn 32nd & 33rd Sts; mains $24-50; ⊙10am-midnight Mon-Fri, from 9am Sat & Sun; 🖉; Ⓢ6 to 33rd St)

🔾 Upper West Side

Jacob's Pickles American $$

On a restaurant-lined stretch of Amsterdam Ave, this inviting and warmly lit eatery serves upscale comfort food, like catfish tacos, wine-braised turkey leg dinner, and St Louis ribs slathered with coffee molasses barbecue sauce. The biscuits and pickles are top-notch, and you'll find two dozen or so craft beers on tap from New York, Maine and beyond. (Map p74; ☏212-470-5566; www. jacobspickles.com; 509 Amsterdam Ave, btwn 84th & 85th Sts; mains $15-26; ⊙10am-2am Mon-Thu, to 4am Fri, 9am-4am Sat, to 2am Sun; Ⓢ1 to 86th St)

PJ Clarke's American $$

Across the street from Lincoln Center, this red-checked-tablecloth spot has a buttoned-down crowd, friendly bartenders and a solid menu. If you're in a rush, belly up to the bar for a Black Angus burger and a Brooklyn Lager. A raw bar offers fresh Long Island Little Neck and Cherry Stone clams, as well as jumbo shrimp cocktails. (Map p74; ☏212-957-9700; www.pjclarkes.com; 44 W 63rd St, cnr Broadway; burgers $13-16, mains $20-26; ⊙11:30am-2am; Ⓢ1 to 66th St-Lincoln Center)

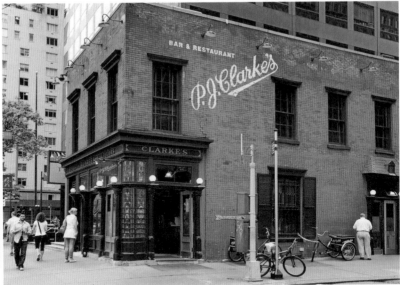

PJ Clarke's

🌆 Upper East Side

Jones Wood Foundry   British $$

Inside a narrow brick building that once housed an ironworks, the Jones Wood Foundry is a British-inspired gastropub serving first-rate beer-battered fish and chips, bangers and mash, lamb and rosemary pie and other hearty temptations. On warm days, grab a table on the enclosed courtyard patio. (Map p74; 📞212-249-2700; www.joneswoodfoundry.com; 401 E 76th St, btwn First & York Aves; mains lunch $16-20, dinner $19-26; ⏱11am-11pm; 🛜; 🚇6 to 77th St)

🍸 DRINKING & NIGHTLIFE

🍹 Downtown

Apothéke   Cocktail Bar

It takes a little effort to track down this former opium-den-turned-apothecary bar. Inside, skilled barkeeps work like careful chemists, using local and organic produce from greenmarkets or the rooftop herb garden to produce intense, flavorful 'prescriptions'. (Map p60; 📞212-406-0400; www.apothekenyc.com; 9 Doyers St; ⏱6:30pm-2am

Mon-Sat, 8pm-2am Sun; 🚇J/Z to Chambers St, 4/5/6 to Brooklyn Bridge-City Hall)

Ten Bells   Bar

This tucked-away tapas bar has flickering candles, dark tin ceilings, brick walls and a U-shaped bar that's an ideal setting for conversation with a new friend. The chalkboard menu features excellent wines by the glass, which go nicely with *boquerones* (marinated anchovies) and other Iberian hits. The entrance is unsigned. (Map p60; 📞212-228-4450; www.tenbellsnyc.com; 247 Broome St, btwn Ludlow & Orchard Sts; ⏱5pm-2am Mon-Fri, from 3pm Sat & Sun; 🚇F to Delancey St, J/M/Z to Essex St)

Wayland   Bar

Whitewashed walls, weathered floorboards and salvaged lamps give this urban outpost a Mississippi flair, which goes just right with the live music (bluegrass, jazz, folk) from Sunday through Wednesday. There are decent drink specials and $1 oysters from 5pm to 7pm on weekdays. (Map p60; 📞212-777-7022; www.thewaylandnyc.com; 700 E 9th St, cnr Ave C; ⏱5pm-4am; 🚇L to 1st Ave)

PETER HORREE / ALAMY STOCK PHOTO ©

ZUMA PRESS, INC / ALAMY STOCK PHOTO ©

Jimmy's Corner

> *stiff drinks and a whiff of nostalgia await at Jimmy's Corner*

Employees Only — Bar

Duck behind the neon 'Psychic' sign to find this hidden hangout. The bar gets busier as the night wears on. Bartenders are ace mixologists, fizzing up crazy, addictive libations like the Ginger Smash and the Mata Hari. Great for late-night drinking, and eating, courtesy of the on-site restaurant that serves until 3:30am. (Map p60; ☏212-242-3021; www.employeesonlynyc.com; 510 Hudson St, near Christopher St; ⊗6pm-4am; ⓈWIto Christopher St-Sheridan Sq)

Buvette — Wine Bar

The rustic-chic decor here (think delicate tin tiles and a swooshing marble countertop) make it the perfect place for a glass of wine – no matter the time of day. For the full experience at this self-proclaimed *gastrotèque*, grab a seat at one of the surrounding tables, and nibble on small plates while enjoying the Old-World wines (mostly from France and Italy). (Map p60; ☏212-255-3590; www.ilovebuvette.com; 42 Grove St, btwn Bedford & Bleecker Sts; ⊗9am-2am; ⓈW1 to Christopher St-Sheridan Sq, A/C/E, B/D/F/M to W 4th St)

Old Town Bar & Restaurant — Bar

It still looks like 1892 in here, with the original tile floors and tin ceilings – the Old Town is an 'old world' drinking-man's classic (and woman's: Madonna lit up at the bar here, when lighting up was still legal, in her 'Bad Girl' video). There are cocktails around, but most come for beers and a burger (from $12). (Map p66; ☏212-529-6732; www.oldtownbar.com; 45 E 18th St, btwn Broadway & Park Ave S; ⊗11:30am-1am Mon-Fri, noon-2am Sat, 1pm-midnight Sun; ⓈW4/5/6, N/Q/R, L to 14th St-Union Sq)

◉ Midtown

Frying Pan — Bar

The Lightship *Frying Pan* and the two-tiered dockside bar where it's parked are fine go-to spots for a sundowner. On warm days, the rustic open-air space brings in the crowds, who come to laze on deck chairs, eat burgers, drink ice-cold beers and admire the waterside views. (Map p66; 212-989-6363; www.fryingpan.com; Pier 66, at W 26th St; noon-midnight May-Oct; C/E to 23rd St)

Jimmy's Corner   Dive Bar
This skinny, welcoming, completely unpretentious dive off Times Square is owned by an old boxing trainer – as if you wouldn't guess by all the framed photos of boxing greats. The jukebox covers Stax to Miles Davis. (Map p66; 212-221-9510; 140 W 44th St, btwn Sixth & Seventh Aves, Midtown West; 11am-4am Mon-Fri, from 12:30pm Sat, from 3pm Sun; N/Q/R, 1/2/3, 7 to 42nd St-Times Sq, B/D/F/M to 42nd St-Bryant Park)

Russian Vodka Room   Bar
Actual Russians aren't uncommon at this swanky and welcoming bar. The lighting is dark and the corner booths intimate, but more importantly the dozens of infused vodkas, from cranberry to horseradish, are fun to experiment with. (Map p66; 212-307-5835; www.russianvodkaroom.com; 265 W 52nd St, btwn Eighth Ave & Broadway, Midtown West; 4pm-2am Mon-Thu, to 4am Fri & Sat; C/E to 50th St)

R Lounge   Bar
It mightn't be the most fashionable spot for a drink in town, but this hotel bar delivers a spectacular, floor-to-ceiling view of Times Square that's hard to beat. (Renaissance Hotel; Map p66; 212-261-5200; www.rlounge timessquare.com; Two Times Square, 714 Seventh Ave, at 48th St, Midtown West; 5-11pm Mon, to 11:30pm Tue-Thu, to midnight Fri, 7:30am-midnight Sat, 7:30am-11pm Sun; N/Q/R to 49th St)

Top of the Strand   Cocktail Bar
For that 'I'm in New York' feeling, head to the Strand hotel's rooftop bar, order a martini and admire the jaw-dropping view of the Empire State Building. (Map p66; www.topof thestrand.com; Strand Hotel, 33 W 37th St, btwn Fifth & Sixth Aves; 5pm-midnight Mon & Sun, to 1am Tue-Sat; B/D/F/M to 34th St)

Where to Watch Sport

Baseball The uber-successful New York Yankees (www.yankees.com) play at Yankee Stadium, while the more historically beleaguered **New York Mets** (www.mets.com) play at Citi Field.

Basketball You can get courtside with the NBA's **New York Knicks** (Map p66; www.nyknicks.com) at **Madison Square Garden** (Map p66; www.thegarden.com), called the 'mecca of basketball,' and with the **Brooklyn Nets** (www.nba.com/nets), who play at the **Barclays Center** (www.barclayscenter.com) near downtown Brooklyn.

Football New York City's NFL (profootball) teams, the **Giants** (www.giants.com) and **Jets** (www.newyorkjets.com), share MetLife Stadium in East Rutherford, New Jersey.

Miami Dolphins vs New York Giants
CHRIS TROTMAN / STRINGER / GETTY IMAGES ©

Uptown
Dead Poet   Bar
This skinny, mahogany-paneled pub has been a neighborhood favorite for over a decade, attracting a mix of locals and students nursing pints of Guinness and cocktails named after dead poets. (Map p74; 212-595-5670; www.thedeadpoet.com; 450 Amsterdam Ave, btwn 81st & 82nd Sts; noon-4am; 1 to 79th St)

Penrose   Bar
The Penrose brings a dose of style to the Upper East Side, with craft beers, vintage mirrors, floral wallpaper and friendly bartenders setting the stage for a fine evening among friends. (Map p74; ☎212-203-2751; www.penrosebar.com; 1590 Second Ave, btwn 82nd & 83rd Sts; ☺noon-4am Mon-Fri, from 10am Sat & Sun; ⑤4/5/6 to 86th St)

ℹ INFORMATION

NYC Information Center's website (www.nycgo.com) has loads of tourist information.

ℹ GETTING THERE & AROUND

With its three bustling airports, two main train stations and a monolithic bus terminal, New York City rolls out the welcome mat for the more than 50 million visitors who come to take a bite out of the Big Apple each year.

The city's three airports are John F Kennedy International Airport (p369), **LaGuardia Airport** (LGA; www.panynj.com/aviation/lgaframe) and **Newark Liberty International Airport** (EWR; ☎973-961-6000; www.panynj.gov). Direct flights are possible from most major American and international cities. Figure six hours from Los Angeles, seven hours from London and Amsterdam, and 14 hours from Tokyo.

Consider getting here by train instead of car or plane to enjoy a mix of bucolic and urban scenery en route, without unnecessary traffic hassles, security checks and excess carbon emissions. Check out train options through **Amtrak** (☎800-872-7245; www.amtrak.com).

Flights, tours and rail tickets can be booked online at lonelyplanet.com/bookings.

TO/FROM THE AIRPORT
Taxis charge a $52 flat rate (plus toll and tip) from JFK to anywhere in Manhattan. Fares are metered from Newark (approximately $55 to $75) and LaGuardia ($40 to $50).

A cheaper and pretty easy option to or from JFK is the AirTrain ($5 one way), which connects to subway lines into the city ($2.50; coming from the city, take the Far Rockaway–bound A train) or to the LIRR ($7 to $10 one way) at Jamaica Station in Queens (this is probably the quickest route to Penn Station in the city).

To or from Newark, the AirTrain links all terminals to a New Jersey Transit train station, which connects to Penn Station in NYC ($13 one way combined NJ Transit/Airtrain ticket).

All three airports are also served by express buses ($16) and shuttle vans ($23); such companies include the New York Airport Service Express Bus, which leaves every 20 or so minutes for Port Authority, Penn Station (NYC) and Grand Central Station; and **Super Shuttle Manhattan** (www.supershuttle.com), which picks you (and others) up anywhere, on demand, with a reservation.

BICYCLE
Citi Bike (www.citibikenyc.com; 24hr/7 days $11/27) is NYC's bike-sharing program.

PUBLIC TRANSPORTATION
The **Metropolitan Transport Authority** (MTA; ☎718-330-1234; www.mta.info) runs both the subway and bus systems (per ride $2.75). To board, you must purchase a MetroCard, available at subway windows and self-serve machines, which accept change, dollars or credit/debit cards; purchasing many rides at once works out cheaper per trip. Check the website for information on buses and subway routes, including a handy travel planner.

Subway Inexpensive, open around the clock and often the fastest way to get round the city, though it can be confusing to the uninitiated. A single ride is $2.75 with a MetroCard.

Bus Convenient during off hours – especially when transferring between the city's east and west sides. Same price as the subway.

Taxi Meters start at $2.50 and increase roughly $4 for every 20 blocks.

Interborough ferry Hop-on-hop-off service and free rides in the harbor to Staten Island. Check out New York Waterway (www.nywaterway.com) and New York Water Taxi (www.nywatertaxi.com).

Where to Stay

The 'city that never sleeps' is home to some of the most inventive and memorable spaces for those who might just want to grab a bit of shut-eye during their stay.

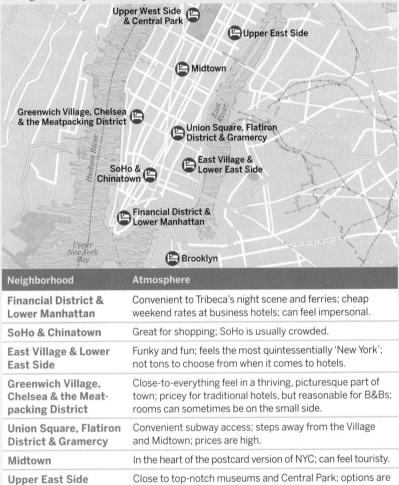

Neighborhood	Atmosphere
Financial District & Lower Manhattan	Convenient to Tribeca's night scene and ferries; cheap weekend rates at business hotels; can feel impersonal.
SoHo & Chinatown	Great for shopping; SoHo is usually crowded.
East Village & Lower East Side	Funky and fun; feels the most quintessentially 'New York'; not tons to choose from when it comes to hotels.
Greenwich Village, Chelsea & the Meat-packing District	Close-to-everything feel in a thriving, picturesque part of town; pricey for traditional hotels, but reasonable for B&Bs; rooms can sometimes be on the small side.
Union Square, Flatiron District & Gramercy	Convenient subway access; steps away from the Village and Midtown; prices are high.
Midtown	In the heart of the postcard version of NYC; can feel touristy.
Upper East Side	Close to top-notch museums and Central Park; options are scarce; prices are high; not particularly central.
Upper West Side & Central Park	Convenient access to Central Park; tends to swing in the familial direction.
Brooklyn	Better prices; great for exploring creative neighborhoods; can be a long commute to Midtown Manhattan.

Fall foliage in the Berkshires (p91)

NEW ENGLAND

New England

New England may look small on a map, but don't let that fool you. From big-city Boston – the cradle of the American experiment – to the rugged shores of Maine, New England packs in a dazzling array of attractions. Historical sites, world-class restaurants and age-old fishing villages are all part of the vibrant mix.

On the coast you'll find sandy beaches begging for a stroll and pristine harbor towns sprinkled with old mansions, wide lawns and quaint antique shops and galleries. The joys here are simple, but amply rewarding – from cracking open a lobster at a weathered seafood shack by the water to hiking a coastal trail past tranquil ponds and along sea cliffs. And if you're lucky enough to be here in autumn, you'll be rewarded with the most brilliant fall foliage you'll ever see.

☑ In This Section

Fall Foliage 90
Acadia National Park 92
Freedom Trail 96
Boston 100
Salem 112
Cape Cod & the Islands 112
Nantucket 115
Martha's Vineyard 117
Vermont 118
New Hampshire 120
Coastal Maine 121

❶ Arriving in New England

Boston is the region's hub. Major US and foreign airlines fly into **Logan International Airport** (p111). The train is another popular way to get here. **Amtrak** (www.amtrak.com) has fast, frequent service connecting Boston to New York City, Washington, DC, and other eastern cities.

Beyond Boston, the best way to get around is by car. The region's highways are good, and distances are short.

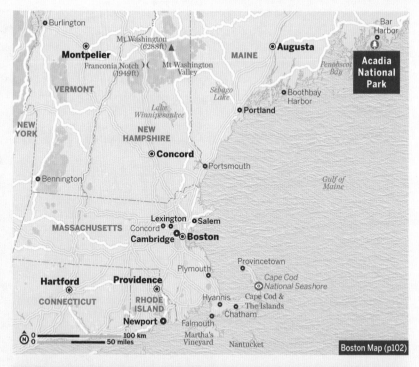

Burlington

Mt Washington
(6288ft) ▲

Montpelier

Franconia Notch) (
(1949ft)

Mt Washington
Valley

MAINE

⊙**Augusta**

Bar
Harbor

Penobscot
Bay

Acadia National Park

VERMONT

Sebago
Lake

Boothbay
Harbor

Lake
Winnipesaukee

⊙**Portland**

**NEW
YORK**

**NEW
HAMPSHIRE**

⊙**Concord**

Bennington

Portsmouth

Gulf of
Maine

MASSACHUSETTS

Lexington ⊙ Salem
Concord ⊙
Cambridge ⊙**Boston**

Provincetown

Plymouth

Cape Cod
⊙ National Seashore

Hartford

Providence

Hyannis

Cape Cod &
The Islands

CONNECTICUT

**RHODE
ISLAND**

Chatham

▲
N
0 —— 100 km
0 —— 50 miles

Newport ⊙

Falmouth

Martha's
Vineyard

Nantucket

Boston Map (p102)

From left: Bar Harbor (p125); Night view of Boston (p100); Cape Cod National Seashore (p113)

Fall in Vermont

DAVE AND LES JACOBS / GETTY IMAGES ©

Fall Foliage

One of New England's greatest natural resources is seasonal change; every fall, the trees fling off that staid New England green and deck their boughs with flaming reds, yellows and oranges. Get ready for leaf-peeping season.

Great For...

☑ **Don't Miss**

Snapping leafy photos in the gorgeous little village of Grafton, VT.

Vermont Leaf Peeps

Here are a few spots to see Vermont's famous fall foliage at its best:

Mt Mansfield Vermont's highest peak is gorgeous when draped in fall colors, especially when an early snowfall dusts the summit white. The best panoramic perspectives are from Stowe, Jeffersonville, Cambridge and Underhill. Hikers can also experience the full sweep of color from the mountaintop; one of the prettiest routes is the Sunset Ridge Trail in Underhill State Park.

Grafton Villages don't get any cuter than Grafton, which looks like it was airlifted in from an earlier century. The white clapboard buildings are even more photogenic when contrasted against fiery leaves and a brilliant blue sky.

Lake Willoughby The Technicolor majesty of changing maples looks especially dramatic on the steep slopes surrounding this fjord-like lake in Vermont's Northeast Kingdom.

Kent Falls State Park

STAN TESS / ALAMY STOCK PHOTO ©

Massachusetts Leaf Peeps

Blanketing the westernmost part of the state, the rounded mountains of the Berkshires turn crimson and gold as early as mid-September.

Great Barrington This former industrial town is now populated with art galleries and upscale restaurants. It's a good base for exploring October Mountain State Forest, a multicolored tapestry of hemlocks, birches and oaks.

Mt Greylock State Reservation The mountain summit offers a panorama stretching up to 100 miles across more than five states.

Connecticut Leaf Peeps

Kent has previously been voted *the* spot in all of New England for fall-foliage viewing. But the fact is the whole of the densely wooded Housatonic River Valley offers numerous opportunities for leaf peeping:

Squantz Pond Shoreline walks with views of bristling mountains carpeted with forests plunging straight down to the pond.

Lake Waramaug Fabulous foliage seen twice over when reflected in the mirror-like expanse of the lake.

Boyd Woods Audubon Sanctuary, Litchfield Gentle walks through deciduous woodland alongside Wigwam Pond.

Kent Falls State Park A leaf-framed waterfall and Technicolor mountain views.

West Cornwall A red covered bridge set against the tree-lined Housatonic River.

Fall Festivals

Big E (www.thebige.com) Officially known as the Eastern States Exposition, this fair in West Springfield, Massachusetts, in the second half of September features animal shows, carnival rides, cheesy performances and more.

Fryeburg Fair (www.fryeburgfair.org) There's something for everyone at this old-fashioned agricultural fair in Maine, from live animals to live music, from fun rides to fireworks. First week in October.

Northern Berkshire Fall Foliage Parade (www.fallfoliageparade.com) If you're in the area for the leaves, catch this festival in North Adams on the first Sunday in October. Music, food and fun.

Cadillac Mountain (p94)

Acadia National Park

The only national park in New England, Acadia encompasses an unspoiled wilderness of undulating coastal mountains, towering sea cliffs, surf-pounded beaches and quiet ponds. The park covers over 62 sq miles, including most of mountainous Mt Desert Island, and holds diverse wildlife including moose, puffins and bald eagles. This dramatic landscape offers a plethora of activities for both leisurely hikers and adrenaline junkies.

Great For...

Mount Desert Island • Bar Harbor

Acadia ◉
National Park

ATLANTIC OCEAN

ⓘ Need to Know

www.nps.gov/acad

★ **Top Tip**

Island Explorer (www.exploreacadia.com; ⊙late Jun-early Oct) **runs eight free shuttle bus routes throughout the park and to adjacent Bar Harbor.**

Acadia National Park was established in 1919 on land John D Rockefeller donated to the national parks system to save from encroaching lumber interests. Today you can hike or cycle along the same carriage roads he once traveled in his horse and buggy.

Start your exploration at **Hulls Cove Visitor Center** (207-288-3338; www.nps.gov/acad; ME 3; 8am-4:30pm mid-Apr–Jun & Oct, to 6pm Jul & Aug, to 5pm Sep), from where the 20-mile Park Loop Rd circumnavigates the eastern portion of the park.

Hiking & Cycling

Some 125 miles of hiking trails crisscross Acadia National Park, from easy half-mile nature walks to steep mountain treks. A standout is the 3-mile round-trip Ocean Trail, which runs between Sand Beach and Otter Cliffs. Pick up a guide describing all the trails at the visitor center.

The park's 45 miles of carriage roads are the prime attraction for cycling. You can rent mountain bikes at **Acadia Bike** (207-288-9605; www.acadiabike.com; 48 Cottage St; per day $23; 8am-6pm Jul & Aug, 9am-6pm May & Jun, Sep & Oct).

Cadillac Mountain

The majestic centerpiece of the park is Cadillac Mountain (1530ft), the highest coastal peak in the eastern US, reached by a 3.5-mile spur road off Park Loop Rd. Four hiking trails lead to the summit from four directions. The 360-degree view of ocean, islands and mountains is a winner any time of the day, but it's truly magical at dawn when hardy souls flock to the top to watch the sun rise over Frenchman Bay.

Cadillac Mountain at sunrise

Cadillac Mountain Summit Trail

Some folks drive up to the summit and somehow miss this view-studded loop trail that crowns Cadillac Mountain. With ocean and mountain vistas galore, this may be the most rewarding 15-minute hike you'll ever make. It begins on a paved footpath at the southern end of the parking lot. As you walk, sweeping views unfold from Southwest Harbor and Great Cranberry Island in the south to Bar Harbor and Frenchman Bay in the east and mainland Maine to the north. Plaques along the way provide insights into the geological origins of Acadia National Park's highest peak.

☑ Don't Miss

The sunrise panorama from atop Cadillac Mountain.

Cadillac Mountain South Ridge Trail

At 7.4 miles (about four hours) round-trip, the South Ridge Trail to the summit of Cadillac Mountain is the longest hike in the park. The trail has a moderate ascent and follows a ridge, rewarding hikers with unobstructed views along the way. It starts in the woods on the north side of ME 3, 100ft south of the Blackwoods Campground entrance.

Witch Hole Pond Cycling Loop

This 3.3-mile carriage-road loop makes a fun, easy outing for families and those looking for a short pedal close to the park's main entrance and Bar Harbor. You'll encounter some gentle hills, but the route is largely flat, skirting bogs and small ponds with log-stacked beaver lodges.

Park Loop Road

Park Loop Rd is the main sightseeing jaunt through Acadia. If you're up for a bracing swim or just want to stroll Acadia's longest beach, stop at Sand Beach. About a mile beyond Sand Beach is Thunder Hole, where wild Atlantic waves crash into a deep, narrow chasm with such force that a thundering boom is created. Look to the south to see Otter Cliffs, a favorite rock-climbing spot that rises vertically from the sea. At Jordan Pond, choose from a 1-mile nature trail loop around the south side of the pond or a 3.5-mile trail that skirts the entire pond. Near the end of Park Loop Rd a side road leads up to Cadillac Mountain.

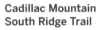

PAT & CHUCK BLACKLEY / ALAMY STOCK PHOTO ©

---

❶ Need to Know

Open year-round, though Park Loop Rd and most facilities close in winter. An admission fee (per car/person $25/12), valid for seven consecutive days, is charged from May through October.

✕ Take a Break

Tea and popovers stoke energy levels at **Jordan Pond House** (www.thejordanpond house.com; ⏰11am-8pm mid-May–Oct).

Freedom Trail marker

GLOWIMAGES / GETTY IMAGES ©

Freedom Trail

The best introduction to revolutionary Boston, the Freedom Trail is a red-brick path that winds past 16 sites that were pivotal to America's independence. The 2.5-mile trail follows the course of the conflict, starting at the Boston Common.

For all intents and purposes, Boston is America's oldest city. The Freedom Trail connects historically significant sites, from the first public school in America to Boston's first church building to sites linked to America's fight for independence from Britain.

The trail is well marked and easy to follow on your own – an ideal strategy if you actually wish to enter some of the historic buildings and museums. Otherwise, there are plenty of tours that follow the trail.

Highlights

Granary Burying Ground

Dating to 1660, the **Granary Burying Ground** (Map p102; Tremont St; ⏲9am-5pm; ⊤Park St) is crammed with historic head-

---

Great For...

☑ **Don't Miss**

Paul Revere's House and the cool bell that was forged in his foundry.

Old State House (p99)

VISIONS OF OUR LAND / GETTY IMAGES ©

Paul Revere House

When silversmith Paul Revere rode to warn
patriots of the British march to Lexington
and Concord, he set out from this 1680
clapboard **house** (Map p102; www.paulrevere
house.org; 19 North Sq; adult/child $3.50/1;
⊙9:30am-5:15pm mid-Apr–Oct, to 4:15pm Nov–
mid-Apr, closed Mon Jan-Mar; 👪; Ⓣ Haymarket).
A self-guided tour gives a glimpse of what
life was like for the Revere family (which
included 16 children!).

Bunker Hill Monument

This 220ft granite obelisk **monument**
(www.nps.gov/bost; Monument Sq; ⊙9am-
5:30pm Jul & Aug, to 4:15pm Sep-Jun; 👪; 🚌93
from Haymarket, Ⓣ Community College) FREE
commemorates the turning-point battle
that was fought on the surrounding hillside
on June 17, 1775. Climb the 294 steps to
the top of the monument to enjoy the
panorama of the city, the harbor and the
North Shore.

stones, many with evocative (and creepy)
carvings. This is the final resting place
of all your favorite revolutionary heroes,
including Paul Revere, Samuel Adams and
John Hancock.

Site of the Boston Massacre

Just outside the Old State House, this **site**
(Map p102; cnr State & Devonshire Sts; Ⓣ State)
marks the spot where the first blood was
shed for the American independence
movement. On March 5, 1770, an angry
mob of colonists swarmed the British
soldiers guarding the State House. Thus
provoked, the soldiers fired into the crowd
and killed five townspeople. The incident
sparked enormous anti-British sentiment
in the lead-up to the revolution.

Tours

Freedom Trail Foundation (www.thefreedomtrail.
org; adult/child $14/8) Excellent tours, broken
up into bite-size portions (eg Boston Common to
Faneuil Hall, North End etc).

NPS Freedom Trail Tour (www.nps.gov/bost)
Free, ranger-led tours.

Boston by Foot (www.bostonbyfoot.com; adult/
child $15/10) Offers a kid-friendly version of the trail.

Walking Tour: Freedom Trail

Trace America's earliest history along the Freedom Trail, which covers Boston's key revolutionary sites.

Distance: 2.5 miles
Duration: 3 hours

✕ Take a Break
After visiting Faneuil Hall, treat yourself to lunch at Union Oyster House (p108).

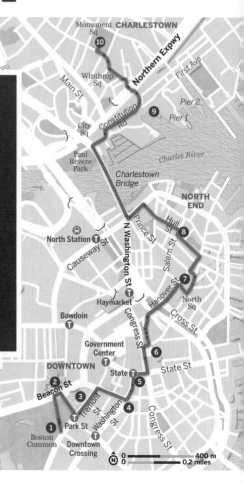

Start Boston Common

❶ Boston Common

The well-trodden route is marked by a double row of red bricks, starting at the Boston Common, America's oldest public park. Follow the trail north.

❷ State House

This gold-domed building was designed by Charles Bulfinch, America's first home-grown architect. As you round Park St, you'll pass the Colonial-era Park Street Church.

❸ Granary Burying Ground

Dating to 1660, this atmospheric spot is crammed with historic headstones, many with evocative carvings. This is the final resting place of all your favorite revolutionary heroes including Paul Revere, Samuel Adams, John Hancock and James Otis.

❹ Old South Meeting House

Walk down School St, past the site of Boston's first public school and the Old Corner Bookstore, a haunt of 19th-century literati. Nearby is the Old South Meeting House. 'No tax on tea!' was the decision on December 16, 1773, when 5000 angry colonists gathered here to protest British taxes, leading to the Boston Tea Party.

Boston Common

HUNTSTOCK / ALAMY STOCK PHOTO ©

❺ Old State House

Dating to 1713, the Old State House is Boston's oldest surviving public building, where the Massachusetts Assembly used to debate the issues of the day before the revolution. Outside, a ring of cobblestones marks the Boston Massacre Site, the first violent conflict of the American Revolution. The building is best known for its balcony, where the Declaration of Independence was first read to Bostonians in 1776.

❻ Faneuil Hall

This public meeting place was the site of so much rabble-rousing that it earned the nickname the 'Cradle of Liberty'. After the revolution, Faneuil Hall was a forum for meetings about abolition, women's suffrage and war.

❼ Paul Revere House

When silversmith Paul Revere rode to warn patriots of the British march to Lexington and Concord, he set out from his home on North Sq. This small clapboard house was built in 1680; it's the oldest house in Boston. A self-guided tour gives visitors a glimpse of what everyday life was like for the Revere family (which included 16 children!)

❽ Old North Church

A lookout in the steeple of Boston's oldest church (it dates back to 1723) signaled to Revere that the British were coming, setting off his famous midnight gallop.

❾ USS Constitution

Walk northwest on Hull St, where you'll find more Colonial graves at Copp's Hill Burying Ground. Then cross the Charlestown Bridge to reach the USS Constitution, the world's oldest commissioned warship.

❿ Bunker Hill Monument

A 220ft granite obelisk monument commemorates the turning-point battle that was fought on the surrounding hillside on June 17, 1775. Ultimately, the Redcoats prevailed, but the victory was bittersweet, as they lost more than one-third of their deployed forces, while the colonists suffered relatively few casualties. Climb the 294 steps to the top of the monument to enjoy the panorama of the city, the harbor and the North Shore.

End Bunker Hill Monument

Boston

One of America's oldest cities is also one of its youngest. A score of colleges and universities add a fresh face to this historic capital and feed a thriving arts and entertainment scene. But don't think for a minute that Boston is all about the literati. Grab a seat in the bleachers at Fenway Park and join the fanatical fans cheering on the Red Sox.

◎ SIGHTS
◎ Beacon Hill & Downtown

Rising above Boston Common is Beacon Hill, one of the city's most historic and affluent neighborhoods.

Boston Common   Park
The Boston Common has served many purposes over the years, including as a campground for British troops during the Revolutionary War and as green grass for cattle grazing until 1830. Although there is still a grazing ordinance on the books, the Common today serves picnickers,

sunbathers and people-watchers. In winter, the **Frog Pond** (www.bostonfrogpond.com; Boston Common; adult/child $5/free, rental $10/5; ⊙10am-4pm Mon, to 9pm Tue-Sun mid-Nov–mid-Mar; ⟨♠⟩; ⟨T⟩Park St) attracts ice-skaters, while summer draws theater lovers for **Shakespeare on the Common** (www.commshakes.org; Boston Common; ⊙8pm Tue-Sat, 7pm Sun Jul & Aug; ⟨T⟩Park St). This is also the starting point for the Freedom Trail. (btwn Tremont, Charles, Beacon & Park Sts; ⊙6am-midnight; ⟨P⟩⟨♠⟩⟨♠⟩; ⟨T⟩Park St)

Rose Kennedy Greenway   Park
The gateway to the newly revitalized waterfront is the Rose Kennedy Greenway. Where once was a hulking overhead highway, now winds a 27-acre strip of landscaped gardens and fountain-lined greens, with an artist market for Saturday shoppers, and food trucks for weekday lunchers. Cool off in the whimsical Rings Fountain, walk the calming labyrinth, or take a ride on the custom-designed Greenway carousel. (www.rosekennedygreenway.org; ⟨♠⟩⟨♠⟩; ⟨T⟩Aquarium or Haymarket)

Faneuil Hall

JOHN CARDASIS / GETTY IMAGES ©

Faneuil Hall Historic Building

This public meeting place was the site of so much rabble-rousing that it earned the nickname the 'Cradle of Liberty.' After the revolution, Faneuil Hall was a forum for meetings about abolition, women's suffrage and war. The historic hall is normally open to the public, who can hear about the building's history from National Park Service (NPS) rangers. (www.nps.gov/bost; Congress St; ☺9am-5pm; T Haymarket or Government Center)

New England Aquarium Aquarium

Teeming with sea creatures of all sizes, shapes and colors, this giant fishbowl is the centerpiece of downtown Boston's waterfront. The main attraction is the newly renovated, three-story Giant Ocean Tank, which swirls with thousands of creatures great and small, including turtles, sharks and eels. Countless side exhibits explore the lives and habitats of other underwater oddities, as well as penguins and seals. (www.neaq.org; Central Wharf; adult/child $25/18; ☺9am-5pm Mon-Fri, to 6pm Sat & Sun, 1hr later Jul & Aug; P ♿; T Aquarium) ✐

◉ North End & Charlestown

An old-world warren of narrow streets, the Italian North End offers visitors an irresistible mix of colorful period buildings and mouthwatering eateries. Colonial sights (linked by the Freedom Trail) spill across the river into Charlestown, home to America's oldest battleship.

◉ Seaport District

Following the HarborWalk, it's a pleasant stroll across the Fort Point Channel and into Boston's newest dining hot spot.

Boston Tea Party Ships & Museum Museum

'Boston Harbor a teapot tonight!' To protest unfair taxes, a gang of rebellious colonists dumped 342 chests of tea into the water. The 1773 protest – the Boston Tea Party – set into motion the events leading to the Revolutionary War. Nowadays, replica Tea

👪 Boston for Children

Boston is one giant history museum, the setting for many lively and informative field trips. Cobblestone streets and costume-clad tour guides can bring to life the events that kids read about in history books, while hands-on experimentation and interactive exhibits fuse education and entertainment.

Great stops for kids:

Public Garden (p104) Swan Boats ply the lagoon and tiny tots climb on the bronze ducklings.

Boston Common Kids can cool their toes in the Frog Pond, ride the carousel and romp at the playground.

New England Aquarium Enjoy face-to-face encounters with underwater creatures.

Boston Tea Party Ships & Museum Hands-on history.

Great tours for kids:

Boston for Little Feet (p106) The only Freedom Trail walking tour designed especially for children aged six to 12.

Urban AdvenTours (p106) Rents kids' bikes and helmets, as well as bike trailers for toddlers.

Boston Duck Tours (p106) Quirky quackiness is always a hit.

Swan Boats in the Public Garden
AMY RILEY / GETTY IMAGES ©

Party Ships are moored at the reconstructed Griffin's Wharf, alongside an excellent experiential museum dedicated to the revolution's most catalytic event. (www.boston teapartyship.com; Congress St Bridge; adult/

Boston

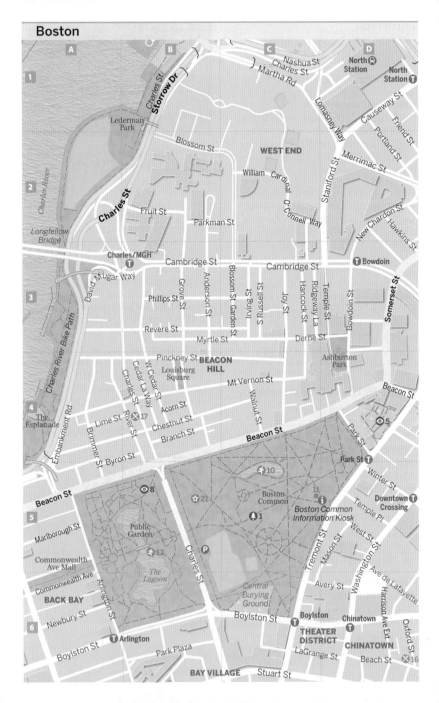

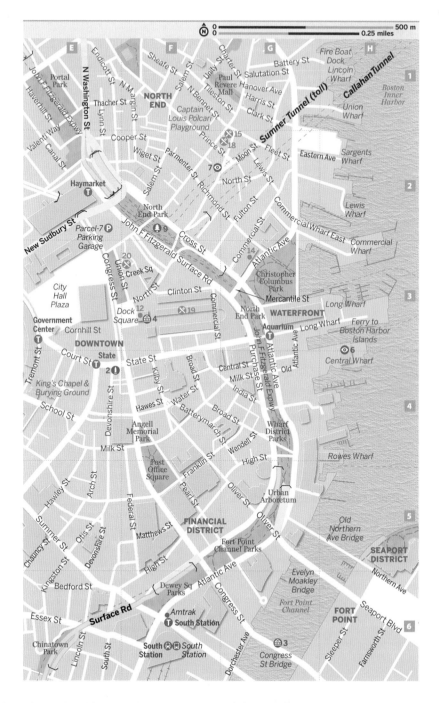

Boston

⊚ **Sights**
1 Boston Common..C5
2 Boston Massacre Site...............................E4
3 Boston Tea Party Ships &
   Museum G6
4 Faneuil Hall F3
5 Granary Burying Ground D4
6 New England Aquarium H3
7 Paul Revere House F2
8 Public Garden...B5
9 Rose Kennedy Greenway..........................F2

⊕ **Activities, Courses & Tours**
10 Boston Common Frog Pond.....................C5
11 Freedom Trail Foundation........................C5

12 NPS Freedom Trail Tour F3
13 Swan Boats...B5
14 Urban AdvenTours....................................G3

⊗ **Eating**
15 Giacomo's Ristorante...............................G2
16 Gourmet Dumpling House........................D6
17 Paramount B4
18 Pomodoro G2
19 Quincy Market...F3
20 Union Oyster House..................................F3

⊕ **Entertainment**
21 Shakespeare on the Common...................B5

child $25/15; ⊙10am-5pm, last tour 4pm; 🚻; T South Station)

Institute of
Contemporary Art Museum
Boston is fast becoming a focal point for contemporary art in the 21st century, with the Institute of Contemporary Art leading the way. The building is a work of art in itself: a glass structure cantilevered over a waterside plaza. The vast light-filled interior allows for multimedia presentations, educational programs and studio space. More importantly, it allows for the development of the ICA's permanent collection. (ICA; www.icaboston.org; 100 Northern Ave; adult/child $15/free; ⊙10am-5pm Tue, Wed, Sat & Sun, to 9pm Thu & Fri; 🚻; 🚌 SL1 or SL2, T South Station)

⊚ Chinatown, Theater District & South End

Compact Chinatown offers enticing Asian eateries and tea houses, while the overlapping Theater District is clustered with performing-arts venues and nightclubs. To the west, the sprawling South End boasts one of America's largest concentrations of Victorian row houses, a dynamic art community and a terrific restaurant scene.

⊚ Back Bay

Extending west from the Boston Common, this well-groomed area boasts graceful brownstone residences, grand edifices and the shopping mecca of Newbury St.

Public Garden Gardens
Adjoining Boston Common, the Public Garden is a 24-acre botanical oasis of Victorian flowerbeds, verdant grass and weeping willow trees shading a tranquil lagoon. The old-fashioned pedal-powered **Swan Boats** (www.swanboats.com; Public Garden; adult/child $3/1.50; ⊙10am-5pm Jun-Aug, to 4pm mid-Apr–May, noon-4pm Sep; T Arlington) have been delighting children for generations. The most endearing statue in the Public Garden is *Make Way for Ducklings,* depicting Mrs Mallard and her eight ducklings, the main characters in the beloved book by Robert McCloskey. (www.friendsofthepublicgarden.org; Arlington St; ⊙6am-midnight; 🚻; T Arlington)

Boston Public Library Library
Dating from 1852, the esteemed Boston Public Library lends credence to Boston's reputation as the 'Athens of America.' The old McKim building is notable for its magnificent facade and exquisite interior art. Pick up a free brochure and take a self-guided tour; alternatively, free guided tours depart from the entrance hall (times vary). (www.bpl.org; 700 Boylston St; ⊙9am-

9pm Mon-Thu, to 5pm Fri & Sat year-round, also 1-5pm Sun Oct-May; 🛜; [T]Copley)

Trinity Church — Church

A masterpiece of American architecture, Trinity Church is the country's ultimate example of Richardsonian Romanesque. The granite exterior, with a massive portico and side cloister, uses sandstone in colorful patterns. The interior is an awe-striking array of vibrant murals and stained glass, most by artist John LaFarge, who cooperated closely with architect Henry Hobson Richardson to create an integrated composition of shapes, colors and textures. Free architectural tours are offered following Sunday service at 11:15am. (www.trinitychurchboston.org; 206 Clarendon St; adult/child $7/free; ⊘9am-4:30pm Mon, Fri & Sat, to 5:30pm Tue-Thu, 1-5pm Sun; [T]Copley)

◉ Fenway & Kenmore Square

Kenmore Sq is best for baseball and beer, while the southern part of the Fenway is dedicated to higher-minded cultural pursuits.

Museum of Fine Arts — Museum

Since 1876, the Museum of Fine Arts has been Boston's premier venue for showcasing art by local, national and international artists. Nowadays, the museum's holdings encompass all eras, from the ancient world to contemporary times, and all areas of the globe, making it truly encyclopedic in scope. Most recently, the museum has added gorgeous new wings dedicated to the Art of the Americas and to contemporary art, contributing to Boston's emergence as an art center in the 21st century. (MFA; www.mfa.org; 465 Huntington Ave; adult/child $25/10; ⊘10am-5pm Sat-Tue, to 10pm Wed-Fri; 🚇; [T]Museum or Ruggles)

Isabella Stewart Gardner Museum — Museum

The magnificent Venetian-style palazzo that houses this museum was home to 'Mrs Jack' Gardner until her death in 1924. A monument to one woman's taste for acquiring exquisite art, the Gardner is

💬 Lexington & Concord

Students of history and lovers of liberty can trace the events of that fateful day that started a revolution – April 19, 1775. Follow in the footsteps of British soldiers and colonial Minutemen, who tromped out to Lexington to face off on the town green, then continued on to Concord for the battle at the Old North Bridge. Much of this area now comprises the **Minute Man National Historic Park** (www.nps.gov/mima; 250 North Great Rd, Lincoln; ⊘9am-5pm Apr-Oct; 🚇) FREE, with an informative visitors center at the eastern end of the park.

Hartwell Tavern, Minute Man National Historical Park
DANITA DELIMONT / GETTY IMAGES ©

filled with almost 2000 priceless objects, primarily European, including outstanding tapestries and Italian Renaissance and 17th-century Dutch paintings. The four-story greenhouse courtyard is a masterpiece and a tranquil oasis that alone is worth the price of admission. (www.gardnermuseum.org; 280 The Fenway; adult/child $15/free; ⊘11am-5pm Mon, Wed & Fri-Sun, to 9pm Thu; 🚇; [T]Museum)

◉ Cambridge

On the north side of the Charles River lies politically progressive Cambridge, home to academic heavyweights Harvard University and Massachusetts Institute of Technology (MIT). At its hub, Harvard Square overflows with cafés, bookstores and street performers.

📖 Must-Sees for JFK Enthusiasts

Boston has several mandatory pilgrimage sites for fans of the 35th president.

John F Kennedy National Historic Site (www.nps.gov/jofi; 83 Beals St; ⊙9:30am-5pm Wed-Sun May-Oct; T Coolidge Corner) FREE Guided tours allow visitors to see furnishings, photographs and mementos that have been preserved from the time the Kennedy family lived here.

John F Kennedy Presidential Library & Museum (www.jfklibrary.org; Columbia Point; adult/child $14/10; ⊙9am-5pm; T JFK/UMass) The official memorial to JFK is a fitting legacy to his storied life.

John F Kennedy Presidential Library & Museum
TRAVEL IMAGES / UIG / GETTY IMAGES ©

Harvard University   University
Founded in 1636 to educate men for the ministry, Harvard is America's oldest college. The original Ivy League school has eight graduates who went on to be US presidents, not to mention dozens of Nobel laureates and Pulitzer Prize winners. It educates 6500 undergraduates and about 12,000 graduates yearly in 10 professional schools. The geographic heart of Harvard University – where red-brick buildings and leaf-covered paths exude academia – is Harvard Yard. (www.harvard.edu; Massachusetts Ave; tours free; ⊙tours hourly 10am-3pm Mon-Sat; T Harvard)

🎯 TOURS

Urban AdvenTours   Bicycle Tour
Founded by avid cyclists who believe the best views of Boston are from a bicycle. The City View Ride provides a great overview of how to get around by bike, but there are other specialty tours such as Bikes at Night and the Emerald Necklace tour. (📞617-379-3590; www.urbanadventours.com; 103 Atlantic Ave; tours $55; 🚴; T Aquarium) 📝

Boston Duck Tours   Boat Tour
These ridiculously popular tours use WWII amphibious vehicles that cruise the downtown streets before splashing into the Charles River. The 80-minute tours depart from the Museum of Science, the Prudential Center or the New England Aquarium. Reserve in advance. (📞617-267-3825; www.bostonducktours.com; adult/child $36/25; 🚴; T Aquarium, Science Park or Prudential)

Boston by Foot   Walking Tour
This fantastic nonprofit offers 90-minute walking tours, with neighborhood-specific walks and specialty theme tours like Literary Landmarks, the Dark Side of Boston and Boston for Little Feet – a kid-friendly version of the Freedom Trail. (www.bostonbyfoot.com; adult/child $15/10; 🚴)

NPS Freedom Trail Tour   Walking Tour
Show up at least 30 minutes early to snag a spot on one of the free, ranger-led Freedom Trail tours provided by the National Park Service. Tours depart from the visitor center in Faneuil Hall, and follow a portion of the Freedom Trail (not including Charlestown), for a total of 90 minutes. Each tour is limited to 30 people. (www.nps.gov/bost; Faneuil Hall; ⊙10am & 2pm Apr-Oct; T State) FREE

🔒 SHOPPING

Newbury St in the Back Bay and Charles St on Beacon Hill are Boston's best shopping destinations for the traditional and trendy. Harvard Sq is famous for bookstores and the South End is the city's up-and-coming art district.

✪ ENTERTAINMENT

Half-price tickets to same-day theater and concerts in Boston are sold at **BosTix** (www.bostix.org; ☻10am-6pm Tue-Sat, 11am-4pm Sun) at Faneuil Hall and Copley Sq. Cash only.

For up-to-the-minute listings, grab a copy of the free *Boston Phoenix*.

Fenway Park   Baseball

From April to September you can watch the Red Sox play at Fenway Park, the nation's oldest and most storied ballpark. Unfortunately, it is also the most expensive – not that this stops the Fenway faithful from scooping up the tickets. There are sometimes game-day tickets on sale starting 90 minutes before the opening pitch. (www.redsox.com; 4 Yawkey Way; bleachers $12-40, grandstand $29-78, box $50-75; ⊤Kenmore)

Club Passim   Live Music

Folk music in Boston seems to be endangered outside of Irish bars, but the legendary Club Passim does such a great job booking top-notch acts that it practically fills in the vacuum by itself. The colorful, intimate room is hidden off a side street in Harvard Sq, just as it has been since 1969. (☏617-492-7679; www.clubpassim.org; 47 Palmer St; tickets $15-30; ⊤Harvard)

Boston Symphony Orchestra   Classical Music

Flawless acoustics match the ambitious programs of the world-renowned Boston Symphony Orchestra. From September to April, the BSO performs in the beauteous **Symphony Hall** (www.bso.org; 301 Massachusetts Ave; ☻tours 4pm Wed & 2pm Sat, reservation required), featuring an ornamental high-relief ceiling and attracting a fancy-dress crowd. In summer months, the BSO retreats to Tanglewood in Western Massachusetts. (BSO; ☏617-266-1200; www.bso.org; 301 Massachusetts Ave; tickets $30-115; ⊤Symphony)

> *grab a seat in the bleachers at Fenway Park and cheer on the Red Sox*

Fenway Park

ISRAEL PABON / SHUTTERSTOCK ©

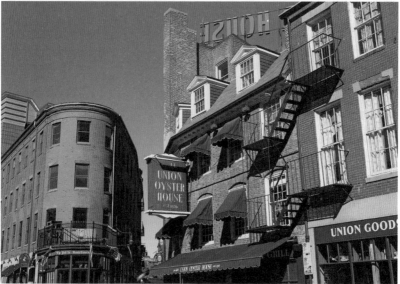

Union Oyster House

✖ EATING

Indulge in affordable Asian fare in China-town and Italian feasts in the North End; or head to the South End for the city's trendiest foodie scene.

✖ Beacon Hill & Downtown

Quincy Market　　　　Food Court **$**
Behind Faneuil Hall, this food court is packed with about 20 restaurants and 40 food stalls. Choose from chowder, bagels, Indian, Greek, baked goods and ice cream, and take a seat at one of the tables in the central rotunda. (www.faneuilhallmarketplace. com; Congress St; ⏰10am-9pm Mon-Sat, noon-6pm Sun; 🛜 🗗 👪; Ⓣ Haymarket)

Paramount　　　　Cafeteria **$$**
This old-fashioned cafeteria is a neighbor-hood favorite. A-plus diner fare includes pancakes, home fries, burgers and sand-wiches, and big, hearty salads. Banana and caramel French toast is an obvious go-to for the brunch crowd. Don't sit down until you get your food! At dinner, add table service and candlelight, and the place goes

upscale without losing its down-home charm. (www.paramountboston.com; 44 Charles St; mains breakfast & lunch $6-12, dinner $15-23; ⏰7am-10pm Mon-Thu, to 11pm Fri, 8am-11pm Sat, to 10pm Sun; 🗗 👪; Ⓣ Charles/MGH)

Union Oyster House　　Seafood **$$$**
The oldest restaurant in Boston has been serving seafood in this red-brick building since 1826. Countless history-makers have propped themselves up at this bar, includ-ing Daniel Webster and John F Kennedy. (Apparently JFK used to order the lobster bisque.) Overpriced but atmospheric. (www.unionoysterhouse.com; 41 Union St; mains lunch $15-20, dinner $22-32; ⏰11am-9:30pm; Ⓣ Haymarket)

✖ North End

Pomodoro　　　　　　Italian **$$**
Pomodoro is one of the North End's most romantic settings for delectable Italian. The food is simple but perfectly prepared: fresh pasta, spicy tomato sauce, grilled fish and meats, and wine by the glass. If you're lucky, you might receive a complimentary tiramisu for dessert. Cash only. (📞617-367-

4348; 351 Hanover St; mains brunch $12, dinner
$23-24; ⏱5-11pm Mon-Fri, noon-11pm Sat & Sun;
T Haymarket)

Giacomo's Ristorante   Italian $$

Customers line up before the doors open
to get a spot in the first round of seating at
this North End favorite. Enthusiastic and
entertaining waiters plus cramped quarters
ensure that you get to know your neigh-
bors. The cuisine is no-frills southern Italian
fare, served in unbelievable portions. Cash
only. (www.giacomosblog-boston.blogspot.com;
355 Hanover St; mains $14-19; ⏱4:30-10:30pm
Mon-Sat, 4-9:30pm Sun; 🖉; T Haymarket)

⊗ Seaport District

Yankee Lobster Co   Seafood $

The Zanti family has been fishing for three
generations, so they definitely know their
stuff. A relatively recent addition is this retail fish market, scattered with a few tables
in case you want to dine in. And you do.
Order something simple like clam chowder
or a lobster roll, accompany it with a cold
beer, and you will not be disappointed.
(www.yankeelobstercompany.com; 300 Northern
Ave; mains $11-20; ⏱10am-9pm Mon-Sat, 11am-
6pm Sun; 🚌SL1 or SL2, T South Station)

Row 34   Seafood $$

In the heart of the new Seaport District, this
is a 'workingman's oyster bar' (by working
man, they mean yuppie). Set in a sharp,
post-industrial space, the place offers a
dozen types of raw oysters and clams,
alongside an amazing selection of craft
beers. There's also a full menu of cooked
seafood. (📞617-553-5900; www.row34.com;
383 Congress St; oysters $2-3, mains lunch
$13-18, dinner $21-28; ⏱11:30am-10pm Mon-Fri,
5-10pm Sat & Sun; T South Station)

⊗ Chinatown, Theater District & South End

Gourmet Dumpling House   Chinese, Taiwanese $

Xiao long bao. That's all the Chinese you
need to know to take advantage of the

🚲 Cycling the Rail Trail

One of the finest cycling trails in all
New England, the Cape Cod Rail Trail
follows a former railroad track for 22
glorious miles past cranberry bogs,
through quaint villages and along sandy
ponds ideal for a dip. The path begins in
Dennis on MA 134 and continues all the
way to Wellfleet. If you have time to do
only part of the trail, begin at Nickerson
State Park in Brewster and head for
the Cape Cod National Seashore in
Eastham. Bicycle rentals are available
at the trailhead in Dennis, at Nickerson
State Park and opposite the **National
Seashore's Salt Pond Visitor Center**
(📞508-255-3421; 50 Doane Rd, cnr US 6 &
Nauset Rd, Eastham; ⏱9am-5pm) FREE.

Cape Cod Rail Trail
STEPHEN SAKS / GETTY IMAGES ©

specialty at the Gourmet Dumpling House
(or GDH, as it is fondly called). They are
Shanghai soup dumplings, of course, and
they are fresh, doughy and delicious. The
menu offers plenty of other options, including scrumptious crispy scallion pancakes.
Come early or be prepared to wait. (52
Beach St; dumplings $2-8, mains $10-15; ⏱11am-
1am; 🖉; T Chinatown)

Myers & Chang   Asian $$

This super-hip Asian spot blends Thai,
Chinese and Vietnamese cuisines, which
means delicious dumplings, spicy stir-fries
and oodles of noodles. The kitchen staff
does amazing things with a wok, and the
menu of small plates allows you to sample

Where to Stay

Choose a place to lay your head in the Boston neighborhoods of Back Bay, Kenmore Square or Fenway; these locales are close to major sights and have great dining, shopping and nightlife, as well as convenient transport links.

---

a wide selection of dishes. The vibe is casual but cool, international and original. (617-542-5200; www.myersandchang. com; 1145 Washington St; small plates $10-18; 11:30am-10pm Sun-Thu, to 11pm Fri & Sat; ; SL4 or SL5, New England Medical Center)

Back Bay

Sweetgreen Vegetarian $

Vegetarians, gluten-free eaters, health nuts and all human beings will rejoice in the goodness that is served at Sweetgreen. Choose a salad or a wrap, then custom-design your own, or choose one of the delicious, fresh combos that have already been invented, including seasonal specialties. So healthy. So satisfying. So good. (www. sweetgreen.com; 659 Boylston St; mains $6-10; 10:30am-10:30pm; ; Copley)

Courtyard Modern American $$

The perfect destination for an elegant luncheon with artfully prepared food is – believe it or not – the Boston Public Library. Overlooking the beautiful Italianate courtyard, this grown-up restaurant serves seasonal, innovative and exotic dishes (along with a few standards). After 2pm, the Courtyard serves a delightful afternoon tea ($32), with a selection of sandwiches, scones and sweets. (www.thecateredaffair. com; 700 Boylston St; mains $17-22; 11:30am-4pm Mon-Fri; ; Copley)

Cambridge

Clover Food Lab Vegetarian $

Clover is on the cutting edge. It's all high-tech with its 'live' menu updates and electronic ordering system. But it's really about the food – local, seasonal, vegetarian food – that is cheap, delicious and fast. How fast? Check the menu. Interesting tidbit: Clover started as a food truck (and still has a few trucks making the rounds). (www. cloverfoodlab.com; 7 Holyoke St; mains $6-7; 7am-midnight Mon-Sat, to 7pm Sun; ; Harvard)

🍸 DRINKING & NIGHTLIFE

Bleacher Bar Sports Bar

Tucked under the bleachers at Fenway Park, this classy bar offers a view onto center field. It's not the best place to watch the game, as the place gets packed, but it's a fun way to experience America's oldest ballpark, even when the Sox are not playing. Gentlemen: enjoy the view from the loo! (www.bleacherbarboston.com; 82a Lansdowne St; 11am-1am Sun-Wed, to 2am Thu-Sat; Kenmore)

Warren Tavern Pub

One of the oldest pubs in Boston, the Warren Tavern has been pouring pints for its customers since George Washington and Paul Revere drank here. It is named for General Joseph Warren, a fallen hero of the Battle of Bunker Hill (shortly after which – in 1780 – this pub was opened). Also recommended as a lunch stop. (www.warren tavern.com; 2 Pleasant St; 11am-1am Mon-Fri, 10am-1am Sat & Sun; Community College)

ℹ️ INFORMATION

Boston Common Information Kiosk (GBCVB Visitors Center; www.bostonusa.com; Boston Common; 8:30am-5pm; Park St) Starting point for the Freedom Trail and many other walking tours.

ℹ️ GETTING THERE & AWAY

The train and bus stations are conveniently side by side, and the airport is a short subway ride away.

Bleacher Bar

AIR

Logan International Airport (☎ 800-235-6426; www.massport.com/logan) is just across Boston Harbor from the city center.

BUS

South Station (700 Atlantic Ave) is the terminal for an extensive network of long-distance buses operated by Greyhound and regional bus companies. To NYC, both **Lucky Star Bus** (www. luckystarbus.com; South Station; one way $20) and **Megabus** (www.megabus.com; South Station; one-way $10-30) depart from South Station, while **Go Bus** (www.gobuses.com; Alewife Brook Pkwy; one way $18-34; T Alewife) departs from Cambridge.

TRAIN

The **MBTA Commuter Rail** (☎ 800-392-6100, 617-222-3200; www.mbta.com) runs to destinations in the greater Boston area, departing from North Station or South Station as appropriate. The **Amtrak** (☎ 800-872-7245; www.amtrak. com; South Station) terminal is at South Station.

ⓘ GETTING AROUND

TO/FROM THE AIRPORT

Logan International Airport is just a few miles from downtown Boston: take the blue-line subway or the silver-line bus.

BICYCLE

Boston's bike-share program is the **Hubway** (www.thehubway.com; 24/72hr membership $6/12, 30/60/90 minutes free/$2/4; ⏱24hr), with 60 Hubway stations around town. For leisurely riding or long trips, rent a bike from Urban AdvenTours (p106).

SUBWAY

The **MBTA** (☎ 617-222-3200; www.mbta.com; per ride $2.10-2.65; ⏱5:30am-12:30am Sun-Thu, to 2am Fri & Sat) operates the 'T.' Five color-coded lines radiate 'outbound' from the downtown stations of Park St, Downtown Crossing and Government Center.

TAXI

Flag taxis on the street, find them at major hotels or taxi stands. For airport transfers, call **Cabbie's Cab** (☎ 617-547-2222; www.cabbies cab.com; airport $35).

Salem

Salem is renowned for the witch hysteria of 1692, when innocent folks were put to death for practicing witchcraft. Nowadays, the town embraces its role as 'Witch City' with witchy museums, spooky tours and Halloween madness. The most poignant site in Salem is the **Witch Trials Memorial** (Charter St), which honors the innocent victims.

These incidents obscure the city's true claim to fame: its glory days as a center for clipper-ship trade with the Far East. The **Salem Maritime National Historic Site** (www.nps.gov/sama; 193 Derby St; ⊘9am-5pm) FREE tells the story. Stroll out to the end of Derby Wharf and peek inside the 1871 lighthouse or climb aboard the tall ship *Friendship*. Get complete information from the **NPS Regional Visitor Center** (www.nps.gov/sama; 2 New Liberty St; ⊘9am-5pm).

The exceptional **Peabody Essex Museum** (www.pem.org; 161 Essex St; adult/child $18/free; ⊘10am-5pm Tue-Sun; 🖐) was founded upon the art, artifacts and curios collected by Salem traders during their early expeditions to the Far East.

Cape Cod & the Islands

Clambering across the National Seashore dunes, cycling the Cape Cod Rail Trail, eating oysters at Wellfleet Harbor – this sandy peninsula serves up a bounty of local flavor. Fringed with 400 miles of sparkling shoreline, 'the Cape,' as it's called by Cape Codders, rates as New England's top beach destination. But there's a lot more than just beaches here. When you've had your fill of sun and sand, get out and explore artist enclaves, take a cruise, or join the free-spirited street scene in Provincetown.

For accommodations options, visit www.capecodchamber.org.

Hyannis

Cape Cod's commercial hub, Hyannis is also a jumping-off point for ferries to Nantucket and Martha's Vineyard. Most famously, Hyannis has long been the summer home of the Kennedy clan. The

Chatham Pier Fish Market

John F Kennedy Hyannis Museum (www.jfkhyannismuseum.org; 397 Main St; adult/child $10/5; ⏱9am-5pm Mon-Sat, noon-5pm Sun) celebrates the 35th president with photographs, videos and mementos.

The town's mile-long Main St is fun to stroll along and is the place for dining, drinking and shopping. Kalmus Beach is popular for windsurfing, while Craigville Beach is where the college set goes. After fun in the sun, head to **Raw Bar** (📞508-539-4858; www.therawbar.com; 230 Ocean St; lobster rolls $26; ⏱11am-8pm Sun-Thu, to 11pm Fri-Sat) for the mother of all lobster rolls – it's like eating an entire lobster in a bun.

Chatham

Upscale inns and shops are a hallmark of the cape's most genteel town. Start your exploration on Main St, with its old sea captains' houses and cool art galleries. At the fish pier, watch fishermen unload their catch and spot seals basking on nearby shoals. A mile south on Shore Rd is Lighthouse Beach, an endless expanse of sea and sandbars that offers some of the finest beach strolling on Cape Cod.

The two uninhabited islands off the elbow comprise the 7600-acre **Monomoy National Wildlife Refuge** (www.fws.gov/northeast/monomoy) 📷 . Take a boat tour with the **Beachcomber** (📞508-945-5265; www.sealwatch.com; Crowell Rd; North Beach water taxi adult/child $20/10, seal-watching trips adult/child $29/25; ⏱10am-5pm) or **Monomoy Island Excursions** (📞508-430-7772; www.monomoysealcruise.com; 702 MA 28, Harwich Port; 1½hr tours adult/child $36/30) to see hundreds of gray seals, harbor seals and shorebirds.

If you like it fresh and local to the core, salt-sprayed **Chatham Pier Fish Market** (📞508-945-3474; www.chathampierfishmarket.com; 45 Barcliff Ave; mains $12-25; ⏱10am-6pm Wed-Sun), with its own sushi chef and day boats, is for you. The chowder is incredible and the fish so fresh it was swimming earlier in the day. It's all takeout, but there are shady picnic tables and a harborful of sights.

🌅 Cape Cod National Seashore

Cape Cod National Seashore extends some 40 miles around the curve of the Outer Cape and encompasses most of the shoreline from Eastham to Provincetown. It's a treasure-trove of unspoiled beaches, dunes, salt marshes and forests. Thanks to President John F Kennedy, this vast area was set aside for preservation in the 1960s, just before a building boom hit the rest of his native Cape Cod. (www.nps.gov/caco; beach pass pedestrian/car $3/20)

Race Point Beach, Provincetown
WALTER BIBIKOW / GETTY IMAGES ©

Provincetown

This is it: as far as you can go on the cape, and more than just geographically. Fringe writers and artists began making a summer haven in Provincetown a century ago. Today this sandy outpost has morphed into the hottest gay and lesbian destination in the Northeast. Flamboyant street scenes, brilliant art galleries and unbridled nightlife paint the town center.

Away from Commercial St, the untamed coastline and vast beaches beg to be explored. Swimmers favor the relatively calm, though certainly brisk, waters of Herring Cove Beach, while Race Point Beach is the kind of beach where you could walk for miles and see no one but the occasional angler casting for bluefish. The beaches are connected by an excellent, paved bike path through the dunes.

Aquinnah Cliffs

Known as Up-Island, the rural western half of Martha's Vineyard is a patchwork of rolling hills, small farms and open fields frequented by wild turkey and deer. The coastal Aquinnah Cliffs, also known as the Gay Head Cliffs, are so special they're a National Natural Landmark. These 150ft-high cliffs glow with an amazing array of colors that can be best appreciated in the late-afternoon light. You can hang out at **Aquinnah Public Beach** (parking $15), just below the multihued cliffs, or walk a mile north along the shore to an area that's popular with nude sunbathers.

Aquinnah Cliffs
DANITA DELIMONT / GETTY IMAGES ©

◎ SIGHTS

Province Lands Visitor Center   Beach

Overlooking Race Point Beach, this Cape Cod National Seashore visitor center has displays on dune ecology and a rooftop observation deck with an eye-popping 360-degree view of the outermost reaches of Cape Cod.

The park stays open to midnight so, even after the visitor center closes, you can still climb to the deck for sunset views and unobstructed stargazing. (www.nps.gov/caco; Race Point Rd; car/bike/pedestrian $15/3/3; ⊙9am-5pm; P)

Provincetown Art Association & Museum   Museum

Founded in 1914 to celebrate the town's thriving art community, this vibrant museum showcases the works of artists who have found their inspiration in Provincetown. Chief among them is Edward Hopper, who had a home and gallery in the Truro dunes. (PAAM; www.paam.org; 460 Commercial St; adult/child $10/free; ⊙11am-8pm Mon-Thu, to 10pm Fri, to 5pm Sat & Sun)

☞ TOURS

Dolphin Fleet Whale Watch   Boat Tour

Provincetown is the perfect launch point for whale-watching, since it's the closest port to Stellwagen Bank National Marine Sanctuary, a summer feeding ground for humpback whales. Dolphin offers as many as 12 whale-watch tours daily. Humpback whales have a flair for acrobatic breaching and come surprisingly close to the boats, offering great photo ops. (☏800-826-9300; www.whalewatch.com; MacMillan Wharf; adult/child $46/31; ⊙Apr-Oct;)

✖ EATING

Cafe Heaven   Café $

Light and airy but small and crowded, this art-filled storefront is an easy-on-the-wallet eating place. The menu ranges from sinful croissant French toast to healthy salads. Don't be deterred by the wait – the tables turn over quickly. (☏508-487-9639; 199 Commercial St; mains $7-12; ⊙8am-10pm;)

Mews Restaurant & Cafe   Modern American $$$

Want affordable gourmet? Skip the excellent but pricey restaurant and go upstairs to the bar for a fab view, great martinis and scrumptious bistro fare. (☏508-487-1500; www.mews.com; 429 Commercial St; mains bistro $13-22, restaurant $27-31; ⊙5:30-10pm)

Lobster Pot   Seafood $$$

True to its name, this bustling fish house is the place for lobster. Service can be s-l-o-w.

Humpback whale

Best way to beat the crowd is to come mid-afternoon. (📞508-487-0842; www. ptownlobsterpot.com; 321 Commercial St; mains $22-37; ⏱11:30am-9pm)

🍷 DRINKING & NIGHTLIFE

Pied Bar   Gay & Lesbian

This woman-owned waterfront lounge is a popular dance spot for all genders. The main event is the 'After Tea T-Dance,' so folks head here after the Boatslip. Also hosts 'Women's Week' in October. (www. piedbar.com; 193 Commercial St; ⏱noon-1am May-Oct)

Crown & Anchor   Gay & Lesbian

The queen of the gay scene, this multiwing complex has a nightclub, a video bar, a leather bar and a steamy cabaret that takes it to the limit. (www.onlyatthecrown.com; 247 Commercial St; ⏱hours vary)

ℹ GETTING THERE & AWAY

Plymouth & Brockton (www.p-b.com) buses connect Boston and Provincetown ($35, 3½

hours). From mid-May to mid-October, **Bay State Cruise Company** (📞877-783-3779; www. boston-ptown.com; 200 Seaport Blvd, Boston) runs a ferry between Boston's World Trade Center Pier and MacMillan Wharf (round-trip $88, 1½ hrs).

Nantucket

Once home port to the world's largest whaling fleet, Nantucket has a storied past that is reflected in its period homes and cobbled streets. The entire town is a National Historic Landmark: stroll up Main St to admire the grand whaling-era mansions lined up in a row. To explore the farther reaches of the island, rent a bike in town and take advantage of the dedicated bike paths.

For information about accommodations, visit http://nantucketlodging.org.

◎ SIGHTS

Nantucket Whaling Museum   Museum

A top sight is this evocative museum in a former spermaceti (whale-oil) candle

Vineyard Haven, Martha's Vineyard

WALTER BIBIKOW / GETTY IMAGES ©

> *you'll find cozy inns and chef-driven restaurants*

factory. (13 Broad St; adult/child $20/5; ⊗10am-5pm mid-May–Oct, 11am-4pm Nov–mid-May)

Nantucket Beaches   Beaches
Right in town, Children's Beach has calm water and a playground. For wilder, less frequented strands, pedal a bike or hop on a bus to Surfside Beach, 2 miles to the south. The best place to catch the sunset is Madaket Beach, 5.5 miles west of town.

❌ EATING

Black-Eyed Susan's   Café $$
No reservations, no credit cards and no alcohol (unless you bring it yourself). Yet islanders line up out the door to get one of a dozen tables at this understated gem. This is New American at its finest: you've

eaten these ingredients, but never before in these creative, decidedly delicious combinations. (☎508-325-0308; www.black-eyedsusans.com; 10 India St; breakfast mains $8-12, dinner $24-26; ⊗7am-1pm daily, 6-10pm Mon-Sat; 🖼)

ℹ️ GETTING THERE & AROUND

BOAT
The **Steamship Authority** (☎508-477-8600; www.steamshipauthority.com) runs ferries throughout the day between Hyannis and Nantucket. The fast ferry (round-trip adult/child $69/35) takes an hour; the slow ferry (round-trip adult/child $37/19) takes 2¼ hours.

BUS
Getting around Nantucket is a snap. **NRTA Wave** (www.nrtawave.com; rides $1-2, day pass $7; ⊗late May-Sep) operates buses around town and to Siasconset, Madaket and the beaches. Buses have bike racks, so cyclists can bus one way and pedal back.

Martha's Vineyard

New England's largest island is untouched by the kind of rampant development you'll see on the mainland, Instead, you'll find cozy inns, chef-driven restaurants and a bounty of green farms and grand beaches.

Vineyard Haven is the island's commercial center, though there's not much to deter visitors there. Most ferries arrive at Oak Bluffs, which is the center of all summer fun in the Vineyard. Edgartown has a rich maritime history and more of a patrician air. A scenic, seaside bike trail connects all three towns.

For information on accommodations, visit http://mvol.com/accommodations.

◎ SIGHTS

Campgrounds & Tabernacle   Historic Site

Oak Bluffs started out in the mid-19th century as a summer retreat by a revivalist church, whose members enjoyed a day at the beach as much as a gospel service. They built some 300 cottages, each adorned with whimsical gingerbread trim. These brightly painted cottages – known today as the Campgrounds – surround Trinity Park and its open-air Tabernacle (1879), a venue for festivals and concerts. For a peek inside one, visit the **Cottage Museum** (www. mvcma.org; 1 Trinity Park; adult/child $2/50¢; ◎10am-4pm Mon-Sat, 1-4pm Sun May-Sep), which contains exhibits on CMA history.

Katama Beach   Beach

The Vineyard's best beach lies 4 miles south of Edgartown center. Also called South Beach, Katama stretches for three magnificent miles. Rugged surf will please surfers on the ocean side, while some swimmers may prefer the protected salt ponds on the inland side. (Katama Rd; 👬)

✖ EATING

Among the Flowers Café   Café $$

This is a sweet spot, hidden among the flowers on a garden patio off the main drag.

🔭 Scenic Drive: VT 100

Following Vermont's rugged spine through the rural heart of the state, VT 100 rambles past rolling pastures speckled with cows, tiny villages with white-steepled churches and green mountains crossed with hiking trails and ski slopes. It's the quintessential side trip for those who want to slow down and experience Vermont's bucolic essence. The road runs north to south all the way from Massachusetts to Canada. If your time is short, cruise the scenic 45-mile stretch between Waterbury and Stockbridge, an easy detour off I-89.

RUSSELL BURDEN / GETTY IMAGES ©

It's a darling setting for delicious foodstuffs, even if it is served on paper plates. Folks line up at breakfast time for decadent cinnamon rolls, waffles and omelets. But you won't be disappointed at lunch, especially if you order the lobster roll. (☎508-627-3233; www.amongtheflowersmv.com; 17 Mayhew Lane, Edgartown; mains $8-20; ◎8am-10pm; 🖋)

Slice of Life   Café $$

The look is casual; the fare is gourmet. At breakfast, there's kick-ass coffee, portobello omelets and fab potato pancakes. At dinner the roasted cod with sun-dried tomatoes is a savory favorite. And the desserts – decadent crème brûlée and luscious lemon tarts – are as good as you'll find anywhere. (☎508-693-3838; www.slice oflifemv.com; 50 Circuit Ave, Oak Bluffs; mains $8-24; ◎8am-9pm; 🖋)

Scenic Drive: Kancamagus Hwy

The winding Kancamagus Hwy (NH 112) runs for 35 miles between Lincoln and Conway, right through the White Mountain National Forest and over Kancamagus Pass (2868ft). Unspoiled by commercial development, the paved road offers easy access to campgrounds, hiking trails and fantastic scenery. There are no services along the highway, so pick up picnic supplies in town before setting out.

RAIMUND LINKE / GETTY IMAGES ©

🛈 GETTING THERE & AROUND

BOAT
Frequent ferries operated by the Steamship Authority (p116) link Woods Hole to both Vineyard Haven and Oak Bluffs (round-trip $17, 45 minutes). If you're bringing a car, book well in advance.

From Hyannis, **Hy-Line Cruises** (📞508-778-2600; www.hylinecruises.com; Ocean St Dock) operates a slow ferry ($45, 1½ hours) once daily to Oak Bluffs and a high-speed ferry ($72, 55 minutes, several daily).

BUS
Martha's Vineyard Regional Transit Authority (www.vineyardtransit.com; per ride $2.50, day-pass $7) operates a bus network with frequent service between towns.

Vermont

Whether under blankets of snow, patchworks of blazing fall leaves or exuberant greens of spring and summer, Vermont's blend of bucolic farmland, ancient mountains and picturesque village have serious traveler appeal. Hikers, bikers, skiers and kayakers will find four-season bliss. For foodies, small farmers have made Vermont a locavore paradise, complemented by America's densest collection of craft brewers.

For tourist information, including accommodations options, visit www.vermontvacation.com.

Burlington

This hip college town on the shores of scenic Lake Champlain is one of those places that makes you think, wouldn't it be great to live here? The café and club scene is on par with a much bigger city, while the slow, friendly pace is pure small town.

◉ SIGHTS

Most of the cafés and pubs are located along Church St Marketplace, a brick-lined pedestrian mall where half of Burlington hangs on a sunny day. The mall sits midway between the University of Vermont and Lake Champlain.

Shelburne Museum   Museum
Wear your walking shoes for this extraordinary 45-acre museum, which showcases a Smithsonian-caliber collection of Americana – 150,000 objects in all. The mix of folk art, decorative arts and more is housed in 39 historic buildings, most of them relocated here from other parts of New England to ensure their preservation. Located 9 miles south of Burlington. (📞802-985-3346; www.shelburnemuseum.org; 6300 Shelburne Rd/US 7, Shelburne; adult/youth 13-17yr/child 5-12yr $24/14/12; ⏱10am-5pm mid-May–Oct; 🚻)

Shelburne Farms   Farm
This 1400-acre estate, designed by landscape architect Frederick Law Olmsted

(who also designed New York's Central Park), was both a country house for the aristocratic Webb family and a working farm, with stunning lakefront perspectives. Still a working farm, the property today welcomes visitors. Guests can milk a cow in the farmyard (at 11am and 2pm), sample the farm's superb cheddar cheese, tour the magnificent barns and walk the network of trails. (☏802-985-8686; www.shelburnefarms. org; 1611 Harbor Rd, Shelburne; adult/child 3-17yr $8/5; ⊙9am-5:30pm mid-May–mid-Oct, 10am-5pm mid-Oct–mid-May; 👬) ⌷

Magic Hat Brewery — Brewery

Drink in the history of one of Vermont's most dynamic microbreweries on the fun, free, self-guided tour. Afterwards, sample a few of the eight brews on tap in the on site Growler Bar. Recent samples included the Peppercorn Pilsner, made with pink peppercorns, and the Electric Peel, a grapefruit IPA. (☏802-658-2739; www.magichat.net; 5 Bartlett Bay Rd, South Burlington; ⊙10am-7pm Mon-Sat Jun–mid-Oct, to 6pm Mon-Thu, to 7pm Fri & Sat mid-Oct-May, noon-5pm Sun year-round)

🜚 ACTIVITIES

Ready for outdoor adventures? Head to the waterfront, where options include boating on Lake Champlain and cycling on the 9-mile shorefront Burlington Bike Path. Rent bikes at **Local Motion** (☏802-652-2453; www.localmotion.org; 1 Steele St; bicycles per day $32; ⊙9am-6pm July & Aug, 10am-6pm May & Jun, Sept & Oct; 👬) ⌷.

Whistling Man Schooner Company — Sailing

Explore Lake Champlain on the *Friend Ship*, a 17-passenger, 43-ft sailboat. (☏802-598-6504; www.whistlingman.com; Boathouse, 1 College St, at Lake Champlain; 2hr cruises adult/child under 13yr $40/25; ⊙3 trips daily, late May–early Oct)

🍴 EATING

Penny Cluse Cafe — Café $

Did somebody say bucket-o-spuds? Oh yes, they did. And that's just the first thing listed on the enticing menu at Penny Cluse, one of Burlington's most popular downtown eateries. The kitchen also whips up

Tall ship, Boston

STEVE DUNWELL / GETTY IMAGES ©

pancakes, biscuits and gravy, omelets and tofu scrambles along with sandwiches, fish tacos, salads and excellent *chile relleno*. Expect long lines on weekends. (802-651-8834; www.pennycluse.com; 169 Cherry St; mains $6-12.25; 6:45am-3pm Mon-Fri, 8am-3pm Sat & Sun)

DRINKING & NIGHTLIFE

Vermont Pub & Brewery
Microbrewery

Specialty and seasonal brews, including weekly limited releases, are made on the premises, accompanied by British-style pub fare. (www.vermontbrewery.com; 144 College St; mains $5-18; 11:30am-1am Sun-Wed, to 2am Thu-Sat)

Splash at the Boathouse
Bar

Perched atop Burlington's floating boathouse, this restaurant-bar with stellar lake views is perfect for kicking back with an evening cocktail or microbrew at sunset. (802-658-2244; www.splashattheboathouse. com; 0 College St; 10am-2am mid-May–Sep)

New Hampshire

New Hampshire's towns are small and personable, its mountains majestic and rugged. Outdoor enthusiasts flock to New England's highest range (6288ft at Mt Washington) for cold-weather skiing, summer hiking and brilliant fall foliage scenery.

For accommodations options, visit www. visitnh.gov.

Mt Washington Valley
New England's loftiest mountain range – the White Mountains – is a magnet for adventurers, with boundless opportunities for hiking, kayaking, skiing and scenic drives.

The most scenic journey, perhaps, is on the **Conway Scenic Railroad** (603-356-5251; www.conwayscenic.com; 38 Norcross Circle; Notch Train adult/child 4-12yr/child 1-3yr from $55/39/11, Valley Train from $16.50/11.50/ free; mid-Jun–Oct;). Climb aboard the 1874 Notch Train and take a spectacular 5½-hour trip through Crawford Notch.

Feeling sleepy after a big day out? North Conway is thick with sleeping options, from resort hotels to cozy inns.

New Hampshire

✪ EATING

Moat Mountain Smoke House & Brewing Co   Pub Food $$

With great food, on-point service and tasty homemade beers, Moat Mountain wins best all around for New Hampshire brewpubs. Come here for a wide array of American fare, with a nod to the South: BBQ sandwiches, beefy chili, juicy burgers, wood-grilled pizzas and a delicious curried crab and corn bisque. (☎603-356-6381; www.moatmountain.com; 3378 White Mountain Hwy; mains $10-23; ☺11:30am-midnight)

Franconia Notch

Franconia Notch is the most celebrated mountain pass in New England, a narrow gorge shaped over the eons by a rushing stream slicing through the craggy granite. I-93 runs straight through the state park. **Franconia Notch State Park visitor center** (☎603-745-8391; www.nhstateparks. org; I-93, exit 34A; ☺9am-5pm mid-May–Oct) can give you details on hikes in the park, including the popular Flume Gorge. Alternatively, the **Cannon Mountain Aerial Tramway** (☎603-823-8800; www.cannonmt. com; I-93, exit 34B; round-trip adult/child 6-12yr $17/14; ☺9am-5pm late May–mid-Oct; 🚠) shoots up the side of the mountain, offering a stunning view of Franconia Notch.

Lincoln and North Woodstock are twin towns at the southern end of the Notch and the western end of Kancamagus Hwy, making for a handy place to stop for a bite or a bed. **Woodstock Inn** (☎603-745-3951; www.woodstockinnnh.com; US 3; r incl breakfast with shared/private bath from $147/178; 🌸🛜) is a good option for either.

Mt Washington

Lofty Mt Washington (6288ft) is the highest peak east of the Mississippi and north of the Smoky Mountains. Hikers need to be prepared: the mountain's weather is notoriously severe and can turn on a dime. Cold temperatures and unrelenting winds can occur at any time of year. One of the most popular trails to the summit

begins at **Pinkham Notch Visitor Center** (☎603-278-4453; www.outdoors.org; NH 16; ☺6:30am-10pm May-Oct, to 9pm Nov-Apr), located on NH16 about 11 miles north of North Conway. It's a strenuous 4.2 miles to the summit, taking four to five hours to reach the top.

If you're not up for hiking, the **Mt Washington Auto Road** (☎603-466-3988; www. mountwashingtonautoroad.com; 1 Mt Washington Auto Rd, off NH 16; car & driver $28, extra adult/ child 5-12yr $8/6; ☺7:30am-6pm early Jun-Aug, shorter hours mid-May–early Jun, Sep–mid-Oct) is a fine alternative to reach the summit, starting 2.5 miles north of the visitor center. And the quaintest way to get to the top of Mt Washington is aboard a coal-fired, steam-powered locomotive, known as the **Mt Washington Cog Railway** (☎603-278-5404; www.thecog.com; 3168 Bass Station Rd; adult/child 4-12yr $68/39; ☺May-Oct). Sit back and enjoy the views!

Coastal Maine

Maine is New England's frontier – a land so vast it could swallow the region's five other states with scarcely a gulp. The sea looms large with mile after mile of sandy beaches, craggy sea cliffs and quiet harbors. Time-honored fishing villages and seaside lobster joints are the fame of Maine.

Portland

The 18th-century poet Henry Wadsworth Longfellow referred to his childhood city as the 'jewel by the sea,' and thanks to a hefty revitalization effort, Portland once again sparkles. Its lively waterfront, burgeoning gallery scene and cutting-edge restaurants add up to great exploring and excellent eating.

Start your explorations in Old Port, where 19th-century brick buildings line the streets and flickering gas lanterns light the way. Eat some wicked fresh seafood, quaff a local microbrew and peruse the local galleries.

For accommodations options, visit www. visitportland.com/accommodations.aspx.

Kayaking in Boothbay Harbor (p124)

◉ SIGHTS

Portland Museum of Art Museum
Founded in 1882, this well-respected
museum houses an outstanding collection
of American artists. Maine artists, including
Winslow Homer, Edward Hopper, Louise
Nevelson and Andrew Wyeth, are well
represented. You'll also find a few works by
European masters, including Degas, Picasso and Renoir. The majority of works are
found in the postmodern Charles Shipman
Payson building, designed by the firm of
famed architect IM Pei. (207-775-6148;
www.portlandmuseum.org; 7 Congress Sq; adult/
child $12/6, 5-9pm Fri free; 10am-5pm Sat-
Thu, to 9pm Fri, closed Mon mid-Oct–May)

Fort Williams Park Lighthouse
Four miles southeast of Portland on Cape
Elizabeth, 90-acre **Fort Williams Park**
(sunrise-sunset) is worth visiting for the
panoramas and picnic possibilities. Stroll
around the ruins of the fort, a late-19th-
century artillery base, checking out the
WWII bunkers and gun emplacements (a
German U-boat was spotted in Casco Bay

in 1942) that still dot the lawns. Strange as
it may seem, the fort actively guarded the
entrance to Casco Bay until 1964. Adjacent
to the fort stands the Portland Head Light,
the oldest of Maine's 52 functioning lighthouses. It was commissioned by George
Washington in 1791 and staffed until 1989,
when machines took over. The keeper's
house has been passed into service as the
Museum at Portland Head Light (20
7-799-2661; www.portlandheadlight.com; 1000
Shore Rd; lighthouse museum adult/child 6-18yr
$2/1; 10am-4pm Jun-Oct), which traces the
maritime and military history of the region.

❸ ACTIVITIES

For a different angle on Portland and Casco
Bay, hop one of the boats offering narrated
scenic cruises out of Portland Harbor.

Casco Bay Lines Cruise
This outfit cruises the Casco Bay islands
delivering mail, freight and visitors looking
to bike or explore. It also offers cruises
to Bailey Island (adult/child 5–9years
$26/12). (207-774-7871; www.cascobaylines.
com; 56 Commercial St; adult $13-24, child $7-11)

Ferry in Casco Bay

A meal at Green Elephant

Sunrise over Portland Harbor

Maine Island Kayak Company — Kayaking

On Peak Island, a 15-minute cruise from downtown on the Casco Bay Lines, this well-run outfitter offers fun day and overnight trips exploring the islands of Casco Bay. (207-766-2373; www.maineislandkayak.com; 70 Luther St, Peak Island; tour $65; May-Nov)

😣 EATING

Green Elephant — Vegetarian $$

They'll spice it as hot as you like it at this Zen-chic, Thai-inspired café, which serves brilliant vegetarian fare in an airy and spare nook downtown. Start with the crispy spinach wontons, then move on to one of the exotic soy creations like garlic and ginger tofu or a flavorful curry like the panang coconut curry with vegetables. (207-347-3111; www.greenelephantmaine.com; 608 Congress St; mains $10-15; 11:30am-2:30pm & 5-9:30pm Mon-Sat, to 9pm Sun;)

J's Oyster — Seafood $$

Maybe not the friendliest place on the planet, but this well-loved dive has the cheapest raw oysters in town. Eat 'em on the deck overlooking the pier. The oyster-averse have plenty of sandwiches and seafood mains to choose from. (207-772-4828; www.jsoyster.com; 5 Portland Pier; sandwiches $5-18, mains $25-31; 11:30am-11pm)

Fore Street — New American $$$

Roasting is a high art at Fore Street, one of Maine's most lauded restaurants. Chickens turn on spits in the open kitchen as chefs slide iron kettles of mussels into the wood-burning oven. Local, seasonal eating is taken very seriously, and the menu changes daily to offer what's freshest. The large, noisy dining room nods toward its warehouse past with exposed brick and pine paneling. (207-775-2717; www.fore street.biz; 288 Fore St; small plates $13-22, mains $28-40; 5:30-10pm Sun-Thu, to 10:30pm Fri & Sat)

🍷 DRINKING & NIGHTLIFE

Gritty McDuff's Brew Pub Brewpub
Gritty is an apt description for this party-happy Old Port pub. You'll find a generally raucous crowd drinking excellent beers – Gritty brews its own award-winning ales downstairs. (www.grittys.com; 396 Fore St; ⏰11am-1am)

ℹ️ INFORMATION

Greater Portland Convention & Visitors Bureau (www.visitportland.com; Ocean Gateway Bldg, 14 Ocean Gateway Pier; ⏰9am-5pm Mon-Fri, to 4pm Sat & Sun Jun-Oct, vary rest of year)

ℹ️ GETTING THERE & AROUND

Portland International Jetport (PWM; 📞207-874-8877; www.portlandjetport.org) has nonstop flights to cities in the eastern US.

Greyhound (www.greyhound.com; 950 Congress St) buses and **Amtrak** (📞800-872-7245; www.amtrak.com; 100 Thompson's Point Rd) trains connect Portland and Boston; both take about 2½ hours and charge $14 to $34 one way.

The local bus Metro (www.gpmetrobus.com; fares $1.50), which runs throughout the city, has its main terminus at Monument Sq, the intersection of Elm and Congress Sts.

Boothbay Harbor

On a fjord-like harbor, this achingly picturesque fishing village with narrow, winding streets is thick with tourists in the summer. Other than eating lobster, the main activity here is hopping on boats.
Balmy Days Cruises (📞207-633-2284; www.balmydayscruises.com; Pier 8; harbor tour adult/child 3-11yr $18/9 (Mar-Nov), day-trip cruise to Monhegan adult/child 3-11yr $39/19 (Jun–early Oct), sailing tour adult/child under 12yr $26/18 (mid-Jun-mid-Sep)) runs one-hour harbor tour cruises, day trips to Monhegan Island and 1½-hour sailing trips around the scenic islands near Boothbay.

Of all the lobster joints in Boothbay Harbor, the sprawling waterfront **Lobster Dock** (www.thelobsterdock.com; 49 Atlantic Ave; mains $6-25; ⏰11:30am-8:30pm) is one of the best. It's also a little different. You don't order at the counter, but a server stops

Bar Harbor

GLENN VAN DER KNIJFF / GETTY IMAGES ©

by your table. Take your pick of traditional fried seafood platters, sandwiches and steamers, plus a couple of seafood pastas, but whole butter-dripping lobster is definitely the main event.

After eating your fill, rest up at **Topside Inn** (📞207-633-5404; www.topsideinn.com; 60 McKown St; r incl breakfast $199-360; 🛜). Under new ownership, this grand gray mansion atop McKown Hill has Boothbay's best harbor views. Rooms are elegantly turned out in crisp nautical prints and beachy shades of sage, sea grass and khaki. Mainhouse rooms have more historic charm, but rooms in the two adjacent modern guesthouses are sunny and lovely, too.

For tourist information, including more accommodations options, visit www.boothbayharbor.com.

Bar Harbor

Set on the doorstep of Acadia National Park, this alluring coastal town once rivaled Newport, RI, as a trendy summer destination for wealthy Americans. Today many of the old mansions have been turned into inviting inns and the town has become a magnet for outdoor enthusiasts.

For accommodations options and tourist information, visit www.barharborinfo.com.

🔵 TOURS

Bar Harbor Whale Watch Co Cruise
Operates four-hour whale-watching and puffin-watching cruises, among other options. (📞207-288-2386; www.barharborwhales.com; 1 West St; adult $29-63, child 6-14yr $18-35, child under 6yr free-$9; 🕐mid-May–Oct)

Downeast Windjammer Cruises Cruise
Offers two-hour cruises on the majestic 151ft, four-masted schooner *Margaret Todd*. (📞207-288-4585; www.downeastwindjammer.com; 19 Cottage St; adult/child 6-11yr/2-5yr $38/30/5)

Acadian Nature Cruises Cruise
See whales, porpoises, bald eagles, seals and more on these narrated two-hour nature cruises. (📞207-801-2300; www.acadiannaturecruises.com; 119 Eden St; adult/child 6-14yr/under 6yr $30/18/5; 🕐mid-May–Oct)

🔵 EATING

Cafe This Way American $$
In a sprawling white cottage, this quirky eatery is the place for breakfast, with plump Maine blueberry pancakes and eggs Benedict with smoked salmon. It also serves eclectic, sophisticated dinners, like roasted duck with blueberries, Moroccan-style squash and tuna tempura. Sit in the garden. (📞207-288-4483; www.cafethisway.com; 14½ Mount Desert St; mains breakfast $6-17, dinner $18-28; 🕐7-11:30am Mon-Sat, 8am-1pm Sun, 5:30-9pm nightly May-Oct; 🖊)

Mâche Bistro French $$$
Almost certainly Bar Harbor's best midrange restaurant, Mâche serves contemporary French-inflected fare in a stylishly renovated cottage. The changing menu highlights the local riches – think pumpkin-seed-dusted scallops, lobster-and-brie-flatbread, and wild blueberry trifle. Specialty cocktails add to the appeal. Reservations are crucial. (📞207-288-0447; www.machebistro.com; 321 Main St; mains $18-29; 🕐5:30pm until close Mon-Sat early May-Oct)

WASHINGTON, DC

Washington, DC

The USA's capital teems with iconic monuments, vast museums and the corridors of power where politicians roam. The president, Congress and Supreme Court are here – the three pillars of US government – and in their orbit float the Pentagon, State Department, World Bank and embassies from most corners of the globe.

A lot of history is concentrated within DC's relatively small confines. In a single day, you could gawp at the Declaration of Independence, stand where Martin Luther King Jr gave his 'I Have a Dream' speech, and see the flag that inspired the 'Star Spangled Banner'. Then there's the numerous artifact-stuffed museums, many lined up in a row along the Mall.

Alongside all of that power and history, Washington's prestigious arts and theatre venues showcase America's talents.

☑ In This Section

National Mall 130
Capitol Hill 136
Sights 140
Activities.. 144
Tours... 145
Entertainment 145
Eating 146
Drinking & Nightlife 150

❶ Arriving in Washington, DC

Ronald Reagan National Airport
Metro trains (around $2.50) depart every 10 minutes from 5am to midnight. Taxis to the center cost $13 to $22.

Dulles International Airport Silver Line Express buses run every 15 to 20 minutes to Wiehle-Reston East Metro. The bus and train combined (around $11 total) takes 60 to 75 minutes to the center. Taxis cost $62 to $73.

Union Station Near the Capitol; trains and many buses arrive here.

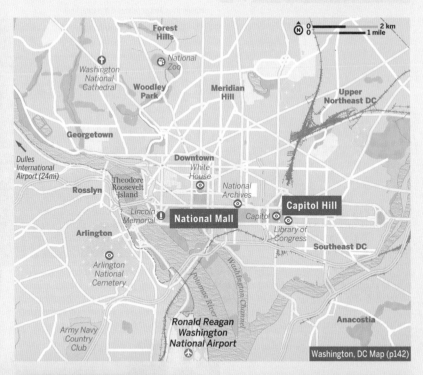

Washington, DC Map (p142)

⇒ Washington, DC in Two Days

Start at the National Mall. Check out the **Air and Space Museum** (p131) and **Museum of Natural History** (p132). Continue to the **Washington Monument** (p131), **Lincoln Memorial** (p131) and **Vietnam Veterans Memorial** (p133). Have dinner Downtown. Next day, tour Capitol Hill, visit the **National Archives** (p140) and saunter by the **White House** (p140). At night go to U St for jazzy clubs.

⇒ Washington, DC in Four Days

On day three, explore Georgetown and have lunch at **Martin's Tavern** (p150). In the evening, catch a show at the **Kennedy Center** (p146). Start day four at Dupont Circle and gape at mansions along Embassy Row (aka Massachusetts Ave NW). Visit the **National Gallery of Art** (p131), **Newseum** (p141) or other sights you might have missed. For dinner, browse 14th St in Logan Circle.

From left: The Capitol (p136); Ronald Reagan National Airport; National Air & Space Museum (p131); Newseum (p141)
ANUSKA SAMPEDRO / GETTY IMAGES ©; PANORAMIC IMAGES / GETTY IMAGES ©; RICHARD I'ANSON / GETTY IMAGES ©; MARK WILLIAMSON / GETTY IMAGES ©

Washington Monument and National Mall

STEVE GOTTLIEB / ALAMY STOCK PHOTO ©

National Mall

This 1.9-mile-long lawn is anchored at one end by the Lincoln Memorial, at the other by Capitol Hill, intersected by the reflecting pool and WWII memorial, and centered by the Washington Monument.

Great For...

☑ Don't Miss

The Lincoln Memorial step where Martin Luther King Jr gave his 'I Have a Dream' speech.

The Mall is the heart of the city, and in some ways, of the American experiment. Perhaps no other symbol has so prominently housed the national ideal of massed voice effecting radical change – from Martin Luther King's 1963 'I Have a Dream' speech to marches for gay marriage in the 2000s. Hundreds of rallies occur here every year. The Mall, framed by great monuments and museums, and shot through with tourists, dog-walkers, Frisbee-tossers and idealists, acts as a loudspeaker for any cause.

Of the Smithsonian Institution's 19 vast museums, 10 are on the Mall, offering everything from dinosaur skeletons to lunar modules to exquisite artworks. All of the sights are free. Whatever places you decide to explore, you'll need to be prepared to walk; the main row of sights is about 2 miles tip to tip.

National Gallery of Art

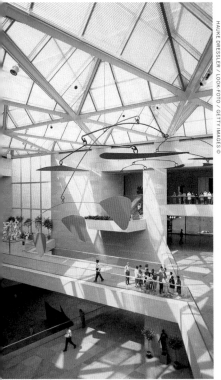

HAUKE DRESSLER / LOOK-FOTO / GETTY IMAGES ©

Constitution Ave NW
National Mall
Independence Ave SW
Potomac River
Tidal Basin
M Smithsonian
3rd St SW

❶ Need to Know

The new DC Circulator (p153) bus route stops by many of the hot spots.

✕ Take a Break

Mitsitam Native Foods Cafe (Map p142; www.mitsitamcafe.com; cnr 4th St & Independence Ave SW, National Museum of the American Indian; mains \$10-18; ⏱11am-5pm; 🚍Circulator, MⓁL'Enfant Plaza) serves unique, indigenous dishes.

★ Top Tip

An atmospheric nighttime walk along Constitution Ave past the dramatically lit monuments.

⏱9am-5pm, to 10pm Jun-Aug; 🚍Circulator, MSmithsonian) FREE

Lincoln Memorial Monument

Anchoring the Mall's west end is the hallowed shrine to Abraham Lincoln, who gazes peacefully across the reflecting pool. To the left of Lincoln you can read the words of the Gettysburg Address, and the hall below highlights other great Lincoln-isms. (www.nps.gov/linc; 2 Lincoln Memorial Circle NW; ⏱24hr; 🚍Circulator, MFoggy Bottom-GWU) FREE

Washington Monument Monument

Just peaking at 555ft (and 5in), the Washington Monument is the tallest building in the district. A 70-second elevator ride whisks you to the observation deck for the city's best views. Same-day tickets for a timed entrance are available at the **kiosk** (Map p142; 15th St, btwn Madison Dr NW & Jefferson Dr SW; ⏱from 8:30am) by the monument. Arrive early. (www.nps.gov/wamo; 2 15th St NW;

National Air & Space Museum Museum

The Air and Space Museum is one of the most popular Smithsonian museums. Everyone flocks to see the Wright brothers' flyer, Chuck Yeager's Bell X-1, Charles Lindbergh's *Spirit of St Louis,* Amelia Earhart's natty red plane and the Apollo Lunar Module. (www.airandspace.si.edu; cnr 6th St & Independence Ave SW; ⏱10am-5:30pm, to 7:30pm mid-Mar–early Sep; 🛜👣; 🚍Circulator, MⓁL'Enfant Plaza) FREE

National Gallery of Art Museum

The staggering collection spans the Middle Ages to the present. The neoclassical west building showcases European art through the early 1900s. The IM Pei–designed east building displays modern art, with works by Picasso, Matisse and Pollock. (www.nga.gov; Constitution Ave NW, btwn 3rd & 7th Sts; ⏱10am-5pm Mon-Sat, 11am-6pm Sun; 🛜; 🚍Circulator, MArchives) FREE

National Museum of Natural History
Museum

Smithsonian museums don't get more popular than this one, so crowds are pretty much guaranteed. The beloved dinosaur hall is under renovation until 2019, but the giant squid and tarantula feedings fill in the thrills at this kid-packed venue. (www.mnh.si.edu; cnr 10th St & Constitution Ave NW; 🕙10am-5:30pm, to 7:30pm Jun-Aug; 👪; 🚌Circulator, Ⓜ Smithsonian) FREE

National Museum of American History
Museum

The museum collects all kinds of artifacts of the American experience. The centerpiece is the flag that flew over Fort McHenry in Baltimore during the War of 1812 – the same flag that inspired Francis Scott Key to pen *The Star-Spangled Banner*. Other highlights include Julia Child's kitchen, Dorothy's ruby slippers and a piece of Plymouth Rock. (www.americanhistory.si.edu; cnr 14th St & Constitution Ave NW; 🕙10am-5:30pm, to 7:30pm Jun-Aug; 📶👪; 🚌Circulator, Ⓜ Smithsonian) FREE

National Museum of African American History & Culture
Museum

This recent addition to the Smithsonian fold covers the diverse African American experience and how it helped shape the nation. The institution is constructing a new building for the museum, to open in 2016. In the meantime, find exhibits on show at the next-door National Museum of American History (on the 2nd floor). (www.nmaahc.si.edu; 1400 Constitution Ave NW; 🕙10am-5:30pm; 🚌Circulator, Ⓜ Smithsonian, Federal Triangle) FREE

Martin Luther King Jr Memorial

National Museum of the American Indian
Museum

This museum makes a striking architectural impression. Inside it offers cultural artifacts, costumes, video and audio recordings related to the indigenous people of the Americas. Exhibits are largely organized and presented by individual tribes, which provides an intimate, if sometimes disjointed, overall narrative. (www.nmai.si.edu; cnr 4th St & Independence Ave SW; ⊙10am-5:30pm; 🛜🚻; 🚇Circulator, Ⓜ️L'Enfant Plaza) FREE

> ★ **Top Tip**
>
> Cycling is one option for navigating the Mall's expanse. Capital Bikeshare (www.capitalbikeshare.com) has handy stations by the Smithsonian Metro and Lincoln Memorial.

GRANT FAINT / GETTY IMAGES ©

United States Holocaust Memorial Museum
Museum

For a deep understanding of the Holocaust this harrowing museum is a must-see. The main exhibit gives visitors the identity card of a single Holocaust victim, whose story is revealed as you take a winding route into a hellish past marked by ghettos, rail cars and death camps. (www.ushmm.org; 100 Raoul Wallenberg Pl SW; ⊙10am-5:20pm, to 6:20pm Mon-Fri Apr & May; Ⓜ️Smithsonian) FREE

Martin Luther King Jr Memorial
Monument

Opened in 2011, this is the Mall's first memorial dedicated to a nonpresident, as well as to an African American. Sculptor Lei Yixin carved the piece. Besides Dr King's image, known as the Stone of Hope, there are two blocks behind him that represent the Mountain of Despair. (www.nps.gov/mlkm; 1850 W Basin Dr SW; ⊙24hr; 🚇Circulator, Ⓜ️Smithsonian) FREE

Vietnam Veterans Memorial
Monument

The opposite of DC's white, gleaming marble is this black, low-lying 'V,' an expression of the psychic scar wrought by the Vietnam War. The monument follows a descent deeper into the earth, with the names of the 58,272 dead soldiers listed in the order in which they died. (www.nps.gov/vive; 5 Henry Bacon Dr NW; ⊙24hr; 🚇Circulator, Ⓜ️Foggy Bottom-GWU) FREE

National WWII Memorial
Monument

Dedicated in 2004, the WWII memorial honors the 400,000 Americans who died in the conflict, along with the 16 million US soldiers who served between 1941 and 1945. The plaza's dual arches symbolize victory in the Atlantic and Pacific theaters. (www.nps.gov/wwii; 17th St; ⊙24hr; 🚇Circulator, Ⓜ️Smithsonian) FREE

> ✕ **Take a Break**
>
> Dining options are thin on the Mall, so bring snacks. Museums typically allow you to bring in food.

National Mall

Folks often call the Mall 'America's Front Yard,' and that's a pretty good analogy. It is indeed a lawn, unfurling scrubby green grass from the Capitol west to the Lincoln Memorial. It's also America's great public space, where citizens come to protest their government, go for scenic runs and connect with the nation's most cherished ideals writ large in stone, landscaping, monuments and memorials.

You can sample quite a bit in a day, though it'll be a full one that requires roughly 4 miles of walking. Start at the **Vietnam Veterans Memorial ❶**, then head counterclockwise around the Mall, swooping in on the **Lincoln Memorial ❷**, **Martin Luther King Jr Memorial ❸** and **Washington Monument ❹**. You can also pause for the cause of the Korean War and WWII, among other monuments that dot the Mall's western portion.

Martin Luther King Jr Memorial

Walk all the way around the towering statue of Dr King by Lei Yixin and read the quotes. His likeness, incidentally, is 11ft taller than Lincoln and Jefferson in their memorials.

Tidal Basin

Smithsonian Castle

Seek out the tomb of James Smithson, the eccentric Englishman whose 1826 financial gift launched the Smithsonian Institution. His crypt is in a room by the Mall entrance.

Department of Agriculture

National Air & Space Museum

Simply step inside and look up, and you'll be impressed. Lindbergh's *Spirit of St Louis* and Chuck Yeager's sound barrier–breaking Bell X-1 are among the machines hanging from the ceiling.

⑤

⑥

West Building

East Building

⑦

National Museum of the American Indian

US Capitol

Then it's onward to the museums, all fabulous and all free. Begin at the **Smithsonian Castle ❺** to get your bearings – and to say thanks to the guy making all this awesomeness possible – and commence browsing through the **National Air & Space Museum ❻**, **National Gallery of Art & National Sculpture Garden ❼** and **National Museum of Natural History ❽**.

TOP TIPS

Start early, especially in summer. You'll avoid the crowds, but more importantly you'll avoid the blazing heat. Try to finish with the monuments and be in the air-conditioned museums by 10:30am. Also, consider bringing snacks, since the only food available is from scattered cart vendors and museum cafes.

Lincoln Memorial

Commune with Abe in his chair, then head down the steps to the marker where Martin Luther King Jr gave his 'Dream' speech. The view of the Reflecting Pool and Washington Monument is one of DC's best.

Korean War Veterans Memorial

National WWII Memorial

National Museum of African American History & Culture

National Museum of American History

National Sculpture Garden

National Gallery of Art & National Sculpture Garden

Beeline to Gallery 6 (West Building) and ogle the Western Hemisphere's only Leonardo da Vinci painting. Outdoors, amble amid whimsical sculptures by Miró, Calder and Lichtenstein. Also check out IM Pei's design of the East Building.

Vietnam Veterans Memorial

Check the symbol that's beside each name. A diamond indicates 'killed, body recovered.' A plus sign indicates 'missing and unaccounted for.' There are approximately 1200 of the latter.

Washington Monument

As you approach the obelisk, look a third of the way up. See how it's slightly lighter in color at the bottom? Builders had to use different marble after the first source dried up.

National Museum of Natural History

Wave to Henry, the elephant who guards the rotunda, then zip to the 2nd floor's Hope Diamond. The 45.52-carat bauble has cursed its owners, including Marie Antoinette, or so the story goes.

EDDIE BRADY / GETTY IMAGES ©

STEVEN GREAVES /GETTY IMAGES ©

Capitol

Capitol Hill

First-time visitors will be forgiven for assuming Capitol Hill, the city's geographic and legislative heart, is all about power-broking and politics. Truth is, it's pretty much a traditional neighborhood, but there's no denying that the big-domed building grabs all the attention.

Great For

☑ Don't Miss

The 1507 Waldseemuller world map (the first to show America) at the Library of Congress.

The Capitol, appropriately, sits atop Capitol Hill (what Pierre L'Enfant called 'a pedestal waiting for a monument') across a plaza from the almost-as-regal Supreme Court and Library of Congress. They're all DC highlights, and touring them requires the better part of a day.

Capitol Landmark
Since 1800, the Capitol is where the legislative branch of American government – ie Congress – has met to write the country's laws. Enter via the underground visitor center below the East Plaza. Guided tours of the building are free, but you need a ticket. Get one at the information desk, or reserve online in advance (there's no fee).

The hour-long jaunt showcases the exhaustive background of a building that fairly sweats history. You'll watch a cheesy

Jefferson Building, Library of Congress

DANITA DELIMONT / GETTY IMAGES ©

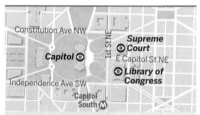

❶ Need to Know

Groovy underground tunnels connect the Capitol and Library of Congress, making for easy, weatherproof access.

✕ Take a Break

Eastern Market (p149) is a short stroll away for butchers, bakers and blue-crab makers.

★ Top Tip

Military bands perform on the Capitol steps weekdays (except Thursday) at 8pm June through August.

film first, then staff members lead you into the ornate halls and chambers cluttered with the busts, statues and personal mementos of generations of Congress members.

To watch Congress in session, you need a separate visitor pass. US citizens must get one from their representative or senator; foreign visitors should take their passports to the House and Senate Appointment Desks on the upper level. Congressional committee hearings are actually more interesting (and substantive) if you care about what's being debated; check for a schedule, locations and to see if they're open to the public (they often are) online at www.house.gov and www.senate.gov. (Map p142; www.visitthecapitol.gov; First St NE & E Capitol St; ⊗8:30am-4:30pm Mon-Sat; Ⓜ Capitol South) FREE

Supreme Court   Landmark

The highest court in the USA, the Supreme Court sits in a pseudo-Greek temple. Arrive early to watch arguments (periodic Monday through Wednesday October to April). You can visit the permanent exhibits and the building's five-story, marble-and-bronze, spiral staircase year-round. When court is not in session you can hear lectures (every hour on the half-hour) in the courtroom. (Map p142; www.supremecourt.gov; 1 1st St NE; ⊗9am-4:30pm Mon-Fri; Ⓜ Capitol South) FREE

Library of Congress   Library

The world's largest library – with 29 million books and counting – awes in both scope and design. The centerpiece is the 1897 Jefferson Building. Gawk at the Great Hall, done up in stained glass, marble and mosaics of mythical characters, then seek out the Gutenberg Bible (c 1455), and Thomas Jefferson's round library. Free tours take place between 10:30am and 3:30pm on the half-hour. (Map p142; www.loc.gov; 1st St SE; ⊗8:30am-4:30pm Mon-Sat; Ⓜ Capitol South) FREE

Eastern Market

HENRY LEDERER / GETTY IMAGES ©

Walking Tour: Capitol Hill

Explore the area around the legislative heart of the United States, taking in historic buildings and local sites.

Distance: 2 miles
Duration: 3 to 4 hours

✕ Take a Break

Popular food stall Market Lunch (www.easternmarket-dc.org; ⊘7:30-2:30pm Tue-Fri, 8am-3pm Sat, 11am-3pm Sun) sits smack in the middle of Eastern Market and uses fresh local ingredients.

Start Eastern Market Ⓜ Eastern Market

❶ Eastern Market

Start by fueling up at **Eastern Market** (p149; about 20m north of Eastern Market Metro). This is the heart of Capitol Hill: a neighborhood hangout, covered bazaar and just great place to soak up local flavor. Walk west on Independence Ave SE toward the Capitol Dome, which is hard to miss.

❷ Folger Shakespeare Library

At 3rd St SE, detour a couple of blocks north to the **Folger Shakespeare Library** (www.folger.edu; 201 E Capitol St SE; ⊘10am-5pm Mon-Sat, noon-5pm Sun; Ⓜ Capitol South). The building, jokingly referred to as 'Stark

Deco,' holds the world's largest collection of Shakespeare's works, along with cool exhibits. Get ready for a literary comparison, because your next stop is the Library of Congress.

❸ Library of Congress

Pop in to the library (p137) for a guided tour of a building that's almost as impressive as its mission: to gather all the knowledge in the world under one roof.

❹ Capitol Hill Visitor Center

Now go underground into the **Capitol Visitor Center** (www.visitthecapitol.gov; 1st St NE & E Capitol St; ⊘8:30am-4:30pm Mon-Sat). You can easily spend two or more hours here learning about the seat of the legislative branch of government (ie Congress).

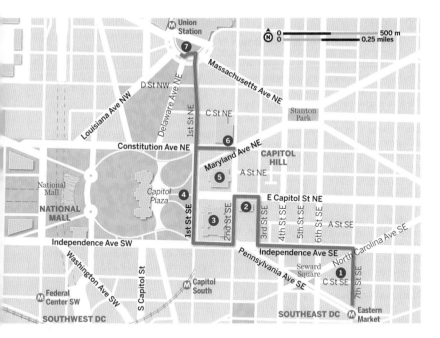

⑤ The Supreme Court

Across the street the government's judiciary branch – the Supreme Court (p137) – rises up in Greek temple-esque splendor. If you happen to stumble upon the day of an interesting case, you may find that your tour has come to an abrupt, albeit serendipitous end – watching verbal arguments conducted in front of the nine justices is an opportunity that shouldn't be passed up.

⑥ Sewell-Belmont House

Make another little detour to **Sewell-Belmont House** (☎202-546-1210; www. sewallbelmont.org; 144 Constitution Ave NE; admission $8; ☺tours 11am, 1pm & 3pm Thu-Sat; Ⓜ Union Station, Capitol South), home base of the National Woman's Party since 1929,

and 43-year residence of the party's legendary founder, suffragette Alice Paul. US women: she's why you can vote.

⑦ Union Station

Return to 1st St NE and head north until you get to **Union Station** (www.unionstation dc.com; 50 Massachusetts Ave NE; Ⓜ Union Station). This is one of the masterpieces of the early-20th-century beaux-arts movement, patterned after the Roman Baths of Diocletian. We like to think even an emperor would be awed by the sights just traversed.

Finish Union Station Ⓜ Union Station

◎ SIGHTS
◎ White House Area & Downtown

White House   Landmark
The White House has survived both fire (the Brits torched it in 1814) and insults (Jefferson groused that it was 'big enough for two emperors, one Pope and the grand Lama'). Tours must be arranged in advance. Americans must apply via one of their state's members of Congress, and non-Americans must apply through either the US consulate in their home country or their country's consulate in DC. Applications are taken from 21 days to six months in advance; three months ahead is the recommended sweet spot. (🕿 tours 202-456-7041; www.whitehouse.gov; ⊙ tours 7:30-11:30am Tue-Thu, to 1:30pm Fri & Sat; Ⓜ Federal Triangle, McPherson Sq, Metro Center) FREE

National Archives   Landmark
It's hard not to feel a little in awe of the big three documents in the National Archives: the Declaration of Independence, the Constitution and the Bill of Rights, plus one of four copies of the Magna Carta. Taken together, it becomes clear just how radical the American experiment was for its time. The Public Vaults, a bare scratching of archival bric-a-brac, make a flashy rejoinder to the main exhibit. (🕿 866-272-6272; www.archives.gov/museum; 700 Pennsylvania Ave NW; ⊙ 10am-5:30pm Sep–mid-Mar, to 7pm mid-Mar–Aug; Ⓜ Archives) FREE

Reynolds Center for American Art & Portraiture   Museum
If you only visit one art museum in DC, make it the Reynolds Center, which combines the National Portrait Gallery and the American Art Museum. There is, simply put, no better collection of American art in the world than at these two Smithsonian museums. Famed works by Edward Hopper, Georgia O'Keeffe, Andy Warhol, Winslow Homer and loads more celebrated artists fill the galleries. (🕿 202-633-1000; www.americanart.si.edu; cnr 8th & F Sts NW; ⊙ 11:30am-7pm; 🛜; Ⓜ Gallery Pl) FREE

Ford's Theatre   Historic Site
On April 14, 1865, John Wilkes Booth assassinated Abraham Lincoln in his box seat

Declaration of Independence at National Archives

here. Timed-entry tickets let you see the flag-draped site. They also provide entry to the basement museum (displaying Booth's .44-caliber pistol, his muddy boot etc) and to Petersen House (across the street), where Lincoln died. Arrive early because tickets do run out. Reserve online ($6.25 fee) to ensure admittance. (📞202-426-6924; www.fords.org; 511 10th St NW; ⊙9am-4:30pm; Ⓜ Metro Center) FREE

Newseum
Museum

This six-story, highly interactive news museum is worth the admission price. You can delve into the major events of recent years (the fall of the Berlin Wall, September 11, Hurricane Katrina), and spend hours watching moving film footage and perusing Pulitzer Prize–winning photographs. The concourse level displays FBI artifacts from prominent news stories, such as the Unabomber's cabin and John Dillinger's death mask. (www.newseum.org; 555 Pennsylvania Ave NW; adult/child $23/14; ⊙9am-5pm; 📶 ⑆; Ⓜ Archives, Judiciary Sq)

White House Visitor Center
Museum

Getting inside the White House can be tough, so here is your backup plan. Browse artifacts like Roosevelt's desk for his fireside chats and Lincoln's cabinet chair. Multimedia exhibits give a 360-degree view into the White House's rooms. It's obviously not the same as seeing the real deal firsthand, but the center does do its job very well, giving good history sprinkled with great anecdotes on presidential spouses, kids, pets and dinner preferences. (www.nps.gov/whho; 1450 Pennsylvania Ave NW; ⊙7:30am-4pm; Ⓜ Federal Triangle) FREE

◉ Dupont Circle

Phillips Collection
Museum

The first modern-art museum in the country (opened in 1921) houses a small but exquisite collection of European and American works. Renoir's *Luncheon of the Boating Party* is a highlight, along with pieces by Gauguin, Van Gogh, Matisse, Pi-

🏛 Smithsonian Institution

The Smithsonian Institution (www. si.edu) is not a single place, as commonly thought; rather, it consists of 19 museums, the National Zoo and nine research facilities. Most are in DC, but others are further flung in the US and abroad. Together they comprise the world's largest museum and research complex – and it's all free to visitors. Thanks go to the curious Englishman James Smithson, who never visited the USA, but willed the fledgling nation $508,318 to found an 'establishment for the increase and diffusion of knowledge' in 1826.

Most Smithsonian museums are open daily (except Christmas Day). Some have extended hours in summer. Be prepared for lines and bag checks.

casso and many other greats. The intimate rooms, set in a restored mansion, put you unusually close to the artworks. The permanent collection is free on weekdays. (www.phillipscollection.org; 1600 21st St NW; Sat & Sun $10, Tue-Fri free, ticketed exhibitions per day $12; ⊙10am-5pm Tue, Wed, Fri & Sat, to 8:30pm Thu, 11am-6pm Sun, chamber-music series 4pm Sun Oct-May; Ⓜ Dupont Circle)

◉ Georgetown

Dumbarton Oaks
Gardens, Museum

The mansion's 10 acres of enchanting formal gardens are straight out of a storybook. In springtime, the blooms – including heaps of cherry blossoms – are stunning. The mansion itself is worth a walk-through to see exquisite Byzantine and pre-Columbian art (including El Greco's *The Visitation*) and the fascinating library of rare books. (www.doaks.org; 1703 32nd St NW; museum free, gardens adult/child $8/5; ⊙museum 11:30am-5:30pm Tue-Sun, gardens 2-6pm)

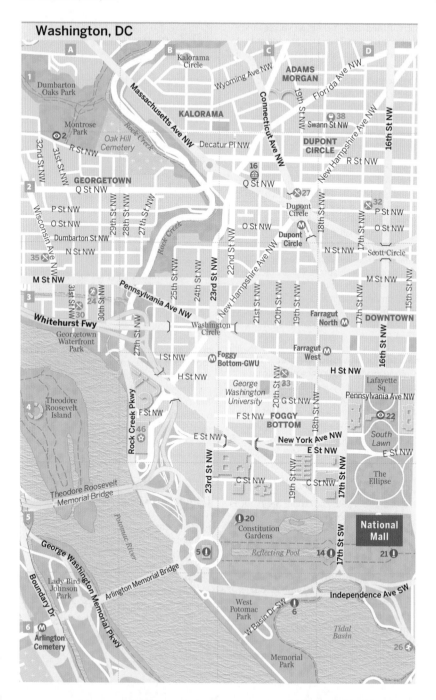

Washington, DC

Kalorama Circle

Wyoming Ave NW

ADAMS MORGAN

Florida Ave NW

Dumbarton Oaks Park

Massachusetts Ave NW

KALORAMA

Connecticut Ave NW

19th St NW

Swann St NW

○38

Montrose Park

Oak Hill Cemetery

Decatur Pl NW

New Hampshire Ave NW

DUPONT CIRCLE

16th St NW

R St NW

○2

R St NW

32nd St NW

31st St NW

GEORGETOWN

Q St NW

16 🏛

Q St NW

R St NW

Wisconsin Ave NW

29th St NW

28th St NW

27th St NW

26th St NW

25th St NW

Dupont Circle

⊗27

18th St NW

17th St NW

⊗32

P St NW

P St NW

O St NW

O St NW

Dupont Circle Ⓜ

O St NW

N St NW

Scott Circle

Dumbarton St NW

N St NW

35⊗

N St NW

M St NW

22nd St NW

New Hampshire Ave NW

21st St NW

20th St NW

19th St NW

17th St NW

15th St NW

M St NW

M St NW

31st St NW

30th St NW

24 🔾

Pennsylvania Ave NW

24th St NW

23rd St NW

DOWNTOWN

30

Whitehurst Fwy

Georgetown Waterfront Park

Washington Circle

Farragut North Ⓜ

16th St NW

27th St NW

I St NW

Ⓜ **Foggy Bottom-GWU**

Farragut West Ⓜ

H St NW

Rock Creek Pkwy

H St NW

George Washington University

20th St NW

⊗33

H St NW

Theodore Roosevelt Island

F St NW

G St NW

18th St NW

Lafayette Sq

Pennsylvania Ave NW

○22

46 🔾

F St NW

FOGGY BOTTOM

E St NW

New York Ave NW

South Lawn

E St NW

E St NW

Theodore Roosevelt Memorial Bridge

23rd St NW

C St NW

19th St NW

17th St NW

C St NW

The Ellipse

○20 Constitution Gardens

5 🔾

Reflecting Pool

14 🔾

17th St SW

National Mall

21 🔾

Potomac River

George Washington Memorial Pkwy

Lady Bird Johnson Park

Arlington Memorial Bridge

West Potomac Park

W Basin Dr SW

🔾 6

Independence Ave SW

Boundary Dr

Ⓜ **Arlington Cemetery**

Tidal Basin

26 🔾

Memorial Park

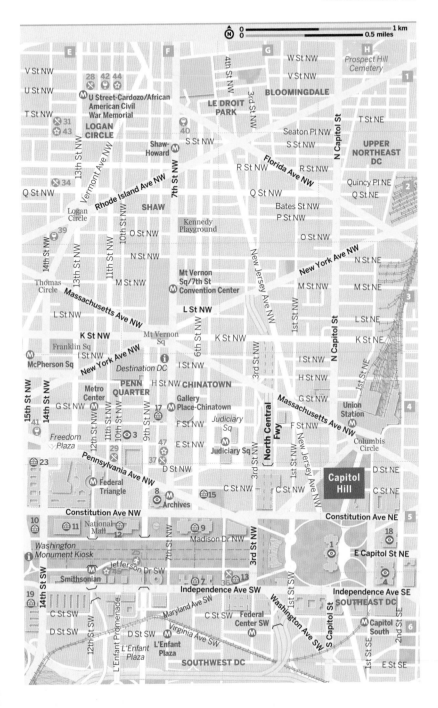

Washington, DC

◎ Sights
1 Capitol..H5
2 Dumbarton Oaks...............................A2
3 Ford's Theatre...................................F4
4 Library of Congress..........................H6
5 Lincoln Memorial..............................B5
6 Martin Luther King Jr Memorial............C6
7 National Air and Space Museum.............F6
8 National Archives..............................F5
9 National Gallery of Art......................F5
10 National Museum of African
   American History and Culture.............E5
11 National Museum of American
   History..E5
12 National Museum of Natural
   History..E5
13 National Museum of the American
   Indian...G6
14 National WWII Memorial....................D5
15 Newseum...F5
16 Phillips Collection............................C2
17 Reynolds Center for American Art
   & Portraiture...................................F4
18 Supreme Court.................................H5
19 United States Holocaust
   Memorial Museum.............................E6
20 Vietnam Veterans Memorial...............C5
21 Washington Monument.....................D5
22 White House.....................................D4
23 White House Visitor Center...............E4

◈ Activities, Courses & Tours
24 C&O Canal Towpath...........................A3
25 Carousel...F5
26 Tidal Basin Boathouse.......................D6

◈ Eating
27 Afterwords Cafe...............................C2
28 Ben's Chili Bowl................................E1
29 Central Michel Richard.......................E4
30 Chez Billy Sud..................................A3
31 Compass Rose...................................E1
32 Duke's Grocery.................................D2
33 Founding Farmers..............................C4
34 Le Diplomate....................................E2
35 Martin's Tavern.................................A3
36 Mitsitam Native Foods Cafe...............G6
37 Red Apron Butchery..........................F4

◉ Drinking & Nightlife
38 Bar Charley......................................D1
39 Churchkey..E2
40 Right Proper Brewing Co....................F1
41 Round Robin.....................................E4
42 U Street Music Hall...........................E1

◈ Entertainment
43 Black Cat...E1
44 Bohemian Caverns............................E1
45 Discovery Theater.............................E5
46 Kennedy Center................................B4
47 Shakespeare Theatre Company..........F4

◎ Upper Northwest DC

National Zoo
Zoo

Home to over 2000 individual animals (400 different species) in natural habitats, the National Zoo is famed for its giant pandas Mei Xiang and Tian Tian, along with their cub Bao Bao (born to Mei Xiang in 2013). Other highlights include the African lion pride, Asian elephants, and dangling orangutans swinging 50ft overhead from steel cables and interconnected towers (aka the 'O Line'). (www.nationalzoo.si.edu; 3001 Connecticut Ave NW; ⏰10am-6pm Apr-Oct, to 4:30pm Nov-Mar, grounds 6am-8pm daily, to 6pm Nov-Mar; Ⓜ Cleveland Park, Woodley Park-Zoo/Adams Morgan) FREE

Washington National Cathedral
Church

This Gothic cathedral, as dramatic as its European counterparts, blends both the spiritual and the profane in its architectural treasures. The stained-glass windows are stunning (check out the 'Space Window' with an imbedded lunar rock); you'll need binoculars to spy the Darth Vader gargoyle on the exterior. Specialized tours delve deeper into the esoteric; call or go online for the schedule. There's also an excellent café here. (☏202-537-6200; www.national cathedral.org; 3101 Wisconsin Ave NW; adult/child $10/6, admission free Sun; ⏰10am-5:30pm Mon-Fri, to 8pm some days May-Sep, 10am-4:30pm Sat, 8am-4pm Sun; ☎; Ⓜ Tenleytown-AU to southbound bus 31, 32, 36, 37)

✦ ACTIVITIES

C&O Canal Towpath
Walking, Cycling

The shaded hiking-cycling path – part of a larger national historic park – runs alongside a waterway constructed in the mid-1800s to transport goods all the way to

West Virginia. Step on at Jefferson St for a lovely green escape from the crowd. (www. nps.gov/choh; 1057 Thomas Jefferson St NW)

Tidal Basin Boathouse   Boating
It rents paddleboats to take out on the Tidal Basin. Make sure you bring a camera. There are great views, of the Jefferson Memorial in particular, from the water. (www. tidalbasinpaddleboats.com; 1501 Maine Ave SW; 2-/4-person boat rental $14/22; ⏱10am-6pm mid-Mar–Aug, Wed-Sun only Sep–mid-Oct, closed mid-Oct–mid-Mar; 🚌Circulator, MSmithsonian)

🜚 TOURS

Bike & Roll   Bicycle Tour
Offers day and evening bike tours around the Mall and Capitol Hill. The 'Monuments at Night' tour is especially atmospheric. The company also arranges combo boat-bike trips to Mt Vernon. (www.bikeandrolldc. com; adult/child from $40/30; ⏱mid-Mar–Nov)

DC by Foot   Walking Tour
Guides for this pay-what-you-want walking tour offer engaging stories and historical details on different jaunts covering the National Mall, Lincoln's assassination, Georgetown's ghosts, U St's food and many more. Most takers pay around $10 per person. (www.dcbyfoot.com)

❂ ENTERTAINMENT

See the free weekly *Washington City Paper* for comprehensive listings.

Don't have the dough for a big-ticket show? No worries. Each evening the Millennium Stage at the Kennedy Center (p146) puts on a first-rate music or dance performance at 6pm in the Grand Foyer. The cost is absolutely nada.

Black Cat   Live Music
A pillar of DC's rock and indie scene since the 1990s, the battered Black Cat has hosted all the greats of years past (White Stripes, the Strokes, Arcade Fire among others). If you don't want to pony up for

Arlington National Cemetery

Arlington National Cemetery
(☎877-907-8585; www.arlingtoncemetery. mil; ⏱8am-7pm Apr-Sep, to 5pm Oct-Mar; MArlington Cemetery) FREE is the somber final resting place for more than 400,000 military personnel and their dependents, with veterans of every US war from the Revolution to Iraq. The cemetery is spread over 612 hilly acres. Departing from the visitor center, bus tours are a handy way to visit the cemetery's memorials. Highlights include the Tomb of the Unknowns with its elaborate changing of the guard ceremony, and the gravesite of John F and Jacqueline Kennedy, marked by an eternal flame.

Graves of JFK and Jacqueline Kennedy Onassis
MALCOLM PARK / GETTY IMAGES ©

$20-a-ticket bands on the upstairs main stage (or the smaller Backstage below), head to the Red Room for jukebox, pool and strong cocktails. (www.blackcatdc.com; 1811 14th St NW; MU St)

Bohemian Caverns   Jazz
Back in the day, Bohemian Caverns hosted the likes of Miles Davis, John Coltrane and Duke Ellington. Today the timeless jazz club stages a mix of youthful renegades and soulful legends. Monday night's swingin' house band draws an all-ages crowd. (www.bohemiancaverns.com; 2001 11th St NW; admission $7-22; ⏱7pm-midnight Mon-Thu, 7:30pm-2am Fri & Sat, 6pm-midnight Sun; MU St)

Washington, DC for Children

The top destination for families is undoubtedly the (free!) National Zoo (p144), and museums around the city will entertain and educate children of all ages. Institutions with especially good programming include the National Air and Space Museum (p131), National Museum of Natural History (p132), Newseum (p141) and National Gallery of Art (p131).

Other kid-friendly spots include the old-fashioned **carousel** (Map p142; tickets $3.50; ☺10am-6pm; ☐Circulator, MSmithsonian) on the Mall, which can be followed with a romp around the wide-open lawn and the Smithsonian's **Discovery Theater** (Map p142; www. discoverytheater.org; 1100 Jefferson Dr SW; tickets $6-12; ♿; ☐Circulator, MSmithsonian), which focuses on storytelling and cultural plays for children.

For more information, check out:
DC Cool Kids (www.washington.org/ dc-cool-kids) Features activity guides, insider tips from local youngsters on things to do, and museum info.

Smithsonian Kids (www.si.edu/kids) Educational games and projects, plus the lowdown on pint-sized activities at the museums.

Kennedy Center   Performing Arts
Sprawled on 17 acres along the Potomac River, the magnificent Kennedy Center hosts a staggering array of performances – more than 2000 each year among its multiple venues including the Concert Hall (home to the National Symphony) and Opera House (home to the National Opera). A free shuttle bus runs to and from the Metro station every 15 minutes from 9:45am (noon on Sunday) to midnight. (☏202-467-4600; www.kennedy-center.org; 2700 F St NW; MFoggy Bottom-GWU)

Shakespeare Theatre Company   Theater
The nation's foremost Shakespeare company presents masterful works by the bard, as well as plays by George Bernard Shaw, Oscar Wilde, Henrik Ibsen, Eugene O'Neill and other greats. The season spans about a half-dozen productions annually, plus a free summer Shakespeare series on-site for two weeks in late August. (☏202-547-1122; www.shakespearetheatre.org; 450 7th St NW; MArchives)

Washington Nationals   Baseball
DC's Major League Baseball team (the Washington Nationals) bats at Nationals Park. Games include the 'running of the president' – an odd, middle-of-the-fourth-inning race between caricatures of George Washington, Abraham Lincoln, Thomas Jefferson and Teddy Roosevelt. It's good fun, more so in the rare event the Nationals win. Grandstand seats start at $5; infield boxes go for around $70. (www.nationals.com; 1500 S Capitol St SE; ☏; MNavy Yard)

⊗ EATING
⊗ Capitol Hill

Toki Underground   Asian $
Spicy ramen noodles and dumplings sum up wee Toki's menu. Steaming pots obscure the busy chefs, while diners slurp and sigh contentedly. The eatery doesn't take reservations, so explore surrounding bars while you wait; Toki will text when your table is ready. The restaurant isn't signposted; look for the Pug bar, and Toki is above it. (☏202-388-3086; www.tokiunderground.com; 1234 H St NE; mains $10-12; ☺11:30am-2:30pm & 5-10pm Mon-Thu, to midnight Fri & Sat; ☐X2 from Union Station)

Ethiopic   Ethiopian $$
In a city with no shortage of Ethiopian joints, Ethiopic stands above the rest. Top marks go to the various *wats* (stews) and the signature *tibs* (sautéed meat and veg), derived from tender lamb that has sat in a bath of herbs and hot spices. Vegans get lots of love here. (☏202-675-2066; www.

ethiopicrestaurant.com; 401 H St NE; mains $12-18; ⏰5-10pm Tue-Thu, from noon Fri-Sun; 🚗; Ⓜ Union Station)

Rose's Luxury   Modern American $$$

Rose's is DC's most buzzed-about eatery – and that was before *Bon Appetit* named it the nation's best new restaurant in 2014. Crowds fork into worldly Southern comfort food as twinkling lights glow overhead and candles flicker around the industrial, half-finished room. Rose's doesn't take reservations, but ordering your meal at the upstairs bar can save time (and the cocktails are delicious). (📞202-580-8889; www.rosesluxury.com; 717 8th St SE; small plates $12-14, family-style plates $28-33; ⏰5:30-10pm Mon-Thu, to 11pm Fri & Sat; Ⓜ Eastern Market)

⊗ White House Area & Downtown

Red Apron Butchery   Deli $

Red Apron makes a helluva breakfast sandwich. Plop into one of the comfy booths and wrap your lips around the ricotta, honey and pine-nut 'aristocrat' or the egg and chorizo 'buenos dias.' They're all heaped

onto tigelle rolls, a sort of Italian flatbread. But you have to order before 10:30am (2:30pm on weekends). (📞202-524-5244; www.redapronbutchery.com; 709 D St NW; mains $5-10; ⏰7:30am-8pm Mon-Fri, 9am-8pm Sat, 9am-5pm Sun; Ⓜ Archives)

Founding Farmers   Modern American $$

A frosty decor of pickled goods in jars adorns this buzzy dining space. The look is a combination of rustic-cool and modern art that reflects the nature of the food: locally sourced, New American fare. Buttermilk fried chicken and waffles and zesty pork and lentil stew are a few of the favorites. The restaurant is in the IMF building. (📞202-822-8783; www.wearefounding-farmers.com; 1924 Pennsylvania Ave NW; mains $14-26; ⏰11am-10pm Mon, 11am-11pm Tue-Thu, 11am-midnight Fri, 9am-midnight Sat, 9am-10pm Sun; 🚗; Ⓜ Foggy Bottom-GWU, Farragut West)

Central Michel Richard   Modern American $$$

Michel Richard is known for his high-end eating establishments in the District, but Central stands out as a special dining

Washington Nationals playing at Nationals Park

experience. It's aimed at hitting a comfort-food sweet spot. You're dining in a four-star bistro where the food is old-school favorites with a twist: lobster burgers, a sinfully complex meatloaf and fried chicken that redefines what fried chicken can be. (20 2-626-0015; www.centralmichelrichard.com; 1001 Pennsylvania Ave NW; mains $19-34; 11:30am-2:30pm Mon-Fri, 5-10:30pm Mon-Thu, 5-11pm Fri & Sat; Federal Triangle)

U Street, Shaw & Logan Circle

Ben's Chili Bowl　　　　American $

Ben's is a DC institution. The main stock in trade is half-smokes, DC's meatier, smokier version of the hot dog, usually slathered in mustard, onions and the namesake chili. For nearly 60 years presidents, rock stars and Supreme Court justices have come in to indulge in the humble diner, but despite the hype, Ben's remains a true neighborhood establishment. Cash only.

> *presidents and rock stars have come in to indulge in the humble diner*

Ben's Chili Bowl

(www.benschilibowl.com; 1213 U St; mains $5-10; 6am-2am Mon-Thu, 6am-4am Fri, 7am-4am Sat, 11am-midnight Sun; U St)

Compass Rose　　　　International $$

Compass Rose feels like a secret garden, set in a discreet townhouse a whisker from 14th St's buzz. The exposed brick walls, rustic wood decor and sky-blue ceiling give it a casually romantic air. The menu is a mash-up of global comfort foods, so dinner might entail, say, a Chilean *lomito* (pork sandwich), Lebanese *kefta* (ground lamb and spices) and Georgian *khachapuri* (buttery, cheese-filled bread). (202-506-4765; www.compassrosedc.com; 1346 T St NW; small plates $10-15; 5pm-2am Sun-Thu, to 3am Fri & Sat; U St)

Le Diplomate　　　　French $$$

This charming French bistro is a relative newcomer, but it has skyrocketed to one of the hottest tables in town. DC celebrities galore cozy up in the leather banquettes and at the sidewalk tables. They come for an authentic slice of Paris, from the *coq au vin* (wine-braised chicken) and aromatic

BRUNO PEROUSSE / ALAMY STOCK PHOTO ©

baguettes to the vintage curios decorating the bathrooms. Make reservations.
(📞202-332-3333; www.lediplomatedc.com; 1601 14th St NW; mains $22-31; 🕙5-10pm Mon & Tue, 5-11pm Wed & Thu, 5pm-midnight Fri, 9:30am-midnight Sat, 9:30am-10pm Sun; 🄼U St)

⊗ Adams Morgan

Diner American $

The Diner serves hearty comfort food, any time of the day or night. It's ideal for wee-hour breakfast scarf-downs, weekend bloody-Mary brunches (if you don't mind crowds) or any time you want unfussy, well-prepared American fare. Omelets, fat pancakes, mac and cheese, grilled Portobello sandwiches and burgers hit the tables with aplomb. It's a good spot for kids, too. (www.dinerdc.com; 2453 18th St NW; mains $9-17; 🕙24hr; 🚼; 🄼Woodley Park-Zoo/Adams Morgan)

Donburi Japanese $

Hole-in-the-wall Donburi has 15 seats at a wooden counter where you get a front-row view of the slicing, dicing chefs. *Donburi* means 'bowl' in Japanese, and that's what arrives steaming hot and filled with, say, panko-coated shrimp atop rice and blended with the house's sweet-and-savory sauce. It's a simple, authentic meal. There's often a line, but it moves quickly. No reservations. (📞202-629-1047; www.facebook.com/donburidc; 2438 18th St NW; mains $9-12; 🕙11am-10pm; 🄼Woodley Park-Zoo/Adams Morgan)

⊗ Dupont Circle

Afterwords Cafe American $$

Attached to Kramerbooks, this buzzing spot is not your average bookstore café. The packed indoor tables, wee bar and outdoor patio overflow with good cheer. The menu features tasty bistro fare and an ample beer selection, making it a prime spot for happy hour, for brunch and at all hours on weekends (open 24 hours, baby!). (📞202-387-3825; www.kramers.com; 1517 Connecticut Ave; mains $15-21; 🕙7:30am-1am Sun-Thu, 24hr Fri & Sat; 🄼Dupont Circle)

🍽 Market Fare

A couple of groovy markets offer good eats:

Union Market (www.unionmarketdc.com; 1309 5th St NE; 🕙11am-8pm Tue-Sun; 🄼NoMa) The cool crowd hobnobs here, where foodie entrepreneurs sell their banana-ginger chocolates, herbed goat cheeses and smoked meats. Pop-up restaurants use the space to try out concepts for everything from Taiwanese ramen to Indian dosas. Craft beers and coffee drinks help wash it all down. Tables dot the sunlit warehouse, and many locals make an afternoon of it, nibbling and reading. The market is about a half-mile walk from the NoMa Metro station in Northeast DC.

Eastern Market (www.easternmarket-dc.org; 225 7th St SE; 🕙7am-7pm Tue-Fri, to 6pm Sat, 9am-5pm Sun; 🄼Eastern Market) One of the icons of Capitol Hill, Eastern Market sprawls with delectable chow and good cheer. The covered arcade holds a bakery, dairy, butcher, blue-crab-and-shrimp company, and produce vendors. It's not that large... until the weekend, when artisans and farmers join the fun and the market spills out onto the street.

Union Market
JOSHUA ZAKARY / ALAMY STOCK PHOTO ©

Duke's Grocery Café $$

'The taste of East London in East Dupont' is the Duke's tagline, and that means black pudding and baked beans in the morning, spiced-lentil rotis in the afternoon and Brick Lane salt-beef sandwiches late night.

Mount Vernon

One of the most visited historic shrines in the nation, **Mount Vernon** (🖉703-780-2000, 800-429-1520; www.mountvernon.org; 3200 Mount Vernon Memorial Hwy; adult/child $17/9; 🕑8am-5pm Apr-Aug, 9am-4pm Nov-Feb, to 5pm Mar, Sep & Oct, gristmill & distillery 10am-5pm Apr-Oct) was the beloved home of George and Martha Washington, who lived here from the time of their marriage in 1759 until Washington's death in 1799. Now owned and operated by the Mount Vernon Ladies Association, the estate offers glimpses of 18th-century farm life and the first president's life as a country planter. Mount Vernon does not gloss over the Founding Father's slave ownership; visitors can tour the slave quarters and burial ground.

Mount Vernon is 16 miles south of DC off the Mount Vernon Memorial Hwy. By public transportation, take the Metro to Huntington, then switch to Fairfax Connector bus 101. **Grayline** (🖉202-289-1999; www.grayline.com; adult/child incl Mt Vernon admission $90/30) and **OnBoard Tours** (🖉301-839-5261; www.onboardtours.com; adult/child incl Mt Vernon admission from $80/70) run bus tours from DC, stopping at Arlington and Mount Vernon.

Several companies offer seasonal boat trips from DC and Alexandria; the cheapest is **Potomac Riverboat Company** (🖉703-684-0580; www.potomacriverboatco.com; adult/child incl Mt Vernon admission $42/22). A healthy alternative is to take a lovely bike ride along the Potomac River from DC (18 miles from Roosevelt Island). You can even bike one way from the Alexandria waterfront and return by boat with **Bike and Roll DC** (🖉202-842-2453; www.bikeandrolldc.com; adult/child $63/40).

Couples on low-maintenance dates and groups of chitchatty friends angle for tables by the bay windows to people watch. The genial vibe invites all-day lingering. (🖉202-733-5623; www.dukesgrocery.com; 1513 17th St NW; mains $11-16; 🕑5:30-10pm Mon, 8am-10pm Tue & Wed, to 1am Thu & Fri, 11am-1am Sat, to 10pm Sun; 🛜; Ⓜ Dupont Circle)

🍴 Georgetown

Chez Billy Sud — French $$

An endearing little bistro tucked away on a residential block, Billy's mint-green walls, gilt mirrors and wee marble bar exude laid-back elegance. Mustachioed servers bring baskets of warm bread to the white linen–clothed tables, along with crackling pork and pistachio sausage, golden trout, tuna Niçoise salad and plump cream puffs. (🖉202-965-2606; www.chezbillysud.com; 1039 31st St NW; mains $17-29; 🕑11:30am-2pm Tue-Fri, 11am-2pm Sat & Sun, 5-10pm Tue-Thu & Sun, 5-11pm Fri & Sat; 🖋)

Martin's Tavern — American $$

John F Kennedy proposed to Jackie in booth three at Georgetown's oldest saloon, and if you're thinking of popping the question there today, the attentive waitstaff keep the champagne chilled for that very reason. With an old-English country scene, including the requisite fox-and-hound hunting prints on the wall, this DC institution serves unfussy classics like thick burgers, crab cakes and icy-cold beers. (🖉202-333-7370; www.martins-tavern.com; 1264 Wisconsin Ave NW; mains $17-32; 🕑11am-1:30am Mon-Thu, 11am-2:30am Fri, 9am-2:30am Sat, 8am-1:30am Sun)

🍸 DRINKING & NIGHTLIFE

🍸 Capitol Hill

Little Miss Whiskey's Golden Dollar — Bar

If Alice had returned from Wonderland so traumatized by her near beheading that she needed a stiff drink, we imagine she'd pop down to Little Miss Whiskey's. She'd love the whimsical-meets-dark-nightmares decor. And she'd probably have fun with the

Mount Vernon

club kids partying on the upstairs dance-floor on weekends. She'd also adore the weirdly fantastic back patio. (www.littlemiss whiskeys.com; 1104 H St NE; ☺5pm-2am; 🚇X2 from Union Station)

Bluejacket Brewery   Brewery
Beer lovers' heads will explode in Bluejacket. Pull up a stool at the mod-industrial bar, gaze at the silvery tanks bubbling up the ambitious brews, then make the hard decision about which of the 25 tap beers you want to try. A dry-hopped kolsch? Sweet-spiced stout? A cask-aged farmhouse ale? Four-ounce tasting pours help with decision-making. (📞202-524-4862; www.bluejacketdc.com; 300 Tingey St SE; ☺11am-1am Sun-Thu, to 2am Fri & Sat; 🚇Navy Yard)

🍺 White House Area
Round Robin   Bar
Dispensing drinks since 1850, the bar at the Willard hotel is one of DC's most storied watering holes. The small, circular space is done up in Gilded Age accents, all dark wood

and velvet green walls, and while it's touristy, you'll still see officials here likely determin-ing your latest tax hike over a mint julep or single-malt Scotch. (1401 Pennsylvania Ave NW, Willard InterContinental Hotel; ☺noon-1am Mon-Sat, to midnight Sun; 🚇Metro Center)

🍺 U Street, Shaw & Logan Circle
Right Proper Brewing Co   Brewery
As if the artwork – a chalked mural of the National Zoo's giant pandas with laser eyes destroying downtown DC – wasn't enough, Right Proper Brewing Co makes sublime ales in a building where Duke Ellington used to play pool. It's the Shaw district's neigh-borhood clubhouse, a big, sunny space filled with folks gabbing at reclaimed wood tables. (www.rightproperbrewery.com; 624 T St NW; ☺5-11pm Tue-Thu, to midnight Fri & Sat, to 10pm Sun; 🚇Shaw-Howard U)

Churchkey   Bar
Coppery, mod-industrial Churchkey glows with hipness. Fifty beers flow from the taps, including five brain-walloping, cask-aged ales. If none of those please you, another

Tidal Basin (p145) with a view of Jefferson Memorial

500 types of brew are available by bottle (including gluten-free suds). Churchkey is the upstairs counterpart to Birch & Barley, a popular nouveau comfort-food restaurant, and you can order much of its menu at the bar. (www.churchkeydc.com; 1337 14th St NW; ⊙4pm-1am Mon-Thu, 4pm-2am Fri, noon-2am Sat, noon-1am Sun; Ⓜ McPherson Sq)

U Street Music Hall   Club

This is the spot to get your groove on sans the VIP/bottle service crowd. Two local DJs own and operate the basement club. It looks like a no-frills rock bar, but it has a pro sound system, cork-cushioned dance-floor and other accoutrements of a serious dance club. Alternative bands also thrash a couple of nights per week to keep it fresh.

Shows start between 7pm and 10pm. Tickets cost $10 to $20. (www.ustreet musichall.com; 1115 U St NW; ⊙hours vary; Ⓜ U St) FREE

🚇 Dupont Circle

Bar Charley   Bar

Bar Charley draws a mixed crowd from the neighborhood – young, old, gay and straight. They come for groovy cocktails sloshing in vintage glassware and ceramic tiki mugs, served at very reasonable prices by DC standards. Try the gin and gingery Suffering Bastard. The beer list isn't huge, but it is thoughtfully chosen with some wild ales. Around 60 wines are available, too. (www.barcharley.com; 1825 18th St NW; ⊙5pm-12:30am Mon-Thu, 4pm-1:30am Fri, 10am-1:30am Sat, 10am-12:30am Sun; Ⓜ Dupont Circle)

ℹ️ INFORMATION

Destination DC (Map p142; 📞202-789-7000; www.washington.org) DC's official tourism site, with the mother lode of online information.

LINGXIAO XIE / GETTY IMAGES ©

ℹ GETTING THERE & AROUND

TO/FROM THE AIRPORT

Ronald Reagan Washington National Airport
(DCA; www.metwashairports.com) Has its own
Metro station; trains (around $2.50) depart
every 10 minutes or so from 5am to midnight
(to 3am Friday and Saturday nights) and reach
downtown in 20 minutes. Taxis cost $13 to $22
and take 10 to 30 minutes.

Dulles International Airport (p369) The Metro
Silver Line is slated to reach Dulles in 2018. In
the meantime, options include taxis (30 to 60
minutes, $62 to $73) and the following bus-and-
metro options.

Metrobus 5A (www.wmata.com) Runs every 30
to 40 minutes from Dulles to the Rosslyn Metro
station (Blue, Orange and Silver Lines) and on
to central DC (L'Enfant Plaza) between 5:50am
(6:30am weekends) and 11:35pm. Total time to
the center is 60 or so minutes, total bus/Metro
fare is about $9.

Washington Flyer (☏ 888-927-4359; www.
washfly.com) The company's Silver Line Express
bus runs every 15 to 20 minutes from Dulles
airport (main terminal, arrivals level door 4) to
the Wiehle-Reston East Metro station between
6am and 10:40pm (from 7:45am weekends).
Total time to DC's center is 60 to 75 minutes,
total bus-Metro cost around $11.

PUBLIC TRANSPORTATION

The system is a mix of Metro subway trains and
buses. The Metro is the main way to go. Buy a
rechargeable SmarTripcard at any station. It
costs $10, with $8 of that stored for fares. You
can add value as needed. The card is also usable
on buses. Another option: buy an unlimited ride
day pass ($14.50).

DC Circulator (www.dccirculator.com; fare
$1) Red Circulator buses run along handy
local routes, including Union Station to/from
the Mall (looping by all major museums and
memorials), Union Station to/from Georgetown
(via K St), Dupont Circle to/from Georgetown
(via M St), and the White House area to/from
Adams Morgan (via 14th St). Buses operate from

🛏 Where to Stay

Lodging is expensive in DC. The
high-season apex is mid-March through
April (cherry-blossom season). Crowds
and rates also peak in May, June,
September and October. Hotel tax adds
14.5% to rates. If you have a car, figure
on $35 to $55 per day for in-and-out
privileges.

Try for a bed in Capitol Hill and Southwest DC, with its range of hotels, suites
and hostels; or Downtown and the Penn
Quarter, which bustles with trendy bars,
restaurants and theaters.

---

roughly 7am to 9pm weekdays (midnight or so
on weekends).

Metrorail (☏ 202-637-7000; www.wmata.com)
The Metro will get you to most sights, hotels
and business districts, and to the Maryland and
Virginia suburbs. Trains start running at 5am Monday through Friday (from 7am on weekends); the
last service is around midnight Sunday through
Thursday and 3am on Fridays and Saturdays.
Machines inside stations sell computerized fare
cards; fares are based on distance traveled.

TAXI

Taxis are relatively easy to find (less so at night),
but costly. **DC Yellow Cab** (☏ 202-544-1212)
is reliable. The rideshare company Uber is used
more in the District.

TRAIN

Union Station (www.unionstationdc.com; 50
Massachusetts Ave NE) is the city's rail hub.
There's a handy Metro station here for transport
onward in the city.

Amtrak (☏ 800-872-7245; www.amtrak.com) Set
inside the magnificent beaux-arts Union Station.
Trains depart at least once per hour for major East
Coast cities, including New York City (3½ hours)
and Boston (six to eight hours).

St Charles Air Line Bridge and the Chicago River

CHICAGO

Chicago

Steely skyscrapers, top chefs, rocking festivals – the Windy City will blow you away with its low-key cultured awesomeness.

High-flying architecture is everywhere, from the stratospheric, glass-floored Willis Tower to Frank Gehry's swooping silver Pritzer Pavilion to Frank Lloyd Wright's stained-glass Robie House. Whimsical public art studs the streets, and is a knock-out feature of the city's much-loved Millennium Park. For an indoor art experience that can't be beat, gaze in wonder at the massive Art Institute's impressionist masterpieces.

Loosen the belt. You've got a lot of eating to do. On the menu: peanut butter and banana topped waffles for breakfast (at Stephanie Izard's Little Goat) and 20 courses of centrifuged, encapsulated molecular gastronomy for dinner (at Grant Achatz' Alinea).

☑ **In This Section**

Millennium Park.................................. 158
Art Institute of Chicago 160
Sights 164
Activities.. 170
Tours.. 170
Shopping 171
Entertainment 171
Eating 173
Drinking & Nightlife 175

ⓘ **Arriving in Chicago**

O'Hare International Airport The Blue Line El train ($5) runs 24/7. Trains depart every 10 minutes and reach downtown in 40 minutes. Shuttle vans cost $32, taxis around $50.

Chicago Midway Airport The Orange Line El train ($3) runs between 4am and 1am every 10 minutes and reaches downtown in 30 minutes. Shuttle vans cost $27, taxis $35 to $40.

Union Station Trains and Megabus arrive at this Loop depot.

Chicago O'Hare International Airport

W Foster Ave

5 km
2.5 miles

Lake Michigan

Uptown
Wrigley Field
Lake View

John F Kennedy Expwy

W Irving Park Rd
N Harlem Ave
W Belmont Ave

N Western Ave
N Lincoln Ave
N Lake Shore Dr

Tri-State Tollway

N Mannheim Rd
W Grand Ave
W Fullerton Ave
Logan Square

Lincoln Park
Lincoln Park Zoo
Chicago History Museum

N 1st Ave
W North Ave
Oak Park
W Chicago Ave
Humboldt Park
Old Town

Millennium Park
Navy Pier

Washington Blvd
Maywood
Union Station
Art Institute of Chicago

Eisenhower Expwy
W Roosevelt Rd
S Cicero Ave
S Western Ave
Pilsen

W Cermak Rd Cicero
Berwyn

W Ogden Ave Hawthorne Race Track
Bridgeport
Dan Ryan Expwy
S Lake Shore Dr
Museum of Science & Industry

Adlai Stevenson Expwy
W 47th St
Bronze-ville
Hyde Park
Robie House

W 55th St
W Garfield Blvd
University of Chicago
Jackson Park

W Joliet Rd
Chicago Midway Airport

Downtown Chicago Map (p166)

compact discs   new music

➡ Chicago in Two Days

Explore the art and greenery of **Millennium Park** (p158), then stop for a deep-dish pizza at **Giordano's** (p174). Take a tour with the **Chicago Architecture Foundation** (p170) to get the lowdown on the city's skyscrapers. On day two explore the **Art Institute of Chicago** (p160). Grab a stylish dinner in the West Loop, then listen to blues at **Buddy Guy's Legends** (p171).

➡ Chicago in Four Days

On your third day, rent a bicycle, visit **North Avenue Beach** (p170) and cruise through **Lincoln Park** (p168). If it's baseball season, go watch the **Cubs** (p172). In the evening yuck it up at **Second City** (p172). Pick a neighborhood for day four: vintage boutiques in Wicker Park, brainy museums in Hyde Park, or Frank Lloyd Wright architecture in Oak Park.

From left: Chicago's skyline; O'Hare International Airport; Jazz Record Mart (p171); View from North Avenue Beach (p170)

KIM KARPELES / ALAMY STOCK PHOTO ©

Millennium Park

One of Chicago's most important new projects in the past 100 years is this stunning art-filled green space in the heart of the Loop.

Lovely views, daring works of sculpture, high-tech fountains, hidden gardens, free summer concerts and a winter skating rink are all part of the allure at the much-loved Millennium Park.

The Bean

The park's biggest draw is the 'Bean' – officially titled *Cloud Gate* – Anish Kapoor's 110-ton, silver-drop sculpture. It reflects both the sky and the skyline, and everyone clamors around to take a picture and to touch its silvery smoothness. Good vantage points for photos are at the sculpture's north and south ends. For great people-watching, go up the stairs on Washington St, on the Park Grill's north side, where there are shady benches.

Great For...

☑ Don't Miss

The Lurie Garden, filled with prairie flowers and a little river to dip your toes in.

ⓘ Need to Know

Map p166; 📞312-742-1168; www.millennium park.org; 201 E Randolph St; 🕑6am-11pm; 🚹; MBrown, Orange, Green, Purple, Pink Line to Randolph; FREE

✕ Take a Break

Toni Patisserie & Cafe (Map p166; www. tonipatisserie.com; 65 E Washington St; 🕑8am-8pm Mon-Sat, to 5pm Sun; MBrown, Orange, Green, Purple, Pink Line to Randolph or Madison) offers wine, coffee and French pastries.

> ★ **Top Tip**
>
> Free walking tours take place at 11:30am and 1pm daily from late May to mid-October.

Crown Fountain

Jaume Plensa's *Crown Fountain* is another crowd-pleaser. Its two, 50ft-high, glass-block towers contain video displays that flash a thousand different faces. The people shown are all native Chicagoans who agreed to strap into Plensa's special dental chair, where he immobilized their heads for filming. Each mug puckers up and spurts water, just like the gargoyles atop Notre Dame Cathedral. A fresh set of non-puckering faces appears in winter, when the fountain is dry. On hot days the fountain crowds with locals splashing around to cool off. Kids especially love it.

Pritzker Pavilion

Pritzker Pavilion is Millennium Park's acoustically awesome band shell.

Architect Frank Gehry designed it and gave it his trademark swooping silver exterior. The pavilion hosts free concerts at 6:30pm most nights June to August. There's indie rock and new music on Monday, world music and jazz on Thursday, and classical music on Wednesday, Friday and Saturday. On Tuesday there's usually a movie beamed onto the huge screen on stage. You can sit up close in the pavilion, or on the grassy Great Lawn that unfurls behind.

For all shows – but especially the classical ones, which the top-notch Grant Park Orchestra performs – folks bring blankets, picnics, wine and beer. There is nothing quite like sitting on the lawn, looking up through Gehry's wild grid and seeing all the skyscraping architecture that forms the backdrop while hearing the music. If you want a seat up close, arrive early.

Art Institute of Chicago

Art Institute of Chicago

The second-largest art museum in the country, the Art Institute of Chicago has the kind of celebrity-heavy collection that routinely draws gasps from patrons.

Great For...

☑ Don't Miss

Grant Wood's *American Gothic* (Gallery 263), one of America's most famous paintings.

Must See Works: Floor 2

First up is *A Sunday Afternoon on the Island of La Grande Jatte* by Georges Seurat (Gallery 201). Get close enough for the painting to break down into its component dots and you'll understand why it took Seurat two long years to complete his pointillist masterpiece. Next seek out *Nighthawks* by Edward Hopper (Gallery 262). His lonely, poignant snapshot of four solitary souls at a neon-lit diner was inspired by a Greenwich Ave restaurant in Manhattan. In the next room you'll find *American Gothic* by Grant Wood (Gallery 263). The artist, a lifelong resident of Iowa, used his sister and his dentist as models for the two stern-faced farmers.

The Berghoff (p176)

CHUCK ECKERT / ALAMY STOCK PHOTO ©

❶ Need to Know

Map p166; ☎312-443-3600; www.artic.edu; 111 S Michigan Ave; adult/child $25/free; ⏱10:30am-5pm Fri-Wed, to 8pm Thu; 🛜♿; Ⓜ Brown, Orange, Green, Purple, Pink Line to Adams

✗ Take a Break

The nearby 1898 **Berghoff** (p176) is tops for a beer and some Chicago history.

★ Top Tip

Ask at the information desk about free talks and tours once you're inside.

Must See Works: Other Floors

Stop by Marc Chagall's *America Windows* (Gallery 144). He created the huge, blue stained-glass pieces to celebrate the USA's bicentennial. Another favorite is *The Old Guitarist* by Pablo Picasso (Gallery 391). The elongated figure is from the artist's Blue Period. Not far away is Salvador Dalí's *Inventions of the Monsters* (Gallery 396). He painted it in Austria before the Nazi annexation. The title refers to a Nostradamus prediction that the apparition of monsters presages the outbreak of war.

More Intriguing Sights

The Thorne Miniature Rooms (Lower Level, Gallery 11) and Paperweight Collection (Lower Level, Gallery 15) are awesome,

overlooked galleries. The Modern Wing, dazzling with natural light, allows works by Miró, Brancusi and the like to shine. It also provides gallery space for new, cutting-edge multimedia works.

Visiting the Museum

Download the Art Institute's free app, either at home or using the museum's wi-fi. It offers more than 50 tours through the collection, including a Half Day Tour, an Impressionist Tour and the Birthday Suit Tour of naked works. Routes are divided by collection, theme or time available. It works off an internal GPS that isn't the world's most accurate, so expect to walk a lot.

Allow two hours to browse the museum's must-sees; art buffs should allocate much longer. The main entrance is on Michigan Ave, but you can also enter via the Modern Wing on Monroe St.

Walking Tour: Art of the City

This tour swoops through the Loop, highlighting Chicago's revered art and architecture, with a visit to Al Capone's dentist thrown in for good measure.

Distance: 3 miles
Duration: 2 hours

✕ Take a Break

Across the road from Millenium Park, Gage (p173) is a good spot for lunch or a drink in classy surroundings.

Start Chicago Board of Trade

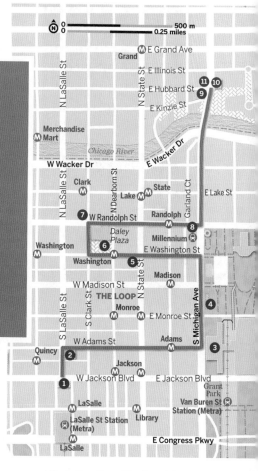

❶ Chicago Board of Trade

Start at the **Chicago Board of Trade** (p165), where futures and options (it has something to do with corn and pork bellies) get swapped inside a stunning art-deco building.

❷ Rookery

A few blocks north, step into the **Rookery** (p165) – a historic 1888 landmark building with a lobby remodeled by Frank Lloyd Wright in 1905. Pigeons used to roost here, hence the name.

❸ Art Institute of Chicago

Head east on Adams St to the **Art Institute of Chicago** (p160), one of the city's most-

visited attractions. The lion statues out front make for a classic, keepsake photo.

❹ Millennium Park

Walk a few blocks north to avant-garde **Millennium Park** (p158) and saunter in to explore the famous Cloud Gate (aka 'the Bean'), human-gargoyle fountains and other contemporary designs.

❺ Hotel Burnham

When you depart Millennium Park, head west on Washington St to **Hotel Burnham**

Preston Bradley Hall, Chicago Cultural Center

ARPAD BENEDEK / GETTY IMAGES ©

(1 W Washington St; www.burnhamhotel.com). It's housed in the Reliance Building, which was the precursor to modern skyscraper design; Capone's dentist drilled teeth in what's now room 809.

❻ Untitled

Just west, **Untitled** (50 W Washington St), created by Pablo Picasso, is ensconced in Daley Plaza. Bird/dog/woman? You decide.

❼ Monument with Standing Beast

Head north on Clark St to Jean Dubuffet's **Monument with Standing Beast** (100 W Randolph St), another head-scratching sculpture.

❽ Chicago Cultural Center

Walk east on Randolph St through the theater district. Pop into the **Chicago Cultural Center** (p164) and have a look at its exquisite interior; its rooms are modeled on the Doge's Palace in Venice and Palazzo Vecchio in Florence.

❾ Wrigley Building

Walk north on Michigan Ave and cross the Chicago River. Just north of the bridge you'll pass the **Wrigley Building** (400 N Michigan Ave), a 1920s construction that ranks among one of Chicago's finest architectural works.

❿ Tribune Tower

Nearby is the Gothic, eye-popping **Tribune Tower** (435 N Michigan Ave). Have a close look when passing to see chunks of the Taj Mahal, Parthenon and other famous structures embedded in the lower walls.

⓫ Billy Goat Tavern

To finish your tour, visit **Billy Goat Tavern** (p174), a vintage Chicago dive that spawned the Curse of the Cubs. Just look around at the walls and you'll get the details. Here it is in short: the tavern's owner, Billy Sianis, once tried to enter Wrigley Field with his pet goat. The smelly creature was denied entry, so Sianis called down a mighty curse on the baseball team in retaliation. They've stunk ever since.

Finish Billy Goat Tavern

◉ SIGHTS
◎ The Loop

Chicago Cultural Center   Building

This block-long building houses ongoing art exhibitions and foreign films, as well as jazz, classical and electronic dance music concerts at lunchtime (12:15pm Monday to Friday). It also contains the world's largest Tiffany stained-glass dome and Chicago's main visitor center. Free building tours take place Wednesday, Friday and Saturday at 1:15pm; meet in the Randolph St lobby. (📞312-744-6630; www.chicagoculturalcenter. org; 78 E Washington St; ⊙9am-7pm Mon-Thu, to 6pm Fri & Sat, 10am-6pm Sun; 📶; Ⓜ Brown, Orange, Green, Purple, Pink Line to Randolph) ᶠᴿᴱᴱ

Maggie Daley Park   Park

Families love the park's fanciful free playgrounds in all their enchanted forest and pirate-themed glory. There's also a rock-climbing wall and 18-hole mini golf course (which becomes an ice-skating ribbon in winter); these features have fees. Multiple picnic tables make the park an excellent spot to relax. It connects to Millennium Park via the pedestrian BP Bridge. (www. maggiedaleypark.com; 337 E Randolph St; ⊙6am-11pm; 👪; Ⓜ Brown, Orange, Green, Purple, Pink Line to Randolph) ᶠᴿᴱᴱ

Willis Tower   Building

This is Chicago's tallest building, and the 103rd-floor Skydeck puts you 1353ft into the heavens. Take the ear-popping, 70-second elevator ride to the top, then step onto one of the glass-floored ledges jutting out in mid-air for a knee-buckling perspective straight down. The entrance is on Jackson Blvd. (📞312-875-9696; www. theskydeck.com; 233 S Wacker Dr; adult/child $19.50/12.50; ⊙9am-10pm Apr-Sep, 10am-8pm Oct-Mar; Ⓜ Brown, Orange, Purple, Pink Line to Quincy)

Buckingham Fountain   Fountain

Grant Park's centerpiece is one of the world's largest squirters, with a 1.5-million-gallon capacity and a 15-story-high spray. It lets loose on the hour from 9am to 11pm mid-April to mid-October, accompanied at night by multicolored lights and music. (301 S Columbus Dr; Ⓜ Red Line to Harrison)

Buckingham Fountain

◎ South Loop

Field Museum of
Natural History   Museum

The mammoth museum houses everything but the kitchen sink – beetles, mummies, gemstones, Bushman the stuffed ape. The collection's rock star is Sue, the largest *Tyrannosaurus rex* yet discovered. She even gets her own gift shop. Special exhibits, like the 3D movie, cost extra. (☎312-922-9410; www.fieldmuseum.org; 1400 S Lake Shore Dr; adult/child $18/13; ☺9am-5pm; ⓘ; ☐146, 130)

Shedd Aquarium   Aquarium

Top draws at the kiddie-mobbed Shedd Aquarium include the Wild Reef exhibit, where there's just 5in of Plexiglas between you and two dozen fierce-looking sharks, and the Oceanarium, with its rescued sea otters. Note the Oceanarium also keeps beluga whales and Pacific white-sided dolphins, a practice that has become increasingly controversial in recent years. (☎312-939-2438; www.sheddaquarium.org; 1200 S Lake Shore Dr; adult/child $31/22; ☺9am-5pm Mon-Fri, to 6pm Sat & Sun Sep-May, to 6pm daily Jun-Aug; ⓘ; ☐146, 130)

Adler Planetarium   Museum

Space enthusiasts will get a big bang (pun!) out of the Adler. There are public telescopes to view the stars, 3D lectures to learn about supernovas and the Planet Explorers exhibit where kids can 'launch' a rocket. The immersive digital films cost $13 extra. The Adler's front steps offer Chicago's primo skyline view. (☎312-922-7827; www.adlerplanetarium.org; 1300 S Lake Shore Dr; adult/child $12/8; ☺9:30am-4pm Mon-Fri, to 4:30pm Sat & Sun; ⓘ; ☐146, 130)

Willie Dixon's
Blues Heaven   Historic Building

From 1957 to 1967, the humble building at 2120 S Michigan Ave was Chess Records, the seminal electric blues label. Muddy Waters, Howlin' Wolf and Bo Diddley cut tracks here, and paved the way for rock 'n' roll with their sick licks and amped-up sound. The studio is now named for the bassist who

🖼 Famous Loop
Architecture

Ever since it presented the world with the first skyscraper, Chicago has thought big with its architecture and pushed the envelope of modern design. The Loop is a fantastic place to roam and gawk at these ambitious structures.

The Chicago Architecture Foundation (p170) runs tours that explain the following buildings and more:

Chicago Board of Trade (141 W Jackson Blvd; Ⓜ Brown, Orange, Purple, Pink Line to LaSalle) A 1930 art-deco gem. Inside, traders swap futures and options. Outside, check out the giant statue of Ceres, the goddess of agriculture, that tops the building.

Rookery (www.flwright.org; 209 S LaSalle St; ☺9:30am-5:30pm Mon-Fri; Ⓜ Brown, Orange, Purple, Pink Line to Quincy) The 1888 Rookery looks fortress-like outside, but the inside is light and airy thanks to Frank Lloyd Wright's atrium overhaul. Tours ($7 to $12) are available at noon on weekdays.

Monadnock Building (www.monadnock building.com; 53 W Jackson Blvd; Ⓜ Blue Line to Jackson) Architectural pilgrims get weak-kneed when they see the Monadnock Building, which is two buildings in one. The north is the older, traditional design from 1891, while the south is the newer, mod half from 1893.

wrote most of the Chess hits. It's pretty ramshackle, with few original artifacts on display. Still, when Willie's grandson hauls out the bluesman's well-worn standup bass and lets you take a pluck, it's pretty cool. Free blues concerts rock the side garden on summer Thursdays at 6pm. The building is about a mile south of the Museum Campus. (☎312-808-1286; www.bluesheaven.com; 2120 S Michigan Ave; tours $10; ☺noon-4pm Mon-Fri, to 3pm Sat; Ⓜ Green Line to Cermak-McCormick Pl)

Downtown Chicago

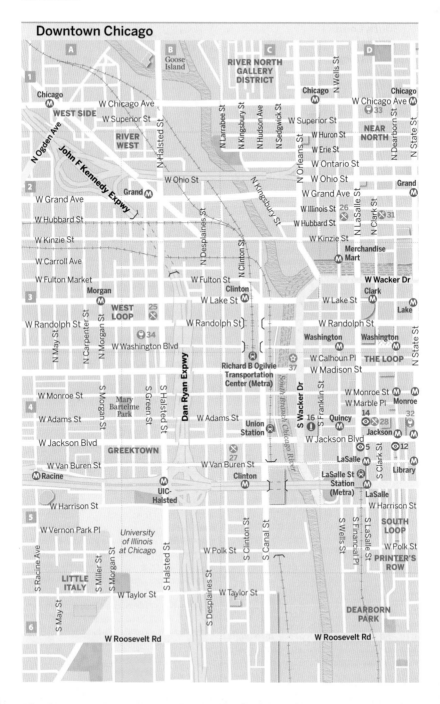

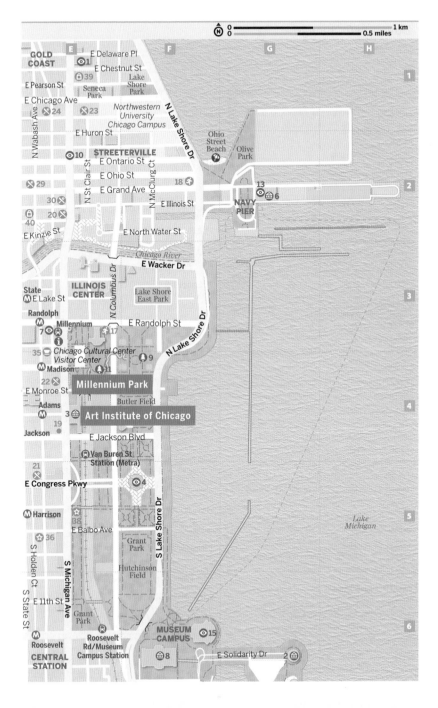

1 km
0.5 miles

GOLD COAST
E Delaware Pl
⊙1
E Chestnut St
🔒39
Lake Shore Park
E Pearson St
Seneca Park
E Chicago Ave
N Wabash Ave
⊗24
⊗23
Northwestern University Chicago Campus
E Huron St
⊙10 **STREETERVILLE**
N St Clair St
E Ontario St
N McClurg Ct
E Ohio St
⊗29
E Grand Ave
18 ⊕
30⊗
E Illinois St
20⊗
40
🔒
E Kinzie St
E North Water St

N Lake Shore Dr
Ohio Street Beach
Olive Park
13
🏛6
NAVY PIER

Chicago River
E Wacker Dr

State
Ⓜ E Lake St
ILLINOIS CENTER
N Columbus Dr
Lake Shore East Park
Randolph
Ⓜ
Millennium
7⊙🏛
ⓘ
35 ▱ Chicago Cultural Center Visitor Center
Ⓜ Madison
17 ⊕
E Randolph St
⊕9
11 ⊕
22⊗
Millennium Park
E Monroe St
Adams
Ⓜ
3🏛 **Art Institute of Chicago**
Butler Field
19
Jackson
E Jackson Blvd
21
⊗
Van Buren St Station (Metra)
E Congress Pkwy
⊙4
N Lake Shore Dr
S Lake Shore Dr

Ⓜ Harrison
☆
38
E Balbo Ave
Grant Park
36
S Holden Ct
S Michigan Ave
Hutchinson Field
E 11th St
S State St
Grant Park
Ⓜ Roosevelt
Roosevelt Rd/Museum Campus Station
CENTRAL STATION
MUSEUM CAMPUS
⊙15
🏛8
E Solidarity Dr
2 🏛

Lake Michigan

Downtown Chicago

⊚ **Sights**
1 360° Chicago E1
2 Adler Planetarium G6
3 Art Institute of Chicago E4
4 Buckingham Fountain F5
5 Chicago Board of Trade D4
6 Chicago Children's Museum G2
7 Chicago Cultural Center E3
8 Field Museum of Natural History F6
9 Maggie Daley Park F4
10 Magnificent Mile E2
11 Millennium Park E4
12 Monadnock Building D4
13 Navy Pier G2
14 Rookery D4
15 Shedd Aquarium F6
16 Willis Tower C4

❂ **Activities, Courses & Tours**
17 Bike Chicago E3
18 Bobby's Bike Hike F2
19 Chicago Architecture Foundation E4
   InstaGreeter .... (see 7)

❂ **Eating**
20 Billy Goat Tavern E2
21 Cafecito E5
22 Gage E4

23 Gino's East E1
24 Giordano's E1
25 Little Goat B3
26 Lou Malnati's D2
27 Lou Mitchell's C4
28 Native Foods Cafe D4
29 Pizzeria Uno E2
30 Purple Pig E2
31 Xoco D2

❂ **Drinking & Nightlife**
32 Berghoff D4
33 Clark Street Ale House D1
34 RM Champagne Salon B3
   Signature Lounge .... (see 1)
35 Toni Patisserie & Cafe E4

❂ **Entertainment**
36 Buddy Guy's Legends E5
37 Lyric Opera Of Chicago C4
38 SummerDance E5

❂ **Shopping**
39 American Girl Place E1
   Chicago Architecture
   Foundation Shop .... (see 19)
40 Jazz Record Mart E2

⊚ Near North

Navy Pier · Waterfront

Half-mile-long Navy Pier is Chicago's most-visited attraction, sporting a 196ft Ferris wheel and carnival rides ($6 to $8 each), an IMAX theater, a beer garden and chain restaurants. Locals groan over its commercialization, but its lakefront view and cool breezes can't be beat. The fireworks displays on summer Wednesdays (9:30pm) and Saturdays (10:15pm) are a treat. (📞312-595-7437; www.navypier.com; 600 E Grand Ave; ⊙10am-10pm Sun-Thu, to midnight Fri & Sat Jun-Aug, 10am-8pm Sun-Thu, to 10pm Fri & Sat Sep-May; 🖼; Ⓜ Red Line to Grand, then trolley) FREE

Magnificent Mile · Street

Spanning Michigan Ave between the river and Oak St, the Mag Mile is the much-touted upscale shopping strip, where Bloomingdales, Neiman's and Saks will lighten your wallet. (www.themagnificentmile.com; N Michigan Ave; Ⓜ Red Line to Grand)

360° Chicago · Observatory

This is the new name for the John Hancock Center Observatory. In many ways the view here surpasses the one at Willis Tower. The 94th-floor lookout has informative displays and the TILT feature (floor-to-ceiling windows that you stand in as they tip out over the ground; it costs $7 extra and is fairly cheesy). Not interested in such frivolities? Shoot straight up to the 96th-floor Signature Lounge, where the view is free if you buy a drink ($8 to $16). (📞888-875-8439; www.360chicago.com; 875 N Michigan Ave; adult/child $19/13; ⊙9am-11pm; Ⓜ Red Line to Chicago)

⊚ Lincoln Park & Old Town

Lincoln Park · Park

The neighborhood gets its name from this park, Chicago's largest. Its 1200 acres stretch for 6 miles, from North Ave north to Diversey Pkwy, where it narrows along the lake and continues until the end of Lake Shore Dr. The park's many lakes, trails and paths make it an excellent place for recreation. Cross-country skiing in the winter and sunbathing in warmer months are just two of the activities Chicagoans enjoy in Lincoln Park. Many buy picnic vittles from the markets on Clark St and Diversey Pkwy. (6am-11pm; ; 151)

Lincoln Park Zoo   Zoo
A local family favorite, filled with gorillas, lions, tigers, snow monkeys and other exotic creatures in the shadow of downtown. Check out the Regenstein African Journey, Ape House and Nature Boardwalk for the cream of the crop. (312-742-2000; www. lpzoo.org; 2200 N Cannon Dr; 10am-4:30pm Nov-Mar, to 5pm Apr-Oct, to 6:30pm Sat & Sun Jun-Aug; ; 151) FREE

Lincoln Park Conservatory   Gardens
Near the zoo's north entrance, the magnificent 1891 hothouse coaxes palms, ferns and orchids to flourish. In winter, it becomes a soothing, 75-degree escape from the icy winds raging outside. (312-742-7736; www.lincolnparkconservancy.org; 2391 N Stockton Dr; 9am-5pm; 151) FREE

Chicago History Museum   Museum
Multimedia displays cover it all, from the Great Fire to the 1968 Democratic Convention. President Lincoln's deathbed is here; so is the chance to 'become' a Chicago hot dog covered in condiments (in the kids' area, but adults are welcome for the photo op). (312-642-4600; www.chicagohistory.org; 1601 N Clark St; adult/child $14/free; 9:30am-4:30pm Mon-Sat, noon-5pm Sun; ; 22)

◉ Lake View & Wrigleyville
North of Lincoln Park, these neighborhoods can be enjoyed by ambling along Halsted St, Clark St, Belmont Ave or Southport Ave, which are well supplied with restaurants, bars and shops. The only real sight is ivy-covered **Wrigley Field** (www.cubs. com; 1060 W Addison St; M Red Line to Addison), named after the chewing-gum guy and home to the much-loved but perpetually losing Chicago Cubs.

Detour: Oak Park

Located 10 miles west of the Loop, Oak Park has two famous sons: novelist Ernest Hemingway was born here, and architect Frank Lloyd Wright lived and worked here from 1889 to 1909.

During Wright's 20 years in Oak Park, he designed many houses. Chief among them is his own, the **Frank Lloyd Wright Home & Studio** (312-994-4000; www.flwright.org; 951 Chicago Ave; adult/child/camera $17/14/5; 10am-4pm), which offers a fascinating, hour-long walk-through that reveals his distinctive style. Tour frequency varies, from every 20 minutes on summer weekends to every hour in winter. The studio also offers guided or self-guided neighborhood walking tours ($15). Or buy an architectural site map ($4.25) from the studio shop, which gives the locations of other Wright-designed abodes. Ten of them cluster nearby.

Despite Hemingway allegedly calling Oak Park a 'village of wide lawns and narrow minds,' the town still pays homage to him at the **Ernest Hemingway Museum** (708-848-2222; www.ehfop. org; 200 N Oak Park Ave; adult/child $15/13; 1-5pm Sun-Fri, from 10am Sat). Admission also includes entry to his birthplace home across the street.

From downtown Chicago, take the CTA Green Line to the Oak Park station, then walk north on Oak Park Ave. It's about a quarter mile to the Hemingway sights and a mile to the Wright home.

Ernest Hemingway Museum
RAYMOND BOYD / GETTY IMAGES ©

Chicago for Children

Chicago is a kid's kind of town. **Chicago Parent** (www.chicagoparent.com) is a dandy resource. Top choices include: **Chicago Children's Museum** (☏312-527-1000; www.chicagochildrensmuseum.org; 700 E Grand Ave; admission $14; ☺10am-5pm Mon-Wed, to 8pm Thu, to 6pm Fri, to 7pm Sat & Sun; ⊞; ⓂRed Line to Grand, then trolley) Climb, dig and splash in this educational playland on Navy Pier; follow with an expedition down the carnival-like wharf itself, including spins on the Ferris wheel and carousel.

Chicago Children's Theatre (☏773-227-0180; www.chicagochildrenstheatre.org) See a show by one of the best kids' theater troupes in the country. Performances take place at venues around town.

Other kid-friendly offerings include North Avenue Beach (p170), Field Museum of Natural History (p165), Shedd Aquarium (p165), Lincoln Park Zoo (p169) and the Museum of Science & Industry (p173).

🟢 ACTIVITIES

Riding along the 18-mile lakefront path is a fantastic way to see the city. Bike-rental companies listed here also offer two- to four-hour tours ($35 to $70, including bikes) that cover themes like the lakefront, beer and pizza munching, or gangster sights. Booking online saves money.

Bike Chicago   Cycling
The company's main location – open year-round – is at Millennium Park. Other outposts include Navy Pier and the Riverwalk. (☏312-729-1000; www.bikechicago. com; 239 E Randolph St; per 1/4hr from $9/30; ☺6:30am-10pm Mon-Fri, from 8am Sat & Sun Jun-Aug, reduced rest of year; ⓂBrown, Orange, Green, Purple, Pink Line to Randolph)

Bobby's Bike Hike   Cycling
Bobby's earns raves from riders; enter through the covered driveway. (☏312-245-9300; www.bobbysbikehike.com; 540 N Lake Shore Dr; per 2/4hr from $20/25; ☺8:30am-8pm Mon-Fri, from 8am Sat & Sun Jun-Aug, 9am-7pm Sep-Nov & Mar-May; ⓂRed Line to Grand)

North Avenue Beach   Beach
Chicago's most popular and amenity-laden stretch of sand wafts a southern California vibe. You can rent kayaks, jet skis, stand up paddleboards (SUPs) and lounge chairs, as well as eat and drink at the pumping, party-orientated beach house. It's 2 miles north of the Loop. (www.cpdbeaches.com; 1600 N Lake Shore Dr; 🛜⊞; 🚌151)

🟢 TOURS

Chicago Architecture Foundation   Boat Tour
The gold-standard boat tours ($40) sail from Michigan Ave's river dock. The popular Evolution of the Skyscraper walking tours ($20) leave from the downtown Michigan Ave address. Weekday lunchtime tours ($15) explore individual landmark buildings. Buy tickets online or at CAF. (CAF; ☏312-922-3432; www.architecture.org; 224 S Michigan Ave; tours $15-50; ⓂBrown, Orange, Green, Purple, Pink Line to Adams)

InstaGreeter   Walking Tour
Provides one-hour Loop tours on the spot from the Chicago Cultural Center visitor center. In summer, free tours of Millennium Park also depart from here daily at 11:30am and 1pm. (www.chicagogreeter.com/insta greeter; 77 E Randolph St; ☺10am-3pm Fri & Sat, 11am-2pm Sun; ⓂBrown, Orange, Green, Purple, Pink Line to Randolph) FREE

Chicago Food Planet Tours   Walking Tour
Go on a guided walkabout in Wicker Park, the Gold Coast or Chinatown, where you'll graze through five or more neighborhood eateries. Departure points and times vary. (☏312-818-2170; www.chicagofoodplanet.com; 3hr tours $45-55)

🔒 SHOPPING

A siren song for shoppers emanates from N Michigan Ave, along the Magnificent Mile (p168).

Chicago Architecture Foundation Shop
Souvenirs

Skyline posters, Frank Lloyd Wright note cards, skyscraper models and more for those with an edifice complex. (www.architecture.org/shop; 224 S Michigan Ave; ⊙9am-6:30pm; Ⓜ Brown, Orange, Green, Purple, Pink Line to Adams)

Jazz Record Mart
Music

One-stop shop for Chicago jazz and blues CDs and vinyl. (www.jazzmart.com; 27 E Illinois St; ⊙10am-7pm Mon-Sat, 11am-5pm Sun; Ⓜ Red Line to Grand)

⭐ ENTERTAINMENT

For same-week theater seats at half price, try **Hot Tix** (www.hottix.org). You can buy them online or in person at the three downtown booths. Check the *Chicago Reader* (www.chicagoreader.com) for listings.The Theater District is a cluster of big, neon-lit venues at State and Randolph Sts. **Broadway in Chicago** (☎800-775-2000; www.broadwayinchicago.com) handles tickets for most.

Hideout
Live Music

Hidden behind a factory at Bucktown's edge, this two-room lodge of indie rock and alt-country is worth seeking out. Music and other events (bingo, literary readings etc) take place nightly. (www.hideoutchicago.com; 1354 W Wabansia Ave; ⊙7pm-2am Tue, 4pm-2am Wed-Fri, 7pm-3am Sat, varies Sun & Mon; 🚌72)

Buddy Guy's Legends
Blues

Top local and national acts wail on the stage of local icon Buddy Guy. Tickets cost $20 Friday and Saturday, $10 on other evenings. The man himself usually plugs in his axe for a series of shows in January. Free, all-ages acoustic performances take place from noon to 2pm Wednesday through Sunday. (www.buddyguy.com; 700 S

> *a siren song for shoppers emanates along the Magnificent Mile*

Jazz Record Mart

CHARLES COOK / GETTY IMAGES ©

Wabash Ave; ⏰5pm-2am Mon & Tue, 11am-2am Wed-Fri, noon-3am Sat, noon-2am Sun; Ⓜ Red Line to Harrison)

Green Mill
Jazz

The timeless Green Mill earned its notoriety as Al Capone's favorite speakeasy. Local and national jazz artists perform nightly; the venue also hosts the nationally acclaimed poetry slam on Sundays. Cover charge is $5 to $15. (www.greenmilljazz.com; 4802 N Broadway; ⏰noon-4am Mon-Sat, 11am-4am Sun; Ⓜ Red Line to Lawrence)

Blues
Blues

This veteran club draws a slightly older crowd that soaks up every crackling, electrified moment. Cover charge is $7 to $10. (www.chicagobluesbar.com; 2519 N Halsted St; ⏰8pm-2am Wed-Sun; Ⓜ Brown, Purple, Red Line to Fullerton)

Chicago Cubs
Baseball

The Cubs last won the World Series in 1908, but that doesn't stop fans from coming out to see them. Part of the draw is atmospheric, ivy-walled Wrigley Field, which dates from 1914. No tickets? Peep through the 'knothole,' a garage door–sized opening on Sheffield Ave, to watch for free. (www.cubs.com; 1060 W Addison St; Ⓜ Red Line to Addison)

Chicago White Sox
Baseball

The Sox are the Cubs' South Side rivals and play in the more modern 'Cell,' aka US Cellular Field. Tickets are usually cheaper and easier to get than at Wrigley Field. (www.whitesox.com; 333 W 35th St; Ⓜ Red Line to Sox-35th)

SummerDance
World Music

Boogie at the Spirit of Music Garden in Grant Park with a multi-ethnic mash-up of locals. Bands play world beats preceded by fun dance lessons – for free. (www.chicagosummerdance.org; 601 S Michigan Ave; ⏰6-9:30pm Fri & Sat, 4-7pm Sun late Jun–mid-Sep; Ⓜ Red Line to Harrison) FREE

Second City
Comedy

Bill Murray, Stephen Colbert, Tina Fey and many more honed their wit at this slick venue. The Main stage and ETC stage host sketch revues (with an improv scene

Second City

thrown in); they're similar in price and quality. The UP stage hosts stand-up and experimental shows. Turn up around 10pm (Friday and Saturday excluded) and watch the comics improv a set for free. (☎312-337-3992; www.secondcity.com; 1616 N Wells St; Ⓜ Brown, Purple Line to Sedgwick)

iO Theater   Comedy
Chicago's other major improv house is a bit edgier than its competition, with four stages hosting bawdy shows nightly. (☎312-929-2401; ioimprov.com/chicago; 1501 N Kingsbury St; Ⓜ Red Line to North/Clybourn)

❌ EATING
🍴 The Loop
Cafecito   Cuban $
Attached to the HI-Chicago hostel and perfect for the hungry, thrifty traveler, Cafecito serves killer Cuban sandwiches layered with citrus-garlic-marinated roasted pork and ham. Strong coffee and hearty egg sandwiches make a fine breakfast. (☎312-922-2233; www.cafecitochicago.com; 26 E Congress Pkwy; mains $6-10; ⊗7am-9pm Mon-Fri, 10am-6pm Sat & Sun; 🛜; Ⓜ Brown, Orange, Purple, Pink Line to Library)

Native Foods Cafe   Vegan $
If you're looking for vegan fast-casual fare downtown, Native Foods is your spot. The meatball sandwich rocks the seitan, while the scorpion burger fires up hot-spiced tempeh. Local beers and organic wines to accompany. (☎312-332-6332; www.nativefoods.com; 218 S Clark St; mains $9-11; ⊗10:30am-9pm Mon-Sat, 11am-7pm Sun; 🍴; Ⓜ Brown, Orange, Purple, Pink Line to Quincy) 🍴

Gage   Modern American $$$
This gastropub dishes up fanciful grub, from Gouda-topped venison burgers to mussels vindaloo to Guinness-battered fish and chips. The booze rocks, too, including a solid whiskey list and small-batch beers. (☎312-372-4243; www.thegagechicago.com; 24 S Michigan Ave; mains $17-36; ⊗11am-10pm Mon, to 11pm Tue-Thu, to midnight Fri & Sat, 10am-10pm Sun; Ⓜ Brown, Orange, Green, Purple, Pink Line to Madison)

💬 Hyde Park

Hyde Park sits on Chicago's south side and makes for a leafy jaunt. In addition to the University of Chicago's grand, gothic campus, the neighborhood holds a couple of top sights.

The **Museum of Science & Industry** (MSI; ☎773-684-1414; www.msichicago.org; 5700 S Lake Shore Dr; adult/child $18/11; ⊗9:30am-5:30pm Jun-Aug, reduced hours Sep-May; 👶; 🚌6 or 10, Ⓜ Metra to 55th-56th-57th) is the largest science museum in the western hemisphere. Highlights include a WWII German U-boat nestled in an underground display ($9 extra to tour it) and the 'Science Storms' exhibit with a mock tornado and tsunami. Kids will love the 'experiments' staff conduct, such as dropping things off the balcony and creating mini explosions.

Nearby is **Robie House** (☎312-994-4000; www.flwright.org; 5757 S Woodlawn Ave; adult/child $17/14; ⊗10:30am-3pm Thu-Mon; 🚌6, Ⓜ Metra to 55th-56th-57th). Of the numerous buildings that Frank Lloyd Wright designed around Chicago, none is more famous or influential than this one. The resemblance of its horizontal lines to the flat landscape of the Midwestern prairie became known as the Prairie style. Inside are 174 stained-glass windows and doors, which you'll see on the hour-long tours (frequency varies by season).

To get here, take the Metra Electric Line trains from Millennium Station downtown, or bus 6 from State St in the Loop.

❌ Near North

This is where you'll find Chicago's mother lode of restaurants.

Xoco   Mexican $
Crunch into warm *churros* (spiraled dough fritters) for breakfast, meaty *tortas* (sandwiches) for lunch and rich *caldos* (soups) for dinner at celeb chef Rick Bayless' Mexican street-food joint. His upscale

Deep-Dish Pizza Icons

Pizzeria Uno (www.unos.com; 29 E Ohio St; small pizzas from $13; ⊙11am-1am Mon-Fri, to 2am Sat, to 11pm Sun; MRed Line to Grand) The deep-dish concept supposedly originated here in 1943.

Lou Malnati's (www.loumalnatis.com; 439 N Wells St; small pizzas from $12; ⊙11am-11pm Sun-Thu, to midnight Fri & Sat; MBrown, Purple Line to Merchandise Mart) It also lays claim to inventing deep dish; famous for its butter crust.

Gino's East (⌧312-266-3337; www. ginoseast.com; 162 E Superior St; small pizzas from $15; ⊙11am-9:30pm; MRed Line to Chicago) Popular spot where you write on the walls while waiting for your pie.

Giordano's (⌧312-951-0747; www. giordanos.com; 730 N Rush St; small pizzas from $15.50; ⊙11am-11pm Sun-Thu, to midnight Fri & Sat; MRed Line to Chicago) Giordano's makes 'stuffed' pizza, a bigger, doughier version of deep dish.

restaurants Frontera Grill and Topolobampo are next door, but you'll need reservations or a whole lot of patience to get in. (www. rickbayless.com; 449 N Clark St; mains $10-14; ⊙8am-9pm Tue-Thu, to 10pm Fri & Sat; MRed Line to Grand) ⊘

Billy Goat Tavern   Burgers $
Tribune and *Sun-Times* reporters have guzzled in the subterranean Billy Goat for decades. Order a 'cheezborger' and Schlitz, then look around at the newspapered walls to get the scoop on infamous local stories, such as the Cubs Curse. (⌧312-222-1525; www.billygoattavern.com; lower level, 430 N Michigan Ave; burgers $4-6; ⊙6am-2am Mon-Fri, 10am-2am Sat & Sun; MRed Line to Grand)

Purple Pig   Mediterranean $$
The Pig's Magnificent Mile location, wide-ranging meat and veggie menu, long list of affordable vinos and late-night serving hours make it a crowd pleaser.

Milk-braised pork shoulder is the hamtastic specialty. No reservations. (⌧312-464-1744; www.thepurplepigchicago.com; 500 N Michigan Ave; small plates $9-19; ⊙11:30am-midnight Sun-Thu, to 1am Fri & Sat; ⊁; MRed Line to Grand)

⊗ Lincoln Park & Old Town
Halsted, Lincoln and Clark Sts are the main veins teeming with restaurants and bars.

Sultan's Market   Middle Eastern $
Neighborhood folks dig the falafel sandwiches, spinach pies and other quality Middle Eastern fare at family-run Sultan's Market. (⌧312-638-9151; www.chicagofalafel. com; 2521 N Clark St; mains $4-7; ⊙10am-10pm Mon-Thu, to midnight Fri & Sat, to 9pm Sun; MBrown, Purple, Red Line to Fullerton)

Alinea   Modern American $$$
Widely regarded as North America's best restaurant, Alinea brings on 20 courses of mind-bending molecular gastronomy. Dishes may emanate from a centrifuge or be pressed into a capsule, à la duck served with a 'pillow of lavender air.' There are no reservations. Instead Alinea sells tickets two to three months in advance via its website. Check the Twitter feed (@Alinea) for last-minute seats. (⌧312-867-0110; www. alinearestaurant.com; 1723 N Halsted St; multicourse menu $210-265; ⊙5-9:30pm Wed-Sun; MRed Line to North/Clybourn)

⊗ Wicker Park, Bucktown & Ukrainian Village
Trendy restaurants open almost every other day in these 'hoods.

Dove's Luncheonette   Tex-Mex $
Grab a seat at the retro diner counter for plates of pork shoulder *pozole* and shrimp-stuffed sweet corn tamales. Dessert? It's pie, of course, maybe lemon cream or peach jalapeño, depending on what they've baked that day. (⌧773-645-4060; www. doveschicago.com; 1545 N Damen Ave; mains $12-15; ⊙9am-10pm Sun-Thu, to 11pm Fri & Sat; MBlue Line to Damen)

Ruxbin Modern American $$$
The passion of the brother-sister team who run Ruxbin is evident in everything from the warm decor made of found items to the artfully prepared flavors in dishes like the pork-belly salad with grapefruit, cornbread and blue cheese. It's BYO. (📞 312-624-8509; www.ruxbinchicago.com; 851 N Ashland Ave; mains $27-32; 🕑 6-10pm Tue-Fri, 5:30-10pm Sat, to 9pm Sun; Ⓜ Blue Line to Division) 🖼

🟢 West Loop

The West Loop booms with hot-chef restaurants. Stroll along Randolph and Fulton Market Sts and take your pick. Greektown extends along S Halsted St (take the Blue Line to UIC-Halsted).

Lou Mitchell's Breakfast $
Lou's is a relic of Route 66, where old-school waitresses deliver eggs and thick-cut French toast just west of the Loop by Union Station. There's usually a queue, but free doughnut holes help ease the wait. (📞 312-939-3111; www.loumitchellsrestaurant.com; 565 W Jackson Blvd; mains $7-11;
🕑 5:30am-3pm Mon-Fri, 7am-3pm Sat & Sun; ♿; Ⓜ Blue Line to Clinton)

Little Goat Diner $$
Top Chef winner Stephanie Izard opened this diner for the foodie masses across the street from her ever-booked main restaurant, Girl and the Goat. Order off the all-day breakfast menu or try lunchtime favorites such as the goat sloppy joe with mashed potato tempura or the pork belly on scallion pancakes. (📞 312-888-3455; www.littlegoatchicago.com; 820 W Randolph St; mains $10-19; 🕑 7am-10pm Sun-Thu, to midnight Fri & Sat; 🛜🖼; Ⓜ Green, Pink Line to Morgan)

🍷 DRINKING & NIGHTLIFE

🍸 The Loop & Near North

Signature Lounge Lounge
Grab the elevator up to the 96th floor of 360° Chicago and order a beverage while

> *The West Loop booms with hot-chef restaurants*

Pizzeria Uno

Hideout (p171)

looking out over the city. (www.signatureroom.com; 875 N Michigan Ave; ⊙11am-12:30am Sun-Thu, to 1:30am Fri & Sat; Ⓜ Red Line to Chicago)

Berghoff   Bar

The Berghoff was the first spot in town to serve a legal drink after Prohibition (ask to see the liquor license stamped '#1'). Little has changed around the antique wood bar since then. Belly up for frosty mugs of the house-brand beer and order sauerbraten from the adjoining German restaurant. (www.theberghoff.com; 17 W Adams St; ⊙11am-9pm Mon-Sat; Ⓜ Blue, Red Line to Jackson)

Clark Street Ale House   Bar

Do as the retro sign advises and 'Stop & Drink Liquor.' Midwestern microbrews are the main draw; order a three beer sampler for $7. (www.clarkstreetalehouse.com; 742 N Clark St; ⊙4pm-4am Mon-Fri, from 11am Sat & Sun; Ⓜ Red Line to Chicago)

🍸 Old Town & Wrigleyville

Old Town Ale House   Bar

This venerated dive bar lets you mingle with beautiful people and grizzled regulars.

It's across the street from Second City. Cash only. (www.theoldtownalehouse.com; 219 W North Ave; ⊙3pm-4am Mon-Fri, from noon Sat & Sun; Ⓜ Brown, Purple Line to Sedgwick)

Gingerman Tavern   Bar

The pool tables, good beer selection and pierced-and-tattooed patrons make Gingerman wonderfully different from the surrounding Wrigleyville sports bars. (3740 N Clark St; ⊙3pm-2am Mon-Fri, from noon Sat & Sun; Ⓜ Red Line to Addison)

Smart Bar   Club

A long-standing, unpretentious favorite for dancing, attached to the Metro rock club. (www.smartbarchicago.com; 3730 N Clark St; ⊙10pm-4am Wed-Sun; Ⓜ Red Line to Addison)

🍸 Wicker Park, Bucktown & Ukrainian Village

Map Room   Bar

At this map-and-globe filled 'traveler tavern' artsy types sip coffee by day and suds from the 200-strong beer list by night. Cash only. (www.maproom.com; 1949 N Hoyne

Ave; ⏱6:30am-2am Mon-Fri, from 7:30am Sat, from 11am Sun; ☎; Ⓜ Blue Line to Western)

Danny's   Bar
Danny's comfortably dim and dogeared ambience is perfect for conversations over a pint early on, then DJs arrive to stoke the dance party as the evening progresses. Cash only. (1951 W Dickens Ave; ⏱7pm-2am; Ⓜ Blue Line to Damen)

🍴 West Loop

RM Champagne Salon   Bar
Sip bubbles at a table in the cobblestoned courtyard and you'll feel like you're in Paris. (✆312-243-1199; www.rmchampagnesalon.com; 116 N Green St; ⏱ 5-11pm Mon-Wed, to 2am Thu & Fri, to 3am Sat, to 11pm Sun; Ⓜ Green, Pink Line to Morgan)

ℹ INFORMATION

Chicago Cultural Center Visitor Center (www. choosechicago.com; 77 E Randolph St; ⏱10am-5pm Mon-Sat, 11am-4pm Sun; ☎; Ⓜ Brown, Orange, Green, Purple, Pink Line to Randolph) It's sparse, but does offer a staffed information desk and sales of discount cards for attractions. Insta-Greeter (Friday through Sunday year-round) and Millennium Park (daily in summer) tours also depart from here.

ℹ GETTING THERE & AROUND

TO/FROM THE AIRPORT

Chicago Midway Airport (MDW; www.fly chicago.com) Eleven miles southwest of the Loop, connected via the CTA Orange Line ($3). Shuttle vans cost $27, taxis cost $35 to $40.

O'Hare International Airport (ORD; www. flychicago.com) Seventeen miles northwest of the Loop. The CTA Blue Line train ($5) runs 24/7. Trains depart every 10 minutes or so; they reach downtown in 40 minutes. Airport Express shuttle vans cost $32, taxis around $50. They can take as long as the train, depending on traffic.

🛏 Where to Stay

Chicago's lodgings rise high in the sky, many in architectural landmarks. Snooze in the building that gave birth to the skyscraper, or in one of Mies van der Rohe's boxy structures, or in a century-old art deco masterpiece.

Choose to stay in the Loop for boutique and architectural hotels and to be near main attractions; or in the Near North and Navy Pier areas for bars, restaurants and big-box stores. For chichi environs (but with the price tag to match), try the Gold Coast.

BICYCLE
Chicago is a cycling-savvy city with a massive bike-share program called **Divvy** (www.divvy bikes.com). Kiosks issue 24-hour passes ($10) on the spot. Insert a credit card, get your ride code, then unlock a bike. The first 30 minutes are free; after that, rates rise fast if you don't dock the bike. Note helmets and locks are not provided.

PUBLIC TRANSPORTATION
The **Chicago Transit Authority** (CTA; www.tran sitchicago.com) operates the city's buses and the elevated/subway train system (aka the El). The standard fare per train is $3 (except from O'Hare, where it costs $5) and includes two transfers; per bus it is $2.25. Unlimited ride passes (one-/three-day pass $10/20) are also available. Get them at rail stations and drug stores.

TAXI
Flash Cab (✆773-561-4444; www.flashcab.com)
Yellow Cab (✆312-829-4222; www.yellowcab chicago.com)
Rideshare company Uber is also popular in Chicago.

TRAIN
Chicago's classic **Union Station** (www.chicago unionstation.com; 225 S Canal St; Ⓜ Blue Line to Clinton) is the hub for **Amtrak** (✆800-872-7245; www.amtrak.com) national and regional services.

MIAMI

Miami

Miami is many things, but to most visitors, it is mainly glamour, condensed into urban form. It is simultaneously an outpost of the Caribbean, the most diverse Latin American city in the world, and a quintessentially American place. Pastel-hued subtropical beauty and brash sexiness are everywhere, from the sun bleeding blood orange over the palm trees to nightclubs where stiletto-heeled models shake to EDM and hip-hop.

On the one hand, everything is striking a pose, from avant-garde gallery hipsters attending a poetry slam in a converted warehouse to the bronzed bodies arrayed along South Beach. On the other hand, the city boasts a wild organic energy distilled from an enormous confluence of immigrants baking under the tropical sun and buffeted by salt breezes.

☑ In This Section

The Everglades 182
Art Deco Miami 186
Sights 193
Activities 196
Entertainment 196
Eating 196
Drinking & Nightlife 198

❶ Arriving in Miami

Most travelers arrive by car or by air to **Miami International Airport** (p199). Having a car makes city explorations easier, and it's vital to visit the Everglades, which are 40 miles inland via the Tamiami Trail (Hwy 41). Rental cars generally come equipped with Sun Pass transponders. These devices carry credit to get you through the region's many tolls.

★ Classic Photo: Art Deco Historic District

Get your best art deco shot when the neon is shining against the sunset, along Ocean Dr and Collins Ave.

Miami Map (p192)

From left: Art-deco buildings; Miami International Airport; Welcome sign, South Beach

PESKYMONKEY / GETTY IMAGES ©; SEAN PAVONE / ALAMY STOCK PHOTO ©; PAUL GIAMOU / GETTY IMAGES ©

The Everglades

Much of America's natural beauty hews toward the dramatic, but here – in this vast tidalscape of mud flats and grassland – the aesthetic is more subtle, but no less magnetic.

Great For...

ⓘ Need to Know

Everglades National Park (☑305-242-7700; www.nps.gov/ever; 40001 SR-9336, Homestead; per vehicle $10; ⊘24hr, visitor center 9am-5pm; 🚻)

Sunset, Everglades

★ **Top Tip**

Year-round it's almost impossible to avoid mosquitoes, but they're ferocious in summer: bring *strong* repellent.

Not a Swamp

Contrary to what you may have heard, the Everglades isn't a swamp. Or at least, it's not *only* a swamp. It's most accurately characterized as a wet prairie – grasslands that happen to be flooded most of the year. Nor is it stagnant. In the wet season, a horizon-wide river creeps ever so slowly beneath the rustling saw grass and around the subtly raised cypress and hardwood hammocks toward the ocean.

Everglades National Park

The park has three main entrances and areas: in the south along Rte 9336 through Homestead and Florida City to Ernest Coe Visitor Center and, at road's end, Flamingo; along the Tamiami Trail/Hwy 41 in the north to Shark Valley; and on the Gulf Coast near Everglades City. Near the entrance

to Ernest Coe, make a pit stop at **Robert is Here** (📞305-246-1592; www.robertishere. com; 19200 SW 344th St, Homestead; mains $3-8; 🕘8am-7pm), a kitschy Old Florida market with a petting zoo, live music and crazy-good milk shakes and fresh produce.

The main park entry points have visitor centers where you can get maps, camping permits and ranger information. You only need to pay the entrance fee (per car/ pedestrian $10/5 for seven days) once to access all points.

Ernest Coe Visitor Center   Park

The main visitor center for the southern portion of the park has excellent, museum-quality exhibits and tons of activity info: the road accesses numerous short trails and lots of top-drawer canoeing opportunities. Call for a schedule of fun ranger-led pro-

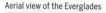

Aerial view of the Everglades

grams, such as the two-hour 'slough slog'. (📞 305-242-7700; www.nps.gov/ever; State Rd 9336; ⏰9am-5pm May-Nov, 8am-5pm Dec-Apr)

Royal Palm Area   Tourist Information

Two trails, the Anhinga and Gumbo Limbo, take all of an hour to walk and put you face to face with a panoply of Everglades wildlife. Gators sun on the shoreline, anhinga spear their prey and wading birds stalk haughtily through the reeds. Come at night for a ranger walk on the boardwalk and shine a flashlight into the water to see one of the coolest sights of your life: the glittering

---

☑ Don't Miss

Keep a sharp eye out for great blue herons, anhingas (aka the snake bird), alligators, crocodiles, manatees and rare Florida panthers.

JUPITERIMAGES / GETTY IMAGES ©

eyes of dozens of alligators prowling the waterways. (📞305-242-7700; Hwy 9336)

Flamingo Visitor Center   Park

From Royal Palm, Hwy 9336 cuts through the belly of the park for 38 miles until it reaches the isolated Flamingo Visitor Center, which has maps of canoeing and hiking trails. **Flamingo Marina** (📞239-695-3101; ⏰store 7am-5:30pm Mon-Fri, from 6am Sat & Sun) offers backcountry boat tours and kayak/canoe rentals for self-guided trips along the coast. (📞239-695-3101; ⏰marina 7am-7pm, from 6am Sat & Sun)

Shark Valley   Park

Shark Valley is a slice of National Park Service grounds heavy with informative signs and knowledgeable rangers. A 15-mile/24km paved trail takes you past small creeks, tropical forest and 'borrow pits' (holes that are basking spots for gators, turtles and birdlife). The pancake-flat trail is perfect for bicycles, which can be rented at the entrance for $7.50 per hour. Bring water. If you don't feel like exerting yourself, the most popular and painless way to immerse yourself in the Everglades is via the two-hour **tram tour** (📞305-221-8455; www.sharkval-leytramtours.com; adult/child under 12yr/senior $22/19/12.75; ⏰departures 9:30am, 11am, 2pm, 4pm May-Dec, 9am-4pm Jan-Apr every hour on the hour) that runs along Shark Valley's entire 15-mile trail. If you only have time for one Everglades activity, this should be it, as you'll likely see gators sunning themselves on the road. Halfway along the trail is the 50ft-high Shark Valley Observation Tower, an ugly concrete tower that offers dramatically beautiful views of the park. (📞305-221-8776; www.nps. gov/ever/planyourvisit/svdirections.htm; 36000 SW 8th St, GPS 25°45'27.60; car/cyclist $10/5; ⏰9:15am-5:15pm; P♿) ✎

---

❶ When to Go

Dry season (December to April) is the prime time to visit: the weather is mild and pleasant, and wildlife abundant. Wet season (May to October) is stiflingly hot, humid and buggy.

Ocean Drive

Art Deco Miami

Modernity with nostalgia for the beaux arts; streamlining coupled with fantastic embellishment; subdued colors and riots of pastel – art deco is South Beach's definitive style.

Great For...

☑ Don't Miss

The Wolfsonian-FIU (p193), an excellent museum with many deco-era treasures.

South Beach's pastel heart is its **Art Deco Historic District** (Map p192), one of the largest in the USA on the National Register of Historic Places. In fact, the area's rejuvenation and rebirth as a major tourist destination results directly from its protection as a historic place in 1979. The National Register designation prevents developers from razing significant portions of what was, in the 1980s, a crime-ridden collection of crumbling eyesores.

Today, hotel and apartment facades are decidedly colorful, with pastel architectural details. The bright buildings catapult you back to the Roaring Twenties or on a wacky tour of American kitsch.

Your first stop should be the **Art Deco Welcome Center** (Map p192; ☑305-672-2014; www.mdpl.org; 1001 Ocean Dr, South Beach; ⏱9:30am-5pm Fri-Wed, to 7pm Thu), which has

A South Beach hotel

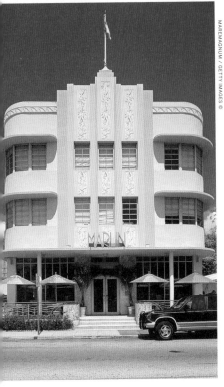

MAREMAGNUM / GETTY IMAGES ©

18th St

**Art Deco
Historic District** ◉

*ATLANTIC
OCEAN*

Collins Ave
Ocean Dr

❶ Need to Know

The **Miami Design Preservation
League** (www.mdpl.org), which runs the
Welcome Center, has the deco lowdown.

✕ Take a Break

Stop by for a burger or milkshake at
24-hour **11th Street Diner** (Map p192;
☏ 305-534-6373; www.eleventhstreetdiner.
com; 1065 Washington Ave; mains $9-18;
◷ 24hr except midnight-7am Wed).

★ Top Tip

Ninety-minute walking tours ($25)
depart from the Art Deco Welcome
Center at 10:30am daily.

tons of art-deco district information and
organizes excellent walking tours.

The Art Deco Historic District

The deco district mostly stretches from
18th St south along Ocean Dr and Collins
Ave. One of the best things about the 1000
or so buildings is their scale: most are no
taller than the palm trees. And while the
architecture is by no means uniform it's all
quite harmonious.

Deco has been a sort of renaissance for
Miami Beach. It caught the eye of Hollywood, which saw something romantically
American in the optimism and innovation
of a style that blends cubism, futurism,
modernism and, most of all, a sense of
movement. Beyond that was a nod to, and
sometimes even reverence for, the elaborate embellishment of Old World decor.

In mid-January, the **Art Deco Weekend**
(www.artdecoweekend.com; Ocean Dr btwn 1st St
& 23rd St) features guided tours, concerts,
auto shows, cafés, arts and antiques.

Classic Designs

There are some unifying themes to classical deco structures that are easy enough
to spot. Perhaps most noticeable is the
sense of streamlined movement, exempli-
fied by rounded walls, racing stripe details,
and 'eyebrows' – rounded buttresses that
provide shade and eye-candy to passersby.
Porthole windows evoke cruise liners, while
lamps and homewares represent long-past
idealizations of a space-age future.

An intimate sense of space is offset by
terrazzo flooring and open verandahs,
which would naturally cool inhabitants in
pre-air-conditioning days. The idea was to
seize on the natural features of the landscape, adding a dash of organic aesthetic
to the overall structure.

/ GETTY IMAGES ©

Walking Tour: Art Deco

It was deco that first made Miami Beach distinctive, and the style remains the sleek signature face of the American Riviera. This quick and easy path takes you to several highlights.

Distance: 1.2 miles
Duration: 2 to 3 hours

Did you Know?
In the early 20th century, art deco's smooth lines were meant to evoke the space-age future.

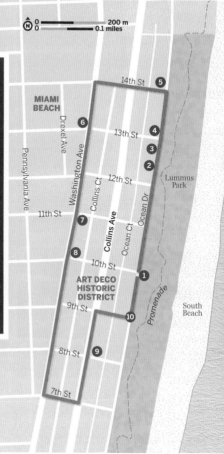

Start Art Deco Welcome Center, 1001 Ocean Drive, Miami Beach

❶ Art Deco Welcome Center

Start at the Welcome Center, at the corner of Ocean Dr and 10th St (named Barbara Capitman Way here, after the founder of the Miami Design Preservation League). Step in for an exhibit on art-deco style.

❷ The Leslie

Head out and go north along Ocean Dr. You'll see several classic deco hotels between 12th St and 14th St. The first one you'll come to is the Leslie, a boxy shape with eyebrows (cantilevered sun shades) wrapped around the side of the building.

❸ The Carlyle

A little further on is the Carlyle, which featured in the film *The Birdcage* and boasts modernistic styling.

❹ The Cardozo Hotel

Finally, pass the graceful Cardozo Hotel. Built by Henry Hohauser and owned by Gloria Estefan, it features sleek, rounded edges.

❺ Winter Haven Hotel

At 14th St, peek inside the sun-drenched Winter Haven Hotel to see its fabulous ter-

Winter Haven Hotel

razzo floors. Al Capone used to stay here; maybe he liked the lobby's deco ceiling lamps.

❻ US Post Office

Turn left and head down 14th St to Washington Ave and the US Post Office, at 13th St. It's a curvy block of white deco in the stripped classical style. Step inside to admire the wall mural, domed ceiling and marble stamp tables.

❼ 11th St Diner

Stop for lunch at the 11th St Diner, a gleaming aluminum Pullman car that was imported in 1992 from Wilkes-Barre, PA. Get a window seat and gaze across the avenue to the corner of 10th St and the stunningly restored Hotel Astor, designed in 1936 by T Hunter Henderson.

❽ Wolfsonian-FIU

After your meal, walk half a block east from there to the imposing Wolfsonian-FIU, an excellent museum of design, formerly the Washington Storage Company. Wealthy snowbirds of the '30s stashed their pricey belongings here before heading back up north.

❾ The Hotel

Continue walking Washington Ave, turn left on 7th St and then continue north along Collins Ave to the Hotel, featuring an interior and roof deck by Todd Oldham. L Murray Dixon designed the hotel as the Tiffany Hotel, with a deco spire, in 1939.

❿ Ocean Drive

Turn right on 9th St and go two blocks to Ocean Dr, where you'll spy nonstop deco beauties; at 960 Ocean Dr (the middling Ocean's Ten restaurant) you'll see an exterior designed in 1935 by deco legend Henry Hohauser.

Finish Ocean Drive

Clockwise from above: Art Deco Historic District (p187);
The Carlyle (p181); Art Deco Historic District (p187);
Art-deco building; Street signs, Design District (p194)

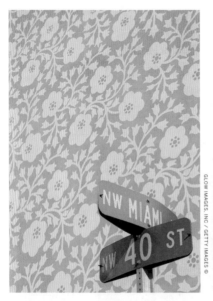

Miami

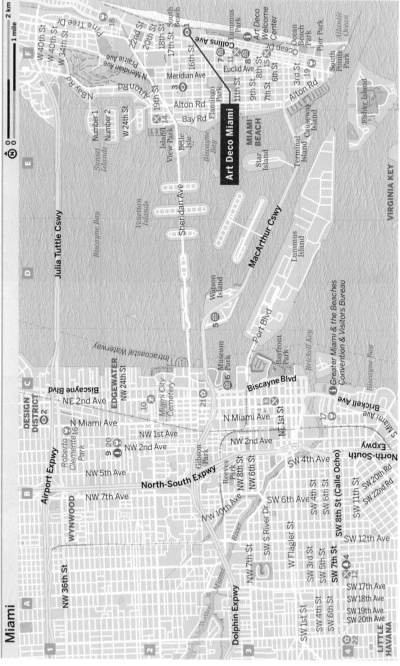

⊙ SIGHTS
◎ Miami Beach

Miami Beach has some of the best beaches in the country, with white sand and warm aquamarine water that rivals the Bahamas. That movie in your head of art-deco hotels, inline-skating models, preening young studs and cruising cars? That's Ocean Dr (from 1st to 11th Sts), where the beach is merely a backdrop for strutting peacocks.

Lincoln Road Mall   Area
This outdoor pedestrian thoroughfare between Alton Rd and Washington Ave is all about seeing and being seen; there are times when Lincoln feels less like a road and more like a runway. Carl Fisher, the father of Miami Beach, envisioned the road as a '5th Ave of the South.' Morris Lapidus, one of the founders of the loopy, neo-Baroque Miami Beach style, designed much of the mall, including shady over-hangs, waterfall structures and traffic barriers that look like the marbles a giant might play with. (www.lincolnroadmall.com)

Wolfsonian-FIU   Museum
A fascinating collection that spans transportation, urbanism, industrial design, advertising and political propaganda from the late 19th to mid-20th century. Visit this excellent design museum early in your stay to put the aesthetics of Miami Beach into fascinating context. By chronicling the interior evolution of everyday life, the Wolfsonian reveals how these trends were architecturally manifested in SoBe's exterior deco. (☏305-531-1001; www.wolfsonian.org; 1001 Washington Ave; adult/child 6-12yr $7/5, free 6-9pm Fri; ◷10am-6pm, to 9pm Thu & Fri)

◎ Downtown
Pérez Art Museum Miami   Museum
The Pérez can claim fine rotating exhibits that concentrate on post-WWII international art, but just as impressive are its location and exterior. This art institution inaugurated Museum Park, a patch of land that oversees the blue swathe of Biscayne Bay. Swiss architects Herzog & de Meuron designed the structure, which integrates tropical foliage, glass and metal – a melding of tropical vitality and fresh modernism that is a nice architectural analogy for Miami itself. (PAMM; ☏305-375-3000; www.pamm.org; 1103 Biscayne Blvd; adult/senior & student $16/12; ◷10am-6pm Tue-Sun, to 9pm Thu, closed Mon; Ⓟ)

◎ Little Havana
As SW 8th St heads away from downtown, it becomes Calle Ocho (pronounced *kah-yeh oh-*cho, Spanish for 'Eighth Street') and heart of Little Havana, the most prominent community of Cuban Americans in the

Miami

◎ Sights
1 Art Deco Historic District............................F2
2 Design District C1
3 Lincoln Road Mall..F2
4 Máximo Gómez Park.....................................A4
5 Miami Children's Museum D3
6 Pérez Art Museum Miami C3
7 Post Office...F3
8 Wolfsonian-FIU...F3
9 Wynwood Walls B2

⊙ Activities, Courses & Tours
10 Wynwood and Design District Arts
      Walks C2

✕ Eating
11 11th St Diner..F3

12 Exquisito Restaurant A4
13 NIU Kitchen..C3
14 Pubbelly E2
15 Puerto Sagua...F3

⊙ Drinking & Nightlife
16 Bardot C1
17 Blackbird Ordinary......................................C4
18 Broken Shaker..F2
19 Room..F4
20 Wood Tavern B2

⊙ Entertainment
21 Adrienne Arsht Center for the
      Performing Arts......................................C3
22 Hoy Como Ayer A4

US. The district remains a living, breathing immigrant enclave, though one whose residents have become more broadly Central American. One of the best times to come is the last Friday of the month during **Viernes Culturales** (www.viernesculturales.org; ⊙7-11pm), or 'Cultural Fridays,' a street fair showcasing Latino artists and musicians.

Máximo Gómez Park   Park

Little Havana's most evocative reminder of Old Cuba is Máximo Gómez Park, or 'Domino Park,' where the sound of elderly men trash-talking over games of chess is harmonized by the quick clack-clack of slapping dominoes. The jarring backtrack, plus the heavy smell of cigars and a sunrise-bright mural of the 1993 Summit of the Americas, combine to make Máximo Gómez one of the most sensory sites in Miami (although it is admittedly one of the most tourist-heavy ones as well). (SW 8th St at SW 15th Ave; ⊙9am-6pm)

> *Little Havana's most evocative reminder of Old Cuba*

Máximo Gómez Park

◉ Design District & Wynwood

Proving that SoBe doesn't hold the lease on hip, these two trendy areas north of downtown – all but deserted 25 years ago – have ensconced themselves as bastions of art and design. **The Design District** (www.miamidesigndistrict.net) is a mecca for interior designers, home to dozens of galleries and contemporary furniture, fixture and design showrooms.

Just south of the Design District, Wynwood is a notable arts district, with myriad galleries and art studios housed in abandoned factories and warehouses. The second Saturday of the month features the Wynwood and **Design District Arts Walks** (www.artcircuits.com; ⊙ 6-9pm 2nd Sat of the month) FREE, with music, food and wine.

Wynwood Walls   Public Art

In the midst of rusted warehouses and concrete blah, there's a pastel-and-graffiti explosion of urban art. Wynwood Walls is a collection of murals and paintings laid out over an open courtyard that invariably bowls people over with its sheer color profile and unexpected location. What's

THE WASHINGTON POST / GETTY IMAGES ©

on offer tends to change with the coming and going of major arts events such as Art Basel, but it's always interesting stuff. (www.thewynwoodwalls.com; NW 2nd Ave, btwn 25th & 26th Sts)

◉ Coral Gables & Coconut Grove

For a slower pace and a more European feel, head inland. Designed as a 'model suburb' by George Merrick in the early 1920s, Coral Gables is a Mediterranean-style village that's centered around the shops and restaurants of the Miracle Mile, a four-block section of Coral Way between Douglas and LeJeune Rds.

Vizcaya Museum
& Gardens   Historic Building

They call Miami the Magic City, and if it is, this Italian villa, the housing equivalent of a Fabergé egg, is its most fairy-tale residence. In 1916, industrialist James Deering started a Miami tradition by making a ton of money and building ridiculously grandiose digs. He employed 1000 people (then 10% of the local population) and stuffed his home with 15th- to 19th-century furniture, tapestries, paintings and decorative arts; today, the grounds are used for the display of rotating contemporary-art exhibitions. (📞305-250-9133; www.vizcayamuseum.org; 3251 S Miami Ave; adult/6-12yr/student & senior $18/6/10; ⏰9:30am-4:30pm Wed-Mon; 🅿)

Venetian Pool   Outdoors

One of the few pools listed on the National Register of Historic Places, this is a wonderland of coral rock caves, cascading waterfalls, a palm-fringed island and Venetian-style moorings. Take a swim and follow in the footsteps (fin-steps?) of stars like Esther Williams and Johnny 'Tarzan' Weissmuller. Opening hours vary depending on the season; call or check the website for details. (📞305-460-5306; www.coralgablesvenetianpool.com; 2701 De Soto Blvd; adult/child $12/7; ⏰hours vary; 🚹)

👪 Miami for Children

The best beaches for kids are in Miami Beach north of 21st St (especially at 53rd St, which has a playground and public toilets) and the beach around 73rd St. Also head south to Matheson Hammock Park.

Miami Children's Museum (📞305-373-5437; www.miamichildrensmuseum.org; 980 MacArthur Causeway; admission $18; ⏰10am-6pm; 🚹) On Watson Island, between downtown Miami and Miami Beach, this hands-on museum has fun music and art studios, as well as some branded 'work' experiences that make it feel a tad corporate.

Zoo Miami (Metrozoo; 📞305-251-0400; www.miamimetrozoo.com; 12400 SW 152nd St; adult/child $18/14; ⏰10am-5pm Mon-Fri, 9:30am-5:30pm Sat & Sun) Miami's tropical weather makes strolling around Zoo Miami almost feel like a day in the wild. For a quick overview (and because the zoo is so big and the sun is broiling), hop on the Safari Monorail; it departs every 20 minutes.

Monkey Jungle (📞305-235-1611; www.monkeyjungle.com; 14805 SW 216th St; adult/child/senior $30/24/28; ⏰9:30am-5pm, last entry 4pm; 🅿🚹) The tagline, 'Where humans are caged and monkeys run free,' tells you all you need to know – except for the fact that it's in far south Miami.

Elephants, Zoo Miami
/GETTY IMAGES ©

★ **Top Five for Art**

Wynwood Walls (p194)

Vizcaya Museum & Gardens (p195)

Wolfsonian-FIU (p193)

Pérez Art Museum Miami (p193)

Lowe Art Museum (p196)

From left: DecoBike stand; Vizcaya Museum & Gardens (p195); Wynwood (p194)

Lowe Art Museum   Museum

The Lowe's tremendous collection satisfies a wide range of tastes, but it's particularly strong in Asian, African and South Pacific art and archaeology, and its pre-Columbian and Mesoamerican collection is stunning. (305-284-3535; www.lowemuseum.org; 1301 Stanford Dr; adult/student $10/5; ☾10am-4pm Tue-Sat, noon-4pm Sun)

😊 ACTIVITIES

DecoBike   Cycling

Flat, architecturally rich Miami Beach and Miami are best accessed via bicycle, and the easiest way of finding a bicycle is through this excellent bike sharing program. (305-532-9494; www.decobike.com; 30min/1hr/2hr/4hr/1-day rental $4/6/10/18/24)

Blue Moon Outdoor Center   Water Sports

The official concessionaire for outdoor rentals in Miami area state parks. (305-957-3040; http://bluemoonoutdoor.com; 3400 NE 163rd St; kayaks per 1½/3hr $23/41; ☾9am-7:30pm Mon-Fri, 8am-8pm Sat & Sun)

🎭 ENTERTAINMENT

Hoy Como Ayer   Live Music

This Cuban hot spot – with authentic music, unstylish wood paneling and a small dancefloor – is enhanced by cigar smoke and Havana transplants. Stop in nightly for *son* (a salsa-like dance that originated in Oriente, Cuba), *boleros* (a Spanish dance in triple meter) and modern Cuban beats. (305-541-2631; www.hoycomoayer.us; 2212 SW 8th St; ☾8:30pm-4am Thu-Sat)

Adrienne Arsht Center for the Performing Arts   Performing Arts

This magnificent venue manages to both humble and enthrall visitors. Today the Arsht is where the biggest cultural acts in Miami come to perform; a show here is a must-see on any Miami trip. Get off the Metromover at the Omni stop. (305-949-6722; www.arshtcenter.org; 1300 Biscayne Blvd)

🍴 EATING

Puerto Sagua   Cuban $

Pull up to the counter for authentic, tasty and inexpensive *ropa vieja* (shredded beef),

PETER PTSCHELINZEW / GETTY IMAGES ©

black beans and *arroz con pollo* (rice with chicken) – plus some of the best Cuban coffee in town – at this beloved Cuban diner. (☎305-673-1115; 700 Collins Ave; mains $6-20; ☺7:30am-2am)

Exquisito Restaurant   Cuban $

For great Cuban cuisine in the heart of Little Havana, this place is exquisite (ha ha). The roast pork has a tangy citrus kick and the *ropa vieja* is wonderfully rich and filling. Even standard sides like beans and rice and roasted plantains are executed with a little more care and tastiness. Prices are a steal, too. (☎305-643-0227; www.elexquisitomiami.com; 1510 SW 8th St; mains $7-13; ☺7am-11pm)

Pubbelly   Fusion $$

Pubbelly's dining genre is hard to pinpoint, besides delicious. It skews between Asian, North American and Latin American, gleaning the best from all cuisines. Examples? Try duck and scallion dumplings, or the mouthwatering udon 'carbonara' with pork belly, poached eggs and parmesan. Hand-crafted cocktails wash down the dishes a treat. (☎305-532-7555; www.pubbellyboys.com/miami/pubbelly; 1418 20th St;

mains $11-26; ☺6pm-midnight Tue-Thu & Sun, to 1am Fri & Sat)

Blue Collar   American $$

It's not easy striking a balance between laid-back and delicious in a city like Miami, where even 'casual' eateries can feel like nightclubs, but Blue Collar has the formula nailed. Friendly staff serve All-American fare sexied the hell up, from crispy snapper to smoky ribs to a superlatively good cheeseburger. A well-curated veg board keeps non-carnivores happy. (☎305-756-0366; www.bluecollarmiami.com; 6730 Biscayne Blvd; mains $15-24; ☺11:30am-3:30pm Mon-Fri, to 3:30pm Sat & Sun, 6-10pm Sun-Thu, to 11pm Fri & Sat; P ⚡ 🚼) ⚡

Versailles   Cuban $$

Versailles *(ver-sigh-yay)* is an institution, one of the mainstays of Miami's Cuban gastronomic scene. Try the ground beef in a gratin sauce or chicken breast cooked in creamy garlic sauce. Older Cubans and Miami's Latin political elite still love coming here, so you've got a real chance to rub elbows with a who's who of Miami's most prominent Latin citizens. (☎305-444-0240;

Where to Stay

The hype surrounding South Beach deco accommodations is justified. This is one of the largest concentrations of boutique hotels in the country, but they're also some of the most expensive in Florida. Choose a spot with a great pool – in Miami they're more about seeing and being seen than swimming, and most of these pools double as bars, lounges or even clubs.

Also check into a retro roadside motel on Biscayne Blvd. Some of the spots in this area are still a little seedy, but savvy motel owners are cleaning up their act and looking to attract the hipsters, artists and gay population flocking to the area, for half the price of South Beach accommodations.

www.versaillesrestaurant.com; 3555 SW 8th St; mains $5-26; ⊗8am-1am Mon-Thu, to 2:30am Fri, to 3:30am Sat, 9am-1am Sun)

NIU Kitchen   Spanish $$

NIU is a small, living room–sized restaurant consistently full of impossibly hip people eating impossibly good contemporary Catalan cuisine. Rarely have we had cuisine that's so compellingly different, from a poached egg with truffled potato foam to manchego and scallop pasta. Wash it all down with good wine and order multiple dishes to share. (✐786-542-5070; http://niukitchen.com; 134 NE 2nd Ave; mains $14-22; ⊗noon-3:30pm Mon-Fri, 6-10pm Sun-Thu, to 11pm Fri & Sat, 1-4pm Sat & Sun; ✐)

🍷 DRINKING & NIGHTLIFE

There are tons of bars along Ocean Dr; a meander at happy hour will get you half-price drinks of extremely varying quality. To increase your chances of getting into the major nightclubs, call ahead to get on the guest list. In South Beach clubs and live-music venues, cover charges can range from $20 to $40; elsewhere you'll get in for around half that.

Broken Shaker   Bar

Craft cocktails are having their moment in Miami, and if mixology is in the spotlight, you can bet Broken Shaker is sharing the glare. Expert bartenders run this spot, located in the back of the **Freehand Miami hotel** (✐305-531-2727; http://thefreehand.com; 2727 Indian Creek Dr; dm $28-49, r $160-214; ❄🐾🛁), which takes up one closet-sized indoor niche and a sprawling outdoor courtyard of excellent drinks and beautiful people. (✐786-325-8974; 2727 Indian Creek Dr; ⊗6pm-3am Mon-Fri, 2pm-3am Sat & Sun)

Wood Tavern   Bar

Wood is a lot of things: local Miami kids who don't want a dive, but who also don't want the long lines and attitude of South Beach. Ergo: a cozy front bar, an outdoor space that includes picnic benches, a wooden stage complete with bleachers and giant Jenga game, and to top it off an attached art gallery with rotating exhibits. (✐305-748-2828; http://woodtavernmiami.com; 2531 NW 2nd Ave; ⊗5pm-3am Tue-Sat, to 11pm Sun)

Room   Bar

This dark, atmospheric, boutique beer bar in SoBe is a gem: hip and sexy as hell but with a low-key attitude. Per the name, it's small and gets crowded. (✐305-531-6061; www.theotheroom.com; 100 Collins Ave; ⊗7pm-5am)

Blackbird Ordinary   Bar

The Ordinary is almost that...well, no. It isn't ordinary at all – this is an excellent bar, with great cocktails (the London Sparrow, with gin, cayenne, lemon juice and passion fruit, goes down well) and an enormous courtyard. But it is 'ordinary' in the sense that it's a come as you are joint that eschews judgment for easy camaraderie. (✐305-671-3307; www.blackbirdordinary.com; 729 SW 1st Ave; ⊗3pm-5am Mon-Fri, 5pm-5am Sat & Sun)

Art-deco hotel, South Beach

Bardot
Club

You really should see the interior of Bardot before you leave the city. It's all sexy French vintage posters and furniture that's been seemingly plucked from a private club that serves millionaires by day, and becomes a scene of decadent excess by night. The entrance looks to be on N Miami Ave, but you'll actually find it in a parking lot behind the building. (☏305-576-5570; www.bardotmiami.com; 3456 N Miami Ave; ⊙8pm-3am Tue & Wed, to 5am Thu-Sat)

ℹ️ INFORMATION

Greater Miami & the Beaches Convention & Visitors Bureau (☏305-539-3000; www.miamiandbeaches.com; 701 Brickell Ave, 27th fl; ⊙8:30am-6pm Mon-Fri) Located in an oddly intimidating high-rise building.

ℹ️ GETTING THERE & AROUND

Miami International Airport (MIA; ☏305-876-7000; www.miami-airport.com; 2100 NW 42nd Ave) is about 6 miles west of downtown, and is accessible by **SuperShuttle** (☏305-871-8210; www.supershuttle.com) as well as by **Tri-Rail** (☏800-874-7245; www.tri-rail.com), a rail link that connects MIA with downtown.

Amtrak (☏305-835-1222, 800-872-7245; www.amtrak.com; 8303 NW 37th Ave) has a main Miami terminal.

Metro-Dade Transit (☏305-891-3131; www.miamidade.gov/transit/routes.asp; tickets $2) runs the local Metrobus and Metrorail ($2), as well as the free **Metromover** (☏305-891-3131; www.miamidade.gov/transit/metromover.asp; ⊙5am-midnight) monorail serving downtown, which is a really great way to see central Miami from a height.

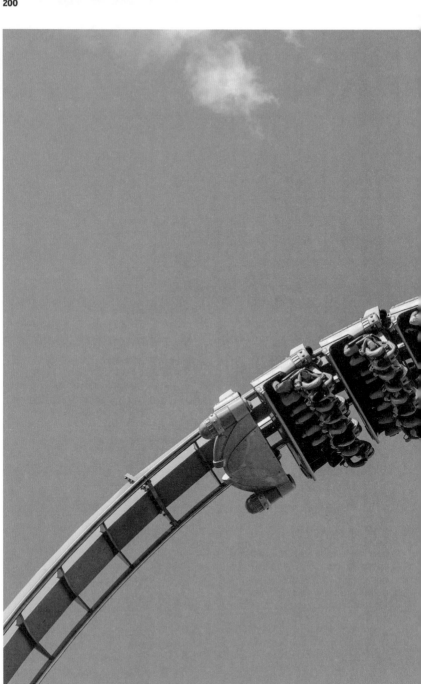

ORLANDO & WALT DISNEY WORLD

Orlando & Walt Disney World

Play quidditch with Harry Potter; disappear into the Twilight Zone; whip through the air on a sea monster: in Orlando, the Theme Park Capital of the World, it's all about adrenaline-fueled fun wrapped up in the mystique of fantasy.

Walt Disney World, Universal Orlando Resort, SeaWorld and Discovery Cove cluster within 15 miles of one another, and Legoland is only an hour's drive from downtown Orlando. These carefully constructed environments, dripping with magic and filled with rides, shows and parades, promise escape from the everyday.

Sure, Orlando has a quieter side, too, with world-class museums, excellent nature preserves and a burgeoning field-to-fork restaurant scene, but as wonderful as it may be, the city will always lie in the shadow of Cinderella's Castle and Hogwarts School of Witchcraft and Wizardry.

☑ In This Section

Walt Disney World Resort 204
Orlando.. 208

❶ Arriving in Orlando and Walt Disney World

If you are flying into **Orlando International Airport** (p211) and are staying at a Walt Disney World resort, arrange in advance for complimentary luxury bus transportation to and from the airport through **Disney's Magical Express** (📞866-599-0951; www.disneyworld.disney. go.com). Disney lies 25 minutes' drive south of downtown Orlando via I-4.

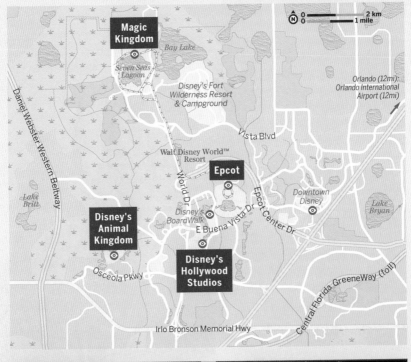

Magic Kingdom

Bay Lake

Seven Seas Lagoon

Disney's Fort Wilderness Resort & Campground

Daniel Webster Western Beltway

Vista Blvd

Orlando (12mi); Orlando International Airport (12mi)

Walt Disney World™ Resort

Epcot

Lake Britt

Disney's BoardWalk

E Buena Vista Dr

World Dr

Epcot Center Dr

Downtown Disney

Lake Bryan

Disney's Animal Kingdom

Disney's Hollywood Studios

Osceola Pkwy

Central Florida GreeneWay (toll)

Irlo Bronson Memorial Hwy

From left: Epcot (p205); Orlando Museum of Art (p209); Downtown Orlando
PAT CANOVA / GETTY IMAGES ©; BERNIE EPSTEIN / ALAMY STOCK PHOTO ©; GIORGIO FOCHESATO / GETTY IMAGES ©

Cinderella Castle, Magic Kingdom

STEPHEN SEARLE / ALAMY STOCK PHOTO ©

Walt Disney World Resort

Go ahead: let your children (and inner child) run rampant. Covering 40 sq miles, Walt Disney World is the largest theme-park resort in the world.

Great For...

☑ Don't Miss

The Enchanted Tiki Room is a Magic Kingdom classic, with talking birds and warbling flowers.

The Theme Parks

The expanse of Walt Disney World includes four theme parks, two water parks, two dozen hotels, 100 restaurants and two shopping and nightlife districts – proving that it's not such a small world after all. With or without kids, you won't be able to inoculate yourself against Disney's infectious enthusiasm and warm-hearted nostalgia.

Disney's Animal Kingdom

Set apart from the rest of Disney both in miles and in tone, **Animal Kingdom** (adult/child $97/91; ⊙9am-7pm, hours vary; 🚊Disney) attempts to blend theme park and zoo, carnival and African safari, all stirred together with a healthy dose of Disney characters, storytelling and transformative magic. The result is, at times, quite odd.

Epcot

DANIELLE GALI / GETTY IMAGES ©

The park is best at animal encounters
and shows, with the 110-acre Kilimanjaro
Safaris as its centerpiece. Don't miss the
iconic Tree of Life, with its fun It's Tough
to Be a Bug! show; the 'must-sea' Finding
Nemo – the Musical; and top thrill rides
Expedition Everest and Kali River Rapids.

Short trails around Animal Kingdom's
Discovery Island lead to quiet spots along
the water, where a handful of benches make
a great place to relax. Keep an eye out for
animals such as tortoises and monkeys.

Epcot

An acronym for 'Experimental Prototype
Community of Tomorrow,' **Epcot** (200 Epcot
Center Dr, Walt Disney World®; adult/child 3-10yr
$97/91; ⏰11am-9pm, hours vary; 🚍Disney,
🚤Disney) was Disney's vision of a high-tech
city when it opened in 1982.

With no roller coasters screeching overhead, no parades, no water rides and plenty
of greenery, things here run a bit slower
than in the rest of Walt Disney World.

Epcot is divided into two halves. Future
World, with rides and corporate-sponsored
interactive exhibits, is comprised of several
pavilions, each holding attractions, restaurants and character greeting spots. World
Showcase comprises 11 re-created nations
featuring country-specific food and shopping. Little ones can cool off in the shooting
water fountains just before the bridge from
Future World to World Showcase.

Magic Kingdom

When most people think of Walt Disney
World, they're thinking of the **Magic Kingdom** (1180 Seven Seas Dr, Walt Disney World®;
adult/child 3-10yr $105/99; ⏰9am-11pm, hours
vary; 🚍Disney, 🚤Disney, monorail Disney). This
is the Disney of commercials, of princesses
and pirates, of Tinkerbell and dreams come
true; this is quintessential old-school Disney with classic rides such as It's a Small
World and Space Mountain.

This is also where the nighttime fireworks and light parade illuminate Main
Street, USA.

Disney's Hollywood Studios

The least charming of Disney's parks, **Disney's Hollywood Studios** (☏407-939-5277; www.disneyworld.disney.go.com; 351 S Studio Dr, Walt Disney World®; adult/child 3-10yr $97/91; ◷9am-10pm, hours vary; 🚌Disney, 🚤Disney) is set for a major transformation: a 14-acre Star Wars land and an 11-acre Toy Story area planned for the next few years. Until then two of Walt Disney World's most exciting rides can be found here: the unpredictable elevator in the Twilight Zone Tower of Terror and the Aerosmith-themed Rock 'n' Roller Coaster.

Food

Theme-park food ranges from OK to awful; the most interesting is served in Epcot's World Showcase. *Always* make reserva-tions; seats can be impossible to get with-out one. For any dining, you can contact central reservations (www.disneyworld. disney.go.com) up to 180 days in advance.

Disney has two dinner shows (a luau and a country-style BBQ) and about 15 charac-ter meals, and these are insanely popular. Book them the minute your 180-day win-dow opens. The most sought-after meal is **Cinderella's Royal Table** (☏407-934-2927; www.disneyworld.disney.go.com; Cinderella's Castle, Magic Kingdom; adult $58-73, child $36-43; ◷8:05-10:40am, 11:45am-2:40pm & 3:50-9:40pm; 📶👶; 🚌Disney, 🚤Disney, 🚌Lynx 50, 56) inside the Magic Kingdom's castle, where you dine with Disney princesses.

What's On

In addition to theme-park events like Magic Kingdom parades and fireworks

Fort Wilderness Resort

and Epcot's Illuminations, Disney has two entertainment districts – Downtown Disney and Disney's Boardwalk – with eats, bars, music, movies, shops and shows.

Mind-blowing acrobatic extravaganza **Cirque du Soleil La Nouba** (407-939-7328, 407-939-7600; www.cirquedusoleil.com; Disney Springs; adult $59-139, child $48-115; 6pm & 9pm Tue-Sat; Disney, Disney, Lynx 50) is one of the best shows at Disney.

Tickets

The minimal base ticket, which allows access to one theme park for one day, costs $97 for adults and $91 for children aged three to nine years ($8 more per person for Magic Kingdom). You can add days and options when you first purchase your ticket or any time within the 14 days after the ticket is first used.

You must purchase tickets to enter the theme and water parks, but activities and entertainment at resort hotels and Disney's entertainment districts don't require park admission.

With FastPass+, visitors can reserve a specific time for up to three attractions per day through My Disney Experience on the website (www.disneyworld.disney.go.com) or by downloading the free app.

Accommodations at Walt Disney World Resort

Walt Disney World has 24 family-friendly sleeping options, from camping to deluxe resorts, and Disney guests receive great perks.

For wilderness on a budget, we love the **Fort Wilderness Resort & Campground** (407-939-5277, 407-824-2900; www.disney world.disney.go.com; 4510 N Fort Wilderness Trail; tent sites $75, RV sites $109-116, 6-person cabins $359; Disney, Disney) with tent sites and cabins that sleep up to six people. The excellent **Art of Animation Resort** (407-939-5277, 407-938-7000; www. disneyworld.disney.go.com; 1850 Animation Way; r $109-199, ste $269-457; Disney) is inspired by animated Disney classics including *The Lion King*, *Cars*, *Finding Nemo* and *The Little Mermaid*. The Yosemite-style **Wilderness Lodge** (407-939-5277, 407-824-3200; www.disneyworld. disney.go.com; 901 Timberline Dr, Walt Disney World; r $289-998; Disney, Disney) traffics in a 'rustic opulence' theme that includes erupting geysers, a swimming area and bunk beds.

Transport Within the Parks

Most hotels in Kissimmee and Orlando – and all Disney properties – offer free transportation to Walt Disney World. The Disney-owned resorts also offer free transportation from the airport. Drivers can reach all four parks via I-4 and park for $20. The Magic Kingdom lot is huge; trams get you to the entrance. Within Walt Disney World, a complex network of monorails, boats and buses get you between the parks, resorts and entertainment districts.

RSBPHOTO1 / ALAMY STOCK PHOTO ©

Orlando

Like Las Vegas, Orlando is almost entirely given over to fantasy. It's a place to come when you want to imagine you're somewhere else: Hogwarts, perhaps, or Cinderella's Castle, or Dr Seuss' world, or an African safari.

Yet there is, in fact, a real city to explore, one with tree-shaded parks of the natural variety, art museums, orchestras, and dinners that don't involve high-fiving Goofy.

◎ SIGHTS

Fashionable Thornton Park has several good restaurants and bars, while Loch Haven Park is home to a cluster of cultural institutions.

> *poke around among the impossibly crooked buidings of Hogsmeade*

Universal Orlando Resort
Theme Park

Universal is giving Disney a run for its money with this mega-complex that features two theme parks, five hotels and Universal CityWalk, an entertainment district that connects the two parks. But where Disney World is all happy and magical, Universal Orlando gets your adrenaline pumping with revved-up rides and entertaining shows.

The first of the two parks, Universal Studios, has a Hollywood backlot feel and simulation-heavy rides dedicated to television and the silver screen, from *The Simpsons* and *Shrek* to *Revenge of the Mummy* and *Twister*. Universal's Islands of Adventure is tops with coaster-lovers, but also has plenty for the little ones in Toon Lagoon and Seuss Landing. But the absolute highlight – and the hottest thing to hit Orlando since Cinderella's Castle – is the Wizarding World of Harry Potter, which features in both parks, connected by the Hogwarts Express. (☎407-363-8000; www.universalorlando.com; 1000 Universal Studios Plaza; single park 1-/2-days $102/150, both parks $147/195, children

Hogsmeade, the Wizarding World of Harry Potter

HOI SHAN WONG / EYEEM / GETTY IMAGES ©

$5-10 less, see website for discounts on multiday passes and Express Pass; ☺daily, hours vary; 🚃Lynx 21, 37 & 40, 🚌Universal)

Discovery Cove   Theme Park

At Discovery Cove, guests spend the day snorkeling in a fish and ray-filled reef, floating on a lazy river through an aviary, and simply relaxing in an intimate tropical sanctuary of white-sand beaches. For an added price beyond the Resort Only package, you can swim with dolphins and walk along the sea floor. It may seem like a fun idea, but since the early 1990s, there has been a growing controversy regarding the ethics of dolphin captivity for the purposes of public display and human interaction. (📞877-434-7268; www.discoverycove.com; 6000 Discovery Cove Way; admission incl SeaWorld and Aquatica from $210, incl dolphin swim from $339, SeaVenture extra $59, prices vary daily; ☺8am-5:30pm, all-day experience, advance reservations required; 👪: 🚃Lynx 8, 38, 50, 111)

Charles Hosmer Morse
Museum of American Art   Museum

Internationally famous, with the world's most comprehensive collection of Tiffany worldwide; the breathtaking centerpiece is a chapel interior, but the stained glass throughout is stunning as well. (📞407-645-5311; www.morsemuseum.org; 445 N Park Ave, Winter Park; adult/child $5/free; ☺9:30am-4pm Tue-Sat, from 1pm Sun, to 8pm Fri Nov-Apr; 👪)

Orlando Museum of Art   Museum

Founded in 1924, Orlando's grand and blindingly white center for the arts boasts a fantastic collection, and hosts an array of adult and family-friendly art events and classes. The popular First Thursday ($10), from 6pm to 9pm on the first Thursday of the month, celebrates local artists with regional work, live music and food from Orlando restaurants. (📞407-896-4231; www.omart.org; 2416 N Mills Ave; adult/child $8/5; ☺10am-4pm Tue-Fri, from noon Sat & Sun; 👪; 🚃Lynx 125, 🚉Florida Hospital Health Village)

🎫 Wizarding World of Harry Potter

Alan Gilmore and Stuart Craig, art director and production designer for the Harry Potter films, collaborated closely with the Universal Orlando Resort engineers to create what is without exception the most fantastically realized themed experience in Florida. The detail and authenticity tickle the fancy at every turn, from the screeches of the mandrakes in the shop windows to the groans of Moaning Myrtle in the bathroom.

Diagon Alley

Diagon Alley, lined with magical shops selling robes, quidditch supplies, wands, brooms and more, leads to the massive Gringotts Bank, home to Universal Studio's newest multisensory thrill ride, Harry Potter and the Escape from Gringotts.

Get your fill of traditional British pub fare such as bangers and mash at the Leaky Cauldron, and save some room for a scoop of wizarding-themed ice cream at Florean Fortescue's Ice-Cream Parlor. Then wander down Knockturn Alley to pick up tools of the dark arts at Borgin and Burkes.

Hogsmeade

Poke around among the cobbled streets and impossibly crooked buildings of Hogsmeade, munch on Cauldron Cakes, and mail a card via Owl Post – all in the shadow of Hogwarts Castle. Two of Orlando's best rides are here – Harry Potter and the Forbidden Journey and a pair of inverted, intertwined rollercoasters called the Dragon Challenge.

If you need a break for a spell (pun intended), then visit Ollivander's Wand Shop to see the selection process, drop by Honeydukes Sweet Shop for some Bertie Botts Every Flavor Beans or pop into the Three Broomsticks & Hog's Head Tavern for pumpkin juice.

From left: A ride at Universal Orlando Resort (p208); A ride at Disney's Animal Kingdom (p204); Zebras at Disney's Animal Kingdom (p204)

Winter Park — Neighborhood
Founded in 1858, this cozy and genteel college-town concentrates some of Orlando's best-kept secrets into a few shaded, pedestrian-friendly streets. Shops, wine bars and sidewalk cafés, including some of the best restaurants in the city and hopping with a mixed crowd of artists, lawyers, families and 30-somethings, line Park Ave, and there are two well-recommended boutique hotels. Don't miss the incredible Charles Hosmer Morse Museum of American Art (p209) or the bucolic Scenic Boat Tour (407-644-4056; www.scenicboattours.com; 312 E Morse Blvd, Winter Park; adult/child $12/6; hourly 10am-4pm;).

❌ EATING

East End Market — Market $
A revolving urban gourmet food court stocking delis, coffee, bars, bakeries and other locally sourced goodness. (231-236-3316; www.eastendmkt.com; 3201 Corrine Dr, Audubon Park; 10am-7pm Tue-Sat, 11am-6pm Sun;)

Yellow Dog Eats — Barbecue $$
Housed in an old, tin-roof general store, this quirky temple of dogs and barbeque is worth the haul for an incredible menu of delectable pulled pork sandwiches in surrounds swarming with local color. Try the Fire Pig (with Gouda, pecan-smoke bacon, slaw, Siracha, and fried onions in a chipotle wrap). (www.yellowdogeats.com; 1236 Hempel Ave, Windermere; mains $8-19; 11am-9pm;)

Cask & Larder — American $$$
From swampy taxidermy-meets-country-chic environs the Cask & Larder serves an innovative menu of locally sourced Southern fare, including an extraordinary kale salad with bacon vinaigrette, charred okra and boar and dumplings. They brew their own craft beer here, and don't mess around when it comes to cocktails ($12). (321-280-4200; www.caskandlarder.com; 565 W Fairbanks Ave, Winter Park; mains $24-46; 5-10pm Mon-Sat, 10:30am-3pm Sun)

HELEN SESSIONS / ALAMY STOCK PHOTO ©

DRINKING & NIGHTLIFE

Woods Cocktail Bar

It's been called Florida's best cocktail bar: a monthly changing menu of craft cocktails hidden in a cozy smoke-free 2nd-floor setting, with exposed brick, a tree-trunk bar and not a smidgeon of mixology pretension. (407-203-1114; www.thewoodsorlando.com; 49 N Orange Ave, 2nd fl, Historic Rose Bldg; cocktails $12; 5pm-2am Mon-Fri, from 7pm Sat, 4pm-midnight Sun)

INFORMATION

For city information, discount tickets to attractions and good multilingual guides and maps, visit Orlando's official **Visitor Center** (407-363-5872; www.visitorlando.com; 8723 International Dr; 8:30am-6pm).

WHERE TO STAY

In addition to the Walt Disney World resorts, Orlando has countless lodging options. Most are clustered around I-Dr, US 192 in Kissimmee and I-4. Reserve Orlando (www.reserveorlando.com) is a central booking agency.

GETTING THERE & AROUND

Orlando International Airport (407-825-8463; www.orlandoairports.net; 1 Jeff Fuqua Blvd) has buses and taxis to major tourist areas. **Amtrak** (www.amtrak.com; 1400 Sligh Blvd) has daily trains south to Miami and north to New York City.

I-Ride Trolley (407-354-5656; www.iridetrolley.com; rides adult/child 3-9yr $2/1, passes 1-/3-/5-/7-/14-days $5/7/9/12/18; 8am-10:30pm) buses run along I-Dr.

French Quarter (p222)

NEW ORLEANS

New Orleans

New Orleans is very much of America, and yet extraordinarily removed from it as well. 'Nola' is something, and somewhere, else. Founded by the French and administered by the Spanish (and then by the French again), she is, with her sidewalk cafés and iron balconies, one of America's most European cities.

But she is also, with her vodoun (voodoo), weekly Second Lines (neigh-borhood parades), Mardi Gras Indians, brass bands and gumbo, the most African and Caribbean city in the country. New Orleans celebrates – while America is on deadline, this city is mixing a cocktail after a long lunch. But after seeing how people here rebuilt their homes after storms and floods, it would be foolish to ever call the locals lazy.

☑ In This Section

Mardi Gras...216
St Charles Avenue Streetcar 220
Sights 222
Tours..228
Entertainment 228
Eating 229
Drinking & Nightlife 232

❶ Arriving in New Orleans

Louis Armstrong New Orleans International Airport (MSY) A taxi to the Central Business District (CBD) costs $34, or $14 per passenger for three or more passengers. Shuttle vans cost $20 per person.

Amtrak & Greyhound Located adjacent to each other downtown; you can walk to the CBD or French Quarter, but don't do so at night. A taxi to the French Quarter should cost around $10.

From left: Mardi Gras (p216); Louis Armstrong New Orleans International Airport (p233); The Tremé (p223)

RAY LASKOWITZ / GETTY IMAGES ©; EQROY / LONELY PLANET ©; FOTOLUMINATE LLC / SHUTTERSTOCK ©

Mardi Gras participant

RAY LASKOWITZ / GETTY IMAGES ©

Mardi Gras

Weird pageantry, West African rituals, Catholic liturgy and massive parade floats, all culminating in the single-most exhausting and exhilarating day of your life – happy Mardi Gras!

Great For...

☑ **Don't Miss**

The all-female Muses krewe, who take over St Charles Ave in one of the best early parades.

Pagan Beginnings

Carnival's pagan origins are deep. Pre-spring festivals of unabashed sexuality and indulgence of appetite are not a rarity around the world, and neither is the concept of denying these appetites as a means of reasserting human forbearance in the face of animalistic cravings. After trying unsuccessfully to suppress these traditions, the early Catholic Church co-opted the spring rite and slotted it into the Christian calendar. Carnival kickoff is rife with costuming, cross-dressing, mistaken identities and satirical, often crude, pokes at people in power. This attitude persists into Fat Tuesday (Mardi Gras).

Modern Mardi Gras

During the mid-19th century, a growing number of krewes (a deliberately quirky

Mardi Gras beads

RAY LASKOWITZ / GETTY IMAGES ©

ℹ Need to Know

Mardi Gras New Orleans (www.mardi grasneworleans.com) has parade and krewe information and tips on visiting the spectacle.

✕ Take a Break

Acme Oyster & Seafood House
(☎ 504-522-5973; www.acmeoyster.com; 724 Iberville St; mains $11-24; ☺ 11am-10pm Sun-Thu, to 11pm Fri & Sat) shucks fine bivalves near the party.

★ Top Tip

Bring the kids: Mardi Gras is surprisingly family-friendly outside of the debauch in the French Quarter.

spelling of 'crews,' or clubs) supplied Mardi Gras with both structure and spectacle; the former made the celebration easily accessible, while the latter gave it popularity and notoriety outside of New Orleans. Rex first appeared in 1872, Momus a year later and Proteus in 1882. Mythological and sometimes satirical themes defined the parades, making these processions coherent theatrical works on wheels. These old-line krewes were (and for the most part remain) highly secretive societies comprising the city's wealthiest, most powerful men.

Many enduring black traditions emerged around the turn of the 20th century. The spectacular Mardi Gras Indians began to appear in 1885; today their elaborate feathered costumes, sewn as a tribute to Native American warriors, are recognized as pieces of folk art. The black krewe of Zulu appeared in 1909, with members initially calling themselves the Tramps and parading on foot. By 1916, when the Zulu Social Aid & Pleasure Club was incorporated, the krewe brought floats, and its antics deliberately spoofed the pomposity of elite white krewes.

Today's 'superkrewes' began forming in the 1960s. Endymion debuted as a modest neighborhood parade in 1967; now its parades and floats are the largest around, with nearly 2000 riders and with one of its immense floats measuring 240ft in length.

Throw Me Something, Mister!

During Mardi Gras, enormous floats crowded with riders representing the city's Carnival 'krewes' proceed up and down thoroughfares such as St Charles Ave and Canal St. The float riders toss 'throws' to the waiting crowds; throws range from strings of beads to plastic cups, blinking baubles and stuffed animals. Here are some locally recognized rules for throw-catching:

● First: Locals never bare their breasts for beads. Most find it crude, and there are kids around.

● Second: If there's a young kid near you, move, or be prepared to give the kid whatever you catch.

○ Third: Many locals will say they'd never touch a throw that hit the street, but we've seen more than a few sneakily bend over to scoop up a cup or a unique string of beads. Rest assured it's not the done thing – even if it is occasionally, well, done.

Twelve Days of Parades

The parade season is a 12-day period beginning two Fridays before Fat Tuesday. Early parades are charming, neighborly processions that whet your appetite for the later parades, which increase in size and grandeur.

Krewe du Vieux By parading before the official parade season and marching on foot, Krewe du Vieux is permitted to pass through the French Quarter. Notoriously bawdy and satirical. Usually held three Saturdays before Fat Tuesday.

Le Krewe d'Etat The name is a clever, satirical pun: d'Etat is ruled by a dictator rather than a king.

Muses An all-women's krewe that parades down St Charles Ave with thousands of members and some imaginative, innovative floats; their throws include coveted hand-decorated shoes.

Mardi Gras weekend is lit up by the entrance of the superkrewes, who arrive with their monstrous floats and endless processions of celebrities, as flashy as a Vegas revue.

Endymion On Saturday night this mega-krewe stages its spectacular parade and 'Extravaganza,' as it calls its ball in the Superdome.

Krewe of Endymion parade

Bacchus On Sunday night the Bacchus superkrewe wows an enraptured crowd along St Charles Ave with its celebrity monarch and a gorgeous fleet of floats.

Zulu On Mardi Gras morning Zulu rolls along Jackson Ave, where folks set up barbecues on the sidewalk and krewe members distribute their prized hand-painted coconuts.

The 'King of Carnival,' Rex, waits further Uptown; it's a much more restrained affair, with the monarch himself looking like he's been plucked from a deck of cards.

☑ Don't Miss

Our favorite of the big parades is Krewe de Vieux, an old-school wallking parade.

MATTHEW D WHITE / GETTY IMAGES ©

Walking Krewe Review

Some of the best parades of Carnival Season are put on by DIY bohemian walking krewes, groups of friends who create a grassroots show. Casual observers are always welcome to participate. Just bring a costume!

Barkus Dress up your furry friends for this all-pet parade (www.barkus.org).

Box of Wine Crazily costumed revelers march up St Charles Ave ahead of the Bacchus (god of wine) parade, distributing free wine from boxes along the way.

Intergalactic Krewe of Chewbacchus Dress up as your favorite sci-fi character at this wonderful parade for geeks, nerds and other people we might hang out with on weekends (www.chewbacchus.org).

Red Beans & Rice On Lundi Gras, folks dress up in costumes made from dry beans or as Louisiana food items.

Society of St Anne Traditionally made up of artists and bohemians, St Anne marches on Mardi Gras morning from the Bywater to the Mississippi and features the best costumes of Carnival Season.

Costume Contests

Mardi Gras is a citywide costume party, and many locals take a dim view of visitors who crash the party without one. For truly fantastic outfits, march with the Society of St Anne on Mardi Gras morning. This collection of artists and misfits prides itself on its DIY outfits, which seem to have marched out of a collision between a David Bowie video and a '60s acid trip. The creativity and pageantry on display really need to be seen to be believed.

❶ Did You Know

Shakespeare gave Carnival celebrations his literary interpretation as far back as 1601 with *Twelfth Night;* the play is named for the holiday that traditionally begins the Carnival Season.

RAY LASKOWITZ / GETTY IMAGES ©

St Charles Avenue Streetcar

Clanging through this bucolic corridor comes the St Charles Ave streetcar, a mobile bit of urban transportation history, bearing tourists and commuters along a street as important to American architecture as Frank Lloyd Wright.

Great For...

☑ Don't Miss

The Tulane and Loyola Universities and several historic churches and synagogues on the streetcar route.

The Streetcar

The clang and swoosh of the St Charles Ave streetcar is as essential to Uptown and the Garden District as live oaks and mansions. New Orleanians are justifiably proud of their moving monument, which began life as the nation's second horse-drawn streetcar line, the New Orleans & Carrollton Railroad, in 1835.

In 1893 the line was among the first streetcar systems in the country to be electrified. Now it is one of the few streetcars in the USA to have survived the automobile era. Millions of passengers utilize the streetcar every day despite the fact the city's bus service tends to be faster. In many ways, the streetcar is the quintessential vehicle for New Orleans public transportation: slow, pretty, and if not entirely efficient, extremely atmospheric.

St Charles
Avenue
Streetcar

St Charles Ave

Mississippi River

❶ Need to Know

Streetcars arrive every 15 minutes or so, 24 hours a day. The cost per ride is $1.25.

✕ Take a Break

Head to the **Columns Hotel** (www. thecolumns.com; 3811 St Charles Ave; ⏱2pm-midnight Mon-Thu, 11am-2am Fri & Sat, to midnight Sun) for a cocktail with a side of Southern gentility.

★ Top Tip

The Jazzy Pass provides unlimited rides on streetcars for one ($3) or three ($9) days; see www.norta.com.

The fleet of antique cars survived the hurricanes of 2005 and today full service has been restored all the way to South Carrollton Ave. In recent times the line has carried more than 3 million passengers a year.

St Charles Avenue

It's only slightly hyperbolic to claim St Charles Ave is the most beautiful street in the USA. Once you enter the Garden District, the entire street is shaded under a tunnel of grand oak trees that look like they could have wiped the floor with an orc army in a Tolkien novel (ie they're old, and they're big).

Gorgeous houses, barely concealed behind the trees, house the most aristocratic elite of the city. Those same elite often ride in the floats that proceed along St Charles during Carnival season; look up to the tree branches and you'll see many are laden with shiny beads tossed from Mardi Gras floats. Within the Neutral Ground, or median space that houses the streetcar tracks, you'll often see joggers and families passing through the verdant corridor. By far the best way of experiencing this cityscape is via the slow, antique rumble of the streetcar; free from driving, you're free to gaze on all the beauty.

Some of the most elegant buildings to keep an eye out for include:
Elms Mansion (3029 St Charles Ave)
Smith House (4534 St Charles Ave)
'Wedding Cake' House (5807 St Charles Ave)
Milton Latter Memorial Library (5120 St Charles Ave)

⊙ SIGHTS

◎ French Quarter

Elegant, Caribbean-colonial architecture, lush gardens and wrought-iron accents are the visual norm in the French Quarter. But this is also the heart of New Orleans' tourism scene. Bourbon St generates a loutish membrane that sometimes makes the rest of the Quarter difficult to appreciate. Look past this. The Vieux Carré (Old Quarter; first laid out in 1722) is the focal point of much of this city's culture and in the quieter back lanes and alleyways there's a sense of faded time shaken and stirred with joie de vivre.

Jackson Square   Square, Plaza

Sprinkled with lazing loungers, surrounded by sketch artists, fortune-tellers and traveling performers, and watched over by cathedrals, offices and shops plucked from a Parisian fantasy, Jackson Sq is one of America's great town greens and the heart of the Quarter. The identical, block-long Pontalba Buildings overlook the scene, and the nearly identical Cabildo and Presbytère structures flank the impressive St Louis Cathedral. In the middle of the park stands the Jackson monument – Clark Mills' bronze equestrian statue of the hero of the Battle of New Orleans, Andrew Jackson, which was unveiled in 1856. (Decatur & St Peter Sts)

Cabildo   Museum

The former seat of government in colonial Louisiana now serves as the gateway to exploring the history of the state in general, and New Orleans in particular. It's also a magnificent building in its own right; the elegant Cabildo marries elements of Spanish colonial architecture and French urban design better than most buildings in the city. Exhibits range from Native American tools, to 'Wanted' posters for escaped slaves, to a gallery's worth of paintings of stone-faced old New Orleanians. (☏800-568-6968, 504-568-6968; http://louisianastatemuseum.org/museums/the-cabildo; 701 Chartres St; adult/child under 12yr/student $6/free/5; ☹10am-4:30pm Tue-Sun, closed Mon; ♿)

St Louis Cathedral   Cathedral

One of the best examples of French architecture in the country, this triple-spired

St Louis Cathedral

cathedral is dedicated to Louis IX, the French king sainted in 1297; it's a most innocuous bit of Gallic heritage in the heart of an American city. In addition to hosting black, white and Creole Catholic congregants, St Louis has also attracted those who, in the best New Orleanian tradition, mix their influences, such as voodoo queen Marie Laveau. (📞504-525-9585; www.stlouis cathedral.org; Jackson Sq; donations accepted, self-guided tour $1; ⊙8am-4pm)

Historic New Orleans Collection   Museum

In several exquisitely restored buildings you'll find thoughtfully curated exhibits with an emphasis on archival materials, such as the original transfer documents of the Louisiana Purchase. Separate home, architecture/courtyard and history tours run at 10am, 11am, 2pm and 3pm, the home being the most interesting of them. (THNOC; 📞504-523-4662; www.hnoc.org; 533 Royal St; admission free, tours $5; ⊙9:30am-4:30pm Tue-Sat, from 10:30am Sun)

◉ The Tremé

The oldest African American neighborhood in the city is steeped in a lot of history. Leafy Esplanade Ave, which borders the neighborhood, is full of Creole mansions, and is one of the prettiest streets in the city.

Backstreet Cultural Museum   Museum

Mardi Gras Indian suits grab the spotlight with dazzling flair – and finely crafted detail – in this informative museum, which examines the distinctive elements of African American culture in New Orleans. The museum isn't terribly big – it's the former Blandin's Funeral Home – but if you have any interest in the suits and rituals of Mardi Gras Indians as well as Second Line parades and Social Aid & Pleasure Clubs (the local black community version of civic associations), you need to stop by. (📞504-522-4806; www.backstreetmuseum.org; 1116 Henriette Delille St (formerly St Claude Ave); per person $8; ⊙10am-5pm Tue-Sat)

🚹🚺 New Orleans for Children

Many of New Orleans' daytime attractions are well suited for kids, including the Audubon Zoo (p227) and Aquarium of the Americas (p226).

Carousel Gardens Amusement Park
(📞504-483-9402; www.neworleanscitypark. com; 7 Victory Ave, City Park; adult/children 36in & under $4/free, each ride $4; ⊙10am-5pm Tue-Thu, 10am-10pm Fri, 11am-10pm Sat, 11am-6pm Sun Jun & Jul, Sat & Sun only spring & fall) The 1906 carousel is a gem of vintage carny-ride happiness. Other thrills include a Ferris wheel, bumper cars and a tilt-a-whirl. Buy an $18 pass for unlimited rides. Open nightly from Thanksgiving through the early new year for Celebration in the Oaks.

Louisiana Children's Museum
(📞504-523-1357; www.lcm.org; 420 Julia St; admission $8.50; ⊙9:30am-4:30pm Tue-Sat, noon-4:30pm Sun mid-Aug–May, 9:30am-5pm Mon-Sat, noon-5pm Sun Jun–mid-Aug) This educational museum is like a high-tech kindergarten where the wee ones can play in interactive bliss till nap time. Lots of corporate sponsorship equals lots of hands-on exhibits. The Little Port of New Orleans gallery spotlights the five types of ships found in the local port. Kids can play in a galley kitchen, or they can load cargo. Elsewhere kids can check out optical illusions, shop in a pretend grocery store or get crafty in an art studio.

Children posing at a feather boa display

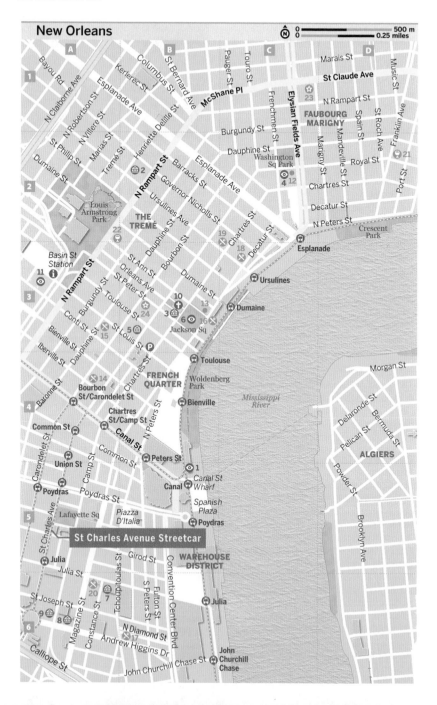

New Orleans

Ⓝ | 0 — 500 m
| 0 — 0.25 miles

Bayou Rd

N Claiborne Ave

Columbus St

St Bernard Ave

Kerlerec St

Esplanade Ave

N Robertson St

N Villere St

St Philip St

Marais St

Treme St

Henriette Delille St

Dumaine St

St Claude Ave

Marais St

Pauger St

Touro St

McShane Pl

Frenchmen St

Burgundy St

Dauphine St

Elysian Fields Ave

N Rampart St

FAUBOURG
MARIGNY

Spain St

St Roch Ave

Franklin Ave

Music St

☆ 23

N Rampart St

🏛 2

Barracks St

Esplanade Ave

Washington
Sq Park

Mandeville St

Marigny St

Royal St

Port St

Governor Nicholls St

Ursulines Ave

◉ 12
◉ 4

Chartres St

🚉 21

N Rampart St

Louis
Armstrong
Park

THE
TREMÉ

Dauphine St

Bourbon St

Chartres St

Decatur St

19

18

Decatur St

N Peters St

Esplanade

Crescent
Park

22

Basin St
Station

St Ann St

Orleans Ave

St Peter St

Dumaine St

🚻 Ursulines

11 ◉

ℹ

N Rampart St

Burgundy St

Toulouse St

10
🅘

13

🚻 Dumaine

Conti St

St Louis St

15

5 🏛

3 🏛

6 ◉ 16

Jackson Sq

24

Bienville St

Iberville St

Dauphine St

Chartres St

🅿

🚻 Toulouse

14

FRENCH
QUARTER

Woldenberg
Park

*Mississippi
River*

Bourbon
St/Carondelet St

N Peters St

🚻 Bienville

Baronne St

Chartres
St/Camp St

Morgan St

Common St

Canal St

Delaronde St

Bermuda St

Pelican St

ALGIERS

Carondelet St

Camp St

Common St

🚻 Peters St

◉ 1

Canal St
Wharf

Powder St

Union St

Poydras

Poydras St

Canal

Spanish
Plaza

Brooklyn Ave

Lafayette Sq

Piazza
D'Italia

🚻 Poydras

St Charles Ave

St Charles Avenue Streetcar

Girod St

WAREHOUSE
DISTRICT

🚻 Julia

Julia St

Tchoupitoulas St

Convention Center Blvd

S Peters St

Fulton St

🚻 Julia

St Joseph St

20

7 🏛

9 🏛

8 🏛

Magazine St

Constance St

N Diamond St

Andrew Higgins Dr

John Churchill Chase St

John
Churchill
Chase

Calliope St

New Orleans

◎ Sights
1 Aquarium of the Americas...................B5
2 Backstreet Cultural Museum B2
3 Cabildo B3
4 Frenchmen Art Market.....................C2
5 Historic New Orleans Collection B3
6 Jackson Square...........................B3
7 Louisiana Children's Museum A6
8 National WWII Museum A6
9 Ogden Museum of Southern Art A6
10 St Louis Cathedral........................B3
11 St Louis Cemetery No 1...................A3

◎ Activities, Courses & Tours
12 Confederacy of Cruisers....................C2
13 Friends of the Cabildo B3

◎ Eating
14 Acme Oyster & Seafood House A4
15 Bayona A3
16 Café du Monde B3
17 Cochon................................B6
18 Coop's Place............................C3
19 Croissant D'Or Patisserie.................C2
20 Peche Seafood Grill......................A6

◎ Drinking & Nightlife
21 Mimi's in the Marigny.....................D2
22 Tonique A2

◎ Entertainment
23 AllWays Lounge.........................C1
24 Preservation Hall........................B3
Spotted Cat ....(see 4)

St Louis Cemetery No 1 Cemetery
This cemetery received the remains of most early Creoles. The shallow water table necessitated above-ground burials, with bodies placed in the family tombs you see to this day. The supposed grave of voodoo queen Marie Laveau is here, scratched with 'XXX's from spellbound devotees. By request of the family that owns the tomb, do not add to this graffiti; to do so is also technically illegal. In 2015, in response to ongoing vandalism, cemetery visitation was limited to relatives of the interred and approved guided tours. (www.noladeadspace.com; 1300 St Louis St; admission by guided tour; ⏰9am-3pm Mon-Sat, to noon Sun; ♿)

◎ Faubourg Marigny, the Bywater & the Ninth Ward

North of the French Quarter are the Creole suburbs (*faubourgs,* which more accurately means 'neighborhoods') of the Marigny and the Bywater. Frenchmen St is a fantastic strip of live-music goodness. Nearby St Claude Ave now boasts a collection of good live-music venues, which is less Dixie-style jazz and more punk and bounce (a local style of frenetic dance music).

Frenchmen Art Market Market
Independent artists and artisans line this alleyway market, which has built a repu-
tation as one of the finest spots in town to find a unique gift to take home as your New Orleans souvenir. 'Art,' in this case, includes clever T-shirts, hand-crafted jewelry, trinkets and, yes, a nice selection of prints and original artwork. (www.facebook.com/frenchmenartmarket; 619 Frenchmen St; ⏰7pm-1am Thu-Sun) 📷

Crescent Park Park
This waterfront park is our favorite spot in the city for taking in the Mississippi. Enter over the enormous arch at Piety and Chartres Sts and watch the fog blanket the nearby skyline. A promenade meanders past an angular metal and concrete conceptual 'wharf'' (placed next to the burned remains of the former commercial wharf); one day, said path will extend to a planned performance space at Mandeville St. A dog park is located near the Mazant St entrance, which also gives disabled access. (Piety, Chartres & Mazant Sts; ⏰8am-6pm, to 7pm mid-Mar–early Nov; 🅿♿🐕) 📷

◎ CBD & Warehouse District
National WWII Museum Museum
This extensive, heart-wrenching museum presents an admirably nuanced and thorough analysis of the biggest war of the 20th century. And its exhibits, which are displayed in three grand pavilions, are amazing. Wall-sized photographs capture

What is Voodoo?

Voodoo as a faith comes from West Africa. It is a belief system that stresses ancestor worship and the presence of the divine via a pantheon of spirits and deities. Slaves from Africa and the Caribbean brought voodoo to Louisiana, where it melded with Roman Catholicism. One faith stressed saints and angels, the other ancestor spirits and supernatural forces; all came under the rubric of voodoo. Hoodoo are the magical implements popularly associated with voodoo, but how much magic they provide and their import to daily worship is often exaggerated (to use the same Christian comparison, many would find it insulting to call a rosary or crucifix a magic talisman).

The most well known voodoo practitioner was Marie Laveau, a 19th-century mixed race woman who married a Haitian free person of color. The legends surrounding Laveau are legion, but she is popularly associated with leading voodoo rituals near Bayou St John and providing magic spells for high-class New Orleans women. It's a fair bet much of this folklore was sensationalized by the popular press of the time; stories of magic brown-skinned women performing devilish rituals sold newspapers and magazines, at least more so than a sober recording of a religion that mixed Western Christianity and African ancestor worship.

the confusion of D-Day. Riveting oral histories tell remarkable stories of survival. A stroll through the snowy woods of Ardennes feels eerily cold. The experience is personal, immersive and educational. Don't miss it. (504-528-1944; www.national ww2museum.org; 945 Magazine St; adult/child/senior $23/14/20, plus 1/2 films $5/10; 9am-5pm)

Ogden Museum of Southern Art Museum

One of our favorite museums in the city manages to be beautiful, educational and unpretentious all at once. New Orleans entrepreneur Roger Houston Ogden has assembled one of the finest collections of Southern art anywhere, which includes huge galleries ranging from impressionist landscapes to outsider folk-art quirkiness, to contemporary installation work. On Thursday nights, pop in for Ogden after Hours, when you can listen to great Southern musicians and sip wine with a fun-loving, arts-obsessed crowd in the midst of the masterpieces. (504-539-9650; www.ogdenmuseum.org; 925 Camp St; adult/child 5-17yr/student $10/5/8; 10am-5pm Wed-Mon, plus 5:30-8pm Thu)

Aquarium of the Americas Aquarium

Part of the Audubon Institute, the immense Aquarium of the Americas is loosely regional, with exhibits that delve beneath the surface of the Mississippi River, Gulf of Mexico, Caribbean Sea and far-off Amazon rainforest. The new and impressive Great Maya Reef lures visitors into a 30ft-long clear tunnel running through a 'submerged' Mayan city, home to exotic fish. Upstairs, the penguin colony, the sea-horse gallery and Parakeet Pointe – where you can feed the colorful birds – are perennially popular. In the Mississippi River Gallery, look for the rare white alligator. (504-581-4629; www.auduboninstitute.org; 1 Canal St; adult/child/senior $24/18/19, with IMAX $29/23/23; 10am-5pm Tue-Sun;)

Garden District & Uptown

The main architectural division in New Orleans is between elegant Creole townhouses and the magnificent mansions of the American district, settled after the Louisiana Purchase. These huge structures, plantationesque in their appearance, are most commonly found in the Garden District and Uptown. Magnificent oak trees arch over St Charles Ave, which cuts through the heart of this sector and where the supremely picturesque St Charles Ave streetcar (p220) runs. The boutiques and galleries of Magazine St form the best shopping strip in the city.

Audubon Zoological Gardens   Zoo
This is among the country's best zoos. It contains the ultracool Louisiana Swamp exhibit, which is full of alligators, bobcats, foxes, bears and snapping turtles. Look for new and improved elephant and orangutan enclosures in late 2015, as well as a Lazy River water feature for kids. Open Mondays March through early September. (📞504-581-4629; www.audoboninstitute.org; 6500 Magazine St; adult/child 2-12yr/senior $19/14/15; ⏱10am-4pm Tue-Fri, to 5pm Sat & Sun Sep-Feb, 10am-5pm Mon-Fri, to 6pm Sat & Sun Mar-Aug; 👪)

◎ City Park & Mid-City
City Park   Park
Live oaks, Spanish moss and lazy bayous frame this masterpiece of urban planning. Three miles long and 1 mile wide, dotted with gardens, waterways, bridges and home to a captivating art museum, City Park is bigger than Central Park in NYC, and it's New Orleans' prettiest green space. It's also a perfect 'local' park, in the sense that it is an only slightly tamed expression of the forest and Louisiana wetlands that are the natural backdrop of the city. (📞504-482-4888; www.neworleans citypark.com; Esplanade Ave & City Park Ave)

New Orleans Museum of Art   Museum
Inside City Park, this elegant museum was opened in 1911 and is well worth a visit both for its special exhibitions and top-floor galleries of African, Asian, Native American and Oceanic art – don't miss the outstanding Qing dynasty snuff-bottle collection. Its **sculpture garden** (⏱10am-4:30pm Sat-Thu, to 8:45pm Fri) FREE contains a cutting-edge collection in lush, meticulously planned grounds. (NOMA; 📞504-658-4100; www.noma. org; 1 Collins Diboll Circle; adult/child 7-17yr $10/6; ⏱10am-6pm Tue-Thu, to 9pm Fri, 11am-5pm Sat & Sun)

New Orleans Museum of Art

FLIPHOTO / SHUTTERSTOCK ©

Preservation Hall

> *one of the most storied live-music venues in New Orleans*

⊙ TOURS

Confederacy of Cruisers   Bicycle Tour
Our favorite bicycle tours in New Orleans set you up on cruiser bikes that come with fat tires and padded seats for Nola's flat, pot-holed roads. The main 'Creole New Orleans' tour takes in the best architecture of the Marigny, Bywater, Esplanade Ave and the Tremé. Confederacy also does a 'History of Drinking' tour (for those aged 21 or over) and a tasty culinary tour. (📞504-400-5468; www.confederacyofcruisers.com; tours from $49)

Friends of the Cabildo   Walking Tour
These excellent walking tours are led by knowledgeable (and often funny) docents who reveal the history of the French Quarter, the stories behind some of the most famous streets and details of the area's many architectural styles. (📞504-523-3939; www.friendsofthecabildo.org; 523 St Ann St; adult/student $20/15; ⊙10am & 1:30pm Tue-Sun) 🖼

✪ ENTERTAINMENT

Jazz Fest (www.nojazzfest.com), a world-famous extravaganza of music, food, crafts and good living, is held on the last weekend of April and the first weekend of May.

Chickie Wah Wah   Live Music
Despite the fact it lies in Mid-City on one of the most unremarkable stretches of Canal St, Chickie Wah Wah is a great jazz club. Local legends such as the Sweet Olive String Band or Meschya Lake, and plenty of international talent, all make their way across the small stage. (📞504-304-4714; www.chickiewahwah.com; 2828 Canal St; ⊙shows around 8pm)

Preservation Hall   Jazz
Preservation Hall, housed in a former art gallery that dates back to 1803, is one of the most storied live-music venues in New Orleans. Barbara Reid and Grayson 'Ken' Mills formed the Society for the Preservation of New Orleans Jazz in 1961, at a time when Louis Armstrong's generation was already getting on in years. The resident performers, the Preservation Hall Jazz

Band, are ludicrously talented, and regularly tour around the world. These white-haired musos and their tubas, trombones and cornets raise the roof every night. (504-522-2841; www.preservationhall.com; 726 St Peter St; cover $15 Sun-Thu, $20 Fri & Sat; showtimes 8pm, 9pm & 10pm)

Spotted Cat   Live Music
It's good the Spotted Cat is across the street from Snug Harbor. They're both great jazz clubs, but where the latter is a swish martini sorta spot, the former is a thumping sweatbox where drinks are served in plastic cups – an ideal execution of the tiny New Orleans music club. (www.spottedcatmusicclub.com; 623 Frenchmen St; 4pm-2am Mon-Fri, from 3pm Sat & Sun)

Tipitina's   Live Music
'Tips,' as locals call it, is one of New Orleans' great musical meccas. The legendary Uptown nightclub, which takes its name from Professor Longhair's 1953 hit single, is the site of some of the city's most memorable shows, particularly when big names such as Dr John come home to roost. Outstanding music from local talent, too. (504-895-8477; www.tipitinas.com; 501 Napoleon Ave)

AllWays Lounge   Theater
In a city full of funky music venues, the AllWays stands out as one of the funkiest. On any given night of the week you may see experimental guitar, local theater, thrash-y rock, live comedy or a '60s-inspired shagadelic dance party. Also: the drinks are supercheap. (504-218-5778; http://theallwayslounge.net; 2240 St Claude Ave; 6pm-midnight Sat-Wed, to 2am Thu & Fri)

Mid-City Rock & Bowl   Live Music
A night here is a quintessential New Orleans experience. The venue is a strange, wonderful combination of bowling alley, deli and huge live-music and dance venue, where patrons get down to New Orleans roots music while trying to avoid that 7-10 split. The best time and place in the city to experience zydeco is the weekly Thursday-night dance party held here. (504-861-1700; www.rockandbowl.com; 3000 S Carrollton Ave; 5pm-late)

Barataria Preserve

This section of the **Jean Lafitte National Historical Park & Preserve**, south of New Orleans near the town of Marrero, provides the easiest access to the dense swamplands that ring New Orleans. The 8 miles of platform trails are a stunning way to tread lightly through the swamp where you can check out gators, nutrias (read: big invasive rats), tree frogs and hundreds of species of birds. It is well worth taking a ranger-led walk to learn about the many ecosystems that make up what are often lumped together as 'wetlands.'

Start at the **NPS Visitors Center**, (504-689-3690; www.nps.gov/jela; Hwy 3134; 9am-5pm, visitor center 9:30am-4:30pm Wed-Sun) 1 mile west of Hwy 45 off the Barataria Blvd exit, where you can pick up a map or join a guided walk or canoe trip (most Saturday mornings and monthly on full-moon nights; call to reserve a spot).

EATING

French Quarter

Croissant D'Or Patisserie   Bakery $
On the quieter side of the French Quarter, this spotlessly clean pastry shop is where many locals start their day. Bring a paper, order coffee and a croissant – or a tart, quiche or sandwich topped with béchamel sauce – and bliss out. Check out the tiled sign on the threshold that says 'ladies entrance' – a holdover from earlier days. (504-524-4663; www.croissantdornola.com; 617 Ursulines Ave; meals $3-5; 6am-3pm Wed-Mon)

Café du Monde   Café $
Du Monde is overrated, but you're probably gonna go there, so here goes: the coffee is decent and the beignets (square, sugar-coated fritters) are inconsistent. The atmosphere is off-putting: you're a number forced through the wringer, trying to shout

over Bob and Fran while they mispronounce 'jambalaya' and a street musician badly mangles John Lennon's 'Imagine.' At least it's open 24 hours. (☏800-772-2927; www.cafedumonde.com; 800 Decatur St; beignets $2; ⊙24hr)

Coop's Place · Cajun $

Coop's is an authentic Cajun dive, but more rocked out. Make no mistake: it's a grotty chaotic place, the servers have attitude and the layout is annoying. But it's worth it for the food: rabbit jambalaya, chicken with shrimp and *tasso* (smoked ham) in a cream sauce – there's no such thing as 'too heavy' here. No patrons under 21. (☏504-525-9053; www.coopsplace.net; 1109 Decatur St; mains $8-17.50; ⊙11am-3am)

Bayona · Louisianan $$$

Bayona is, for our money, the best splurge in the Quarter. It's rich but not overwhelming, classy but unpretentious, innovative without being precocious, and all round just a very fine spot for a meal. The menu changes regularly, but expect fresh fish, fowl and game prepared in a way that comes off as elegant and deeply cozy at the same time. (☏504-525-4455; www.bayona.com; 430 Dauphine St; mains $29-38; ⊙11:30am-1:30pm Wed-Sun, 6-9:30pm Mon-Thu, 5:30-10pm Fri & Sat)

The Tremé

Willie Mae's Scotch House · Southern $

Willie Mae's has been dubbed some of the best fried chicken in the world by the James Beard Foundation, the Food Network and other media. It thus sees a steady flow of tourist traffic. The chicken, served in a basket, is pretty damn good, as are the butter beans. (2401 St Ann St; fried chicken $11; ⊙10am-5pm Mon-Sat)

Bywater

Red's Chinese · Chinese $

Red's has upped the Chinese cuisine game in New Orleans in a big way. The chefs aren't afraid to add lashings of Louisiana flavor, yet this isn't what we'd call 'fusion' cuisine. The food is grounded deeply in spicy Sichuan flavours, which pairs well with the occasional flash of cayenne. The General Lee's chicken is stupendously

good. (📞504-304-6030; www.redschinese. com; 3048 St Claude Ave; mains $8-16; ⊙noon-3pm & 5-11pm)

Joint   Barbecue $
The Joint's smoked meat has the olfactory effect of the Sirens' sweet song, pulling you, the proverbial traveling sailor, off course and into savory meat-induced blissful death (classical Greek analogies ending *now*). Knock back some ribs, pulled pork or brisket with some sweet tea in the backyard garden and learn to love life. (📞504-949-3232; http://alwayssmokin.com; 701 Mazant St; mains $7-17; ⊙11:30am-10pm Mon-Sat)

Bacchanal   Modern American $
From the outside, Bacchanal looks like a leaning Bywater shack; inside are racks of wine and stinky but sexy cheese. Musicians play in the garden, while cooks dispense delicious meals on paper plates from the kitchen in the back; on any given day you may try chorizo-stuffed dates or seared diver scallops that will blow your gastronomic mind. (📞504-948-9111; www. bacchanalwine.com; 600 Poland Ave; mains $8-16, cheese from $5; ⊙11am-midnight)

✖ CBD & Warehouse District

Cochon   Cajun $$
The phrase 'everything but the squeal' springs to mind when perusing the menu at Cochon, regularly named one of New Orleans' best restaurants. At this bustling eatery Donald Link pays homage to his Cajun culinary roots, and the menu revels in most parts of the pig. Other meats include rabbit, alligator and oysters. (📞504-588-2123; www.cochonrestaurant.com; 930 Tchoupitoulas St; small plates $8-14, mains $19-26; ⊙11am-10pm Mon-Thu, to 11pm Fri & Sat)

Peche Seafood Grill   Seafood $$
We're not sure why, but there's a split opinion locally about this latest venture from Donald Link. Put us in the lick-the-plate and order-more category. Seafood dishes are prepared simply here, but unexpected flourishes – whether from salt, spices or magic – sear the deliciousness onto your tastebuds. The vibe is convivial, with a happy, stylish crowd sipping and savoring. (📞504-522-1744; www.pecherestaurant.com; 800 Magazine St; small plates $9-14, mains $14-27; ⊙11am-10pm Mon-Thu, to 11pm Fri & Sat)

★ Top Five for Local Eats
Coop's Place (p230)
Bayona (p230)
Cochon (p231)
Willie Mae's Scotch House (p230)
Croissant D'Or Patisserie (p229)

From left: Cajun cuisine at Cochon; Cafe du Monde (p229); Hot chocolate and beignets

St Joe's Bar

Garden District & Uptown

Ba Chi Canteen
Vietnamese $

Do not be skeptical of the bacos. These pillowy bundles of deliciousness – a *banh bao* crossed with a taco – successfully merge the subtle seasonings of Vietnamese fillings with the foldable convenience of a taco-shaped steamed flour bun. Pho and *banh mi* – dubbed po'boys here – round out the menu. (www.facebook.com/bachi canteenla; 7900 Maple St; mains $4-15; ⊘11am-2:30pm Mon-Fri, to 3:30pm Sat, 5:30-9pm Mon-Wed, 5:30-10pm Thu-Sat)

Boucherie
Southern $$

The thick, glistening cuts of bacon on the BLT can only be the work of the devil – or chef Nathanial Zimet, whose house-cured meats and succulent Southern dishes are lauded citywide. Savor boudin balls with garlic aioli, blackened shrimp in bacon vinaigrette, and smoked Wagyu brisket with garlic-parmesan fries. The Krispy Kreme bread pudding with rum syrup is a wonder. (☑504-862-5514; www.boucherie-nola.com; 1596 S Carrollton Ave; lunch $10-18, dinner $15-18; ⊘11am-3pm & 5:30-9:30pm Tue-Sat)

Gautreau's
Modern American $$$

There's no sign outside Gautreau's, just the number 1728 discreetly marking a nondescript house in a residential neighborhood. Cross the threshold to find a refined but welcoming dining room where savvy diners, many of them New Orleanian food aficionados, dine on fresh, modern American fare. Chef Sue Zemanick has won every award a rising young star can garner in American culinary circles. (☑504-899-7397; www. gautreausrestaurant.com; 1728 Soniat St; mains $22-42; ⊘6-10pm Mon-Sat)

DRINKING & NIGHTLIFE

Skip loutish Bourbon St and get into the neighborhoods, where you can experience some of the best bars in America.

Tonique
Bar

Tonique is a bartender's bar. Seriously: on a Sunday night, when the weekend rush is over, we've seen no less than three of the city's top bartenders arrive here to unwind. Why? Because this gem mixes some of the best drinks in the city, and it has a spirits menu as long as a Tolstoy novel to draw upon. (☎504-324-6045; http://bartonique. com; 820 N Rampart St; ⊗noon-2am)

Mimi's in the Marigny   Bar
The name of this bar could justifiably change to 'Mimi's *is* the Marigny'; we can't imagine the neighborhood without this institution. Mimi's is as attractively disheveled as Brad Pitt on a good day, all comfy furniture, pool tables, an upstairs dance hall decorated like a Creole mansion gone punk, and dim, brown lighting like a fantasy in sepia. (☎504-872-9868; 2601 Royal St; ⊗6pm-2am Sun-Thu, to 4am Fri & Sat)

St Joe's Bar   Bar
The bartender might make a face when you order a blueberry mojito – mojitos are hard to make. But dang, dude, you make 'em so good. They've been voted the best in town by New Orleanians several times. Patrons at this dark-but-inviting place are in their 20s and 30s, and friendly and chatty, as are the staff. (www.stjoesbar.com; 5535 Magazine St; ⊗4pm-3am Mon-Fri, noon-3am Sat, to 1am Sun)

ⓘ INFORMATION

The city's official visitor website is www. neworleansonline.com.

Basin St Station (☎504-293-2600; www. basinststation.com; 501 Basin St; ⊗9am-5pm) Affiliated with the New Orleans CVB, this interactive tourist info center inside the former freight administration building of the Southern Railway has loads of helpful info and maps as well as an historical overview film and a small rail museum component. It's next door to St Louis Cemetery No 1.

ⓘ GETTING THERE & AWAY

Louis Armstrong New Orleans International Airport (MSY; ☎504-303-7500; www.flymsy. com; 900 Airline Hwy), 11 miles west of the city, handles primarily domestic flights.

The **Union Passenger Terminal** (☎504-299-1880; 1001 Loyola Ave) is home to **Greyhound** (☎504-525-6075; www.greyhound.com; 1001 Loyola Ave; ⊗5:15-10:30am, 11:30am-1pm &

2:30-9:25pm) bus services and **Amtrak** (☎800-872-7245, 504-528-1610; ⊗ticketing 5:45am-10pm) train services.

ⓘ GETTING AROUND
TO/FROM THE AIRPORT
The **Airport Shuttle** (☎866-596-2699; www. airportshuttleneworleans.com; one way/round-trip $20/38) runs to downtown hotels.

Taxis downtown cost $34 for one or two people, $14 more for each additional passenger.

BICYCLE
Rent bicycles at **Bicycle Michael's** (☎504-945-9505; www.bicyclemichaels.com; 622 Frenchmen St; per day from $35; ⊗10am-7pm Mon & Tues, Thu-Sat, to 5pm Sun).

PUBLIC TRANSPORTATION
The **Regional Transit Authority** (RTA; ☎504-248-3900; www.norta.com; fares $1.25 plus 25¢ per transfer) runs the local bus service. Bus and streetcar fares are $1.25, plus 25¢ for transfers. RTA Visitor Passes for one/three days cost $5/12.

TAXI
For a taxi, call **United Cabs** (☎504-522-9771; www.unitedcabs.com; ⊗24hr).

LAS VEGAS

Las Vegas

Vegas, baby: it's the ultimate escape. This is the only place you can spend the night partying in ancient Rome, wake up in Egypt, take brunch beneath the Eiffel Tower, watch an erupting volcano at sunset and get married in a pink Cadillac at midnight. Double down with the high rollers, browse couture and sip a frozen vodka martini from a bar made of ice – it's all here for the taking.

So, is Vegas America's dirty little secret or its dream factory? It is, of course, both – and remains a bastion of hangover-inducing weekends for people from all walks of life. It doesn't matter if you play the penny slots or drop a bankroll every night – either way you'll leave town convinced you've had the time of your life.

☑ In This Section

Cruising the Strip 238
Sights & Activities 240
Entertainment 241
Eating 242
Drinking & Nightlife 243

❶ Arriving in Las Vegas

By car Most travelers approach the Strip (Las Vegas Blvd) off the I-15 Fwy. Try to avoid exiting onto busy Flamingo Rd; opt for quieter Tropicana Ave or Spring Mountain Rd.

McCarran International Airport The easiest and cheapest way to reach your hotel is via **airport shuttle bus** (one-way to the Strip/downtown hotels from $7/9). Taxis cost at least $20, plus tip, to the Strip.

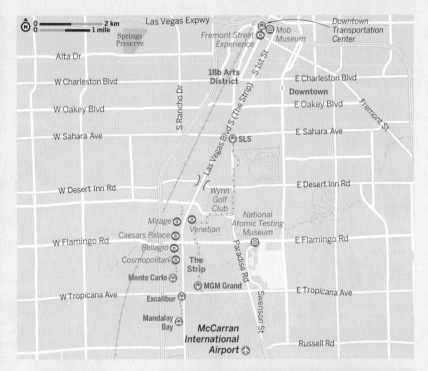

From left: The Strip (p238); Welcome to Fabulous Downtown Las Vegas sign; Elvis impersonator in a Las Vegas chapel
GARY COOK / ROBERTHARDING / GETTY IMAGES ©;   PAUL MORTON / GETTY IMAGES ©;   LONELY PLANET / GETTY IMAGES ©

Venetian

Cruising the Strip

The Strip, a 4.5-mile stretch of Las Vegas Blvd lined with hulking casino hotels and mega-resorts, is so hypnotizing that few visitors venture beyond it – this is where Vegas is at.

This famous boulevard is always changing. The themed casinos built on Las Vegas Blvd in the last half of the 20th century drove home the idea that bigger is better. In 1989 Steve Wynn opened the Mirage, with its erupting volcano and 20,000-gallon tropical aquarium. Other spectacular resorts soon followed, and many classic casinos were abandoned and imploded. In 2005 Wynn reset the Strip's standard with his namesake casino hotel, embodying a new, sophisticated resort style, free of campy themes. Today, all three varieties of casinos – vintage, themed and high-fashion – are worth your time on a stroll down the Strip.

Great For...

☑ Don't Miss

The Bellagio's dancing fountains (free shows take place at least twice hourly) and its blockbuster Gallery of Fine Art.

Cosmopolitan   Casino

Like the new Hollywood 'It' girl, the Cosmopolitan looks fabulous at all times. A steady stream of ingenues and entourages parade

Caesars Palace

RICHARD I'ANSON / GETTY IMAGES ©

ⓘ Need to Know

See www.lasvegas.com for the lowdown on restaurants, bars and events.

✕ Take a Break

The Cosmopolitan's **Chandelier Bar** (p243) rolls out three levels of other-worldly drinks.

★ Top Tip

Distances are deceiving; a walk to what looks like a nearby casino usually takes longer than expected.

Out front are the same spritzing fountains that daredevil Evil Knievel made famous when he jumped them on a motorcycle on December 31, 1967 (and ended up with a shattered pelvis and a fractured skull). More than two decades later, his son Robby repeated the attempt – more successfully. (☏702-731-7110; www.caesarspalace.com; 3570 Las Vegas Blvd S; ⊙24hr; 🛜)

Venetian   Casino
The Venetian's regal 120,000-sq-foot casino has marble floors, hand-painted ceiling frescoes and 120 table games, including a high-limit lounge and an elegant no-smoking poker room, where women are very welcome (unlike at many other poker rooms in town). (☏702-414-1000; www.venetian.com; 3355 Las Vegas Blvd S; ⊙24hr)

Mirage   Casino
Inside, the Mirage's paradisiacal setting is replete with a huge **rainforest atrium** under a conservatory dome filled with jungle foliage, meandering streams and soothing cascades. Woven into the tropical waterscape are scores of bromeliads. Tropical scents also waft through the hotel lobby, which features a 20,000-gallon saltwater **aquarium** filled with 60 species of coral-reef critters from Fiji to the Red Sea, including puffer fish, tangs and pygmy sharks. (☏702-791-7111; www.mirage.com; 3400 Las Vegas Blvd S; ⊙24hr)

through the lobby, along with anyone else who adores contemporary art and design. (☏702-698-7000; www.cosmopolitanlasvegas.com; 3708 Las Vegas Blvd S; ⊙24hr)

Bellagio   Casino
This posh European-style casino has high-limit gaming tables and 2400 slot machines with very comfortable seats, but highly unfavorable odds. A stop on the World Poker Tour, Bellagio's tournament-worthy poker room even offers 24-hour tableside food delivery for card sharks. (☏888-987-6667; www.bellagio.com; 3600 Las Vegas Blvd S; ⊙24hr)

Caesars Palace   Casino
Despite recent upgrades that have lent the once-gaudy Palace a more sophisticated air, some of the resort's original features from the swinging '60s have survived.

⊙ SIGHTS & ACTIVITIES

Beyond the Strip, downtown Las Vegas – the original city center – focuses on fun-loving Fremont St, and is home to the oldest hotels and casinos: expect a retro feel, cheaper drinks and lower table limits.

Mob Museum   Museum

It's hard to say what's more impressive: the museum's physical location in a historic federal courthouse where mobsters sat for federal hearings in 1950–51, the fact that the board of directors is headed up by a former FBI Special Agent, or the thought-fully curated exhibits telling the story of organized crime in America. In addition to hands-on FBI equipment and mob-related artifacts, the museum boasts a series of multimedia exhibits featuring interviews with real-life Tony Sopranos. (☏702-229-2734; www.themobmuseum.org; 300 Stewart Ave; adult/child 11-17yr $20/14; ⊗10am-7pm Sun-Thu, to 8pm Fri & Sat; ☐Deuce)

National Atomic Testing Museum   Museum

Fascinating multimedia exhibits focus on science, technology and the social history of the 'Atomic Age' which lasted from WWII until atmospheric bomb testing was driven underground in 1961 and a worldwide ban on nuclear testing was declared in 1992. View historical footage of atomic testing and examine southern Nevada's past, present and future, from Native American ways of life to the environmental legacy of atomic testing. Don't miss the cool muse-um shop near the ticket booth, a Nevada Test Site guard station replica. (☏702-794-5151; www.nationalatomictestingmuseum.org; 755 E Flamingo Rd, Desert Research Institute; adult/child 7-17yr $14/12; ⊗10am-5pm Mon-Sat, noon-5pm Sun; ☐202)

Arts Factory   Arts Center

Las Vegas' fractured art scene received an enormous boost in the late 1990s, when commercial photographer Wes Isbutt established this arts complex downtown. Today, it hosts **First Friday** (www.firstfriday lasvegas.com; ⊗5-11pm) events, with as many

Fremont Street Experience

SYLVAIN SONNET / GETTY IMAGES ©

as 10,000 people attending gallery exhibits on the first Friday evening of every month. Next door, **Art Square** (📞702-483-8844; www. artsquarelv.com; 1025 S 1st St; ⏱most galleries 1-7pm Wed-Fri, to 4pm Sat) has even more galleries, eclectic shops, experimental theater space and an arty bar. (📞702-383-3133; www.theartsfactory.com; 107 E Charleston Blvd; ⏱9am-6pm daily, to 10pm 1st Fri of month; 🚌Deuce, SDX)

Fremont Street Experience   Mall

A five-block pedestrian mall that's topped by an arched steel canopy and filled with computer-controlled lights, the Fremont Street Experience, between Main St and Las Vegas Blvd, has brought life back to downtown. Every evening, the canopy is transformed by hokey six-minute light-and-sound shows enhanced by 550,000 watts of wraparound sound and a larger-than-life screen lit up by 12.5 million synchronized LEDs. (www.vegasexperience.com; Fremont St, btwn Main St & Las Vegas Blvd; ⏱hourly dusk-midnight; 🚌Deuce, SDX) FREE

Slotzilla   Ziplining

Soar through the air on ziplines strung underneath the Fremont Street canopy. Billed as the world's largest slot machine, Slotzilla is a 12-story, slot-machine-themed platform. (📞844-947-8342; www.vegasexperience.com; Fremont Street Experience; rides from $20; ⏱noon-midnight Sun-Thu, to 2am Fri & Sat), a

⊕ ENTERTAINMENT

With several locations around town, **Tix 4 Tonight** (📞877-849-4868; www.tix4tonight.com; 3743 Las Vegas Blvd S, Hawaiian Marketplace; ⏱10am-8pm; gDeuce) offers half-price tix for a limited lineup of same-day shows and small discounts on 'always sold-out' shows.

Beatles LOVE   Theater

Another smash hit from Cirque du Soleil, *Beatles LOVE* started as the brainchild of the late George Harrison. Using *Abbey Road* master tapes, the show psychedelically fuses the musical legacy of the

ⓘ Gambling Terms

Learn the lingo before you hit the casinos.

All in To bet everything you've got.

Ante A starting wager required to play table games.

Comps Freebies (eg buffet passes, show tickets, hotel rooms) given to players.

Cooler An unlucky gambler who makes everyone else lose.

Double down In blackjack, to double your bet after getting your first two cards.

Eye in the sky High-tech casino surveillance systems.

Fold To throw in your cards and stop betting.

High roller A gambler who bets big (aka a 'whale').

Let it ride To roll over a winning wager into the next bet.

Low roller A small-time gambler.

Marker Credit-line debt owed to a casino.

One-armed bandit Old-fashioned nickname for a slot machine.

Pit boss A card dealer's supervisor on the casino floor.

Sucker bet A gamble on nearly impossible odds.

Toke A tip or gratuity.

Where to Stay

Megaresorts on the Center Strip are where the most action is, and you'll pay a premium to sleep there. But the South Strip can be as much of a blast, not to mention more affordable. Hotels on the North Strip advertise bargain prices, but have the most disappointing rooms and location. Downtown is for die-hard gamblers, locals and repeat visitors who've tired of the Strip scene; it's now experiencing something of a revival.

South Strip
ELEANOR SCRIVEN / ROBERTHARDING / GETTY IMAGES ©

Beatles with Cirque's high-energy dancers and signature aerial acrobatics. Come early to photograph the trippy, rainbow-colored entryway and grab drinks at Abbey Road bar, next to Revolution Lounge. (702-792-7777, 800-963-9634; www.cirquedusoleil.com; Mirage; tickets $79-180; 7pm & 9:30pm Thu-Mon;)

Le Rêve The Dream Theater
Underwater acrobatic feats by scuba-certified performers are the centerpiece of this intimate 'aqua-in-the-round' theater, which holds a one-million-gallon swimming pool. Critics call it a less-inspiring version of Cirque's *O*, while devoted fans find the romantic underwater tango, thrilling high dives and visually spectacular adventures to be superior. Beware: the cheapest seats are in the 'splash zone.' (888-320-7110, 702-770-9966; http://boxoffice.wynnlasvegas.com; Wynn; tickets $105-195; 7pm & 9:30pm Fri-Tue)

🍴 EATING

The Strip

Earl of Sandwich Deli $
Pennypinchers sing the praises of this super-popular deli next to the casino, which pops out sandwiches on toasted artisan bread, tossed salads, wraps and a kids' menu, all with quick service, unbeatable opening hours and some of the lowest prices on the Strip. (www.earlofsandwichusa.com; Planet Hollywood; menu $2-7; 24hr;)

Bouchon French $$$
Napa Valley wunderkind Thomas Keller's rendition of a Lyonnaise bistro features a seasonal menu of French classics. The poolside setting complements the oyster bar (open 3pm to 10:30pm daily) and an extensive raw seafood selection. Decadent breakfasts and brunches, imported cheeses, caviar, foie gras and a superb French and Californian wine list all make appearances. Reservations essential. (702-414-6200; www.bouchonbistro.com; Venezia Tower, Venetian; mains breakfast & brunch $12-26, dinner $19-51; 7-10:30am & 5-10pm Mon-Fri, 8am-2pm & 5-10pm Sat & Sun)

Gordon Ramsay Steak Steak $$$
Carnivores, leave Paris behind and stroll through a miniaturized Chunnel into British chef Gordon Ramsay's steakhouse. Ribboned in red and domed by a jaunty Union Jack, this is one of the top tables in town. Fish, chops and signature beef Wellington round out a menu of Himalayan salt room-aged steaks. No reservation? Sit at the bar instead. (877-346-4642, 702-946-4663; www.gordonramsay.com; Paris Las Vegas; mains $32-105, tasting menu without/with wine pairings $145/220; 4:30-10:30pm daily, bar to midnight Fri & Sat)

Sage American $$$
Chef Shawn McClain brings seasonal Midwestern farm-to-table cuisine to the Strip. The backlit mural over the bar almost steals the scene, but creative twists on meat-and-potatoes classics – imagine pork terrine with blue corn succotash and

Chandelier Bar

salsa verde – and seafood and pasta also shine. After dinner, sip absinthe poured from a rolling cart. Reservations essential; business casual dress. (702-590-8690; Aria, CityCenter; mains $35-54, tastings menus $59-150; 5-11pm Mon-Sat)

Downtown & off The Strip

Lotus of Siam   Thai $$
Saipin Chutima's authentic northern Thai cooking has won almost as many awards as her distinguished European and New World wine cellar. Renowned food critic Jonathan Gold once called it 'the single best Thai restaurant in North America.' Although the strip-mall hole-in-the-wall may not look like much, foodies flock here. Reservations essential. (702-735-3033; www.saipinchutima. com; 953 E Sahara Ave; mains $9-30; 11:30am-2:30pm Mon-Fri, 5:30-10pm daily; ; SDX)

Firefly   Tapas $$
Firefly is always packed with a fashionable local crowd, who come for well-prepared Spanish and Latin American tapas, such as *patatas bravas,* chorizo-stuffed empanadas

and vegetarian bites like garbanzo beans seasoned with chili, lime and sea salt. A backlit bar dispenses the house specialty sangria – red, white or sparkling – and fruity mojitos. Reservations recommended. (702-369-3971; www.fireflylv.com; 3824 Paradise Rd; shared plates $5-12, mains $15-20; 11:30am-midnight; 108)

DRINKING & NIGHTLIFE

Before shelling out the cover charge for a nightclub, look for the club's own promoters, usually standing on the casino floor of the corresponding hotel or resort – they're giving out passes for expedited entry and free drinks, especially to well-dressed women. Alternatively, consider booking ahead with a club promoter such as Chris Hornak of **Free Vegas Club Passes** (www.freevegas clubpasses.com).

The Strip

Chandelier Bar   Cocktail Bar
Towering high in the center of the Cosmopolitan, this ethereally designed cocktail bar is inventive yet beautifully simple,

👍 Going to the Chapel

A blushing bride says 'I do' every five minutes in Sin City. Scores of celebrity couples have exchanged vows in Vegas, from Elvis Presley and Priscilla Beaulieu to Andre Agassi and Steffi Graf.

If you're thinking of tying the knot and want to know what's required, contact **Clark County's Marriage License Bureau** (📞 702-671-0600; www. clarkcountynv.gov/Depts/clerk/Services/ Pages/MarriageLicenses.aspx; 201 E Clark Ave; marriage license from $60; ⏰ 8am-midnight), which gets jammed during crunch times such as weekends, holidays and 'lucky' number days. For an inexpensive, no-fuss civil ceremony, make an appointment with the county's **Office of Civil Marriages** (📞 702-671-0577; www. clarkcountynv.gov/depts/clerk/services/ pages/civilmarriages.aspx; 330 S 3rd St, 6th fl; wedding ceremonies from $75; ⏰ 2-6pm Sun-Thu, 10am-9pm Fri, 12:30pm-9pm Sat). Expect to pay at least $200 for a basic ceremony at an old-school Vegas wedding chapel. Operating for more than 50 years, **Graceland Wedding Chapel** (📞 800-824-5732, 702-382-0091; www. gracelandchapel.com; 619 Las Vegas Blvd S) created the original Elvis wedding. **Little Church of the West** (📞 800-821-2452, 702-739-7971; www.littlechurchlv. com; 4617 Las Vegas Blvd S; ⏰ 8am-11pm) features a quaint, quiet little wooden chapel built in 1942 and pictured in *Viva Las Vegas*. At zany **Viva Las Vegas Wedding Chapel** (📞 800-574-4450, 702-384-0771; www.vivalasvegasweddings.com; 1205 Las Vegas Blvd S), you can invite your family and friends to watch your wacky themed ceremony broadcast live online.

with three levels connected by romantic curved staircases, all draped with glowing strands of glass beads. The second level is headquarters for molecular mixology (order a martini made with liquid nitrogen),

while the third specializes in floral and fruit infusions. (Cosmopolitan; ⏰ 24hr; 🚌 Deuce)

Mix Lounge   Lounge
High atop one of M-Bay's hotel towers, this is *the* place to go for sunset cocktails. The glassed-in elevator has amazing views on the ride up to the rooftop, and that's before you even glimpse the mod interior design with chocolate-brown leather sofas or the roofless balcony opening up soaring views of the Strip, desert and mountains. (64th fl, Mandalay Bay; cover after 10pm $20-25; ⏰ 5pm-midnight Sun-Tue, to 3am Wed-Sat)

XS   Club
XS is *the* hottest nightclub in Vegas – at least for now. Its extravagantly gold-drenched decor and over-the-top design means you'll be waiting in line for cocktails at a bar towered over by ultra-curvaceous, larger-than-life golden statues of female torsos. Famous-name electronica DJs make the dancefloor writhe, while high rollers opt for VIP bottle service at private poolside cabanas. (📞 702-770-0097; www.xslasvegas. com; Encore; cover $20-50; ⏰ 9:30pm-4am Fri & Sat, from 10:30pm Sun & Mon)

Marquee   Club
The Cosmopolitan's glam nightclub cashes in on its multimillion-dollar sound system and a happening dancefloor surrounded by towering LED screens displaying light projections that complement EDM tracks handpicked by famous-name DJs. From late spring through early fall, Marquee's mega-popular daytime pool club heads outside to a lively party deck overlooking the Strip, with VIP cabanas and bungalows. (📞 702-333-9000; www.marqueelasvegas.com; Cosmopolitan; ⏰ 10pm-5am Thu-Sat & Mon)

🍸 Downtown & off the Strip
Want to chill out with the locals? Head to one of their go-to favorites.

Beauty Bar   Bar
Swill a cocktail or just chill with the cool kids inside the salvaged innards of a 1950s New Jersey beauty salon. DJs and live

XS

bands rotate nightly, spinning everything from tiki lounge tunes, disco and '80s hits to punk, metal, glam and indie rock. Check the website for special events like 'Karate Karaoke.' (702-598-3757; www.thebeautybar.com; 517 Fremont St; cover free-$10; 10pm-4am; Deuce)

Frankie's Tiki Room   Bar

At the only round-the-clock tiki bar in town, insanely inventive tropical cocktails are rated in strength by skulls on the menu. Renowned tiki designers, sculptors and painters have their work on display all around, and the souvenir tiki mugs are crazy cool. Walk in wearing a Hawaiian shirt on 'Aloha Friday' between 4pm and 8pm, and your first drink is half-off. (702-385-3110; www.frankiestikiroom.com; 1712 W Charleston Blvd; 24hr; 206)

ⓘ GETTING THERE & AROUND

McCarran International Airport (LAS; 702-261-5211; www.mccarran.com; 5757 Wayne Newton Blvd) has direct flights from many US cities, and some from Canada and Europe. **Bell Trans** (800-274-7433; www.bell-trans.com) offers a shuttle service between the airport and the Strip.

Fast, fun and fully wheelchair accessible, the **monorail** (702-699-8299; www.lvmonorail.com; single-ride $5, 72hr pass $40; 7am-midnight Mon, to 2am Tue-Thu, to 3am Fri-Sun) connects the SLS Station (closest to Circus Circus) to the MGM Grand, stopping at major Strip megaresorts along the way.

GRAND CANYON NATIONAL PARK

Grand Canyon National Park

Why do folks become giddy when describing the Grand Canyon? One peek over the edge makes it clear. The canyon captivates travelers with its sheer immensity; it is a tableau of rugged plateaus, crumbling spires and shadowed ridges that reveals the earth's history layer by dramatic layer.

Snaking along its floor are 277 miles of the Colorado River, which has carved the canyon over the past six million years and exposed rocks up to two billion years old.

The two rims of the Grand Canyon offer different experiences, and are rarely visited on the same trip. Most visitors choose the South Rim with its easy access, abundant services and vistas that don't disappoint. The quieter North Rim has its own charms; 1000ft higher than the South Rim, its cooler temperatures support wildflower meadows and tall, thick stands of aspen and spruce.

☑ In This Section

South Rim Overlooks........................250
South Rim...252
North Rim...255
Route 66...257
Flagstaff 257

❶ Arriving in Grand Canyon National Park

Grand Canyon Village is 6 miles north of the South Rim Entrance Station. The North Rim has one entrance, 30 miles south of Jacob Lake on Hwy 67. The North Rim and South Rim are 215 miles apart by car, or 21 miles on foot through the canyon.

A park **entrance ticket** (vehicles/cyclists and pedestrians $25/12) is valid for seven days and provides access to both rims.

From left: View from Shoshone Point; Grand Canyon South Rim entrance; View of Grand Canyon from Mather Point

PANORAMIC IMAGES / GETTY IMAGES ©; LAURA CIAPPONI / GETTY IMAGES ©; MEINZAHN / GETTY IMAGES ©

Grand Canyon at sunrise, seen from Yaki Point

WWW.FERPECTSHOTZ.COM / GETTY IMAGES ©

South Rim Overlooks

The Grand Canyon doesn't have a photographic bad side, but it has to be said that the views from the South Rim are stunners.

Each of the South Rim's overlooks has its individual beauty, with some unique angle that sets it apart from the rest – a dizzyingly sheer drop, a view of river rapids or a felicitous arrangement of jagged temples and buttes. Sunrises and sunsets are particularly sublime, with the changing light creating depth and painting the features in rich hues of vermilion and purple.

Great For...

☑ Don't Miss

Incredible sunsets illuminating the canyon at Hopi Point. It's worth the crowd jostling.

Top Five Overlooks

Mohave Point (Hermit Rd; Hermits Rest) Overlooks the river and three rapids; great for sunrise or sunset.

Hopi Point (Hermit Rd; Hermits Rest) Gorgeous sunset spectacle; juts further into the canyon than any other South Rim overlook, offering magnificent east–west views. During the summer peak, there

Desert View Watchtower

GARY WEATHERS / GETTY IMAGES ©

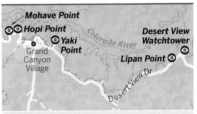

ℹ Need to Know

Check the park website (www.nps.gov/grca) for updates on sights and events.

✕ Take a Break

Fuel up on pancakes or fresh trout at **El Tovar Dining Room & Lounge** (p254).

★ Top Tip

The park no longer sells bottled water; fill your thermos at filling stations along the rim.

Reading the Formations

The distinctive sequence of color and texture that layers the canyon is worth learning, as you'll see it over and over again.

Kaibab limestone Starting at the top, a layer of creamy white Kaibab limestone caps the rim on both sides of the canyon.

Toroweap formation The vegetated slope between the cliffs of Kaibab limestone above and the massive Coconino cliffs below.

Coconino sandstone Note how sandstone erodes differently from limestone when you see these sheer 350ft cliffs.

Hermit shale Next lies a slope of crumbly red Hermit shale; today it supports a distinctive band of shrubs and trees.

Supai Group Just below the Hermit shale are these red cliffs and ledges, similar in composition, but differing in hardness.

Redwall limestone One of the canyon's most prominent features; the huge red cliff forms a dividing line between forest habitats above and desert habitats below.

Finally comes the small slope of **Muav limestone**, followed by the soft greenish **Bright Angel shale** and **Tapeats sandstone**, the last and oldest layer.

can be more than 1000 people waiting for shuttle pick-up after sunset.

Lipan Point (Desert View Dr) Creeks, palisades, rapids and sunrises.

Desert View Watchtower (Desert View, East Entrance; ⊙ 8am-sunset mid-May–Aug, 9am-6pm Sep–mid-Oct, 9am-5pm mid-Oct–Feb, 8am-6pm Mar–mid-May; 🚻) The marvelously worn winding staircase of Mary Colter's 70ft stone tower, built in 1932, leads to the highest spot on the rim (7522ft). From here, unparalleled views take in not only the canyon and the Colorado River, but also the San Francisco Peaks, the Navajo Reservation and the Painted Desert.

Yaki Point (Yaki Rd, off Desert View Dr; 🚌 Kaibab/Rim) A favorite point to watch the sunrise warm the canyon's features; because it's accessible year-round by shuttle or bicycle only, it tends to be quieter.

South Rim

To escape the throngs, visit during fall or winter. You'll also gain some solitude by walking a short distance from the viewpoints on the Rim Trail or by heading into the canyon itself.

Summer temperatures inside the canyon soar above 100°F (38°C). While the South Rim is open year-round, most visitors come between late May and early September. The North Rim is open from mid-May to mid-October.

◉ SIGHTS & ACTIVITIES

A 7-mile scenic route follows the rim along Hermit Rd west of Grand Canyon Village. Closed to private vehicles March through November, it's serviced by free shuttle buses; cycling is encouraged. Stops offer spectacular views, and interpretive signs explain canyon features.

Hiking along the South Rim offers options for every fitness level. The easy Rim Trail dips in and out of the scrubby pines of Kaibab National Forest to connect scenic

points and historical sights over 13 miles. Portions are paved, and every viewpoint is accessible by shuttle.

Desert View Drive follows the canyon rim for 26 miles east of Grand Canyon Village to reach Desert View, the park's east entrance, with wonderful viewpoints en route.

The most popular route into the canyon itself is the steep and scenic Bright Angel Trail. Don't try to hike to the Colorado River and back in a single day; summer heat can be crippling. The 8-mile descent is punctuated with four turnaround spots. Day hikers should turn around at one of the two resthouses (a 3- to 6-mile round-trip), or hit the trail at dawn for the longer hikes to Indian Garden and Plateau Point (9.2 and 12.2 miles round-trip respectively).

Rough, grueling and exposed, the stunning South Kaibab Trail combines staggering scenery with 360-degree views. Rangers discourage all but the shortest day hikes – it's a 12.6-mile round-trip to the river and back. For the park's finest

Cyclists on the Rim Trail

DANITA DELIMONT / GETTY IMAGES ©

day hike, turn around at Cedar Ridge (3 miles round-trip).

Bright Angel Bicycles
& Café at Mather Point Bicycle Rental

Half-or full-day bicycle rentals, with helmets and add-on pull-along trailer option, can be reserved in advance online or by phone; with the exception of the peak stretch from July through mid-August, however, walk-ins can usually be accommodated. Hermit Rd bicycle/shuttle packages allow you to ride past overlooks one-way, and hop one of their private shuttles the other. (928-638-3055, 928-814-8704; www.bikegrandcanyon.com; Visitor Center Plaza, Grand Canyon Village; 24hr rental adult/child 16yr & under $40/30, 5hr rental $30/20, wheelchair $10, single/double stroller up to 8hrs $18/27; Apr-Nov; @; Village, Kaibab/Rim)

TOURS

Grand Canyon
Mule Rides Guided Tour

The Canyon Vistas Mule Ride takes groups of up to 20 mules 4 miles along the East Rim Trail. If you want to descend into the canyon, the only option is an overnight trip to Phantom Ranch. These trips follow the Bright Angel Trail 10.5 miles (5½ hours) down, spend one or two nights in Phantom Ranch, and return 7.8 miles (five hours) along the South Kaibab Trail. (888-297-2757, same day/next day reservation 928-638-3283; www.grandcanyonlodges.com; Bright Angel Lodge; 3hr mule ride $120, 1-/2-night mule ride $533/758 incl meals & accommodations; rides available year-round, hours vary;)

DAY TRIPS FROM LAS VEGAS

Day tours from Sin City are popular, but check the itinerary very closely. The West Rim, on the Hualapai Reservation and not part of the national park, is closest to Las Vegas and is very busy with bus and helicopter tours. It does not offer any sights beyond a handful of overlooks and the glass skywalk, and because it sits several

 Best Places to Spot Wildlife

California condors In front of Bright Angel Lodge at the South Rim, look for California condors hanging out on the ledges below. From any viewpoint on either rim, you will often see them wheeling around on thermals.

Elk and mule deer It's not uncommon to encounter roaming elk and mule deer in wooded areas on both rims, even in the middle of the day. Show up in the early morning around El Tovar, on the South Rim, or around dusk.

Bighorn sheep More elusive, but we have encountered one grazing placidly in a drainage off the heavily trafficked Bright Angel Trail. You'll have a better chance of spotting them from a river vantage point.

California condor
MWKPHOTO / GETTY IMAGES ©

thousand feet lower than either rim, views are less grand. Worthy operators:

Canyon Tours (702-260-0796; www.canyontours.com) Bus, plane and helicopter tours from Las Vegas, including a $79 day trip bus-only tour to the South Rim. All tours to the North Rim include a helicopter or airplane leg.

Grand Canyon Tour Company (702-655-6060, 800-222-6966; www.grandcanyontourcompany.com; Las Vegas) A massive variety of tours depart from Las Vegas, Sedona and Phoenix.

👍 Rafting the Colorado River

A boat trip down the Colorado is an epic, adrenaline-pumping adventure in which you experience the Grand Canyon by looking up, not down from the rim. Its human history comes alive in ruins, wrecks and rock art. At night you camp under stars on sandy beaches. Commercial trips take two or three weeks to run the entire 279 miles of river; operators also offer shorter segments.

The multigenerational, family-run **Arizona Raft Adventures** (📞800-786-7238, 928-526-8200; www.azraft.com; 6-day Upper Canyon hybrid/paddle trips $2050/2150, 10-day Full Canyon motor trips $3000) offers paddle, oar, hybrid (with opportunities for both paddling and floating) and motor trips. Music fans can join one of the folk and bluegrass trips, with professional pickers and banjo players providing background tunes.

Arizona River Runners (📞602-867-4866, 800-477-7238; www.raftarizona.com; 6-day Upper Canyon oar trip $1984, 8-day Full Canyon motor trip $2745) have been at their game since 1970, offering oar-powered and motorized trips. It specializes in family trips as well as 'Hiker's Special' trips that take place over six to 12 days in the cooler temperatures of April. The company also caters to travelers with special needs, offering departures for people with disabilities.

White-water rafting

⊗ EATING

El Tovar Dining Room & Lounge   American $$$
Dark-wood tables are set with china and white linen, eye-catching murals spotlight Native American tribes and huge windows frame views of the Rim Trail and canyon beyond. Breakfast options include El Tovar's pancake trio (buttermilk, blue cornmeal and buckwheat pancakes with pine-nut butter and prickly pear syrup) and blackened trout with two eggs. (📞928-638-2631; www.grandcanyonlodges.com; El Tovar, National Historic Landmark District, Grand Canyon Village; mains $17-35; ⊙restaurant 6:30-10:45am, 11:15am-2pm & 4:30-10pm, lounge 11am-11pm; ♿; 🚐Village)

Arizona Room   American $$$
Antler chandeliers hang from the ceiling and windows overlook the Rim Trail and canyon beyond. Try to get on the waitlist when doors open at 4:30pm, because by 4:40pm you may have an hour's wait – reservations are not accepted. Bison and black bean chile and ribs with prickly pear barbecue give a Western vibe. (www.grandcanyonlodges.com; Bright Angel Lodge, National Historic Landmark District, Grand Canyon Village; mains $12-29; ⊙11:30am-3pm & 4:30-10pm Jan-Oct; ♿; 🚐Village)

❶ INFORMATION

Grand Canyon Visitor Center (📞928-638-7888; www.nps.gov/grca; Visitor Center Plaza, Grand Canyon Village; ⊙8am-5pm Mar-Nov, 9am-5pm Dec-Feb; 🚐Village, 🚐Kaibab/Rim) The South Rim's main visitor center. On the plaza here, bulletin boards and kiosks display information about ranger programs, the weather, tours and hikes. Inside is a ranger-staffed information desk, a lecture hall and a theater screening a 20-minute movie, *Grand Canyon: A Journey of Wonder*.

ℹ GETTING THERE & AROUND

Summer visitors can park their vehicle at the National Geographic Visitor Center in Tusayan, buy a park ticket there, and ride a free **park shuttle** (www.nps.gov/grca; Tusayan & Grand Canyon Visitor Center; ⏰8am-9.30pm mid-May–early Sep) to the main Grand Canyon Visitor Center.

Inside the park, free shuttles operate along three routes: around Grand Canyon Village, west along Hermits Rest Route and east along Kaibab Trail Route. Buses run at least twice per hour, from one hour before sunset to one hour afterward.

North Rim

Head here for blessed solitude; of the park's 4.4 million annual visitors, only 400,000 make the trek to the North Rim. Meadows are thick with wildflowers and dense clusters of willowy aspen and spruce trees, and the air is often crisp, the skies big and blue.

Facilities on the Canyon's North Rim are closed from mid-October until mid-May,

but the road itself remains open until blocked by snow.

◎ SIGHTS & ACTIVITIES

The short and easy paved trail (0.5 miles) to Bright Angel Point is a canyon must. Beginning from the back porch of Grand Canyon Lodge, it goes to a narrow finger of an overlook with fabulous views.

The North Kaibab Trail, the North Rim's only maintained rim-to-river trail, connects with trails to the South Rim. The first 4.7 miles are the steepest, dropping 3050ft to Roaring Springs – a popular all-day hike. For a shorter day hike below the rim, walk just 0.75 miles down to Coconino Overlook or 2 miles to the Supai Tunnel to get a taste of steep inner-canyon hiking. The 28-mile round-trip to the Colorado River is a multi-day affair.

Canyon Trail Rides (📞435-679-8665; www.canyonrides.com; North Rim; 1hr/half-day mule ride $40/80; ⏰schedules vary mid-May–mid-Oct) offers mule rides. One half-day trip goes along the rim, the other drops into the canyon on the North Kaibab Trail.

Toroweap overlook, North Rim

Grand Canyon Lodge

> *views from the dining room are huge*

⊗ EATING

The lodge will prepare sack lunches ($15), ready for pickup as early as 5:30am, for those wanting to picnic on the trail.

Grand Canyon Lodge Dining Room   American $$

Although seats beside the window are wonderful, views from the dining room are so huge it really doesn't matter where you sit. While the solid dinner menu includes buffalo steak, western trout and several vegetarian options, don't expect culinary memories – the view is the thing. Make reservations in advance of your arrival to guarantee a spot for dinner. (✆928-638-2611, off-season 928-645-6865; www.grandcanyonlodgenorth.com; mains

breakfast $6-13, lunch $10-15, dinner $13-33; ⊗6:30-10am, 11:30am-2:30pm & 4:45-9:45pm mid-May–mid-Oct; ⊛)

Grand Canyon Cookout Experience   American $$$

Feast on smoked beef brisket, roasted chicken, skillet cornbread and all the fixings – served with a side of Western songs and jokes. It might sound cheesy, but it's a lot of fun, old-school national park-style, and it's great for kids. Take the Bridle Trail to the cookout site, or catch the complimentary train or shuttle van. (✆928-638-2611; Grand Canyon Lodge; adult/child 6-15yr $30/15; ⊗5:45pm Jun 1-Sep 30; ⊛)

ⓘ INFORMATION

North Rim Visitor Center (✆928-638-7864; www.nps.gov/grca; North Rim; ⊗8am-6pm) Beside Grand Canyon Lodge, this is the place to get information on the park, and the starting point for ranger-led nature walks.

ℹ GETTING THERE & AROUND

The **Transcanyon Shuttle** (📞877-638-2820, 928-638-2820; www.trans-canyonshuttle.com; one way rim-to-rim $85, one-way South Rim to Marble Canyon $70; ⊙mid-May–mid-Oct) departs daily from Grand Canyon Lodge for the South Rim (five hours) and is perfect for rim-to-rim hikers. Reserve well in advance.

Route 66

Running for 2400 miles from Chicago to Los Angeles, Route 66 (aka the 'Mother Road') was the first cross-country highway to be paved, in 1937. Families fled west on it during the Dust Bowl; after WWII, they got their kicks road-tripping. The route was bypassed by Interstate 40 in 1985, but some original parts remain, including approximately 875 miles across New Mexico and Arizona. Some highlights: the Grand Canyon, classic diners and kitschy delights like the Wigwam Motel in Holbrook, Arizona. Check www.historic66.com for details.

Flagstaff

Flagstaff's laid-back charms are myriad, from its pedestrian-friendly historic downtown crammed with eclectic vernacular architecture and vintage neon to its high-altitude pursuits such as skiing and hiking. Throw in a healthy appreciation for craft beer, freshly roasted coffee beans and an all-round good time and you have the makings of a town you want to slow down and savor.

◎ SIGHTS

Museum of Northern Arizona   Museum

An attractive Craftsman-style stone building amid a pine grove, this small but excellent museum spotlights local Native American archaeology, history and culture, as well as geology, biology and the arts. It's on the way to the Grand Canyon, and makes a wonderful introduction to human and natural history of the region.

⌖ Monument Valley

Like a classic movie star, Monument Valley has a face known around the world. The epic beauty of its fiery red spindles, sheer-walled mesas and grand buttes is heightened by the desolation that stretches all around.

Straddling the Arizona–Utah border, this fantasyland of crimson sandstone towers soaring up to 1200ft is traversed by Hwy 163. Its most famous formations are best admired from the rough 17-mile dirt road that loops through **Monument Valley Navajo Tribal Park** (📞435-727-5874; www.navajonationparks.org; per 4-person vehicle $20; ⊙drive 6am-8:30pm May-Sep, 8am-4:30pm Oct-Apr; visitor center 6am-8pm May-Sep, 8am-5pm Oct-Apr). Expect a dusty, bumpy drive, during which you can get out at several overlooks to take photos and buy trinkets and jewelry from Navajo vendors. Allow at least 1½ hours for the drive, which starts from the visitor center at the end of a 4-mile paved road off Hwy 163. There's also a restaurant, gift shop, small museum and the View Hotel.

To get into the backcountry, join a Navajo-led tour on foot, on horseback or by vehicle. Tours leave frequently from booths alongside the visitor center, costing from $55 for a 90-minute motorized trip.

Monument Valley is 180 miles northeast of the Grand Canyon; to drive from the South Rim takes around 3½ hours.

Where to Stay

Advance or same-day reservations are required for the South Rim's six lodges, which are operated by **Xanterra** (☏888-297-2757, 303-297-2757, 928-638-3283; www.grandcanyonlodges.com). If you can't find accommodations in the national park, try Tusayan, Valle (31 miles south), Cameron (53 miles east), Williams (60 miles south) or Flagstaff (80 miles southeast).

For North Rim, accommodations are limited to one lodge (Grand Canyon Lodge; www.grandcanyonlodgenorth.com) and one campground. If these are booked, try your luck 80 miles north in Kanab, UT, or 84 miles northeast in Lees Ferry.

Hiking & Camping Permits

All overnight hikes and backcountry camping in Grand Canyon National Park require a permit. The **Backcountry Information Center** (☏928-638-7875; www.nps.gov/grca/planyourvisit/backcountry-permit.htm; Grand Canyon National Park, PO Box 129, Grand Canyon, AZ 86023; ◷8am-5pm daily, seasonal variation) accepts applications ($10, plus $5 per person per night) up to four months in advance, in person or by mail or fax. If you arrive without a permit, join the center's waiting list.

(☏928-774-5213; www.musnaz.org; 3101 N Fort Valley Rd; adult/senior/child 10-17yr $10/9/6; ◷10am-5pm Mon-Sat, noon-5pm Sun; ⊞)

Lowell Observatory　　Observatory
Sitting atop a hill just west of downtown, this national historic landmark was built by Percival Lowell in 1894. The first sighting of Pluto occurred here in 1930. Weather permitting, visitors can stargaze through on-site telescopes, including the famed 1896 Clark Telescope, the impetus behind the now-accepted theory of an expanding universe. (☏main phone 928-774-3358, recorded information 928-233-3211; www.lowell.edu; 1400 W Mars Hill Rd; adult/child 5-17yr $12/6; ◷9am-10pm Jun-Aug, shorter hours Sep-May; ⊞)

⊗ ENTERTAINMENT

Charly's Pub & Grill　　Live Music
Inside the Weatherford Hotel, with regular live blues, jazz and folk. (☏928-779-1919; www.weatherfordhotel.com; 23 N Leroux St; ◷8am-2am)

⊗ EATING

Macy's　　Café $
The delicious house-roasted coffee at this Flagstaff institution has kept the city buzzing for more than 30 years now. The vegetarian menu includes many vegan choices, along with traditional café grub like pastries, steamed eggs, waffles, yogurt and granola, salads and veggie sandwiches. (www.macyscoffee.net; 14 S Beaver St; mains under $8; ◷6am-8pm; ⊛⊘)

Criollo Latin Kitchen　　Fusion $$
This intimate Latin fusion spot has a romantic, industrial setting for cozy cocktail dates and tasty small plates, but the blue-corn blueberry pancakes make a strong argument for showing up for brunch on weekends. The popular weekday Happy Hour (3pm to 6pm) features $4 margaritas (try a raspberry basil) and $3 sliders. (☏928-774-0541; www.criollolatinkitchen.com; 16 N San Francisco St; mains $15-28; ◷11am-10pm Mon-Fri, from 9am Sat & Sun) ⊘

⊙ DRINKING & NIGHTLIFE

Follow the 1-mile Flagstaff Ale Trail (www.flagstaffaletrail.com) to sample craft beer at downtown breweries and a pub or two.

Museum Club　　Bar
This honky-tonk roadhouse on Route 66 has been kicking up its heels since 1936.

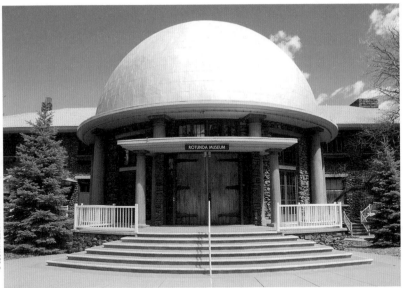

Lowell Observatory

Inside what looks like a huge log cabin, you'll find a large wooden dancefloor, animal mounts and a sumptuous elixir-filled mahogany bar. The origins of the name? In 1931 it housed a taxidermy museum. (✆928-526-9434; www.themuseumclub.com; ⊙11am-2am)

ℹ INFORMATION

Visitor Center (✆928-774-9541, 800-842-7293; www.flagstaffarizona.org; 1 E Route 66; ⊙8am-5pm Mon-Sat, 9am-4pm Sun) Located inside the Amtrak station, the visitor center has a great Flagstaff Discovery map as well as tons of information on things to do.

ℹ GETTING THERE & AROUND

Arizona Shuttle (✆928-226-8060, 800-888-2749; www.arizonashuttle.com; ⊙year-round) runs shuttles to the Grand Canyon South Rim ($30 one way), Sedona ($39) and Phoenix Sky Harbor Airport ($45).

Operated by **Amtrak** (✆800-872-7245, 928-774-8679; www.amtrak.com; 1 E Route 66; ⊙3am-10:45pm), the *Southwest Chief* stops at Flagstaff on its daily run between Chicago and Los Angeles.

Forecourt of the TCL Chinese Theatre (p266)

LOS ANGELES

Los Angeles

If you think you've already got LA figured out – celebrities, smog, traffic, bikini babes and pop-star wannabes – think again. Although it's an entertainment capital, the city's truths aren't delivered on movie screens or reality shows; rather, they're glimpsed in everyday experiences on the streets. The one thing that brings Angelenos together is that they're seekers – or the descendants of seekers – drawn by a dream of fame, fortune or rebirth.

Now is an exciting time to visit LA: Hollywood and Downtown are undergoing an urban renaissance, and the art, music, food and fashion scenes are all in high gear. Chances are, the more you explore, the more you'll love 'La-La Land.'

☑ **In This Section**

Santa Monica Pier 264
Hollywood 266
Griffith Park 268
Sights 274
Activities 277
Shopping 279
Entertainment 279
Eating 280
Drinking & Nightlife 283

ℹ **Arriving in LA**

Los Angeles International Airport
There is no direct rail connection from the airport to the city, but shuttles and taxis pick up the slack. Shared-ride vans leave 7am to 11pm from the terminals' lower level; fares start from $16 to Downtown. **LAX FlyAway Buses** (www.lawa.org/FlyAway) travel nonstop to Downtown's Union Station ($8, 45 minutes). Flat-rate taxis to Downtown cost $46.50 (around 30 minutes).

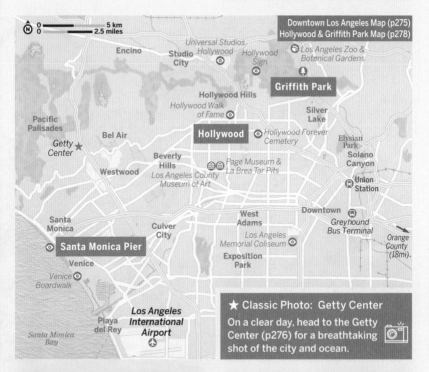

N
0 —————— 5 km
0 —————— 2.5 miles

Downtown Los Angeles Map (p275)
Hollywood & Griffith Park Map (p278)

Universal Studios
Hollywood

Encino

Studio
City

Hollywood
Sign

Los Angeles Zoo &
Botanical Gardens

Griffith Park

Hollywood Hills

*Hollywood Walk
of Fame*

Silver
Lake

Pacific
Palisades

Bel Air

Hollywood

Hollywood Forever
Cemetery

Elysian
Park

Getty
Center

Beverly
Hills

Page Museum &
La Brea Tar Pits

Solano
Canyon

Westwood

Los Angeles County
Museum of Art

Union
Station

Santa
Monica

Culver
City

West
Adams

Downtown

Greyhound
Bus Terminal

Orange
County
(18mi)

Santa Monica Pier

Los Angeles
Memorial Coliseum

Venice

Exposition
Park

*Venice
Boardwalk*

★ Classic Photo: Getty Center

On a clear day, head to the Getty
Center (p276) for a breathtaking
shot of the city and ocean.

Playa
del Rey

*Santa Monica
Bay*

Los Angeles
International
Airport

◐ LA in Two Days

Begin in Hollywood. Star-search on the
Walk of Fame (p267) and take a tour
at **Paramount** (p267) or **Sony** (p267).
Later, get a dose of nature at **Griffith
Park** (p268). Spend day two around
Downtown LA. Start with its roots at **El
Pueblo de Los Angeles** (p274), then
catch up with the present at the **Walt
Disney Concert Hall** (p274). Have
dinner in Little Tokyo.

◐ LA in Four Days

Head to the **Venice Boardwalk** (p272)
and **Santa Monica Pier** (p264), where
beaches, carnival rides and superb
people-watching fill day three. On the
last day, visit the **Los Angeles County
Museum of Art** (p276) and environs.
Then stroll along glamorous **Rodeo
Drive** (p276) before heading to the lofty
Getty Center (p276). At night, catch a
show at the **Hollywood Bowl** (p280).

From left: Santa Monica Pier (p264); Los Angeles International Airport; Rodeo Drive (p276), Venice Boardwalk (p272)

IAN DAGNALL / ALAMY STOCK PHOTO ©

Santa Monica Pier

Once the very end of Route 66, Santa Monica Pier dates back to 1908 and is the city's most compelling landmark. Extending almost a quarter mile over the Pacific, it's all about the view: stroll to the edge and gaze out over the rolling, blue-green sea.

Great For...

☑ Don't Miss

The free, eclectic concert program on Thursday nights (from 7pm to 10pm) in summer.

Pacific Park

Kids get their kicks at **Pacific Park** (🖉310-260-8744; www.pacpark.com; ⏰11am-9pm Sun-Thu, to midnight Fri & Sat Jun-Aug, shorter hours Sep-May; 👪), a small amusement park with a solar-powered Ferris wheel, kiddy rides, midway games and food stands. Rides cost between $3 and $5 each; a day of unlimited spins costs $21.95/15.95 (over/under 42in tall); check the website for discount coupons.

Carousel

Near the pier entrance, nostalgic souls and their offspring can giddy up the beautifully hand-painted horses of the 1922 carousel featured in the movie *The Sting*.

South Bay Bicycle Trail

JON HICKS / CORBIS ©

Santa Monica
Pier

Santa Monica
State Beach

Ocean Ave

Santa Monica
Bay

❶ Need to Know

📞310-458-8900; www.santamonicapier.
org; 🚻

✕ Take a Break

Indulge in seafood specials at lively **Lobster** (📞310-458-9294; www.thelobster.com;
1602 Ocean Ave; mains $12-38; ⏱11:30am-
10pm Sun-Thu, to 11pm Fri & Sat; 🚌BBB 1).

★ Top Tip

Perry's Café (📞310-939-0000; www.
perryscafe.com; Ocean Front Walk; mountain
bikes & Rollerblades per hr/day $10/30, body-
boards per hr/day $7/17; ⏱9:30am-5:30pm),
about 1 mile south on the beach, is
a great place for equipment rentals,
with easy bicycle trail access.

Aquarium

Peer under the pier – just below the carousel – for Heal the Bay's **Santa Monica Pier
Aquarium** (📞310-393-6149; www.healthebay.
org; 1600 Ocean Front Walk; adult/child $5/free;
⏱2-5pm Tue-Fri, 12:30-5pm Sat & Sun; 🚻).
Sea stars, crabs, sea urchins and other
critters and crustaceans scooped from
the bay stand by to be petted – ever so
gently, please – in their adopted touch-tank
homes.

Seaside Cinema

Catch the Pacific sea breeze while camping
out on the Santa Monica Pier where the
Front Porch Cinema at the Pier (www.
santamonicapier.org/frontporchcinema) FREE
presents populist faves every Friday night
from late September through October.

Tickets are free but must be picked up at
the Santa Monica Visitors Center (📞800-
544-5319; www.santamonica.com; 2427 Main St,
Santa Monica)

What's Nearby

South of the pier is the Original Muscle
Beach, where the Southern California
exercise craze began in the mid-20th century, and new equipment now draws a new
generation of fitness fanatics. Close by, the
search for the next Bobby Fischer is on at
the International Chess Park. Anyone can
join in. Following the **South Bay Bicycle
Trail**, a paved bike and walking path, south
for about 1.5 miles takes you straight to
Venice Beach. Bike or in-line skates are
available to rent on the pier and at beachside kiosks.

Mausoleum, Hollywood Forever Cemetery

GOHOLLYWOOD / ALAMY STOCK PHOTO ©

Hollywood

Just as an aging movie star gets the occasional facelift, so too does Hollywood. While it hasn't recaptured its 'Golden Age' glamour, its modern seediness is disappearing.

Great For...

☑ **Don't Miss**

The multistory mall **Hollywood & Highland** (6801 Hollywood Blvd) for nicely framed views of the hillside Hollywood sign.

TCL Chinese Theatre

Even the most jaded visitor may thrill in the famous forecourt of the **TCL Chinese Theatre** (Map p278; ☎ 323-463-9576; www.tclchinesetheatres.com; 6925 Hollywood Blvd; tours & movie tickets adult/child/senior $13.50/6.50/11.50), where screen legends have left their imprints in cement: feet, hands, dreadlocks, and even magic wands. The exotic pagoda theater – complete with temple bells and stone heaven dogs from China – has shown movies since 1927.

Dolby Theatre

Real-life celebrities sashay along the red carpet of this **theater** (Map p278; www.dolbytheatre.com; 6801 Hollywood Blvd; tours adult/child, senior & student $19/15; ⊗10:30am-4pm) that hosts the Academy Awards.

TCL Chinese Theatre

IAN DAGNALL / ALAMY STOCK PHOTO ©

Pricey 30-minute tours take you inside the auditorium, VIP room and past an actual Oscar statuette.

Hollywood Forever Cemetery
Hollywood Forever (Map p278; ☑323-469-1181; www.hollywoodforever.com; 6000 Santa Monica Blvd; ☺8am-5pm; ℗) boasts lavish landscaping, over-the-top tombstones, epic mausoleums and a roll call of departed superstars. Rock-and-roll faithfuls flock to the graves of Johnny and Dee Dee Ramone at this historic boneyard, whose other famous residents include Rudolph Valentino, Cecil B DeMille and Jayne Mansfield. For a full list of residents, pick up a map ($5) at the flower shop (open from 9am to 5pm).

ℹ Need to Know
You can visit Hollywood Blvd by day, but it's richer at night, when the stars glitter.

✕ Take a Break
Thai Town, a small section of Hollywood Blvd that's packed with spicy kitchens, is a short drive east.

★ Top Tip
New stars hit the Walk of Fame once or twice monthly. Check the website for upcoming ceremonies.

Movie & TV Studios
Half the fun of visiting Hollywood is hoping you'll see stars. Up the odds by joining the studio audience of a sitcom or game show, which usually tape between August and March. For free tickets, contact **Audiences Unlimited** (☑818-260-0041; www.tvtickets. com). For an authentic behind-the-scenes look, take a shuttle tour at **Warner Bros Studios** (☑877-492-8687, 818-972-8687; www. wbstudiotour.com; 3400 W Riverside Dr, Burbank; tours from $54; ☺8:15am-4pm Mon-Sat, hours vary Sun) or **Paramount Pictures** (Map p278; ☑323-956-1777; www.paramountstudiotour. com; 5555 Melrose Ave; tours from $53; ☺tours 9:30am-2pm Mon-Fri, hours vary Sat & Sun), or a walking tour of **Sony Pictures Studios** (☑310-244-8687; www.sonypicturesstudios tours.com; 10202 W Washington Blvd; tour $38; ☺tours usually 9:30am, 10:30am, 1:30pm & 2:30pm Mon-Fri). Book ahead.

Hollywood Walk of Fame
Big Bird, Bob Hope, Marilyn Monroe and Aretha Franklin are among the stars along the **Hollywood Walk of Fame** (Map p278; www.walkoffame.com; Hollywood Blvd). Since 1960 more than 2400 performers have been honored with a pink-marble sidewalk star. The galaxy extends along Hollywood Blvd between La Brea Ave and Gower St, and along Vine St between Yucca St and Sunset Blvd.

Griffith Park

Even some locals don't know that LA's Griffith Park is five times the size of NYC's Central Park, making it one of the largest urban green spaces in the country. The park contains an outdoor theater, a zoo, an observatory, a museum, children's playgrounds, golf, tennis, and over 50 miles of hiking paths.

Great For...

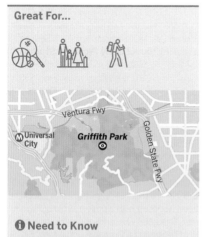

❶ Need to Know

Map p278; ☏323-913-4688; www.laparks. org/dos/parks/griffithpk; ☺5am-10:30pm, trails sunrise-sunset; P ⫯⫯ FREE

Griffith Observatory (p270)

★ **Top Tip**

Park access is easiest via the Griffith Park Dr or Zoo Dr exits off I-5 (Golden State Fwy). Parking is plentiful and free.

Griffith Observatory

The park's sparkling white art-deco centerpiece is Griffith Observatory (Map p278; ☏213-473-0800; www.griffithobservatory.org; 2800 E Observatory Rd; admission free, planetarium shows adult/child $7/3; ⏰noon-10pm Tue-Fri, from 10am Sat & Sun; P 🛜 ♿) FREE, on the slopes of Mt Hollywood. The city views from the terrace are unmatched (as long as it's not smoggy).

The public is welcome to peer into the Zeist Telescope on the east side of the roof where sweeping views of the Hollywood Hills and the gleaming city below are spectacular, especially at sunset. After dark, staff wheel additional telescopes out to the front lawn for stargazing.

You'll definitely want to grab a seat in the Planetarium – the aluminum-domed ceiling becomes a massive screen where lasers are projected to offer a tour of the cosmos, while another laser-projection show allows you to search for water, and life, beyond earth.

The observatory has starred in many movies, most famously *Rebel Without a Cause* with James Dean. Outside, have your picture snapped beside the actor's bust with the Hollywood sign caught neatly in the background. The carless can hop on the LADOT Observatory Shuttle (35 minutes, $.50) from the Red Line station on Vermont and Sunset Blvd.

Hollywood Sign

The Griffith Observatory is one of the best viewing spots for LA's most famous landmark. The **Hollywood sign** (Map p278) first appeared in the hills in 1923 as an advertising gimmick for a real-estate devel-

Griffith Observatory

opment called 'Hollywoodland.' Each letter is 50ft tall and made of sheet metal. Once aglow with 4000 light bulbs, the sign even had its own caretaker, who lived behind the 'L' until 1939.

The last four letters were lopped off in the '40s as the sign started to crumble. In the late '70s Alice Cooper and Hugh Hefner joined forces with fans to save the famous symbol, and Hef was back at it again in 2010 when the hills behind the sign became slated for a housing development. The venerable Playboy donated the last $900,000 of the necessary $12.5 million it took to buy and preserve the land.

★ Top Tip

For information and maps stop by the Griffith Park Ranger Station (Map p278; ☎ 323-665-5188; 4730 Crystal Springs Dr).

JOSEPH BRODERICK / EYEEM / GETTY IMAGES ©

For Kids

The richly festooned 1926 **Merry-Go-Round** (Map p278; www.laparks.org/DOS/parks/griffithPK/mgr.htm; Griffith Park center; rides $2; ⊙11am-5pm daily May-Sep, Sat & Sun Oct-Apr; 🚼) was brought to its current home in 1937. It has 68 carved and painted horses sporting real horsehair tails.

The **Griffith Park Southern Railroad** (Map p278; www.griffithparktrainrides.com/content/griffith-park-southern-railroad; 4400 Crystal Springs Dr; adult & child/senior $2.75/2.25; ⊙10am-4:15pm Mon-Fri, to 4:45pm Sat & Sun; P 🚼) has a fleet of miniature trains that have ferried generations of children around a 1-mile loop past pony rides, a Native American village and an old Western town since 1948.

Get to the Greek

A more intimate version of the Hollywood Bowl, the 5800-seat **Greek Theatre** (Map p278; ☎323-665-5857; www.greektheatrela.com; 2700 N Vermont Ave; ⊙May-Oct) is an outdoor amphitheater tucked into a woodsy hillside of Griffith Park. It is much beloved for its vibe and variety – Los Lobos to MGMT to Willie Nelson. Parking is stacked, so plan on a post-show wait.

LA Well Being

Mineral Wells (www.laparks.org; Griffith Park Dr; ⊙6am-dusk) is one of our favorite picnic spots in Griffith Park. If you've been looking for the real LA, you'll find it here.

✕ Take a Break

Get picnic fixings at the **Oaks Gourmet** (Map p278; ☎323-871-8894; www.theoaksgourmet.com; 1915 N Bronson Ave; mains $9-13; ⊙7am-midnight; P), a five-minute drive from the observatory.

☑ Don't Miss

Head to the observatory roof to peek through the telescopes housed in the smaller domes. Also here: sweeping Hollywood Hills views.

Walking Tour: Venice

Step into the Venice lifestyle and discover that there are more moments of Zen packed into this tiny beach community than in most other 'hoods combined.

Distance: 3.5 miles
Duration: 2 hours

✖ Take a Break

Put your feet up at one of the many cafés or restaurants along Abbot Kinney Blvd.

Start Ocean Front Walk and Washington Blvd; 🚌BBB 1

❶ South Venice Beach
South of the Venice Pier is the un-trammeled **beach** of South Venice.

❷ Venice Canals
Even many Angelenos have no idea that just a couple of blocks away from the boardwalk madness is an idyllic neighborhood that preserves 3 miles of **canals** of the late developer and tobacco mogul Abbot Kinney.

❸ Venice Boardwalk
The famed **Venice Boardwalk** (Venice Pier to Rose Ave; ⊙24hr), officially known as Ocean Front Walk, is a vortex for the loony, the free-spirited, the hip and athletic. Here are outdoor gyms, beach rentals, skate parks and drum circles.

❹ Muscle Beach
Gym rats with an exhibitionist streak can get a tan and a workout at this famous **outdoor gym** right on the Venice Boardwalk where Arnold once bulked up alfresco.

❺ Venice Beach Graffiti Park
Keep your camera at the ready as you approach the tagged-up towers and free-standing concrete wall of **Venice Beach Graffiti Park**, forever open to aerosol artists to curb vandalism.

Skateboarders, Venice Beach

KYLIE MCLAUGHLIN / GETTY IMAGES ©

⑥ Venice Beach Skate Park

Long the destination of local skate punks, the concrete at **Venice Beach Skate Park** has been molded and steel-fringed into 17,000 sq feet of vert, tranny and street terrain with unbroken ocean views.

⑦ Fig Tree's Café

If you're hungry already, **Fig Tree's Café** (www.figtreescafe.com; 429 Ocean Front Walk; ☺8am-8pm) serves the best eats on the Boardwalk.

⑧ Ballerina Clown & the Binoculars Buildings

On Main St are two of Venice's more capti-vating buildings. The **ballerina clown** rises like a twisted god/goddess from the corner of Main and Rose on an otherwise pedes-trian building. Across the street is Frank Gehry's eye-popping **Binoculars Building**.

⑨ Abbot Kinney Boulevard

Abbot Kinney, the man who dug the canals and christened the town, would probably be delighted to find the stretch of his namesake **boulevard** stacked with unique, individually owned boutiques, galleries and sensational restaurants.

Finish Abbot Kinney Blvd; 🚌MTA 33

◎ SIGHTS

◎ El Pueblo de Los Angeles

Compact, colorful and car-free, this historic district is an immersion in LA's Spanish-Mexican roots. Its spine is **Olvera Street**, a festive kitsch-o-rama where you can snap up handmade folkloric trinkets, then chomp on tacos or sugar-sprinkled churros.

La Plaza de Cultura y Artes   Museum

This museum chronicles the Mexican-American experience in Los Angeles, from the Mexican–American War when the border crossed the original pueblo, to the Zoot Suit Riots to Cesar Chavez and the Chicana movement. (Map p275; 📞213-542-6200; www.lapca.org; 501 N Main St; ⊘noon-5pm Mon, Wed & Thu, to 6pm Fri-Sun) FREE

◎ Grand Avenue Cultural Corridor

Walt Disney Concert Hall   Building

A molten blend of steel, music and psychedelic architecture, this iconic concert venue is the home base of the Los Angeles Philharmonic, but has also hosted contemporary bands such as Phoenix and classic jazz men like Sonny Rollins. Frank Gehry pulled out all the stops: the building is a gravity-defying sculpture of heaving and billowing stainless-steel. (Map p275; 📞info 213-972-7211, tickets 323-850-2000; www.laphil.org; 111 S Grand Ave; ⊘guided tours usually noon & 1pm Tue-Sat; P) FREE

Museum of Contemporary Art   Museum

A collection that arcs from the 1940s to the present and includes works by Mark Rothko, Dan Flavin, Joseph Cornell and other big-shot contemporary artists is housed in a postmodern building by Arata Isozaki. Galleries are below ground, yet skylit bright. (Map p275; MOCA; 📞213-626-6222; www.moca.org; 250 S Grand Ave; adult/child $12/free, 5-8pm Thu free; ⊘11am-5pm Mon & Fri, to 8pm Thu, to 6pm Sat & Sun)

◎ Little Tokyo

Little Tokyo swirls with shopping arcades, Buddhist temples, public art, traditional gardens, authentic sushi bars and noodle shops and a provocative branch of MOCA, **Geffen Contemporary at MOCA** (Map p275; 📞213-626-6222; www.moca.org; 152 N Central Ave; adult/student/child 12 yr & under $12/7/free; ⊘11am-5pm Mon & Fri, to 8pm Thu, to 6pm Sat & Sun).

Japanese American National Museum   Museum

A great first stop in Little Tokyo, this is the country's first museum dedicated to the Japanese immigrant experience. You'll be moved by galleries dealing with the painful chapter of the WWII internment camps. Afterward relax in the tranquil garden, and browse the well-stocked gift shop. Admission is free on Thursdays from 5pm to 8pm, and all day on the third Thursday of each month. (Map p275; 📞213-625-0414; www.janm.org; 100 N Central Ave; adult/child $9/5; ⊘11am-5pm Tue-Wed & Fri-Sun, noon-8pm Thu)

◎ South Park

South Park isn't actually a park but an emerging Downtown LA neighborhood around **LA Live** (Map p275; www.lalive.com; 800 W Olympic Blvd), a dining and entertainment hub.

Grammy Museum   Museum

It's the highlight of LA Live. Music lovers will get lost in interactive exhibits, which define, differentiate and link musical genres, while live footage strobes. You can glimpse such things as GnR's bass drum, Lester Young's tenor, Yo Yo Ma's cello and Michael's glove (though exhibits and collections do rotatparame). (Map p275; 📞213-765-6800; www.grammymuseum.org; 800 W Olympic Blvd; adult/child $13/11, after 6pm $8; ⊘11:30am-7:30pm Mon-Fri, from 10am Sat & Sun; 👪)

◎ Exposition Park & Around

Just south of the University of Southern California (USC) campus, this park has a full day's worth of kid-friendly museums. Outdoor landmarks include the **Rose**

Downtown Los Angeles

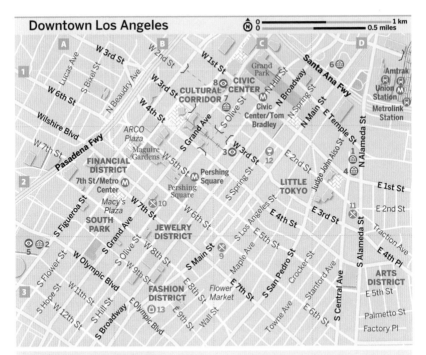

Downtown Los Angeles

⊙ Sights
1 Geffen Contemporary at MOCA D2
2 Grammy Museum A3
3 Grand Central Market C2
4 Japanese American National
    Museum D2
5 LA Live A3
6 La Plaza de Cultura y Artes D1
7 Museum of Contemporary Art C1
8 Walt Disney Concert Hall C1

⊗ Eating
9 Cole's C3
10 Q Sushi B2
11 Sushi Gen D2

⊖ Drinking & Nightlife
12 Edison C2

⊕ Shopping
13 Fashion District B3

Garden (www.laparks.org; 701 State Dr;
🕑9am-sunset Mar 16-Dec 31) FREE and the
1923 **Los Angeles Memorial Coliseum**
(www.lacoliseum.com; 3939 S Figueroa St),
site of the 1932 and 1984 Summer Olympic Games.

Natural History Museum
of Los Angeles   Museum
From dinos to diamonds, bears to beetles,
hissing roaches to African elephants –
this museum will take you around the
world and back, across millions of years
in time. It's all housed in a beautiful 1913

Spanish Renaissance-style building that
stood in for Columbia University in the
first Tobey Maguire *Spider-Man* movie – yup, this was where Peter Parker
was bitten by the radioactive arach-
nid. (📞213-763-3466; www.nhm.org; 900
Exposition Blvd; adult/student & senior/child
$12/9/5; 🕑9:30am-5pm; 👪)

California Science Center   Museum
A simulated earthquake, baby chicks
hatching and a giant techno-doll named
Tess bring out the kid in all of us at this
multimedia museum with plenty of buttons

Los Angeles for Kids

Keeping kids happy is child's play in LA. The sprawling **Los Angeles Zoo** (☏323-644-4200; www.lazoo.org; 5333 Zoo Dr; adult/senior/child $18/15/13; ⏰10am-5pm, closed Christmas; [P][🚻]) in family-friendly Griffith Park (p276) is a sure bet. Or cycle around the park; the **Bike-rental Concession** (Map p278; ☏323-662-6573; www.laparks.org; bikes per hour/day $8/25; ⏰2-6pm Mon-Fri, 10:30am-dusk Sat & Sun) is adjacent to the Crystal Springs picnic area. Dino-fans will dig the La Brea Tar Pits (p276) and the Natural History Museum (p275), while budding scientists crowd the **Griffith Observatory** (p270) and California Science Center (p275). For under-the-sea creatures, head to the **Aquarium of the Pacific** (☏tickets 562-590-3100; www.aquariumofpacific.org; 100 Aquarium Way, Long Beach; adult/senior/child $29/26/15; ⏰9am-6pm; [🚻]) in Long Beach. The amusement park at Santa Monica Pier (p276) is fun for all ages. Activities for younger kids are more limited at tween/teen-oriented **Universal Studios Hollywood** (www.universalstudioshollywood.com; 100 Universal City Plaza, Universal City; admission from $87, under 3yr free; ⏰open daily, hours vary; [P][🚻]). In neighboring Orange County, **Disneyland** (☏714-781-4565; disneyland.disney.go.com; 1313 Disneyland Dr; adult/child $99/93, 1-day pass to both parks $155/149; [🚻]) has two ever-popular theme parks.

Collared lories at Los Angeles Zoo
GARY VESTAL / GETTY IMAGES ©

to push, lights to switch on and knobs to pull. Don't miss seeing the space shuttle *Endeavour,* which requires a timed-ticket reservation ($2). (☏film schedule 213-744-2109, general info 323-724-3623; www.californiasciencecenter.org; 700 Exposition Park Dr; IMAX movie adult/child $8.25/5; ⏰10am-5pm; [🚻])
FREE

◉ Mid-City

Some of LA's best museums line 'Museum Row,' a short stretch of Wilshire Blvd east of Fairfax Ave.

Los Angeles County Museum of Art
Museum

LA's premier art museum, LACMA's galleries are stuffed with all the major players – Rembrandt, Cézanne, Magritte, Mary Cassatt and Ansel Adams, to name a few – plus several millennia worth of ceramics from China, woodblock prints from Japan, pre-Columbian art, and ancient sculpture from Greece, Rome and Egypt. (Map p278; LACMA; ☏323-857-6000; www.lacma.org; 5905 Wilshire Blvd; adult/child $15/free; ⏰11am-5pm Mon, Tue & Thu, to 9pm Fri, 10am-7pm Sat & Sun; [P])

Page Museum & La Brea Tar Pits
Museum

Mammoths and saber-toothed cats used to roam LA's savannah in prehistoric times. We know this because of an archaeological trove of skulls and bones unearthed at La Brea Tar Pits, one of the world's most fecund and famous fossil sites. (Map p278; www.tarpits.org; 5801 Wilshire Blvd; adult/child/student & senior $12/5/9, 1st Tue of month Sep-Jun free; ⏰9:30am-5pm; [P][🚻])

◉ Beverly Hills & West LA

No trip to LA would be complete without a saunter along pricey, pretentious **Rodeo Drive**, a three-block ribbon where sample-size fembots browse for fashions from international houses – from Armani to Zegna – in couture-design stores.

Getty Center
Museum

In its billion-dollar, in-the-clouds perch, high above the city grit and grime, the Getty

Center presents triple delights: a stellar art collection (everything from renaissance artists to David Hockney), Richard Meier's cutting-edge architecture, and the visual splendor of seasonally changing gardens. (310-440-7300; www.getty.edu; 1200 Getty Center Dr, off I-405 Fwy; 10am-5:30pm Tue-Fri & Sun, to 9pm Sat; P) FREE

Santa Monica

The belle by the beach mixes urban cool with a laid-back vibe. Tourists, teens and street performers throng car-free, chainstore-lined **Third Street Promenade**. For more local flavor, shop posh **Montana Avenue** or eclectic **Main Street**, backbone of the neighborhood once nicknamed 'Dogtown,' the birthplace of skateboard culture.

ACTIVITIES

CYCLING & IN-LINE SKATING

Get scenic exercise in-line skating or pedaling along the paved **South Bay Bicycle Trail**, which parallels the beach for most of the 22 miles between Santa Monica and Pacific Palisades. Rental outfits are plentiful in busier beach towns. Warning: it's crowded on weekends.

HIKING

Turn on your celeb radar while strutting it with the hot bods along Runyon Canyon Park above Hollywood. Griffith Park is also laced with trails.

SWIMMING & SURFING

Top beaches for swimming are Malibu's **Leo Carrillo State Park**, **Santa Monica State Beach** and the South Bay's **Hermosa Beach**. Malibu's **Surfrider Beach** is a legendary surfing spot. Beach parking rates vary seasonally.

'Endless summer' is, sorry to report, a myth; much of the year you'll want a wet suit in the Pacific. Water temperatures become tolerable by June and peak just under 70°F (21°C) in August. Water quality varies; check the 'Beach Report Card' at http://brc.healthebay.org.

> *the visual splendour of seasonally changing gardens*

Getty Center

P. EOCHE / GETTY IMAGES ©

Hollywood & Griffith Park

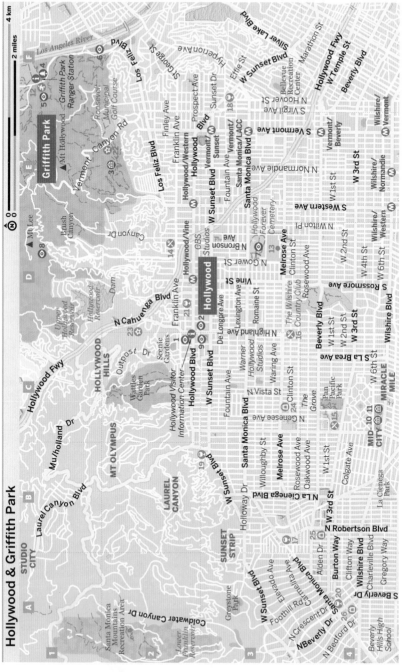

Hollywood & Griffith Park

◎ **Sights**
1 Dolby Theatre.. C2
2 Egyptian Theatre D3
3 Griffith Observatory E2
4 Griffith Park F1
5 Griffith Park Merry-Go-Round F1
6 Griffith Park Southern Railroad.................F1
7 Hollywood Forever Cemetery D3
8 Hollywood Sign D1
9 Hollywood Walk of Fame C3
10 Los Angeles County Museum of Art C4
11 Page Museum & La Brea Tar Pits............. C4
TCL Chinese Theatre ....(see 1)

◉ **Activities, Courses & Tours**
12 Bike-rental Concession...............................F1
13 Paramount Pictures D3
TMZ Tours ....(see 1)

◉ **Eating**
14 Oaks Gourmet.. D2

15 Original Farmers Market........................... C4
16 Pizzeria & Osteria Mozza C3
Ray's ....(see 10)

◉ **Drinking & Nightlife**
17 Abbey... B3
18 Akbar..F3
19 Bar Marmont B3
20 Nic's Beverly Hills...................................... A4
21 No Vacancy... D2

◉ **Entertainment**
American Cinematheque..................(see 2)
22 Greek Theatre... E2
23 Hollywood Bowl.. D2

◉ **Shopping**
24 Melrose Avenue.. C3
25 Robertson Boulevard................................. B4
26 Rodeo Drive A4

🔒 SHOPPING

Although Beverly Hills' Rodeo Drive is the most iconic shopping strip in LA, the city abounds with other options for retail therapy. Fashionistas and their paparazzi piranhas flock to Mid-City's Robertson Blvd. You also might spot celebs shopping on nearby 3rd St. Unusual and unique local boutiques line Main St in Santa Monica, Venice's Abbot Kinney Blvd and Sunset Blvd in Silver Lake.

Rodeo Drive   Shopping
The city's most famous shopping street, spanning three glittery blocks in Beverly Hills. If browsing for fashions from international houses of couture is simply too exhausting, take a break on Via Rodeo. It's a cobbled lane lined with outdoor cafés that's perfect for people-watching. (Map p278; btwn Wilshire & Santa Monica Blvds)

Robertson Boulevard   Fashion
Fashionistas, and their paparazzi piranhas, flock to this spot near Beverly Hills. If sassy, ultrachic clothing's your thing, you'll head here, too. Robertson Boulevard is also a

good spot for celebrity spotting. (Map p278; btwn Beverly Blvd & 3rd St)

Melrose Avenue   Fashion
A popular shopping strip as famous for its epic people-watching as it is for its consumer fruits. You'll see hair (and people) of all shades and styles, and everything from gothic jewels to custom sneakers to medical marijuana to stuffed porcupines available – for a price. The strip is located between Fairfax and La Brea Aves. (Map p278)

Fashion District   Fashion
Bargain hunters with couture taste head to this 90-block nirvana in Downtown LA. Bounded by Main and Wall Sts and 7th St and Pico Blvd, the district's prices prices are lowest in bazaar-like Santee Alley, but the styles are grooviest in the Gerry Building and Cooper Design Space. (Map p275; www.fashiondistrict.org)

⭐ ENTERTAINMENT

For discounted and half-price tickets, check **Goldstar** (www.goldstar.com) or **LA Stage**

From left: Sushi at Q Sushi (p282); Grand Central Market; Stall at Original Farmers Market

MEL MELCON / GETTY IMAGES ©

P. EOCHE / GETTY IMAGES ©

Tix (www.lastagetix.com), the latter strictly for theater.

Hollywood Bowl   Concert Venue
Summers in LA just wouldn't be the same without this chill spot for music under the stars, from symphonies to big-name acts such as Baaba Maal, Sigur Ros, Radiohead and Paul McCartney. A huge natural amphitheater, the Hollywood Bowl has been around since 1922 and has great sound. (Map p278; ☑323-850-2000; www.hollywood bowl.com; 2301 N Highland Ave; rehearsals free, performance costs vary; ☺Jun-Sep)

Dodger Stadium   Baseball
Few clubs can match the Dodgers when it comes to history (Jackie Robinson, Sandy Koufax, Kirk Gibson and Vin Scully), success and fan loyalty. The club's newest owners bought the organization for roughly two billion dollars, an American team sports record. (☑866-363-4377; www. dodgers.com; 1000 Elysian Park Ave; ☺Apr-Sep)

American Cinematheque   Cinema
A nonprofit screening tributes, retrospectives and foreign films in the **Egyptian**

Theatre (Map p278; www.egyptiantheatre.com; 6712 Hollywood Blvd). Directors, screenwriters and actors often swing by for post-show Q&As. (Map p278; www.americancinematheque. com; 6712 Hollywood Blvd; adult/senior & student $11/9)

TMZ Tours   Bus Tour
Cut the shame. If you really want to spot celebrities, glimpse their homes, and gawk and laugh at their dirt, then join this branded tour imagined by the paparazzi made famous. Tours are two hours long, and you will likely meet some of the TMZ stars and perhaps even celebrity guests on the bus. (Map p278; ☑855-486-9868; www.tmz.com/ tour; 6925 Hollywood Blvd; adult/child $59/49; ☺approximately 10 tours daily)

🍴 EATING
LA's culinary scene is California's most eclectic, from celebrity chefs whipping up farmers-market menus to authentic global cuisine.

For cheap, fast meals-on-the-go, graze the international food stalls of the historic **Grand Central Market** (Map p275; www.

grandcentralmarket.com; 317 S Broadway;
🕙8am-6pm Sun-Wed, to 9pm Thu-Sat).

Original Farmers Market   Market $

The Farmers Market is a great spot for a
casual meal any time of day, especially
if the rug rats are tagging along. There
are lots of options here, from gumbo to
Singapore-style noodles to tacos. (Map p278;
www.farmersmarketla.com; 6333 W 3rd St; mains
$6-12; 🕙9am-9pm Mon-Fri, to 8pm Sat, 10am-
7pm Sun; P 🚼)

Lemonade   Californian $

The first incarnation of an imaginative, local
market café with a line-up of tasty salads
(watermelon radish and chili or tamarind
pork and spicy carrots), and stockpots
bubbling with lamb and stewed figs or
miso-braised short ribs. It has six kinds of
lemonade augmented with blueberries and
mint or watermelon and rosemary. Yummy
sweets too. (http://lemonadela.com; 1661 Abbot
Kinney Blvd; meals $8-13; 🕙11am-9pm)

Cole's   Sandwiches $

A funky old basement tavern known for
originating the French Dip sandwich way

back in 1908, when those things cost a
nickel. You know the drill – french bread
piled with sliced lamb, beef, turkey, pork or
pastrami, dipped once or twice in *au jus*.
(Map p275; www.213nightlife.com/colesfrench
dip; 118 E 6th St; sandwiches $6-9; 🕙11am-10pm
Sun-Wed, to midnight Thu, to 1am Fri & Sat)

Sushi Gen   Japanese $$

Come early to grab a table, and know that
they don't do the uber-creative 'look at me'
kind of rolls. In this Japanese classic sushi
spot, seven chefs stand behind the blonde
wood bar, carving thick slabs of melt-in-
your-mouth salmon, buttery toro and a
wonderful Japanese snapper, among other
staples. Their sashimi special at lunch
($18) is a steal. It's set in the Honda Plaza.
(Map p275; 📞213-617-0552; www.sushigen.org;
422 E 2nd St; sushi $11-21; 🕙11:15am-2pm &
5:30-9:45pm)

Fishing with Dynamite   Seafood $$

You'll love this place for their oysters and
raw bar, the miso black cod, the serrano
scallops seared and garnished with uni, and
for their fried oyster po'boy, which is soul
stirring. The menu is constantly rotating,

but trust us, if you like binge eating on fine seafood, starve yourself for a day, then come here. (☏310-893-6299; www.eatfwd.com; 1148 Manhattan Ave; oysters from $2.25, dishes $9-19; ⊘11:30am-10pm Sun-Wed, to 10:30pm Thu-Sat)

Phoenicia   Lebanese $$
OK, the design lacks charm, but this is where local Lebanese and Armenian families land on Sunday nights for homeland delicacies such as *soujouk* (a spicy Armenian beef sausage, dried, sliced and sautéed with onion and tomato), *maanek* (Lebanese beef sausage with a lemon glaze), *lessanat* (lamb tongue sliced thin) and *nekhat* (lamb brains cooked in olive oil, lemon juice and garlic, served cold). (☏818-956-7800; www.phoeniciala.com; 343 N Central Ave, Glendale; appetizers $5-8, meals $11-23; ⊘11:30am-11pm Sun-Thu, to midnight Fri & Sat)

Abigaile   Pub Food $$
Hermosa's gastropub dux. Sandwiches include the 'dirty bird' – a fried chicken number garnished with pickles and maple syrup. It gets healthy with *pho* and soba noodles, and goes all out at breakfast too. One wall is tagged with anarchy, the bar is stainless steel and there's ample seating at wooden tables scattered throughout the hardwood interior and on a sunny patio. (☏310-798-8227; www.abigailerestaurant.com; 1301 Manhattan Ave; mains $10-30; ⊘5pm-late Mon-Fri, from 11am Sat & Sun)

Yakitoriya   Japanese $$
Simple and real, this chef-owned and family-operated *yakitori* (Japanese grilled chicken) joint crafts the most tender and savory grilled-chicken skewers you can imagine. We love the wings, neck, chicken skin, meatballs and the minced chicken bowl topped with quail egg. (☏310-479-5400; 11301 W Olympic Blvd; dishes $2.50-27; ⊘6-10:30pm Mon & Wed-Sun; ♿)

Q Sushi   Sushi $$$
A slender wedge of exquisite sushi. This stunning dark and blonde wood sushi bar is all *omakase* (chef's selections) all the time. At dinner there will be 20 courses (lunch about half that) all created by Japanese sushi savant Hiro Naruke, who lost his business in the 2011 tsunami aftermath. Two LA lawyers, who've done business in Tokyo for years and have always loved his

Phoenicia

food, bankrolled his move. (Map p275; ☎213-225-6285; www.qsushila.com; 521 W 7th St; per person lunch/dinner $75/165)

Ray's   Modern American $$$

They change the menu twice daily, but if they offer it, order the shrimp and grits: it's rich and buttery, with chunks of andouille sausage, okra and two king prawns. Their burrata melts with tang, the yellow-tail collar is crisp and moist, and the bacon-wrapped rabbit sausage will wow you. (Map p278; ☎323-857-6180; www.raysandstarkbar.com; 5905 Wilshire Blvd; dishes $11-27; ⊙11:30am-3pm & 5-10pm Mon-Fri, from 10am Sat & Sun; P; ▣MTA 20)

Waterloo & City   Gastropub $$$

At the forefront of LA's gastropub movement, Waterloo & City remains one of the city's best – if not the undisputed champ – thanks to pork shank ravioli served with grilled apples, grilled octopus, shishito peppers and squid-ink aioli, and a beef Wellington that will make you cry tears of joy. The sticky toffee pudding is a must. (☎310-391-4222; www.waterlooandcity.com; 12517 Washington Blvd; small plates $12-15, mains $20-29; ⊙5-11pm Sun & Mon, to midnight Tue-Thu, to 1am Fri & Sat)

Pizzeria & Osteria Mozza   Italian $$$

Osteria Mozza is all about fine cuisine crafted from market fresh, seasonal ingredients; but being a Mario Batali joint, you can expect adventure (squid-ink chitarra freddi with Dungeness crab, sea urchin and jalapeño) and consistent excellence. Reservations are recommended. (Map p278; ☎323-297-0100; www.mozza-la.com; 6602 Melrose Ave; pizzas $11-19, dinner mains $27-38; ⊙pizzeria noon-midnight daily, osteria 5:30-11pm Mon-Fri, 5-11pm Sat, 5-10pm Sun)

🍷 DRINKING & NIGHTLIFE

Hollywood has been legendary sipping territory since before the Rat Pack days. Creative cocktails are the order of the day at reinvented watering holes in Downtown LA and edgier neighborhoods. Beachside

⚧ LGBT Los Angeles

'Boystown,' along Santa Monica Blvd in West Hollywood (WeHo), is gay ground zero, with dozens of high-energy bars, cafés, restaurants, gyms and clubs. The diverse, multiethnic crowd in Silver Lake is all-inclusive, from leather-and-Levi's bars to hipster haunts.

Out & About (www.outandabout-tours.com) Leads weekend walking tours of the city's lesbi-gay cultural landmarks. The festival season kicks off in May with Long Beach Pride (http://longbeach-pride.com) and continues with WeHo's LA Pride (http://lapride.org) in June.

Abbey (Map p278; www.abbeyfoodandbar.com; 692 N Robertson Blvd; mains $9-13; ⊙11am-2am Mon-Thu, from 10am Fri, from 9am Sat & Sun) At WeHo's essential gay bar and restaurant, take your pick of preening on an outdoor patio, in a chill lounge or on the dancefloor, and enjoy flavored martinis. A dozen other bars and nightclubs are a short stumble away.

Akbar (Map p278; www.akbarsilverlake.com; 4356 W Sunset Blvd; ⊙4pm-2am) A killer jukebox, casbah-style atmosphere and a Silver Lake crowd that's been known to change from hour to hour – gay, straight or just hip, but not too-hip-for-you.

Gay Pride Parade, Santa Monica Blvd

bars run the gamut from surfer dives to candlelit cocktail lounges.

From left: Fuego; Bar Marmont; Basement Tavern

To confirm all of your preconceived prejudices about LA, look no further than a velvet-roped nightclub in Hollywood. Come armed with a hot bod or a fat wallet to impress the bouncers.

Federal Bar
Bar

This converted, historic bank with its weighty granite bar, crystal chandeliers, and burly wooden columns offers craft beers and booze behind the bar. They also have a venue downstairs where they host DJs and local bands, including nationally known stand-outs like Dengue Fever. (www.lb.thefederalbar.com; 102 Pine Ave, Long Beach; ⏰11:30am-11pm)

Fuego
Tequila Bar

Fuego is the place to be for Sunday brunch, Happy Hour or whenever you're thirsty. Here are 30-plus tequila labels, seven fire-pits and cushioned Balinese day beds on the tiki-themed patio. Then there's sweet, funny, old-school Linda. She's usually got a story and is always pouring something promising. (www.fuegolongbeach.com; 700 Queens Way, Long Beach; ⏰10am-11pm Mon-Thu, to 1am Fri-Sun)

Bar Marmont
Bar

Elegant, but not stuck up; been around, yet still cherished. With high ceilings, molded walls and terrific martinis, the famous, and wish-they-weres, still flock here. If you time it right you might see Tom Yorke, or perhaps Lindsay Lohan? Come midweek. Weekends are for amateurs. (Map p278; ☏323-650-0575; www.chateaumarmont.com/barmarmont.php; 8171 Sunset Blvd; ⏰6pm-2am)

Stronghold
Speakeasy

The Stronghold had a brief life as a killer newschool speakeasy set in a loft above the Stronghold leather shop. It was famous for a consistent line-up of some of LA's best local musicians trying out their new material between gigs. Sadly, The Man shut them down, so now it's taken its ethos on the road, and is promoting the same kind of gigs at venues in Venice, the Marina and beyond. Check its Facebook page for details. (www.facebook.com/the stronghold; 1625 Abbot Kinney Blvd; ⏰varies)

Basement Tavern
Bar

A creative speakeasy, housed in the basement of the Victorian, and our favorite well

in Santa Monica. We love it for the craftsman cocktails, cozy booths, island bar and nightly live-music calendar that features blues, jazz, bluegrass and rock bands. It gets way too busy on weekends for our taste, but week-nights can be special. (www.basementtavern. com; 2640 Main St; ☺5pm-2am)

No Vacancy   Bar

An old, shingled Victorian has been con-verted into LA's hottest night out. Even the entrance is theatrical: you'll follow a rickety staircase into a narrow hall and enter the room of a would-be madame, dressed in fishnet and hospitality who will soon press a button to reveal another staircase down into the living room and out into a court-yard. (Map p278; ☎323-465-1902; www.no vacancyla.com; 1727 N Hudson Ave; ☺8pm-2am)

Mermaid   Dive Bar

The bad old granddad of the Hermosa strand, this divey classic with black-vinyl booths and a circle bar patrolled by grizzled vets who make a mean martini, is the perfect antidote to the varying degrees of fromage found beyond its grimy windows,

which do open on occasion to reveal ocean views. (☎310-374-9344; 11 Pier Ave; ☺10am-10:30pm)

Nic's Beverly Hills   Bar

Martinis for every palate lure the cocktail crowd to upscale, but fun-loving, Nic's, the only decent watering hole in all of Beverly Hills, where the libations and crowd range from the colorful and sassy to the no-frills and classy. (Map p278; ☎310-550-5707; www.nicsbeverlyhills.com; 453 N Canon Dr; ☺4pm-midnight Mon-Wed, to 2am Thu-Sat)

Edison   Bar

Metropolis meets *Blade Runner* at this industrial-chic basement boîte where you'll be sipping mojitos surrounded by turbines and other machinery back from its days as a boiler room. Don't worry, it's all tarted up nicely with cocoa leather couches and three cavernous bars. No athletic wear, flip-flops or baggy jeans tolerated. (Map p275; ☎213-613-0000; www.edisondowntown.com; 108 W 2nd St, off Harlem Pl; ☺5pm-2am Wed-Fri, from 7pm Sat)

Orange County Beaches

If you've seen *The OC* or *Real Housewives*, you may think you already know what to expect from this giant quilt of suburbia connecting LA and San Diego, lolling beside 42 miles of glorious coastline. In reality, Hummer-driving hunks and Botoxed beauties mix it up with hang-loose surfers and beatnik artists to give each of Orange County's beach towns a distinct vibe.

Just across the LA–OC county line, old-fashioned **Seal Beach** is refreshingly noncommercial, with a quaint walkable downtown. Less than 10 miles further south along the Pacific Coast Hwy (Hwy 1), **Huntington Beach** – aka 'Surf City, USA' – epitomizes SoCal's surfing lifestyle. Fish tacos and happy-hour specials abound at bars and cafés along downtown HB's Main St, not far from a shortboard-sized **surfing museum** (www.surfingmuseum.org).

Next up is the ritziest of the OC's beach communities: yacht-filled **Newport Beach**. Families and teens steer toward Balboa Peninsula for its beaches, vintage wooden pier and quaint amusement center. From nearby the 1906 Balboa Pavilion, **Balboa Island Ferry** (www.balboaislandferry.com) shuttles across the bay to Balboa Island for strolls past historic beach cottages and boutiques along Marine Ave.

Continuing south, Hwy 1 zooms past the wild beaches of **Crystal Cove State Park** (www.parks.ca.gov; 8471 N Coast Hwy) before winding downhill into **Laguna Beach**, the OC's most cultured seaside community. There, secluded beaches, glassy waves and eucalyptus-covered hillsides create a Riviera-like feel.

Another 10 miles south, detour inland to **Mission San Juan Capistrano** (www.missionsjc.com), one of California's most beautifully restored Spanish colonial missions, with flowering gardens and a fountain courtyard.

ℹ INFORMATION

VISITOR CENTERS

Hollywood Visitor Information Center
(Map p278; ☎ 323-467-6412; http://discoverlosangeles.com; Hollywood & Highland complex, 6801 Hollywood Blvd, Hollywood; ☺ 10am-10pm Mon-Sat, to 7pm Sun) In the Dolby Theatre walkway.

Santa Monica Visitor Information Center (☎ 800-544-5319; www.santamonica.com; 2427 Main St, Santa Monica) Roving information officers patrol the promenade on Segways!

WHERE TO STAY

For seaside life, base yourself in Santa Monica or Venice. Cool-hunters and party people will be happiest in Hollywood or WeHo; culture vultures, in Downtown LA.

ℹ GETTING THERE & AROUND

LA's gateway hub is Los Angeles International Airport (p369), the USA's second busiest airport. Door-to-door shared-ride vans operated by **Prime Time** (☎ 800-733-8267; www.primetimeshuttle.com) and **Super Shuttle** (☎ 800-258-3826; www.supershuttle.com) leave from the lower level of LAX terminals. Destinations include Santa Monica ($21), Hollywood ($27) and Downtown LA ($16). Curbside dispatchers summon taxis at LAX. A flat fare applies to Downtown LA ($46.50). Otherwise, metered fares (including $4 airport surcharge) average $30 to $35 to Santa Monica or $50 to Hollywood, plus tip.

Long-distance Amtrak trains roll into Downtown LA's historic **Union Station** (☎ 800-872-7245; www.amtrak.com; 800 N Alameda St).

Greyhound's **main bus terminal** (☎ 213-629-8401; www.greyhound.com; 1716 E 7th St) is in an unsavory part of Downtown LA, so avoid arriving after dark.

Right: Surfers, Huntington Beach
MATTHEW MICAH WRIGHT / GETTY IMAGES ©

Golden Gate Bridge (292)

SAN FRANCISCO

San Francisco

Psychedelic drugs, newfangled technology, gay liberation, green ventures, free speech and culinary experimentation all became mainstream long ago in San Francisco. Good times and social revolutions have often started here, from manic gold rushes to blissful hippie be-ins. Grab your coat and a handful of glitter, and enter the land of fog and fabulousness. So long, inhibitions; hello, San Francisco.

If California is one grand, sweeping gesture, a long arm cradling the Pacific, then San Francisco – that seven-by-seven-mile peninsula – is a forefinger pointing upward. Take this as a hint to look up: you'll notice San Francisco's crooked Victorian rooflines, wind-sculpted treetops and fog tumbling over the Golden Gate Bridge.

☑ In This Section

Golden Gate Bridge 292
Cable Cars 294
Alcatraz 296
Ferry Building 300
Chinatown 302
Sights 304
Tours 309
Shopping 310
Entertainment 311
Eating 313
Drinking & Nightlife 316

ℹ Arriving in San Francisco

San Francisco Airport (SFO) Fast, 30-minute rides to Downtown on BART cost $8.65; door-to-door shuttle vans cost $17 to $20; express bus fare to the Temporary Transbay Bus Terminal is $5; taxis cost $40 to $55.

Oakland International Airport (OAK) Catch BART from the airport to Downtown ($10.05, every 10 to 20 minutes, 25 minutes to center) or take a shared van for $30 to $40. A taxi to SF destinations is $60 to $75.

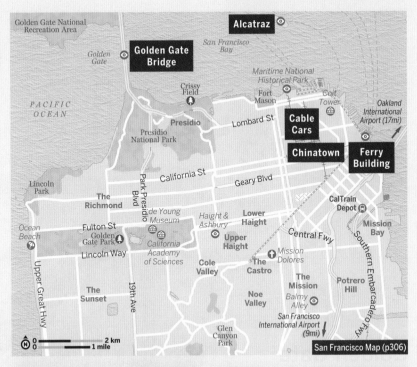

Golden Gate National Recreation Area

Alcatraz ◉

Golden Gate Bridge

Golden Gate ◉

San Francisco Bay

PACIFIC OCEAN

Maritime National Historical Park

Crissy Field ◉

Fort Mason ◉

Colt Tower 🏛

Cable Cars

Oakland International Airport (17mi)

Lombard St

Presidio

Presidio National Park

Chinatown

Ferry Building

Lincoln Park

The Richmond

California St

Park Presidio Blvd

de Young Museum 🏛

Geary Blvd

CalTrain Depot 🚉

Ocean Beach ◉

Fulton St

Golden Gate Park ◉

California Academy of Sciences

Haight & Ashbury

Upper Haight ◉

Lower Haight

Central Fwy

Mission Bay

Lincoln Way

Southern Embarcadero Fwy

Upper Great Hwy

The Sunset

19th Ave

Cole Valley

The Castro

Mission Dolores 🏛

The Mission

Potrero Hill

Noe Valley

Balmy Alley ◉

San Francisco International Airport (9mi) ↓

Glen Canyon Park

Ⓝ ⊙ 0 ___ 2 km
⊙ 0 ___ 1 mile

San Francisco Map (p306)

◗ San Francisco in Two Days

On day one, hop aboard the Powell-Mason cable car and hold on for hills and thrills. Have lunch in the **Ferry Building** (p300), then catch your pre-booked ferry to spooky **Alcatraz** (p296). On day two, get the camera ready for **Golden Gate Bridge** (p292) vistas. Make a trip across the spanner, or visit **Golden Gate Park** (p309) for views from **de Young Museum** (p309).

◗ San Francisco in Four Days

Start day three in Chinatown (p302). Hit Fisherman's Wharf in the afternoon; take the **Powell-Hyde cable car** (p295) past zigzagging **Lombard Street** (p305) to **Maritime National Historical Park** (p305). Begin day four ogling **Balmy Alley** (p308) in the Mission. Explore the hippie-historic **Haight** (p309), and end the evening at the **Castro Theatre** (p312).

From left: Cable car (p294); San Francisco Airport; Golden Gate Park (p309); Castro Theatre (p312)

PHOTO BY MIKE SHAW / GETTY IMAGES ©

Golden Gate Bridge

Other suspension bridges impress with engineering, but none can touch the Golden Gate Bridge for showmanship. Romantics and photographers rejoice over its magical scenery. When afternoon fog rolls in, the bridge performs its disappearing act: now you see it, now you don't and, abracadabra, it's sawn in half. Return the next morning for its dramatic unveiling.

Great For...

☑ Don't Miss

Fort Point for fab bridge vistas with the bonus of intriguing Civil War displays.

Construction

San Francisco's famous suspension bridge was almost nixed by the navy in favor of concrete pylons and yellow stripes. Joseph B Strauss rightly receives praise as the engineering mastermind behind this iconic marvel, but without the aesthetic intervention of architects Gertrude and Irving Morrow and incredibly quick work by daredevil workers, this 1937 landmark might have been just another traffic bottleneck.

International Orange

On sunny days it transfixes crowds with its radiant glow – thanks to 25 daredevil painters, who reapply 1000 gallons of International Orange paint weekly.

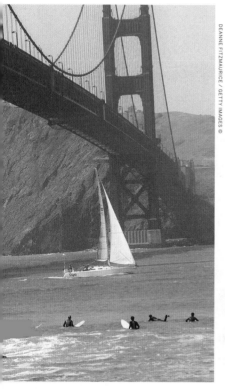

DEANNE FITZMAURICE / GETTY IMAGES ©

PACIFIC OCEAN

ⓞ **Golden Gate Bridge**

101

ⓘ Need to Know

www.goldengatebridge.org/visitors; off Lincoln Blvd; northbound free, southbound toll $6, billed electronically to vehicle's license plate; for details, see www.goldengate.org/tolls; 🚌28, all Golden Gate Transit buses

✕ Take a Break

Stop by the **Warming Hut** (983 Marine Dr, Presidio; ⊙9am-5pm) for fair-trade coffee and pastries.

★ Top Tip

Dress warmly before crossing the bridge, with a water-resistant outer layer to break the fog.

Views of the Bridge

As far as best views go, cinema buffs believe Hitchcock had it right: seen from below at **Fort Point**, the bridge induces a thrilling case of *Vertigo*. Fog aficionados prefer the north-end lookout at **Marin's Vista Point**, to watch gusts billow through bridge cables like dry ice at a Kiss concert.

To see both sides of the debate, hike or bike the 1.7-mile span. MUNI bus 28 runs to the parking lot, and pedestrians and cyclists can cross the bridge on sidewalks.

Crossing the Bridge

Walking or cycling across the Golden Gate Bridge to Sausalito is a fun way to avoid traffic, get some great ocean views and bask in that refreshing Marin County air. It's a fairly easy journey, mostly flat or downhill when heading north from San Francisco (cycling back to the city involves one big climb out of Sausalito). You can also simply hop on a ferry back to SF.

The trip is about 4 miles from the south end of the bridge and takes less than an hour. Pedestrians have access to the bridge's east walkway between 5am and 9pm daily (until 6pm in winter). Cyclists generally use the west side, except on weekdays between 5am and 3:30pm, when they must share the east side with pedestrians (who have the right-of-way). After 9pm (6pm in winter), cyclists can still cross the bridge on the east side through a security gate. Check the bridge **website** (www.goldengatebridge.org/bikesbridge/bikes.php) for changes.

More information is available at the websites of the **San Francisco Bicycle Coalition** (www.sfbike.org) and the **Marin County Bicycle Coalition** (www.marinbike.org).

DAVID CLAPP / GETTY IMAGES ©

Cable Cars

A creaking hand brake seems to be the only thing between you and cruel fate as your 15,000-pound cable car picks up speed downhill, careening toward oncoming traffic.

Great For...

☑ Don't Miss

The view of twisty Lombard St on the Powell-Hyde line.

Vintage Public Transport

Andrew Hallidie's 1873 contraptions have held up miraculously well on San Francisco's giddy slopes, and groaning brakes and clanging brass bells only add to the carnival-ride thrills.

Novices slide into strangers' laps, but regulars just grip the leather hand-straps, lean back, and ride downhill slides like pro surfers. Follow their lead and you'll soon master the San Francisco stance.

The Powell-Hyde Cable Car

The ascent up Nob Hill feels like the world's longest roller-coaster climb – but on the Powell-Hyde cable car (red signs), the biggest thrills are still ahead. This cable car bobs up and down hills, with the Golden Gate Bridge popping in and out of view

FRANCESCO RICCARDO IACOMINO / GETTY IMAGES ©

California Street Cable Car

History buffs and crowd-shy visitors prefer San Francisco's oldest cable car line: the California St cable car, in operation since 1878. This divine ride west heads through Chinatown past Old St Mary's Cathedral and climbs Nob Hill to Grace Cathedral. Hop off at Polk St for Swan Oyster Depot, tempting boutiques and cocktail bars. The Van Ness Ave terminus is a few blocks west of Alta Plaza Park and Lafayette Park, which are both ringed by stately Victorians. From here, brave the gauntlet of Fillmore St boutiques to reach a moment of Zen in Japantown's Peace Plaza.

Riding the Cable Cars

Boarding The Powell St and California St cable car turnarounds usually have queues, but they move fast. To skip the queue, head further up the line and jump on when the cable car stops. Cable cars may make rolling stops, especially on downhill runs. To board on hills, act fast: leap onto the baseboard and grab the closest leather hand strap.

Stops Cable cars stop at almost every block on the California St and Powell-Mason lines, and every block on the north–south stretches of the Powell-Hyde line; see www.sfmuni.com for maps.

Accessibility Cable cars are not wheelchair accessible.

on Russian Hill. Hop off the cable car at Lombard St to walk the zigzagging route to North Beach. Otherwise, stop and smell the roses along stairway walks to shady Macondray Lane and blooming Ina Coolbrith Park.

The Powell-Mason Cable Car

The Powell-Hyde line may have multimillion-dollar vistas, but the Powell-Mason line (yellow signs) has more culture. Detour atop Nob Hill for tropical cocktails at the vintage tiki Tonga Room, then resume the ride to Chinatown. The route cuts through North Beach at Washington Sq, where you're surrounded by pizza possibilities and alleyways named after Beat poets. The terminus at Bay and Taylor Sts is handy to visit two truly riveting attractions: the USS *Pampanito* and Musée Mécanique.

Cells in Alcatraz

152   150

Alcatraz

Over the decades, Alcatraz has been the nation's first military prison, a forbidding maximum-security penitentiary and disputed territory between Native American activists and the FBI.

Great For...

☑ Don't Miss

The feeling of isolation in the chilling cell blocks; D-Block was for the most notorious inmates.

Early History

It all started innocently enough back in 1775, when Spanish lieutenant Juan Manuel de Ayala sailed the *San Carlos* past the 22-acre island that he called Isla de Alcatraces (Isle of the Pelicans). In 1859 a new post on Alcatraz became the first US West Coast fort and it soon proved handy as a holding pen for Civil War deserters, insubordinates and the court-martialed.

By 1902 the four cell blocks of wooden cages were rotting, unsanitary and ill-equipped for the influx of US soldiers convicted of war crimes in the Philippines. The army began building a new concrete military prison in 1909, but upkeep was expensive and the US soon had other things to worry about.

Tourists at Alcatraz

DERRICK ALDERMAN / ALAMY STOCK PHOTO ©

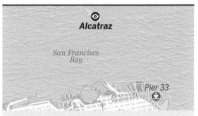

❶ Need to Know

📞Alcatraz Cruises 415-981-7625; www.
alcatrazcruises.com; day tours adult/child/
family $30/18/90, night tours adult/child
$37/22; ⏱call center 8am-7pm, ferries
depart Pier 33 half-hourly 8:45am-3:50pm,
night tours 5:55pm & 6:30pm

✕ Take a Break

Bring your own snacks; note that eating
is allowed only at the ferry dock.

★ Top Tip
Book a month ahead for self-guided
daytime visits, and even earlier for
night tours.

Native American Occupation

Native Americans claimed sovereignty over
Alcatraz in the '60s, noting it had long been
used by the Ohlone people as a spiritual
retreat. In 1969, 79 Native American activists swam to the island and took it over.
During the next 19 months, some 5600
Native Americans would visit the occupied
island. Public support eventually pressured
President Richard Nixon in 1970 to restore
Native American territory and strengthen
self-rule for Native American nations.

Visiting Alcatraz

It's often windy and much colder on Alcatraz; wear extra layers, long pants and a cap.

Visiting Alcatraz means walking – a lot.
The ferry drops you off at the bottom of a
130ft-high hill, which you must ascend to
reach the cell block. For people with mobility impairment, there's a twice-hourly tram
from dock to cell house. Wear sturdy shoes.

Prison Life

In 1934 the Federal Bureau of Prisons took
over Alcatraz as a prominent showcase for
its crime-fighting efforts. The Rock aver-
aged only 264 inmates, but its roster read
like a list of America's Most Wanted. A-list
criminals doing time on Alcatraz included
Chicago crime boss Al 'Scarface' Capone,
dapper kidnapper George 'Machine Gun'
Kelly and hot-headed Harlem mafioso and
sometime-poet 'Bumpy' Johnson.

Although Alcatraz was considered
escape-proof, in 1962 the Anglin brothers
and Frank Morris stuffed their beds with
dummies, floated away on a makeshift raft
and were never seen again.

Security and upkeep proved prohibitively
expensive and finally the island prison was
abandoned to the birds in 1963.

Alcatraz

Book a ferry from Pier 33 and ride 1.5 miles across the bay to explore America's most notorious former prison. The trip itself is worth the money, providing stunning views of the city skyline. Once you've landed at the **Ferry Dock & Pier 1**, you begin the 580-yard walk to the top of the island and prison; if you're out of shape, there's a twice-hourly tram.

As you climb toward the **Guardhouse 2**, notice the island's steep slope; before it was a prison, Alcatraz was a fort. In the 1850s, the military quarried the rocky shores into near-vertical cliffs. Ships could then only dock at a single port, separated from the main buildings by a sally port (a drawbridge and moat in what became the guardhouse). Inside, peer through floor grates to see Alcatraz' original prison.

Volunteers tend the brilliant **Officer's Row Gardens 3** – an orderly counterpoint to the overgrown rose bushes surrounding the burned-out shell of the **Warden's House 4**. At the top of the hill, by the front door of the **Main Cellhouse 5**, beautiful shots unfurl all around, including a **view of the Golden Gate Bridge 6**. Above the main door of the administration building, notice the **historic signs & graffiti 7**, before you step inside the dank, cold prison to find the **Frank Morris cell 8**, former home to Alcatraz' most notorious jail-breaker.

TOP TIPS

➡ Book at least one month prior for self-guided daytime visits, longer for ranger-led night tours. For info on garden tours, see www.alcatraz gardens.org.

➡ Be prepared to hike; a steep path ascends from the ferry landing to the cell block. Most people spend two to three hours on the island. You need only reserve for the outbound ferry; take any ferry back.

➡ There's no food (just water) but you can bring your own; picnicking is allowed at the ferry dock only. Dress in layers as weather changes fast and it's usually windy.

EMMA DURNFORD / GETTY IMAGES ©

Historic Signs & Graffiti
During their 1969–71 occupation, Native Americans graffitied the water tower: 'Home of the Free Indian Land.' Above the cellhouse door, examine the eagle-and-flag crest to see how the red-and-white stripes were changed to spell 'Free.'

Warden's House
Fires destroyed the warden's house and other structures during the Indian Occupation. The government blamed the Native Americans; the Native Americans blamed federal agents provocateurs acting on behalf of the Nixon Administration to undermine public sympathy.

Parade Grounds

DAVID CLAPP / GETTY IMAGES ©

Ferry Dock & Pier
A giant wall map helps you get your bearings. Inside nearby Bldg 64, short films and exhibits provide historical perspective on the prison and details about the Indian Occupation.

View of Golden Gate Bridge

The Golden Gate Bridge stretches wide on the horizon. Best views are from atop the island at Eagle Plaza, near the cellhouse entrance, and at water level along the Agave Trail (September to January only).

Main Cellhouse

During the mid-20th century, the maximum-security prison housed the day's most notorious troublemakers, including Al Capone and Robert Stroud, the 'Birdman of Alcatraz' (who actually conducted his ornithology studies at Leavenworth).

Power House

6

Recreation Yard   **Water Tower**

5

8

Officers' Club

Frank Morris Cell

Peer into cell 138 on B-Block to see a re-creation of the dummy's head that Frank Morris left in his bed as a decoy to aid his notorious – and successful – 1962 escape from Alcatraz.

7   **3**

Lighthouse

4

2

Guard Tower

1

Guardhouse

Alcatraz' oldest building dates to 1857 and retains remnants of the original drawbridge and moat. During the Civil War the basement was transformed into a military dungeon – the genesis of Alcatraz as prison.

Officer's Row Gardens

In the 19th century soldiers imported topsoil to beautify the island with gardens. Well-trusted prisoners later gardened – Elliott Michener said it kept him sane. Historians, ornithologists and archaeologists choose today's plants.

Inside the Ferry Building

AMANDA AHN / ALAMY STOCK PHOTO ©

Ferry Building

Other towns have gourmet ghettos, but San Francisco puts its love of food front and center at the Ferry Building.

Great For...

☑ Don't Miss

Recchiuti Chocolates, which sends out its siren song among the stalls in the arrivals hall.

Restoration

Like a grand salute, the Ferry Building's trademark 240ft tower greeted dozens of ferries daily after its 1898 inauguration. But with the opening of the Bay Bridge and Golden Gate, ferry traffic subsided in the 1930s. An overhead freeway was built, obscuring the building's stately facade and turning it black with exhaust. Only after the 1989 earthquake did city planners realize what they'd been missing: with its grand halls and bay views, this was the perfect place for a new public commons.

Ferry Plaza Farmers Market

Even before building renovations were completed in 2003, the **Ferry Plaza Farmers Market** (Map p306; ☎415-291-3276; www.cuesa.org; Market St & the Embarcadero;

Ferry Building at night

ℹ️ Need to Know

Map p306; 📞415-983-8030; www.ferrybuildingmarketplace.com; Market St & the Embarcadero; 🕙10am-6pm Mon-Fri, 9am-6pm Sat, 11am-5pm Sun; 🅿️🚻; 🚌2, 6, 9, 14, 21, 31, Ⓜ️Embarcadero, Ⓑ Embarcadero

✖️ Take a Break

Sustainable fish tacos reign supreme at Mexican **Mijita** (Map p306; www.mijitasf.com; 1 Ferry Bldg).

★ Top Tip

For bayside picnics, find benches flanking the bronze Gandhi statue by the ferry docks.

🕙10am-2pm Tue & Thu, 8am-2pm Sat; Ⓜ️Embarcadero) began operating out front on the sidewalk, offering seasonal, sustainable gourmet treats and local specialty foods not found elsewhere. Artisanal goat cheese, fresh-pressed California olive oil, wild boar and organic vegetables soon captured the imagination of SF's chefs and eaters.

Foodie Destination

Today the local gourmet action continues indoors, where select local stalls sell artisanal cheese, wild-harvested mushrooms, locally roasted espresso, and organic ice cream in foodie-freak flavors like barley wine and foie gras. People-watching wine bars and award-winning restaurants provide enticing reasons to miss your ferry.

What's Nearby

Justin Herman Plaza (Map p306; www.sfrecpark.org) The plaza across the Embarcadero from the Ferry Building is a crowd-pleaser, and its central Vaillancourt Fountain is SF's favorite eyesore. Join the scene already in progress here among wild parrots, local craft-makers, lunchtime concert-goers, Friday-night roller skaters and wintertime ice-skaters.

Bay Bridge Lights In 2013 lighting artist Leo Villareal strung 25,000 LED lights onto the vertical suspension cable of the Bay Bridge's western span, transforming it into a 1.8-mile-long nightly light show – the world's largest and most psychedelic display of LED lights.

Rincon Park A sliver of green south of the Ferry Building, Rincon Park borders the bay with a wide promenade luring hand-holding sweethearts, families and skateboarders. The centerpiece is a five-story-high sculpture San Franciscans love to hate: *Cupid's Span*, Claes Oldenburg's giant yellow bow with a red arrow buried in the ground.

Waverly Place

BARRY WINIKER / GETTY IMAGES ©

Chinatown

Forty-one historic alleyways, packed into Chinatown's 22 blocks, have seen it all since 1849: gold rushes and revolution, incense and opium, fire, and icy receptions. The narrow backstreets are lined with towering buildings because there was nowhere to go but up in Chinatown after 1870, when laws limited Chinese immigration, employment and housing.

Great For...

☑ **Don't Miss**

Spofford Alley at sundown, when gossiping shopkeepers and mah-jong players provide lots of local color.

Waverly Place

Off Sacramento St are the flag-festooned balconies of Chinatown's historic temples, where services have been held since 1852 – even in 1906, while the altar was still smoldering at **Tin How Temple** (Tien Hau Temple; Map p306; 125 Waverly Place; donation customary; ⊙10am-4pm, except holidays; ⌑1, 8, 30, 45, ⌑California St, Powell-Mason, Powell-Hyde). Downstairs are noodle shops, laundries and traditional Chinese apothecaries.

Ross Alley

Ross Alley (Map p306; ⌑1, 30, 45) was known as Mexico, Spanish and Manila St after the women who staffed its notorious back-parlor brothels. Colorful characters now fill alleyway murals, and anyone can make a fortune the easy way at **Golden**

Ross Alley

ROBERTO SONCIN GEROMETTA / GETTY IMAGES ©

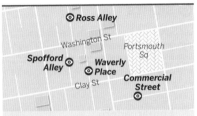

⊙ **Ross Alley**

Washington St

Portsmouth Sq

Spofford Alley ⊙

Waverly Place ⊙

Clay St

Commercial Street ⊙

❶ Need to Know

Map p306; btwn Grant Ave & Stockton St, California St & Broadway; 🚊1,30,45, 🚋Powell-Hyde, Powell-Mason, California St

✕ Take a Break

Load up on dim sum in the sunny upstairs room at **City View** (p313).

★ Top Tip
Explore the area with the young local guides of Chinatown Alleyway Tours (p309).

Spofford Alley

As sunset falls on sociable **Spofford Alley** (Map p306; 🚊1, 15, 30, 45), you'll hear clicking mah-jong tiles and a Chinese orchestra warming up. But generations ago, you might have overheard Sun Yat-sen and his conspirators at number 36 plotting the 1911 overthrow of China's last dynasty.

Find out More

Picture what it was like to be Chinese in America during the Gold Rush, transcontinental railroad construction or Beat heyday at the **Chinese Historical Society of America** (CHSA; Map p306; 📞415-391-1188; www.chsa.org; 965 Clay St; ⊙noon-5pm Tue-Fri, 11am-4pm Sat; 🚊1, 8, 30, 45, 🚋California St, Powell-Mason, Mason-Hyde) 𝗙𝗥𝗘𝗘. This 1932 landmark was built as Chinatown's YWCA by Julia Morgan (chief architect of Hearst Castle). Exhibits reveal once-popular views of Chinatown, including the sensationalist opium den exhibit at San Francisco's 1915 Panama-Pacific International Expo, inviting fairgoers to 'Go Slumming' in Chinatown.

Gate Fortune Cookie Company (Map p306; 📞415-781-3956; 56 Ross Alley; ⊙8am-6pm; 🚊8, 30, 45, 🚋Powell-Mason, Powell-Hyde). You may luck into a concert at Jun Yu's barbershop at 32 Ross Alley, where the octogenarian barber often plays the *erhu* (Chinese lap violin) between customers on weekends.

Commercial Street

Across Portsmouth Square from San Francisco's City Hall, this euphemistically named hot spot caught fire in 1906. The city banned the 25¢ Chinese brothels of **Commercial Street** (Map p306; 742 Commercial St; 🚊1, 15, 41, 45) in favor of 'parlor houses,' where basic services were raised to $3 and watching cost $10.

⊙ SIGHTS

Let San Francisco's 43 hills stretch your legs and your imagination as they deliver breathtaking views. Keep your city smarts and wits about you in the Tenderloin and South of Market (SoMa) neighborhoods.

⊙ Embarcadero

Exploratorium   Museum

Is there a science to skateboarding? Do toilets really flush counterclockwise in Australia? Find answers to questions you wished you'd learned in school, at San Francisco's thrilling hands-on science museum. Combining science with art, and investigating human perception, the Exploratorium nudges you to question how you perceive the world around you. The setting is thrilling – a 9-acre, glass-walled pier jutting straight into San Francisco Bay, with large outdoor portions you can explore free of charge, 24 hours a day. (☑415-528-4444; www.exploratorium.edu; Pier 15; adult/child $29/19, 6-10pm Thu $15; ⊙10am-5pm Tue-Sun, over 18yr only Thu 6-10pm; Pⓜ; ⓂF) ⊘

⊙ North Beach & Chinatown

Coit Tower   Historic Building, Art

Adding an exclamation mark to San Francisco's skyline, Coit Tower offers views worth shouting about – especially after you've climbed the giddy, steep **Filbert Steps** to get here. (Map p306; ☑415-249-0995; http://sfrecpark.org/destination/telegraph-hill-pioneer-park/coit-tower; Telegraph Hill Blvd; elevator entry (nonresident) adult/child $8/5; ⊙10am-6pm May-Oct, 9am-5pm Nov-Apr; 🚌39)

Beat Museum   Museum

The closest you can get to the Beat experience without breaking a law. The 1000+ artifacts in this museum's literary ephemera collection include the sublime (the banned edition of Ginsberg's *Howl*) and the ridiculous (those Kerouac bobble-head dolls are definite head-shakers). Downstairs, watch Beat-era films in ramshackle theater seats redolent with the odors of literary giants, pets and pot. Upstairs, pay your respects at shrines to individual Beat writers. Guided two-hour walking tours cover the museum,

Exploratorium

LAWRENCE MIGDALE / GETTY IMAGES ©

Beat history and literary alleys. (Map p306; 📞 800-537-6822; www.kerouac.com; 540 Broadway; adult/student $8/5, walking tours $25; 🕑museum 10am-7pm, walking tours 2-4pm Mon, Wed & Sat; 🚌8, 10, 12, 30, 41, 45, 🚋Powell-Mason)

◎ Russian Hill & Nob Hill

Lombard Street   Street
You've seen its eight switchbacks in a thousand photographs. The tourist board has dubbed this 'the world's crookedest street', which is factually incorrect. Vermont St in Potrero Hill deserves that award, but Lombard is much more scenic, with its red-brick pavement and lovingly tended flowerbeds. It wasn't always so bent; before the arrival of the automobile it lunged straight down the hill. (900 block of Lombard St; 🚋Powell-Hyde)

◎ Fisherman's Wharf

Maritime National
Historical Park   Historic Site
Four historic ships are floating museums at this national park, the Wharf's most authentic attraction. Moored along Hyde St Pier, standouts include the 1891 schooner *Alma*, 1890 steamboat *Eureka*, paddle-wheel tugboat *Eppleton Hall* and iron-hulled *Balclutha*, which brought coal to San Francisco. It's free to walk the pier; pay only to board ships. (www.nps.gov/safr; 499 Jefferson St, Hyde St Pier; 7-day ticket adult/child $5/free; 🕑9:30am-5pm Oct-May, to 5:30pm Jun-Sep; 👪; 🚌19, 30, 47, 🚋Powell-Hyde, Ⓜ️F)

◎ The Marina & Presidio

Crissy Field   Park
War is for the birds at Crissy Field, a military airstrip turned waterfront nature preserve with knockout Golden Gate views. Where military aircraft once zoomed in for landings, bird-watchers now huddle in the silent rushes of a reclaimed tidal marsh. Joggers pound beachside trails and the only security alerts are raised by puppies suspiciously sniffing surfers. On foggy days, stop by the certified-green Warming

👪 San Francisco for Kids

San Francisco is packed with family-friendly attractions, including the California Academy of Sciences (p309) in Golden Gate Park and the waterfront Exploratorium and Crissy Field.

   In SoMa, the **Children's Creativity Museum** (Map p306; 📞415-820-3320; http://creativity.org/; 221 4th St; admission $12; 🕑10am-4pm Tue-Sun; 👪; 🚌14, Ⓜ️Powell, Ⓑ️Powell) has technology that's too cool for school: robots, live-action video games and 3-D animation work-shops.

   At the **Aquarium of the Bay** (Map p306; www.aquariumofthebay.org; Pier 39; adult/child/family $21.95/12.95/64; 🕑9am-8pm late May-early Sep, shorter off-season hours; 👪; 🚌49, 🚋Powell-Mason, Ⓜ️F) on Pier 39, wander through underwater glass tubes as sharks circle overhead, then let tots gently touch tidepool critters.

Children's Creativity Museum
RICHARD CUMMINS / GETTY IMAGES ©

Hut to browse regional-nature books and warm up with fair-trade coffee. (www.crissy field.org; 1199 East Beach; 🅿️; 🚌30, PresidiGo Shuttle)

Presidio Officers'
Club   Historic Building
The Presidio's oldest building dates to the late 1700s, and was renovated in 2015, revealing gorgeous Spanish-Moorish adobe architecture. The free Heritage Gallery shows the history of the Presidio, from

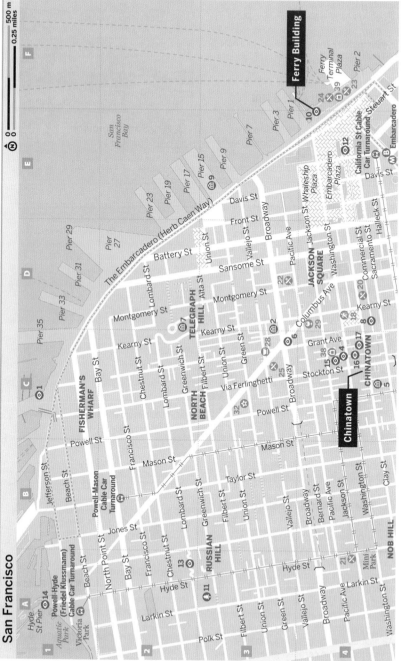

San Francisco

0 0.25 miles

0 500 m

San Francisco Bay

Ferry Building

Ferry Terminal Plaza

Pier 2

Pier 1

Pier 3

Pier 7

Pier 9

Pier 15

Pier 17

Pier 19

Pier 23

Pier 27

Pier 29

Pier 31

Pier 33

Pier 35

The Embarcadero (Herb Caen Way)

Davis St

Front St

Battery St

Sansome St

Montgomery St

Lombard St

Kearny St

Greenwich St

Filbert St

Union St

Green St

Broadway

Pacific Ave

Jackson St

Washington St

Clay St

JACKSON SQUARE

Whaleship Plaza

Embarcadero Plaza

California St Cable Car Turnaround

Davis St

Steuart St

Embarcadero

Sacramento St

Commercial St

Halleck St

Kearny St

Grant Ave

Stockton St

Columbus Ave

CHINATOWN

Chinatown

TELEGRAPH HILL

Alta St

Montgomery St

NORTH BEACH

Via Ferlinghetti

Powell St

Mason St

FISHERMAN'S WHARF

Bay St

Chestnut St

Lombard St

Francisco St

Kearny St

Jefferson St

Beach St

Powell-Mason Cable Car Turnaround

North Point St

Jones St

RUSSIAN HILL

Taylor St

Filbert St

Union St

Vallejo St

Broadway

Bernard St

Pacific Ave

Jackson St

Washington St

NOB HILL

Mini Park

Larkin St

Hyde St

Powell-Hyde (Friedel Klussmann) Cable Car Turnaround

Aquatic Park

Victoria Park

Hyde St Pier

Beach St

Bay St

Chestnut St

Francisco St

Greenwich St

Filbert St

Union St

Green St

Vallejo St

Broadway

Pacific Ave

Washington St

Polk St

Larkin St

Hyde St

San Francisco

◎ **Sights**
1	Aquarium of the Bay	C1
2	Beat Museum	D3
3	Children's Creativity Museum	D7
4	Chinatown Alleyways	C4
5	Chinese Historical Society of America	C4
6	City Lights Bookstore	C3
7	Coit Tower	D2
8	Commercial Street	D4
9	Exploratorium	E3
10	Ferry Building	E4
11	George Sterling Park	A3
12	Justin Herman Plaza	E4
13	Lombard Street	A2
14	Maritime National Historical Park	A1
15	Ross Alley	C4
16	Spofford Alley	C4
17	Tin How Temple	C4

◉ **Activities, Courses & Tours**
18	Chinatown Alleyway Tours	D4

✖ **Eating**
19	Brenda's French Soul Food	A7
20	City View	D4
21	Cocotte	A4
22	Cotogna	D3
23	Ferry Plaza Farmers Market	F4
24	Mijita	F4
25	Molinari	C3
26	Swan Oyster Depot	A5

◉ **Drinking & Nightlife**
27	Aunt Charlie's Lounge	C7
28	Caffe Trieste	C3
29	Comstock Saloon	D4
30	Tonga Room	C5
31	Top of the Mark	C5

◉ **Entertainment**
32	Beach Blanket Babylon	C3
33	San Francisco Giants	F8
34	San Francisco Opera	A8
35	SFJAZZ Center	A8

◉ **Shopping**
36	Britex Fabrics	C6
37	Electric Works	B8
38	Golden Gate Fortune Cookie Company	C4
39	Heath Ceramics	F4

Native American days to present. Moraga Hall – the former officers' club lounge – is a lovely spot to sit fireside and also has free wi-fi. Thursday and Friday evenings, the Club hosts a dynamic line-up of events and lectures. (☏415-561-4165; www.presidio officersclub.com; 50 Moraga Ave; ◷10am-6pm Tue-Sun; ☏; ☐PresidiGo Shuttle) FREE

◎ The Mission & the Castro

Balmy Alley   Murals
Inspired by Diego Rivera's 1930s San Francisco murals and outraged by US foreign policy in Central America, 1970s Mission muralistas set out to transform the political landscape, one mural-covered garage door at a time. Today, Balmy Alley murals span three decades, from an early memorial for El Salvador activist Archbishop Óscar Romero to an homage to Frida Kahlo, Georgia O'Keeffe and other trailblazing women modern artists. (☏415-285-2287; www.precitaeyes.org; btwn 24th & 25th Sts; ☐10, 12, 14, 27, 48, Ⓑ24th St Mission)

Mission Dolores   Church
The city's oldest building and its namesake, whitewashed adobe Misión San Francisco de Asís, was founded in 1776 and rebuilt in 1782 with conscripted Ohlone and Miwok labor – a graveyard memorial hut commemorates 5000 Ohlone and Miwok laborers who died in mission measles epidemics in 1814 and 1826. Today the modest adobe mission is overshadowed by the ornate adjoining 1913 basilica, featuring stained-glass windows of California's 21 missions. (Misión San Francisco de Asís; ☏415-621-8203; www.missiondolores.org; 3321 16th St; adult/child $5/3; ◷9am-4pm Nov-Apr, to 4:30pm May-Oct; ☐22, 33, Ⓑ16th St Mission, ⓂJ)

GLBT History Museum   Museum
America's first gay-history museum cobbles ephemera from the community – Harvey Milk's campaign literature, matchbooks from long-gone bathhouses, photographs of early activists – together with harder-hitting installations that focus on various aspects of queer history, incorporating electronic media to tell personal stories

that illuminate the evolution of the struggle to gain rights and acceptance into the larger culture. (415-621-1107; www.glbthistory. org/museum; 4127 18th St; admission $5, 1st Wed of month free; 11am-7pm Mon-Sat, noon-5pm Sun, closed Tue fall-spring; Castro)

The Haight

Haight & Ashbury   Landmark

This legendary intersection was the epicenter of the psychedelic '60s and remains a counterculture magnet. On average Saturdays here you can sign Green Party petitions, commission a poem, hear Hare Krishna on keyboards and Bob Dylan on banjo. The clock overhead always reads 4:20 – better known in herbal circles as International Bong-Hit Time. A local clockmaker recently fixed it; within a week it was stuck at 4:20. (6, 7, 33, 37, 43)

Golden Gate Park & Around

In 1865, the city voted to turn more than 1000 acres of sand dunes into **Golden Gate Park** (www.golden-gate-park.com; Stanyan St to Great Hwy; ; 5, 7, 18, 21, 28, 29, 33, 44, MN) . The park ends at **Ocean Beach** (415-561-4323; www.parksconservan cy.org; Great Hwy; sunrise-sunset; ; 5, 18, 31, MN), where **Cliff House** (415-386-3330; www.cliffhouse.com; 1090 Point Lobos Ave; 9am-11pm Sun-Thu, to midnight Fri & Sat; 5, 18, 31, 38) FREE overlooks the splendid ruin of **Sutro Baths** (www.nps.gov/goga/history culture/sutro-baths.htm; 680 Point Lobos Ave; sunrise-sunset, visitor center 9am-5pm; ; 5, 31, 38) FREE. Follow the partly paved trail around **Lands End** for shipwreck sightings and Golden Gate Bridge views.

California Academy of Sciences   Museum

Architect Renzo Piano's 2008 landmark LEED–certified green building houses 40,000 weird and wonderful animals in a four-story rainforest and split-level aquarium under a 'living roof' of California wildflowers. After the penguins nod off to sleep, the wild rumpus starts at kids-only Academy Sleepovers ($109; ages five

to 17, plus adult chaperones; 6pm to 8am, including snack and breakfast) and over-21 NightLife Thursdays ($12), when rainforest-themed cocktails encourage strange mating rituals among shy internet daters. (415-379-8000; www.calacademy. org; 55 Music Concourse Dr; adult/child $35/25; 9:30am-5pm Mon-Sat, 11am-5pm Sun; ; 5, 6, 7, 21, 31, 33, 44, MN)

de Young Museum   Museum

Follow sculptor Andy Goldsworthy's artificial fault line in the sidewalk into Herzog & de Meuron's sleek, copper-clad building that's oxidizing green to blend into the park. Don't be fooled by the de Young's camouflaged exterior: shows here boldly broaden artistic horizons, from Oceanic ceremonial masks and Oscar de la Renta gowns to James Turrell's domed 'Skyspace' installation, built into a hill in the sculpture garden. (415-750-3600; http://deyoung. famsf.org/; 50 Hagiwara Tea Garden Dr; adult/ child $10/6, discount with Muni ticket $2, 1st Tue of month free, online booking fee $1 per ticket; 9:30am-5:15pm Tue-Sun, to 8:45pm Fri Apr-Nov; 5, 7, 44, MN)

TOURS

Precita Eyes Mission Mural Tours   Walking Tour

Muralists lead weekend walking tours covering 60 to 70 Mission murals in a six- to 10-block radius of mural-bedecked Balmy Alley. Tours last 90 minutes to 2¼ hours for the more in-depth Classic Mural Walk. Proceeds fund mural upkeep at this community arts nonprofit. (415-285-2287; www.precitaeyes.org; adult $15-20, child $3; see website calendar for tour dates; ; 12, 14, 48, 49, B 24th St Mission)

Chinatown Alleyway Tours   Walking Tour

On these two-hour tours, teenage Chinatown residents guide you through backstreets that have seen it all – Sun Yat-sen plotting China's revolution, '49ers squandering fortunes on opium, services held in temple ruins after the 1906 earthquake.

LGBT San Francisco

Doesn't matter where you're from, who you love or who's your daddy: if you're here, and queer, welcome home.

The Castro is the historic heart of the gay scene. South of Market (SoMa) has leather bars and thump-thump clubs. The Mission is the preferred 'hood for many women and a diverse transgender community.

Cafe Flore (p317) You haven't done the Castro till you've idled on the sun-drenched patio – everyone winds up here sooner or later.

Stud (www.studsf.com; 399 9th St; admission $5-8; ☉noon-2am Tue, 5pm-3am Thu-Sat, 5pm-midnight Sun; 🚍12, 19, 27, 47) Rocking SoMa's gay scene since 1966. Anything goes here, especially on 'Club Some Thing' Fridays.

Aunt Charlie's Lounge (Map p306; 📞415-441-2922; www.auntcharlieslounge. com; 133 Turk St; admission free-$5; ☉noon-2am Mon-Fri, from 10am Sat, 10am-midnight Sun; 🚍27, 31, Ⓜ Powell, Ⓑ Powell) Tenderloin drag dive bar for fabulously seedy glamour and a vintage pulp fiction vibe.

Your presence here helps the community remember its history and shape its future – Chinatown Alleyway Tours are a nonprofit youth-led program of the Chinatown Community Development Center. Credit cards are accepted for advance online reservations only; drop-ins must pay with exact change. (📞415-984-1478; www.chinatown alleywaytours.org/; tours depart Portsmouth Sq, near Washington & Kearny Sts; adult/student $26/16; ☉tours 11am Mon, Tue & Sat, 3pm Thu & Fri; 🚹; 🚍1, 8, 10, 12, 30, 41, 45, 🚃California St, Powell-Mason, Powell-Hyde)

🛍 SHOPPING

City Lights Bookstore Books
Ever since manager Shigeyoshi Murao and founder and Beat poet Lawrence Ferlinghetti successfully defended their right to 'willfully and lewdly print' Allen Ginsberg's magnificent *Howl and Other Poems* in 1957, this bookstore has been a free-speech landmark. Celebrate your freedom to read freely in the designated Poet's Chair upstairs overlooking Jack Kerouac Alley, load up on 'zines on the mezzanine or entertain radical ideas downstairs in the Muckracking and Stolen Continents sections. (📞415-362-8193; www.citylights.com; 261 Columbus Ave; ☉10am-midnight)

Local Take Gifts
This marvelous little shop, next to the F-Market terminus, carries the perfect gifts to take home: SF-specific merchandise, all made locally. Our favorite items include a miniature scale model of Sutro Tower; T-shirts emblazoned with iconic SF locales; cable car and Golden Gate Bridge jewelry; woodcut city maps; knit caps; and snappy one-of-a-kind belt buckles. (localtakesf.com; 3979 B 17th St; ☉11am-7pm; Ⓜ Castro) 🖉

Heath Ceramics Housewares
No local, artisanal SF restaurant tablescape is complete without handmade modern Heath stoneware, thrown by local potters in Heath's Sausalito studio since 1948. Chef Alice Waters has served her definitive California fare on Heath dishware for decades – hence the popular Chez Panisse ceramics in earthy, food-friendly shades. Pieces are priced for fine dining except studio seconds, sold here on weekends. (📞415-399-9284; www.heathceramics.com; 1 Ferry Bldg; ☉10am-7pm Mon-Fri, 8am-6pm Sat, 11am-5pm Sun; Ⓜ Embarcadero, Ⓑ Embarcadero)

Amoeba Records   Music

A bowling-alley-turned-superstore of new and used records in all genres, plus free in-store concerts and *Music We Like* 'zine for great new finds. (📞415-831-1200; www.amoeba.com; 1855 Haight St; 🕑11am-8pm)

Britex Fabrics   Fabric

Runway shows can't compete with Britex's fashion drama. First floor: designers bicker over dibs on caution-orange chiffon. Second floor: glam rockers dig through velvet goldmines. Third floor: Hollywood costumers make vampire movie magic with jet buttons and silk ribbon. Top floor: fake fur flies as costumers prepare for Burning Man, Halloween or an average SF weekend. (📞415-392-2910; www.britexfabrics.com; 146 Geary St; 🕑10am-6pm Mon-Sat; 🚌38, 🚋Powell-Mason, Powell-Hyde, Ⓜ Powell, Ⓑ Powell)

Electric Works   Art, Books

Everything a museum store aspires to be, with a fascinating collection of arty must-haves – beeswax crayons, East German ice-cream spoons, Klein bottles, vintage wind-up toys – plus limited-edition prints and artists' books by David Byrne, Enrique

Chagoya and other contemporary artists. Sales of many artworks printed on-site – including Dave Eggers' panda drawing, tragicomically titled *Doomed by Charm* – benefit nonprofits. (📞415-626-5496; www.sfelectricworks.com; 1360 Mission St; 🕑11am-6pm Tue-Fri, to 5pm Sat; ♿; 🚌14, Ⓜ Van Ness)

✪ ENTERTAINMENT

SFJAZZ Center   Jazz

Jazz greats coast-to-coast and legends from Argentina to Yemen are showcased at America's newest, largest jazz center. Hear fresh takes on classic jazz albums like *Ah Um* and *Getz/Gilberto* downstairs in the Lab, or book ahead for extraordinary main-stage collaborations like Laurie Anderson with David Coulter playing the saw, or pianist Jason Moran's performance with skateboarders improvising moves on indoor ramps. (📞866-920-5299; www.sfjazz.

> *a bowling-alley-turned-superstore of records, plus free in-store concerts*

Amoeba Records

RANAPICS / ALAMY STOCK PHOTO ©

A San Francisco Giants game

org; 201 Franklin St; tickets $25-120; ☺show-times vary; 🚌5, 6, 7, 21, 47, 49, 🇲Van Ness)

San Francisco Opera — Opera

Opera was SF's Gold Rush soundtrack – and today, SF rivals the Met with world premieres of original works covering WWII Italy (*Two Women,* or *La Ciociara*), Stephen King thrillers (*Dolores Claiborne),* and Qing Dynasty Chinese courtesans (*Dream of the Red Chamber*). Don't miss Tuscany-born musical director Nicola Luisotti's signature Verdi operas. Score $10 same-day standing-room tickets at 10am and two hours before curtain. (☎415-864-3330; www. sfopera.com; War Memorial Opera House, 301 Van Ness Ave; tickets $10-350; 🚌21, 45, 47, 🅱Civic Center, 🇲Van Ness)

Beach Blanket Babylon — Cabaret

Snow White searches for Prince Charming in San Francisco: what could possibly go wrong? The Disney-spoof musical-comedy cabaret has been running since 1974, but topical jokes keep it outrageous and wigs as big as parade floats are gasp-worthy. Spectators must be over 21 to handle racy

humor, except at cleverly sanitized Sunday matinees. Reservations essential; arrive one hour early for best seats. (BBB; ☎415-421-4222; www.beachblanketbabylon.com; 678 Green St; admission $25-100; ☺shows 8pm Wed, Thu & Fri, 6:30pm & 9:30pm Sat, 2pm & 5pm Sun; 🚌8, 30, 39, 41, 45, 🚋Powell-Mason)

Castro Theatre — Cinema

The Mighty Wurlitzer organ rises from the orchestra pit before evening performances and the audience cheer for the Great American Songbook, ending with: 'San Francisco open your Golden Gate/You let no stranger wait outside your door...' If there's a cult classic on the bill, say, *Whatever Happened to Baby Jane?,* expect participation. Otherwise, crowds are well-behaved and rapt. (☎415-621-6120; www.castrotheatre.com; 429 Castro St; adult/child $11/8.50; ☺showtimes vary; 🇲Castro)

San Francisco Giants — Baseball

Watch and learn how the World Series is won – bushy beards, women's underwear and all. (☎415-972-2000; www.sfgiants.com; AT&T Park, 24 Willie Mays Plaza; tickets $5-135)

⊗ EATING

Off the Grid
Food Truck **$**

Some 30 food trucks circle their wagons at SF's largest mobile-gourmet hootenannys on Friday night at Fort Mason Center, and Sunday midday for Picnic at the Presidio and Thursday evenings for Twilight at the Presidio (both on the Main Post Lawn). Arrive early for best selection and to minimize waits. Cash only. (www.offthegridsf.com; items $5-12; ⏰Fort Mason Center 5-10pm Fri Apr-Oct, Presidio 5-9pm Thu & 11am-4pm Sun Apr-Oct; 🚺; 🚌22, 28)

Humphry Slocombe
Ice Cream **$**

Indie-rock organic ice cream may permanently spoil you for Top 40 flavors. Once Thai Curry Peanut Butter and Magnolia Brewery Stout have rocked your taste buds, cookie dough seems so obvious, and ordinary sundaes can't compare to Secret Breakfast (bourbon and corn flakes) and Vietnamese Coffee drizzled with hot fudge, olive oil and sea salt. (🟢415-550-6971; www.humphryslocombe.com; 2790 Harrison St; ice cream $4-6; ⏰noon-9pm Mon-Thu, to 10pm Fri-Sun; 🚺; 🚌12, 14, 49, 🅱24th St Mission) 🖥

Craftsman & Wolves
Bakery, Californian **$**

Conventional breakfasts can't compare to the Rebel Within: savory sausage-spiked asiago cheese muffin with a silken soft-boiled egg baked inside. SF's surest pick-me-up is Highwire macchiato and matcha snickerdoodle cookies, and Thai coconut curry scone, chilled pea soup, and Provence rose makes a sublime lunch. Exquisite horchata/hazelnut cube cakes are ideal for celebrating SF half-birthdays, foggy days and imaginary holidays. (🟢415-913-7713; http://craftsman-wolves.com; 746 Valencia St; pastries $3-7; ⏰7am-7pm Mon-Thu, to 8pm Fri, 8am-8pm Sat, to 7pm Sun; 🚌14, 22, 33, 49, 🅱16th St Mission, Ⓜ J)

City View
Chinese **$**

Take your seat in the sunny dining room and your pick from carts loaded with delicate shrimp and leek dumplings,

---

🍽 Foodie Detour

Foodies come to worship at **Chez Panisse**. Housed in a lovely Arts and Crafts house in the Gourmet Ghetto, it's run by Alice Waters, the inventor of California cuisine, Pull out all the stops with a prix-fixe meal downstairs, or go less expensive and a tad less formal in the café upstairs. Reservations accepted one month ahead. (🟢café 510-548-5049, restaurant 510-548-5525; www.chezpanisse.com; 1517 Shattuck Ave; café dinner mains $19-32, restaurant prix-fixe dinner $75-125; ⏰café 11:30am-2:45pm & 5-10:30pm Mon-Thu, 11:30am-3pm & 5-11:30pm Fri & Sat, restaurant seatings 5:30pm & 8pm Mon-Sat) 🖥

---

garlicky Chinese broccoli, tangy spare ribs, coconut-dusted custard tarts and other tantalizing dim sum. Arrive before the midday lunch rush, so you can nab seats in the sunny upstairs room and get first dibs from passing carts. (🟢415-398-2838; http://cityviewdimsum.com; 662 Commercial St; dishes $3-8; ⏰11am-2:30pm Mon-Fri, from 10am Sat & Sun; 🚺; 🚌1, 8, 10, 12, 30, 45, 🚋California St)

La Taqueria
Mexican **$**

SF's definitive burrito has no debatable saffron rice, spinach tortilla or mango salsa, just perfectly grilled meats, slow-cooked beans and classic tomatillo or mesquite salsa wrapped in a flour tortilla. They're purists at La Taqueria – you'll pay extra without beans, because they pack in more meat – but spicy pickles and *crema* (Mexican sour cream) bring complete burrito bliss. (🟢415-285-7117; 2889 Mission St; burritos $6-8; ⏰11am-9pm Mon-Sat, to 8pm Sun; 🚺; 🚌12, 14, 48, 49, 🅱24th St Mission)

Swan Oyster Depot
Seafood **$$**

Superior flavor without the superior attitude of typical seafood restaurants – Swan's downside is an inevitable wait for the few stools at the vintage lunch counter, but the upside of high turnover is incredibly fresh seafood.

Marin County

Majestic redwoods cling to coastal hills just across San Francisco's Golden Gate Bridge in laid-back Marin. The windswept, rugged **Marin Headlands** are laced with hiking trails, providing panoramic views of the city and bay. To find the **visitor center** (☎415-331-1540; www.nps.gov/goga/marin-headlands.htm; Fort Barry; ⏱9:30am-4:30pm), take the Alexander Ave exit after crossing north over the Golden Gate Bridge, turn left under the freeway and follow the signs. Nearby attractions include **Point Bonita Lighthouse** (www.nps.gov/goga/pobo. htm; off Field Rd; ⏱12:30-3:30pm Sat-Mon) FREE, **Rodeo Beach** and the educational **Marine Mammal Center** (☎415-289-7325; www.marinemammalcenter.org; 2000 Bunker Rd; ⏱10am-5pm; ❖) ☐FREE.

Wander among an ancient stand of the world's tallest trees at 550-acre **Muir Woods National Monument** (☎415-388-2595; www.nps.gov/muwo; 1 Muir Woods Rd, Mill Valley; adult/child $10/ free; ⏱8am-sunset), 10 miles northwest of the Golden Gate Bridge. Easy hiking trails loop past thousand-year-old redwoods at Cathedral Grove. Come midweek to avoid crowds or arrive early morning or before sunset. Take Hwy 101 to the Hwy 1 exit, then follow the signs.

The tiny bayside town of **Sausalito** (www.sausalito.org) is where houseboats are docked. It's a popular destination for cycling trips over the bridge (take the ferry back to San Francisco).

Point Bonita Lighthouse, Marin Headlands
JOHN ELK III / GETTY IMAGES ©

Sunny days, place your order to go, browse Polk St boutiques, then breeze past the line to pick up crab salad with Louie dressing and the obligatory top-grade oysters with mignonette sauce. Hike or bus up to **George Sterling Park** (Map p306; www. rhn.org/pointofinterestparks.html; Greenwich & Hyde Sts; ❖; ☐Powell-Hyde) for superlative seafood with ocean views. (☎415-673-1101; www.sfswanoysterdepot.com/; 1517 Polk St; dishes $8-24; ⏱10:30am-5:30pm Mon-Sat; ☐1, 19, 47, 49, ☐California St)

Cotogna Italian $$
Chef-owner Michael Tusk is racking up James Beard Awards for best chef, and you'll discover why: he balances a few pristine flavors in rustic pastas, wood-fired pizzas and authentic Florentine steak. Reserve ahead or plan to eat late (2pm to 5pm) to score the bargain $28 prix-fixe lunch. On the excellent wine list all bottles cost $50, including hard-to-find Italian cult wines. (☎415-775-8508; www.cotognasf. com; 490 Pacific Ave; mains $17-38; ⏱11:30am-10:30pm Mon-Thu, to 11pm Fri & Sat, 5-9:30pm Sun; ☎; ☐10, 12)

Molinari Deli $$
Grab a number and a crusty roll, and when your number rolls around, wise-cracking deli staff in paper hats will stuff it with translucent sheets of *prosciutto di Parma*, milky buffalo mozzarella, tender marinated artichokes or slabs of the legendary house-cured salami. Enjoy yours hot from the panini press at sidewalk tables or in Washington Sq. (☎415-421-2337; www.moli narisalame.com; 373 Columbus Ave; sandwiches $10-12.50; ⏱9am-6pm Mon-Fri, to 5:30pm Sat, 10am-4pm Sun; ☐8, 10, 12, 30, 39, 41, 45, ☐Powell-Mason)

Greens Vegetarian, Californian $$
Career carnivores won't realize there's zero meat in the hearty black-bean chili, or in the other flavor-packed vegetarian dishes, made using ingredients from a Zen farm in Marin. And oh!, what views – the Golden Gate rises just outside the window-lined

Swan Oyster Depot (p313)

dining room. The on-site café serves to-go lunches. For sit-down meals, including Sunday brunch, reservations are essential. (☏415-771-6222; www.greensrestaurant.com; Bldg A, Fort Mason Center, cnr Marina Blvd & Laguna St; lunch $15-18, dinner $18-25; ⊗11:45am-2:30pm & 5:30-9pm Tue-Fri, from 11am Sat, 10:30am-2pm & 5:30-9pm Sun, 5:30-9pm Mon; ⚲♿; ☐28) ⬚

Brenda's French Soul Food   Creole, Southern $$

Chef-owner Brenda Buenviaje blends New Orleans–style Creole cooking with French technique into 'French soul food.' Expect updated classics like beignets, serious biscuits and grits, impeccable Hangtown Fry (eggs with bacon and fried oysters) and fried chicken with collard greens and hot-pepper jelly. Long waits on sketchy sidewalks are unavoidable – but Brenda serves takeaway sandwiches two doors down. (☏415-345-8100; www.frenchsoulfood. com; 652 Polk St; mains lunch $9-13, dinner $12-17; ⊗8am-3pm Mon & Tue, to 10pm Wed-Sat, to 8pm Sun; ☐19, 31, 38, 47, 49)

Cocotte   French $$$

This tiny French bistro on Russian Hill has an open kitchen, lined with copper pots, where the French-born chef-owner creates fabulous lobster salad, hearty coq au vin, and the house-specialty rotisserie chicken, served with dipping sauces, including an outstanding mushroom-cream demi-glace that merits an extra serving of bread to mop up the plate. (☏415-292-4415; www. cocottesf.com; 1521 Hyde St; dinner mains $21-32; ⊗5:30-9:30pm Tue-Sat; ☐10, 12, ☐Powell-Hyde)

State Bird Provisions   Californian $$$

Even before winning back-to-back James Beard Awards, State Bird attracted lines for 5:30pm seatings not seen since the Dead played neighboring Fillmore Auditorium. The draw is a thrilling play on dim sum, wildly inventive with seasonal-regional ingredients and esoteric flavors, like fennel pollen or garum. Plan to order multiple dishes. Book exactly 60 days ahead. (☏415-795-1272; statebirdsf.com; 1529 Fillmore

St; dishes $9-26; ⏱5:30-10pm Sun-Thu, to 11pm Fri & Sat; 🚌22, 38)

🍸 DRINKING & NIGHTLIFE

For a pub crawl, start with North Beach saloons or Mission bars around Valencia and 16th Sts. The Castro has historic gay bars; SoMa adds dance clubs. Downtown and around Union Sq mix dives with speakeasies. Marina bars are preppy, while Haight bars draw mixed alterna-crowds.

Comstock Saloon   Bar
Relieving yourself in the marble trough below the bar is no longer advisable, but otherwise this 1907 Victorian saloon revives the Barbary Coast's glory days. Get the authentic Pisco Punch or martini-precursor Martinez (gin, vermouth, bitters, maraschino liqueur). Reserve booths or back-parlor seating, so you can hear dates when ragtime-jazz bands play. Call it dinner with pot pie and buckets of shrimp. (📞415-617-0071; www.comstocksaloon.com; 155 Columbus Ave; ⏱noon-2am Mon-Fri, 4pm-2am Sat, 4pm-midnight Sun; 🚌8, 10, 12, 30, 45, 🚋Powell-Mason)

Bar Agricole   Bar
Drink your way to a history degree with well-researched cocktails: Bellamy Scotch Sour with house bitters and egg whites passes the test, but El Presidente with white rum, farmhouse curaçao and California pomegranate grenadine takes top honors. This overachiever racks up James Beard Award nods for its spirits and eco-savvy design, and pairs decadent drink with local oysters and excellent California cheeses. (📞415-355-9400; www.baragricole.com; 355 11th St; ⏱6-10pm Sun-Thu, 5:30-11pm Fri & Sat; 🚌9, 12, 27, 47) ✏

Toronado   Pub
Glory hallelujah, beer lovers: your prayers have been answered. Be humbled before the chalkboard altar that lists 45-plus beers on tap and hundreds more bottled, including spectacular seasonal microbrews. Bring cash and order sausages from **Rosamunde** (📞415-437-6851; http://rosamundesausagegrill.com) next door to accompany ale made by Trappist monks. It may get too loud to hear your date talk, but you'll hear angels

sing. (415-863-2276; www.toronado.com; 547 Haight St; 11:30am-2am; 6, 7, 22, N)

Tonga Room Lounge

Tonight's San Francisco weather: 100% chance of tropical rainstorms every 20 minutes, but only around the top-40 band playing on the island in the middle of the indoor pool – you're safe in your grass hut. For a more powerful hurricane, order one in a plastic coconut. Come before 8pm to beat the cover charge. (reservations 415-772-5278; www.tongaroom.com; Fairmont San Francisco, 950 Mason St; cover $5-7; 5:30-11:30pm Sun, Wed & Thu, 5pm-12:30am Fri & Sat; 1, California St, Powell-Mason, Powell-Hyde)

Top of the Mark Bar

So what if it's touristy? Nothing beats twirling in the clouds in your best cocktail dress on the city's highest dancefloor. Fridays are best, when a full jazz orchestra plays, but there's music other nights, too: call ahead to make sure. Expect $15 drinks. (www.topofthemark.com; 999 California St; cover $10-15; 4:30-11:30pm Sun-Thu, 4:30pm-12:30am Fri & Sat; 1, California St)

Caffe Trieste Café

Poetry on bathroom walls, opera on the jukebox, live accordion jams and sightings of Beat poet laureate Lawrence Ferlinghetti: this is North Beach at its best, since the 1950s. Linger over legendary espresso and scribble your screenplay under the Sardinian fishing mural just as young Francis Ford Coppola did. Perhaps you've heard of the movie: *The Godfather.* Cash only. (415-392-6739; www.caffetrieste.com; 601 Vallejo St; 6:30am-10pm Sun-Thu, to 11pm Fri & Sat; ; 8, 10, 12, 30, 41, 45)

Cafe Flore Café

You haven't done the Castro till you've idled on the sun-drenched patio at the Flore – everyone winds up here sooner or later. Weekdays present the best chance to meet neighborhood regulars, who colonize the tables outside. Weekends get packed. Great happy-hour drink specials, like two-for-one margaritas. The food's okay, too. Wi-fi weekdays only; no electrical outlets. (415-621-8579; www.cafeflore.com; 2298 Market St; 7am-1am Sun-Thu, to 2am Fri & Sat; ; Castro)

★ Top Five for Eating

Chez Panisse (p313)

Ferry Building (p300)

Craftsman & Wolves (p313)

City View (p313)

La Taqueria (p313)

From left: Top of the Mark; Ferry Building (p300); Caffe Trieste

IAN SHAW / ALAMY STOCK PHOTO ©

STEFANO POLITI MARKOVINA / ALAMY STOCK PHOTO ©

Sonoma Valley

More laid-back and less commercial than Napa, Sonoma Valley shelters more than 40 wineries off Hwy 12 – and, unlike in Napa, most don't require appointments. Note that there are actually three Sonomas: the town, the valley and the county. The area is about a 90-minute drive from San Francisco.

Some recommended wineries are:

Gundlach-Bundschu Winery California's oldest family-run winery looks like a castle, but has a down-to-earth vibe. Founded in 1858 by a Bavarian immigrant, its signatures are Gewürztraminer and Pinot Noir, but 'Gun-Bun' was the first American winery to produce 100% Merlot. Down a winding lane, it's a terrific bike-to winery, with picnicking, hiking and a lake. Tour the 1800-barrel cave by reservation only. Bottles are $21 to $90. (707-939-3015; www.gunbun.com; 2000 Denmark St, Sonoma; tasting $10-25, incl tour $30-50; 11am-4:30pm, to 5:30pm Jun–mid-Oct)

Benziger If you're new to wine, make Benziger your first stop for Sonoma's best crash course in winemaking. The worthwhile, non-reservable tour includes an open-air tram ride (weather permitting) through biodynamic vineyards, and a five-wine tasting. Great picnicking, plus a playground, make it tops for families. The large-production wine's OK (head for the reserves); the tour's the thing. Bottles are $15 to $80. (707-935-3000, 888-490-2739; www.benziger.com; 1883 London Ranch Rd, Glen Ellen; tasting $15-40, tours $25-50; 10am-5pm, tram tours 11am-3:30pm;)

ℹ INFORMATION

San Francisco Visitor Information Center

(Map p306; 415-391-2000; www.sanfrancisco.travel; Hallidie Plaza, Market & Powell Sts, lower level; 9am-5pm Mon-Fri, to 3pm Sat & Sun;

Powell-Mason, Powell-Hyde, M Powell St, B Powell St) Provides multilingual information, sells transportation passes, publishes glossy maps and booklets, and provides interactive touch screens.

ℹ GETTING THERE & AWAY

AIR

San Francisco International Airport (p369) is 14 miles south of Downtown off Hwy 101, while **Oakland International Airport** (OAK; www.oaklandairport.com; 1 Airport Dr) is 15 miles east of Downtown.

TRAIN

Amtrak (800-872-7245; www.amtrakcalifornia.com) trains stop at Jack London Sq in Oakland, from where Amtrak's Thruway buses connect with San Francisco.

ℹ GETTING AROUND

TO/FROM THE AIRPORT

From a station connected to the SFO international terminal, **BART** (Bay Area Rapid Transit; www.bart.gov; one way $8.65) is a 30-minute train ride to Downtown. An airport taxi to Downtown costs $40 to $55, plus tip. **SuperShuttle** (800-258-3826; www.supershuttle.com) offers shared van rides (per person $17).

Oakland International Airport (OAK) is also connected to the city by BART; to get to Downtown, change at Coliseum Station for a San Francisco/Daly City–bound train. An airport taxi costs upward of $70; SuperShuttle also operates from OAK.

PUBLIC TRANSPORTATION

MUNI (Municipal Transit Agency; %511; www.sfmta.com) operates bus, streetcar and cable-car lines. Standard fare for buses or streetcars is $2.25; cable-car rides are $7 each.

Where to Stay

San Francisco hotel rates are among the world's highest. Plan ahead – well ahead – and grab bargains when you see them.

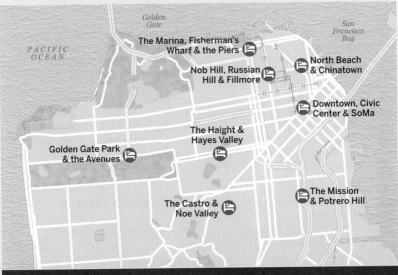

Neighborhood	Atmosphere
The Marina, Fisherman's Wharf & the Piers	Good for kids; lots of restaurants and nightlife at the Marina; many motels on Lombard St with parking. Very touristy; parking at the Marina and Wharf is a nightmare.
Downtown, Civic Center & SoMa	Biggest selection of hotels; near all public transportation; walkable to many sights. Civic Center feels rough.
North Beach & Chinatown	Culturally colorful; great strolling; lots of cafés and restaurants. Limited choices and transportation.
Nob Hill, Russian Hill & Fillmore	Stately, classic hotels atop Nob Hill; good restaurants and shopping in Pacific Heights and Japantown. Steep hills.
The Mission & Potrero Hill	Mission's flat terrain makes it good for walking and biking; easy access to BART. Limited choice of accommodations.
The Castro & Noe Valley	Great nightlife, especially for GLBT travelers; easy access to Market St transit. Far from major tourist sights.
The Haight & Hayes Valley	Lots of bars and restaurants; Hayes Valley near cultural sights; the Haight near Golden Gate Park. Limited choices.
Golden Gate Park & the Avenues	Quiet nights; good for outdoor recreation; easier parking. Far from major sights; foggy and cold in summer.

YOSEMITE NATIONAL PARK

Yosemite National Park

There's a reason why everybody's heard of it (and why four million visitors wend their way here annually): the granite-peak heights are dizzying, the mist from thunderous waterfalls drenching, the Technicolor wildflower meadows amazing and the majestic silhouettes of El Capitan and Half Dome almost shocking against a crisp blue sky. It's a landscape of dreams, surrounding oh-so-small people on all sides.

The jaw-dropping, head-turning, Unesco World Heritage–listed Yosemite garners the devotion of all who enter. From the waterfall-striped granite walls buttressing emerald-green Yosemite Valley and the gemstone lakes of the high country's subalpine wilderness to the skyscraping giant sequoias at Mariposa Grove and Hetch Hetchy's pristine pathways, America's third-oldest national park truly inspires a sense of awe and reverence.

☑ In This Section

Glacier Point	324
Half Dome	326
Yosemite Valley Waterfalls	328
Sights	330
Activities	332
Tours	332
Eating	332

❶ Arriving in Yosemite

Car Yosemite is accessible year-round from the west (via Hwys 120 W and 140) and south (Hwy 41), and also in summer from the east (via Hwy 120 E).

Bus and train Yosemite can easily be reached by public transportation. Greyhound buses and Amtrak trains serve Merced, west of the park, where they are met by buses operated by **Yosemite Area Regional Transportation System** (☏877-989-2787; www.yarts.com).

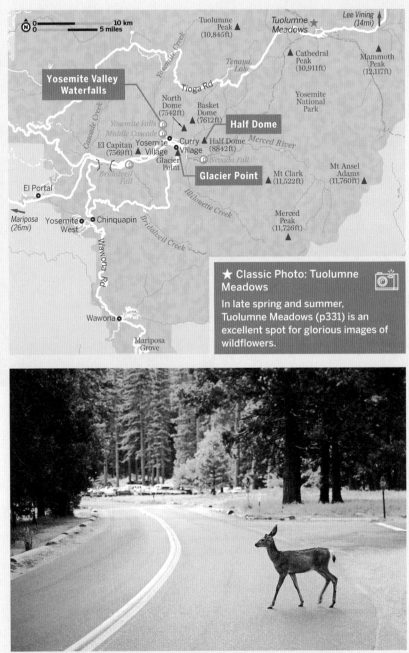

Yosemite Valley Waterfalls

Half Dome

Glacier Point

Tuolumne Peak ▲ (10,845ft)

Tuolumne Meadows ★

Lee Vining ↑ (14mi)

▲ Cathedral Peak (10,911ft)

Mammoth Peak (12,117ft)

Tenaya Lake

Tioga Rd

Yosemite National Park

North Dome (7542ft) ▲

Basket Dome ▲ (7612ft)

Yosemite Falls ◉

Middle Cascade ◉

El Capitan (7569ft) ▲

Yosemite Village ◉

Curry Village ◉

▲ Half Dome (8842ft)

Merced River

Glacier Point ◉

Nevada Fall ◉

Bridalveil Fall

Mt Clark ▲ (11,522ft)

Mt Ansel Adams (11,760ft) ▲

El Portal ◉

Illilouette Creek

Mariposa (26mi)

Yosemite West ◉

Chinquapin ◉

Bridalveil Creek

Wawona Rd

Merced Peak (11,726ft) ▲

Wawona ◉

Mariposa Grove

Cascade Creek

Yosemite Creek

★ Classic Photo: Tuolumne Meadows

In late spring and summer, Tuolumne Meadows (p331) is an excellent spot for glorious images of wildflowers.

From left: Yosemite Falls (p328); Eastern entrance to Yosemite National Park; Deer, Curry Village

JASON TODD / GETTY IMAGES ©

Glacier Point

A lofty 3200ft above the valley floor, Glacier Point presents one of the park's most eye-popping vistas and practically puts you at eye level with Half Dome.

Great For...

☑ Don't Miss

Trying to spot the teensy-looking hikers on Half Dome's summit.

The View

If you drove up here, the views from Glacier Point can make you feel like you cheated somehow – a huge array of superstar sights present themselves without any physical effort. A quick mosey up from the parking lot and you'll find the entire eastern Yosemite Valley spread out before you, from Yosemite Falls to Half Dome, as well as the distant peaks that ring Tuolumne Meadows. Half Dome looms practically at eye level, and if you look closely you can spot ant-sized hikers on its summit.

To the left of Half Dome lies the glacially carved Tenaya Canyon, and to its right are the wavy white ribbons of Nevada and Vernal Falls. On the valley floor, the Merced River snakes through green meadows and

View of Half Dome

KANWARJIT SINGH BOPARAI / ALAMY STOCK PHOTO ©

ⓘ Need to Know

Glacier Point Rd is typically open from May to November only.

✕ Take a Break

There's a **snack and drink stand** (⏱10am-5pm) near the car park.

★ Top Tip

Hikers can book a one-way ticket on the shuttle bus up to Glacier Point, then hike down.

groves of trees. Sidle up to the railing, hold on tight and peer 3200ft straight down at Curry Village. Basket Dome and North Dome rise to the north of the valley, and Liberty Cap and the Clark Range can be seen to the right of Half Dome.

Glacier Point Road

Almost from the park's inception, Glacier Point has been a popular destination. It used to be that getting up here was a major undertaking. That changed once the Four Mile Trail opened in 1872. A wagon road to the point was completed in 1882, and the current Glacier Point Rd was built in 1936.

It's at least an hour's drive from Yosemite Valley up Glacier Point Rd (which is usually open from May into November) off Hwy

41, or a strenuous hike along the Four Mile Trail (actually, 4.6 miles one way) or the less-crowded, waterfall-strewn Panorama Trail (8.5 miles one way). To hike one-way downhill from Glacier Point, reserve a seat on the hikers' shuttle bus (adult/child $25/15).

Overhanging Rock

At the tip of the point is Overhanging Rock, a huge granite slab protruding from the cliff edge like an outstretched tongue, defying gravity and once providing a scenic stage for daredevil extroverts. Through the years, many famous photos have been taken of folks performing handstands, high kicks and other wacky stunts on the rock. The precipice is now off-limits.

Half Dome

There's no doubt that Half Dome is Yosemite's most distinctive natural monument. It is 87 million years old and has a 93% vertical grade – the sheerest cliff in North America.

Great For...

☑ **Don't Miss**

The 1-mile trail to Mirror Lake for Half Dome views (though the lake dries up by late summer).

Mythical Origins

According to Native American legend, one of Yosemite Valley's early inhabitants went down from the mountains to Mono Lake, where he wed a Paiute named Tesaiyac. The journey back to the valley was difficult, and by the time they reached what was to become Mirror Lake, Tesaiyac had decided that she wanted to go back down to live with her people at Mono Lake. However, her husband refused to live on such barren, arid land with no oak trees from which to get acorns.

With a heart full of despair, Tesaiyac began to run toward Mono Lake, and her husband followed her. When the powerful spirits heard quarreling in Yosemite, they became angry and turned the two into stone: he became North Dome and she became Half Dome. The tears she cried made marks as they ran down her face, thus forming Mirror Lake.

Cable handrails leading to the summit

JOHN MOCK / GETTY IMAGES ©

Hiking

At 8842ft, Half Dome is Yosemite's spiritual centerpiece – its rounded granite pate forms an unmistakable silhouette. Geology left a one-of-a-kind imprint on the mega-rock, rendering it round and smooth on three sides, with that crazy-steep vertical face on the fourth side.

Climbers come from around the world to grapple with that legendary north face, but good hikers can reach the Half Dome summit via a 17-mile round-trip trail from Yosemite Valley. The trail gains 4900ft in elevation and has cable handrails for the last 200yd. The hike can be done in one day, but is more enjoyable if you break it up by camping along the way (Little Yosemite Valley is the most popular spot).

ⓘ Need to Know

You can only climb Half Dome when the cables are up, generally from late May to mid-October.

✕ Take a Break

Pick up snacks at **Curry Village**, three-quarters of a mile from the trailhead.

★ Top Tip

Aim to reach the summit early in the day; thunderstorms become more prevalent in the afternoon.

Permits

To stem lengthy lines (and increasingly dangerous conditions) on the vertiginous cables of Half Dome, the park now requires that all-day hikers obtain an advance permit to climb the cables. There are currently three ways to do this, though check www.nps.gov/yose/planyourvisit/hdpermits.htm for the latest information.

Preseason permit lottery (☎877-444-6777; www.recreation.gov; application fee online/by phone $4.50/6.50) Lottery applications for the 300 daily spots must be completed in March, with confirmation notification sent in mid-April.

Daily lottery Approximately 50 additional permits are distributed by lottery two days before each hiking date. Apply online or by phone between midnight and 1pm Pacific Time. It's easier to score weekday permits.

Backpackers Those with Yosemite-issued wilderness permits that *reasonably include* Half Dome can request Half Dome permits ($8 per person) without going through the lottery process.

DON SMITH / GETTY IMAGES ©

Yosemite Valley Waterfalls

Yosemite's waterfalls mesmerize even the most jaded traveler, especially when the spring runoff turns them into thunderous cataracts.

Great For...

☑ **Don't Miss**

The quiet Yosemite Falls Trail – it's a tough 3.4 miles, but it pays off with nifty views.

Yosemite Falls

Yosemite Falls is considered the tallest in North America, dropping 2425ft in three tiers. A slick wheelchair-accessible trail leads to the bottom of this cascade or, if you prefer solitude and different perspectives, you can also clamber up the Yosemite Falls Trail, which puts you atop the falls after a grueling 3.4 miles.

No less impressive are nearby Bridalveil Fall and others scattered throughout the valley.

Bridalveil Fall

At the southwest end of the valley, Bridalveil Fall tumbles 620ft. The Ahwahneechee people call it Pohono (Spirit of the Puffing Wind), as gusts often blow the fall from side to side, even lifting water back up into the

Bridalveil Fall

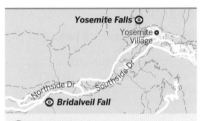

Yosemite Falls ◎
Yosemite ●
Village
Northside Dr   Southside Dr
◎ **Bridalveil Fall**

❶ Need to Know
Spring is the best time to see the falls at their most dramatic, as snowmelt amps up the flow.

✕ Take a Break
Yosemite Village, with quick-bite cafés and shops, is about 5 miles east of Bridalveil Fall.

★ Top Tip
Ditch the car and let the Valley or El Capitan shuttle do the driving for you.

Yosemite Valley Drive

The only driving route in Yosemite Valley takes you past the valley's classic sights and viewpoints, including Bridalveil Fall and Yosemite Falls. Most of this route is covered by the free Yosemite Valley and El Capitan shuttles (the latter goes as far west as the El Capitan Bridge), so consider parking the car, freeing up your hands, and doing this by public transport.

The 12.5-mile loop follows the only two roads in and out of Yosemite Valley: Northside Drive and Southside Drive. Each is (mostly) one way and, as their names suggest, they sit on either side of the Merced River. Without traffic, you can easily drive the loop in less than an hour, but budget more time as you'll want to stop frequently. Despite the fact that the park service has tried to limit the number of cars in the valley, it remains a popular driving tour.

air. This waterfall usually runs year-round, though it's often reduced to a whisper by midsummer. Bring rain gear or expect to get soaked when the fall is heavy.

Park at the large lot where Wawona Rd (Hwy 41) meets Southside Dr. From the lot, it's a quarter-mile walk to the base of the fall. The path is paved, but probably too rough for wheelchairs, and there's a somewhat steep climb at the very end. Avoid climbing on the slippery rocks at its base – no one likes a broken bone.

If you'd rather walk from the valley, a trail (part of the Loop Trails) follows Southside Dr, beginning near the LeConte Memorial Lodge and running about 3.8 miles west to the falls.

⊙ SIGHTS

The main entrances to the **park** (☏20 9-372-0200; www.nps.gov/yose; 7-day entry per car $30) are at Arch Rock (Hwy 140), Wawona (Hwy 41) and Big Oak Flat (Hwy 120 west). Tioga Pass (Hwy 120 east) is open only seasonally.

Yosemite Valley

From the ground up, this dramatic valley cut by the meandering Merced River is song-inspiring: rippling green meadow-grass; stately pines; cool, impassive pools reflecting looming granite monoliths; and cascading ribbons of glacially cold white-water.

Spring snowmelt turns the valley's famous waterfalls into thunderous cataracts; most are reduced to a mere trickle by late summer. Yosemite Falls is North America's tallest, dropping 2425ft in three tiers. A wheelchair-accessible trail leads to the bottom of this cascade or, for solitude and different perspectives, you can trek the grueling switchback trail to the top (6.8 miles round-trip). No less impressive are other waterfalls around the valley. A strenuous granite staircase beside Vernal Fall leads you, gasping, right to the waterfall's edge for a vertical view – look for rainbows in the clouds of mist.

You can't ignore the valley's monumental El Capitan (7569ft), an El Dorado for rock climbers. Toothed Half Dome (8842ft) soars above the valley as Yosemite's spiritual centerpiece. The classic panoramic photo-op is at Tunnel View on Hwy 41 as you drive into the valley.

El Capitan

At nearly 3600ft from base to summit, El Capitan ranks as one of the world's largest granite monoliths. Its sheer face makes it a world-class destination for experienced climbers, and one that wasn't 'conquered' until 1958. Since then, it's been inundated. Look closely and you'll probably spot climbers reckoning with El Cap's series of cracks and ledges, including the famous 'Nose.' At night, park along the road and dim your headlights; once your eyes adjust, you'll

DAVID COURTENAY / GETTY IMAGES ©

easily make out the pinpricks of headlamps dotting the rock face. Listen, too, for voices.

The road offers several good spots from which to ogle El Capitan. The Valley View turnout is one. For a wider view, try the pullout along Southside Dr just east of Bridalveil Fall. You can also park on Northside Dr, just below El Capitan, perhaps the best vantage point from which to see climbers, though you'll need binoculars for a really good view. Look for the haul bags first – they're bigger, more colorful and move around more than the climbers, making them easier to spot. The Yosemite Climbing Association (www.yosemiteclimbing.org) began an 'Ask-a-Climber' program in 2011, where it sets up a telescope at El Capitan Bridge for a few hours a day (mid-May through mid-October) and answers visitors' questions.

Tuolumne Meadows

A 90-minute drive from Yosemite Valley, high-altitude Tuolumne Meadows (pronounced TWOL-uh-mee) draws hikers, backpackers and climbers to the park's northern wilderness. The Sierra Nevada's largest subalpine meadow (8600ft), it's a vivid contrast to the valley, with wildflower fields, azure lakes, ragged granite peaks, polished domes and cooler temperatures. Hikers and climbers have a paradise of options; lake swimming and picnicking are also popular. Access is via scenic Tioga Rd (Hwy 120), which is only open seasonally (usually June through October). West of Tuolumne Meadows and Tenaya Lake, stop at Olmsted Point for epic vistas of Half Dome.

Yosemite Village & Gateway Towns

Though it's often overrun and traffic-choked, you'll likely find yourself in Yosemite Village at some point. It is home to the park's main visitor center and general store, and it offers just about every amenity – from pizzas and ice cream to firewood and wilderness permits. In addition, there are many gateway towns outside the park that have a mix of lodgings and amenities. These include Fish Camp, Oakhurst, El Portal, Mariposa, Groveland and Lee Vining.

★ Top Five for Wildlife Spotting

Black bears

Mule deer

Gray fox

Steller's jays

Bobcats

From left: Mule deer; Tuolumne River; Bobcat

DON SMITH / GETTY IMAGES ©

Yosemite Valley at night

go for moonlit hikes with stargazing

✈ ACTIVITIES

With over 800 miles of varied hiking trails, you're spoiled for choice. Easy valley-floor routes can get jammed; escape the teeming masses by heading up. The ultimate hike summits Half Dome (14 to 16 miles round-trip), but be warned: it's very strenuous, and advance lottery permits are required even for day hikes. Without a permit, it's rewarding to hike just as far as the top of Vernal Fall (2.4 miles round-trip) or Nevada Fall (5.4 miles round-trip) via the Mist Trail.

Yosemite Mountaineering School
Rock Climbing

Offers top-flight instruction for novice to advanced climbers, plus guided climbs and equipment rental. During peak summer season, it also operates at Tuolumne

Meadows. (☏209-372-8344; Curry Village; ⊙Apr-Oct)

⊙ TOURS

The nonprofit **Yosemite Conservancy** (☏209-379-2317; www.yosemiteconservancy.org) has scheduled tours of all kinds, plus custom trips available.

First-timers often appreciate the year-round, two-hour Valley Floor Tour run by **Yosemite Hospitality/Aramark** (☏20 9-372-4386, 209-372-1240), which covers the valley highlights. Call or check the *Yosemite Guide* for pricing.

For other tour options stop at the tour and activity desks at Yosemite Lodge at the Falls, Curry Village or Yosemite Village.

✴ EATING

Concessionaire **Aramark** (www.aramark.com) has a monopoly on park lodging and eating establishments, including fast-food courts and snack bars. Lodging reservations (up to 366 days in advance) are essential for peak season (May through September).

Mountain Room Restaurant
American $$$

With a killer view of Yosemite Falls, the window tables at this casual and elegant contemporary steakhouse are a hot commodity. The chefs whip up the best meals in the park, with flat-iron steak and locally caught mountain trout wooing diners under a rotating display of nature photographs. Reservations are accepted only for groups larger than eight; casual dress is okay. (209-372-1403; Yosemite Lodge; mains $17-36; 5:30-9:30pm;)

ℹ INFORMATION

Yosemite Valley Visitor Center (209-372-0200; Yosemite Village; 9am-5pm) The main office, with exhibits and free film screenings in the theater.

TOP TIPS

The following tips will help you avoid the worst of the Yosemite crowds:

Avoid summer in the valley. Spring's best, especially when waterfalls gush in May. Autumn is blissfully peaceful, and snowy winter days can be magical too.

Park your car and leave it – simply by hiking a short distance up almost any trail, you'll lose car-dependent hordes.

Get up for sunrise, or go for moonlit hikes with stargazing.

ACCOMMODATIONS

More than four million people visit Yosemite each year, many as day visitors but many also vying for the small number of campsites and tent cabins available in the park. It gets especially crowded in Yosemite Valley. Overnighters looking for a quieter, more rugged experience are better off in spots like Bridalveil Creek, Yosemite Creek

⌖ Detour: Wawona

At Wawona, an hour's drive south of Yosemite Valley, drop by the **Pioneer Yosemite History Center** (rides adult/child $5/4; 24hr, rides Wed-Sun Jun-Sep;) FREE, with its covered bridge, historic buildings and horse-drawn stagecoach rides. Further south stands towering Mariposa Grove, home of the Grizzly Giant and other giant sequoia trees. Note the grove is closed to visitors for restoration until spring 2017.

JASON TODD / GETTY IMAGES ©

and Porcupine Flat. Reservations are essential; book through Aramark (www.aramark.com).

For lodgings outside the park, try the gateway towns of Fish Camp, Oakhurst, El Portal, Midpines, Mariposa, Groveland and, in the Eastern Sierra, Lee Vining.

ℹ GETTING AROUND

Free shuttle buses loop around Yosemite Valley and, in summer, the Tuolumne Meadows/Tioga Rd and Wawona/Mariposa Grove areas. Bike rentals (per hour/day $12/34) are available seasonally at Yosemite Lodge and Curry Village, both in the valley.

Faneuil Hall (p101), Boston

In Focus

USA Today 336
Find out what's happening with equality, healthcare and the environment.

History 338
The American story, from struggling colony to world superpower.

Food & Drink 348
Be tempted by America's diverse offerings, from award-winning restaurants to locally made wine and beer.

Sport 352
Beer, hotdogs and baseball, football and basketball: what could be more American?

Arts & Culture 355
Music, film, literature and visual arts: the US has made a huge footprint on the world's cultural scene.

View from the High Line (p50), New York City

USA Today

A historic ruling by the Supreme Court heralded a new era of equality for the world's largest democracy – this on the heels of another high court ruling on healthcare, a pivotal legacy of President Obama. Other hot topics of the day are greener lifestyles and the ever-increasing allure of city life – resulting in a lack of affordable housing, among other things.

A Rainbow Nation

No one who witnessed the Stonewall Riots – which sparked the gay liberation movement in 1969 – could have imagined that he or she would live to see the day when gay marriage would become legal in the United States. Yet on June 26, 2015, that's exactly what happened when the US Supreme Court ruled that all states must recognize same-sex marriage licenses. The historic ruling was the culmination of a long legal battle by gay rights advocates, and there was much euphoria on the streets – especially since the ruling coincided with Pride events happening across the nation.

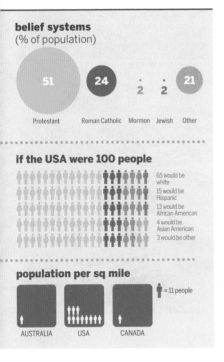

belief systems
(% of population)

51 Protestant
24 Roman Catholic
2 Mormon
2 Jewish
21 Other

if the USA were 100 people

65 would be white
15 would be Hispanic
13 would be African American
4 would be Asian American
3 would be other

population per sq mile

🚶 ≈ 11 people

AUSTRALIA USA CANADA

Healthcare for All

The ruling on same-sex marriages came just days after another important ruling. This one related to the Affordable Care Act (ACA), President Obama's program to extend healthcare through subsidies to millions of uninsured Americans. The court upheld key provisions of the law (the second time the Supreme Court had ruled on Obamacare), though the future of the ACA remains far from certain. Since the law's implementation the House and Senate had tried (unsuccessfully) to repeal Obamacare more than 50 times. Despite congressional obstructionism, the program has been a success, allowing over 16 million uninsured Americans to obtain coverage.

Changing Cityscapes

Cities are booming in America, growing at a faster rate than the rest of the country. Far from being the burned-out hulls of decades past, American cities are safer, and have wide-ranging appeal (in the realm of culture, food, nightlife, liveability). Yet with more people moving from the suburbs to the exurbs to city centers, this has brought many challenges – particularly as the wealthy displace low- and middle-income residents. Some mayors, like Bill De Blasio of New York City and Ed Lee of San Francisco, have launched ambitious programs to create more affordable housing. De Blasio stated that unless New York acted boldly the city risked becoming a gated community of exclusivity rather than opportunity. The same could be said for many American cities.

Greener Futures

With more people moving to urban areas, cities have also grappled with transportation. Building more roads has never helped alleviate traffic congestion – as engineers have known since the 1960s. The answer has been greater investment in public transit. Cities, once deeply married to the automobile (Houston, we're looking at you), have great expanded public transport options, with new light rail lines, express bus lines and dedicated bus lanes. Bike-sharing programs have also exploded across the country, with more than 50 cities offering easy rental (usually by the day and week) for residents and visitors. The benefits – fewer cars on the streets, a bit of exercise for commuters, less carbon in the atmosphere – are obvious, though critics worry about injuries (no bike-sharing programs provide helmets), as well as the long-term financial viability of these often expensive programs.

Plaque commemorating the Declaration of Independence

History

Demagogues, visionaries and immigrants all contribute to the American story. Early colonists arrive in the 1600s, planting the seeds of independence, which later blossom into full nationhood. Westward expansion follows, along with bloody civil war and the emancipation of slaves. In modern times, the US struggles through the Great Depression and horrific wars, and enacts great changes during the Civil Rights movement. After the USSR's demise, the US becomes the world's leading superpower.

8000 BC

Widespread extinction of Ice Age mammals. Indigenous peoples hunt smaller game and start gathering native plants.

7000 BC–100 AD

During the 'Archaic period,' the agricultural 'three sisters' (corn, beans, squash) and permanent settlements become established.

1492

Italian explorer Christopher Columbus 'discovers' America, eventually making three voyages throughout the Caribbean.

Sign at the Boston Tea Party Ships & Museum (p101), Boston

KUMAR SRISKANDAN / ALAMY STOCK PHOTO ©

Enter the Europeans

In 1492 the Italian explorer Christopher Columbus, backed by the monarchy of Spain, voyaged west by sea, looking for the East Indies. With visions of gold, Spanish explorers quickly followed: Hernán Cortés conquered much of today's Mexico; Francisco Pizarro conquered Peru; Juan Ponce de León wandered through Florida looking for the fountain of youth. Not to be left out, the French explored Canada and the Midwest, while the Dutch and English cruised North America's eastern seaboard.

Of course, they weren't the first ones on the continent. When Europeans arrived, between two million and 18 million Native American people occupied the lands north of present-day Mexico and spoke more than 300 languages. European explorers left in their wake diseases to which indigenous peoples had no immunity. More than any other factor – war, slavery or famine – disease epidemics devastated indigenous populations, by anywhere from 50% to 90%. By the 17th century, Native North Americans numbered only about one million, and many of the continent's once-thriving societies were in turmoil and transition.

1607	**1620**	**1773**
Jamestown is founded, though life there is grim: 80 of 108 settlers die during the first year.	The *Mayflower* lands at Plymouth with 102 English Pilgrims. Native Americans save them from starvation.	Bostonians protest British taxes by dumping tea into the harbor, called the 'Boston Tea Party.'

★ **The Best Historic Sites**

Freedom Trail (p96), Boston

National Mall (p130), Washington, DC

Alcatraz (p296), San Francisco

John F Kennedy National Historic Site
(p106), Boston

Freedom Trail (p96) marker, Boston

RICHARD CUMMINS / GETTY IMAGES ©

In 1607, English nobles established North America's first permanent European settlement, in Jamestown, Virginia. Eventually the colony came to be run by a representative assembly of citizens, and it brought the first African slaves to the continent to work the tobacco fields.

In 1620, a boatload of radically religious Puritans established a colony at Plymouth, Massachusetts. Their settlement – intended to be a religious and moral beacon to the world – was notable for its 'Mayflower Compact,' an agreement to govern themselves by consensus. Sadly, the harmony did not extend to the colonists' relationships with local Native American tribes, and their eventual falling out led to bloody warfare.

Thus, at Jamestown and Plymouth, the seeds of the 'American paradox' were sown: white political and religious freedom would come to be founded through the enslavement of blacks and the displacement of Native Americans.

The American Revolution

For the next 150 years, European powers – particularly England, France, Portugal and Spain – competed for position and territory, bringing all their Old World political struggles to the new one. In the south, English businessmen developed a cotton and tobacco plantation economy that became entirely dependent on the use of forced labor, and slavery was eventually legalized into a formal institution. By 1800, one out of every five persons in America was a slave.

Meanwhile, in the 1760s – after winning the Seven Years' War with France and finally gaining control of the eastern seaboard – England started asking the American colonies to chip in to the Crown's coffers. Up to then, Britain had mostly left the colonists alone to govern themselves, but now England raised new taxes and stationed a permanent army.

This didn't sit well, to put it mildly. Colonists protested and boycotted English policies (arguing for 'no taxation without representation'), and openly questioned the benefits of monarchy. Who needed a king imposing rules from abroad when they were doing quite well without one?

1775	1781	1787
Paul Revere warns colonial militia that British troops are coming. The Revolutionary War begins.	General Washington leads his ragtag troops to victory at Yorktown as the British surrender.	US Constitution establishes a democratic form of government, with power vested in the hands of the people.

In 1774, fired by increasing conflict and the era's Enlightenment ideas of individualism, equality and liberty, the colonists convened the First Continental Congress in Philadelphia to decide what to do. Before they could agree, in April 1775, British troops skirmished with armed colonists in Massachusetts, and both sides were at war.

It wasn't until July 4, 1776, that the Revolutionary War's ultimate treasonous goal – independence from England – was first articulated in the Declaration of Independence. Unfortunately, the Continental army, led by George Washington, was underfunded, poorly armed, badly trained and outnumbered by Britain's troops, who were the largest professional army in the world. If not for a 1778 alliance with France, which provided the materials and sea power that eventually won the war for the colonists, America might very well have been a short-lived experiment.

Westward Expansion

After winning independence, the Founding Fathers came to the hard part: fashioning a government. The US Constitution wasn't adopted until 1787. While the democratic government it created amounted to a radical political revolution, economic and social relationships were not revolutionized: rich landholders kept their property, including slaves; Native Americans were excluded from the nation; and women were excluded from politics. As a result, following the ratification of the Constitution, US life has pulsed with the ongoing struggle to define 'all' and 'equal' and 'liberty' – to take the universal language of America's founding and either rectify or justify the inevitable disparities that bedevil any large society.

It would be 70 years before the first real troubles surfaced. In the meantime, America looked west, and its ambitions grew to continental size. Believers in 'manifest destiny' felt that it was divinely fated that the United States should occupy all the land from sea to shining sea – and through wars, purchase and outright theft, they succeeded. Particularly after the discovery of gold in California in 1848 (the Spanish explorers just hadn't known where to look), groaning wagon trains brought fevered pioneers west, a motley collection of miners, farmers, entrepreneurs, immigrants, outlaws and prostitutes, all seeking their fortunes on the frontier. This made for exciting, legendary times, but throughout loomed a troubling question: as new states joined the USA, would they be slave states or free states? The nation's future depended on the answer.

The Civil War

The US Constitution hadn't ended slavery, but it had given Congress the power to approve (or not) slavery in new states. Public debates raged constantly over the expansion of slavery, particularly since this shaped the balance of power between the industrial North and the agrarian South.

1803–06	**1849**	**1865**
France sells the US the Louisiana Purchase; Lewis and Clark then trailblaze west through it to reach the Pacific Ocean.	An epic cross-country gold rush sees 60,000 'Forty-Niners' flock to California's Mother Lode.	The Civil War ends, though celebration is curtailed by President Lincoln's assassination five days later.

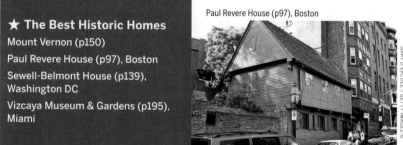

Paul Revere House (p97), Boston

GARY D ERCOLE / GETTY IMAGES ©

★ **The Best Historic Homes**
Mount Vernon (p150)
Paul Revere House (p97), Boston
Sewell-Belmont House (p139),
Washington DC
Vizcaya Museum & Gardens (p195),
Miami

Since the founding, Southern politicians had dominated government and defended slavery as 'natural and normal,' which an 1856 *New York Times* editorial called 'insanity.' The Southern pro-slavery lobby enraged Northern abolitionists. But even many Northern politicians feared that ending slavery would be ruinous. Limit slavery, they reasoned, and in the competition with industry and free labor, slavery would wither without inciting a violent slave revolt – a constantly feared possibility. Indeed, in 1859, radical abolitionist John Brown tried unsuccessfully to spark an uprising to free the slaves at Harpers Ferry, West Virginia.

The economics of slavery were undeniable. In 1860, there were more than four million slaves in the US, most held by Southern planters, who grew 75% of the world's cotton, accounting for over half of US exports. Thus, the Southern economy supported the nation's economy, and it required slaves. The 1860 presidential election became a referendum on this issue, and the election was won by a young politician who favored limiting slavery: Abraham Lincoln.

In the South, even the threat of federal limits was too onerous and, as President Lincoln took office, 11 states seceded from the Union and formed the Confederate States of America. Lincoln faced the nation's greatest moment of crisis. He had two choices: let the Southern states secede or wage war to keep the Union intact. He chose the latter.

The war began in April 1861, when the Confederacy attacked Fort Sumter in Charleston, South Carolina, and raged for the next four years in some of the most gruesome combat the world had known. By the end, more than 600,000 soldiers – nearly an entire generation of young men – were dead, and Southern plantations and cities (most notably Atlanta) lay sacked and burned. The North's industrial might provided an advantage, but its victory was not preordained; it unfolded battle by bloody battle.

As fighting progressed, Lincoln recognized that if the war didn't end slavery outright, victory would be pointless. In 1863, his Emancipation Proclamation expanded the war's aims and freed all slaves. In April 1865, Confederate General Robert E Lee surrendered to Union General Ulysses S Grant in Appomattox, Virginia. The Union had been preserved, but at a staggering cost.

1870

Freed black men are given the vote, vote, but the South's segregationist 'Jim Crow' laws remain until the 1960s.

1880–1920

Millions of immigrants flood in to the US' cities from Europe and Asia, fueling a new age of urban living.

1917

President Woodrow Wilson plunges the US into WWI, pledging that 'the world must be made safe for democracy.'

Immigration & Industrial Revolution

The Civil War ended an economic system of forced labor. But American society remained largely, and often deeply, racist. During Reconstruction (1865–77), the civil rights of ex-slaves were protected by the federal government, which also extracted reparations from Southern states, creating Civil War grudges that lingered for a century.

After Reconstruction, Southern states developed a labor system of indentured servitude (called 'sharecropping') and enacted laws aimed at keeping whites and blacks 'separate but equal.' The South's segregationist 'Jim Crow' laws (which remained in place until the 1960s Civil Rights movement) effectively disenfranchised African Americans in every sphere of daily life.

Meanwhile, with the rapid, post–Civil War settlement of the West, the US appeared like a mythic 'land of opportunity' to immigrants, who flooded in from Europe and Asia. In total, about 25 million people arrived between 1880 and 1920. Poles, Germans, Irish, Italians, Russians, Eastern Europeans, Chinese and more fed an urban migration that made the late 19th century the age of cities. New York was transformed into a buzzing, multi-ethnic 'melting pot,' and the nation's undisputed capital of commerce and finance.

America's industrialists became so rich, and so effective at creating monopolies in steel, oil, banking and railroads, that they became known as 'robber barons,' and not always disparagingly. These paragons of capitalism fueled the industrial revolution, even as choking factories and sweatshops consigned many to lives of poverty and pain. Through the turn of the century, the rise of labor unions and progressive reformers, such as President Woodrow Wilson, led to new laws that broke up the monopolies and softened workplace abuses.

After the US' brief involvement in WWI, the prosperity of the 'roaring' 1920s led to a wave of optimism and good times. The Jazz Age bloomed: flappers danced the Charleston, radio and movies captivated millions, and stock prices went up, up, up.

Americans Get a New Deal

America reached its lowest point in history during the Great Depression. By 1932, nearly one-third of all US workers were unemployed. National output fell by 50%, hundreds of banks shuttered, and great swaths of the country seemed to disappear beneath enormous dust storms.

Franklin D Roosevelt, elected president in 1932, helped rescue the nation from collapse. He bailed out banks, saved homeowners from foreclosure and added millions of jobs. He created massive projects like the Civilian Conservation Corps, which planted more than two billion trees, and the Works Progress Administration, a 600,000-strong workforce that built bridges, dams and other infrastructure.

1920	1920s	1941–45
The 19th Amendment is passed, giving US women the right to vote.	The Harlem Renaissance inspires a burst of African American literature, art, music and cultural pride.	The US enters WWII, deploying more than 16 million troops and suffering around 400,000 deaths.

Brown vs Board of Education National Historic Site

Great Depression, the New Deal & World War II

In October 1929, investors, worried about a gloomy global economy, started selling stocks. But all that selling caused everyone to panic, until they'd sold everything. The stock market crashed, and the US economy collapsed like a house of cards.

Thus began the Great Depression. Frightened banks called in their dodgy loans, people couldn't pay, and the banks folded. Millions lost their homes, farms, businesses and savings, and as much as 50% of the American workforce became unemployed in certain parts of the country (the overall rate at its peak was nearly 33%). In 1932, Democrat Franklin D Roosevelt was elected president on the promise of a 'New Deal' to rescue the US from its crisis, which he did with resounding success.

When war once again broke out in Europe in 1939, the isolationist mood in the US was as strong as ever. But the extremely popular President Roosevelt, elected to an unprecedented third term in 1940, understood that the US couldn't sit by and risk victory for the fascist armies in Europe. Roosevelt sent aid to Britain and persuaded a skittish Congress to go along with it.

On December 7, 1941, Japan launched a surprise attack on Hawaii's Pearl Harbor, killing more than 2000 Americans and sinking several battleships. As US isolationism trans-

1954	1959–75	1963
In *Brown v Board of Education*, the Supreme Court ends segregation in public schools.	The US fights the Vietnam War, supporting South Vietnam against communist North Vietnam.	President John F Kennedy is assassinated while riding in a motorcade in Dallas, Texas.

WALTER BIBIKOW / GETTY IMAGES ©

formed overnight into outrage, Roosevelt suddenly had the support he needed. Germany declared war on the US, and America joined the Allied fight against Hitler and the Axis powers, putting almost its entire will and industrial prowess into the war effort.

Initially, neither the Pacific nor European theaters went well for America. Fighting in the Pacific didn't turn around until the US unexpectedly routed the Japanese navy at Midway Island in June 1942. In Europe, the US dealt the fatal blow to Germany with its massive D-Day invasion of France on June 6, 1944. Germany surrendered the following year.

Nevertheless, Japan continued fighting. Rather than invade the country, President Harry Truman chose to drop experimental atomic bombs (created by the government's top-secret Manhattan Project) on Hiroshima and Nagasaki in August 1945, destroying both cities. Japan surrendered, but the nuclear age was born.

The Civil Rights Movement

From the 1950s, a movement got under way in African American communities to fight for equality. Rosa Parks, who refused to give up her seat to a white passenger on a bus, inspired the Montgomery bus boycott. There were sit-ins at lunch counters where blacks were excluded; massive demonstrations led by Martin Luther King Jr in Washington, DC; and harrowing journeys by 'freedom riders' aiming to end bus segregation. The work of millions paid off: in 1964, President Lyndon Johnson signed the Civil Rights Act, which banned discrimination and racial segregation by federal law.

The Red Scare, Civil Rights & the Wars in Asia

In the decades after WWII, the US enjoyed unprecedented prosperity but little peace.

Formerly wartime allies, the communist Soviet Union and the capitalist USA soon engaged in a running competition to dominate the globe. The superpowers engaged in proxy wars – notably the Korean War (1950–53) and Vietnam War (1959–75) – with only the mutual threat of nuclear annihilation preventing direct war. The UN, founded in 1945, couldn't overcome this worldwide ideological split and was largely ineffectual in preventing Cold War conflicts.

Meanwhile, with its continent unscarred and its industry bulked up by WWII, the American homeland entered an era of growing affluence. In the 1950s, a mass migration left the inner cities for the suburbs, where affordable single-family homes sprang up. Americans drove cheap cars using cheap gas over brand-new interstate highways. They relaxed with the comforts of modern technology, swooned over TV, and got busy, giving birth to a 'baby boom.'

Middle-class whites did, anyway. African Americans remained segregated, poor and generally unwelcome at the party. Echoing 19th-century abolitionist Frederick Douglass, the Southern Christian Leadership Coalition (SCLC), led by African American preacher

1964	**1974**	**1989**
Congress passes the Civil Rights Act, outlawing discrimination on the basis of race, color, religion, sex or national origin.	President Richard Nixon resigns after being connected to the Watergate burglary of Democratic headquarters.	The 1960s-era Berlin Wall is torn down, marking the official end of the decades-long Cold War.

National Museum of the American Indian (p133)

PAUL FRANKLIN / GETTY IMAGES ©

★ **The Best Ethnic & Cultural Sites**

Ellis Island (p45), NYC

National Museum of the American Indian (p133), Washington DC

La Plaza de Cultura y Artes (p274), Los Angeles

Martin Luther King Jr, aimed to end segregation and 'save America's soul': to realize color-blind justice, racial equality and fairness of economic opportunity for all.

Beginning in the 1950s, King preached and organized nonviolent resistance in the form of bus boycotts, marches and sit-ins, mainly in the South. White authorities often met these protests with water hoses and batons, and demonstrations sometimes dissolved into riots, but with the 1964 Civil Rights Act, African Americans spurred a wave of legislation that swept away racist laws and laid the groundwork for a more just and equal society.

Meanwhile, the 1960s saw further social upheavals: rock and roll spawned a youth rebellion, and drugs sent Technicolor visions spinning in their heads. President John F Kennedy was assassinated in Dallas in 1963, followed by the assassinations in 1968 of his brother Senator Robert Kennedy and of Martin Luther King Jr. Americans' faith in their leaders and government was further tested by the bombings and brutalities of the Vietnam War, as seen on TV, which led to widespread student protests.

Yet President Richard Nixon, elected in 1968 partly for promising an 'honorable end to the war,' instead escalated US involvement and secretly bombed Laos and Cambodia. Then, in 1972, the Watergate scandal broke. A burglary at the Democratic Party offices was, through dogged journalism, tied to 'Tricky Dick,' and in 1974 he became the first US president to resign from office.

The tumultuous 1960s and '70s also witnessed the sexual revolution, women's liberation, struggles for gay equality, energy crises over the supply of crude oil from the Middle East and, with the 1962 publication of Rachel Carson's *Silent Spring,* the realization that the USA's industries had created a polluted, diseased environmental mess.

Pax Americana & the War on Terror

In 1980, Republican California governor and former actor Ronald Reagan campaigned for president by promising to make Americans feel good about America again. The affable Reagan won easily, and his election marked a pronounced shift to the right in US politics.

1990s	2001	2005
The internet revolution creates the biggest boom and bust since the Great Depression.	The September 11 terrorist attacks destroy NYC's World Trade Center and kill nearly 3000 people.	Hurricane Katrina ruptures levees, flooding New Orleans and killing more than 1800 people.

Reagan wanted to defeat communism, restore the economy, deregulate business and cut taxes. To tackle the first two, he launched the biggest peacetime military build-up in history, and dared the Soviets to keep up. They went broke trying, one of the many factors that led to the eventual dissolution of the USSR at the end of the decade.

Reagan's military spending and tax cuts created enormous federal deficits, but these were largely erased during the 1990s high-tech internet boom, which seemed to augur a 'new US economy' based on white-collar telecommunications. These hopes and surpluses vanished in 2000, when the high-tech stock bubble burst. That year, after one of the most divisive elections in modern US politics, President George W Bush enacted tax cuts that returned federal deficits to amounts greater than before.

On September 11, 2001, Islamic terrorists flew hijacked planes into New York's World Trade Center and the Pentagon in Washington, DC. This catastrophic attack united Americans behind their president as he vowed revenge and declared a 'war on terror.' Bush soon attacked Afghanistan in an unsuccessful hunt for Al-Qaeda terrorist cells, then he attacked Iraq in 2003 and toppled its president, Saddam Hussein. Meanwhile, Iraq descended into civil war.

Bush's second term was marred by scandals and failures – torture photos from Abu Ghraib, the federal response in the aftermath of Hurricane Katrina and the inability to bring the Iraq War to a close.

Promising hope and change, Democrat Barack Obama was elected as the nation's first African American president in 2008, in itself a hopeful sign that the US' long-standing racial divides were healing. However, Obama's New Deal–style initiatives – such as a massive economic stimulus bill and an overhaul of the broken US healthcare system – were met with widespread protests from a growing anti-government, conservative 'Tea Party' movement.

President Obama won reelection in 2012, aided in large part by the most ethnically and racially diverse coalition in American history. Over 90% of African Americans and nearly 70% of Latinos voted for the man who described himself as 'a mutt.'

Although stymied by congressional obstructionists, Obama had many notable successes during his two terms. He helped open relations with Cuba, oversaw the raid that brought down Osama bin Laden and passed a significant stimulus program that helped create jobs and kept the US out of a major economic meltdown. Perhaps most importantly, he oversaw the passage of the Affordable Care Act, which brought healthcare to millions of previously uninsured Americans.

2008–9	2012	2015
Barack Obama becomes the first African American president.	Hurricane Sandy devastates the East Coast. More than 80 Americans die (plus 200 more in other countries).	In a landmark decision, the US Supreme Court legalizes same-sex marriage. Gay couples can now wed in all 50 states.

Katz's Delicatessen (p75), New York City

Food & Drink

Long before the dawn of competitive cooking shows, molecular gastronomy and organic farm stands, Wampanoag tribespeople brought food to help the Pilgrims stave off certain famine over the winter of 1620, thus kicking off the very first Thanksgiving. Since then Americans have mixed myriad food cultures to create their own distinct culinary traditions, based in part on the rich bounty of the continent.

Staples & Specialties

These days you can get almost every type of food nearly everywhere in the US, but regional specialties are always best in the places they originated.

NYC: Culinary Powerhouse

They say that you could eat at a different restaurant every night of your life in New York City and not exhaust the possibilities. Considering that there are more than 23,000 restaurants in the five boroughs, with constant openings and closings, it's true. Owing to its huge immigrant population and an influx of over 50 million tourists annually, New York captures the title of America's greatest restaurant city, hands down. Its diverse neighborhoods

Clambake

serve authentic Italian food and thin crust–style pizza, all manner of Asian food, French *haute cuisine*, and classic Jewish deli food, from bagels to piled-high pastrami on rye. And the list goes around the globe: Moroccan, Indian, Vietnamese, Russian, Cuban, Brazilian and more. Plus, Manhattan boasts street-cart dining that puts some city restaurant scenes to shame.

Mid-Atlantic: Global Cooking, Crab Cakes & Cheesesteaks

Washington, DC, has a wide array of global fare – not surprising given its ethnically diverse population. In particular, you'll find some of the country's best Ethiopian food. DC also makes fine use of its position near the Chesapeake Bay, offering top crab cakes and seafood. In Philadelphia you can gorge on 'Philly cheese steaks': thin sautéed beef, fried onions and melted cheese on a bun.

New England: Clambakes & Lobster Boils

New England's claim of having the nation's best seafood is hard to beat, because the North Atlantic offers up clams, mussels, oysters and huge lobsters, along with shad, bluefish and cod. New Englanders love a good chowder (seafood stew) and a good clambake, an almost ritual meal where the shellfish are buried in a pit fire with corn, chicken, potatoes and sausages. Fried clam fritters and lobster rolls (lobster meat with mayonnaise served in a bread bun) are served throughout the region. There are excellent cheeses made in Vermont, cranberries (a Thanksgiving staple) harvested in Massachusetts, and maple syrup from

Chicago deep-dish pizza

ANNA ANDRES / GETTY IMAGES ©

★ **The Best Local Temptations**
Boston clam chowder
Maine lobster
Cajun crawfish
Memphis barbecue
Chicago deep-dish pizza
Santa Fe chili stew

New England's forests. Maine's coast is lined with lobster shacks, while baked beans and brown bread are Boston specialties.

The South: Barbecue, Biscuits & Gumbo

No region is prouder of its food culture than the South, which has a long history of mingling Anglo, French, African, Spanish and Native American foods in dishes such as slow-cooked barbecue, which has as many meat and sauce variations as there are towns in the South. Southern fried chicken is crisp outside and moist inside. Breakfasts are as big as can be, and treasured dessert recipes tend to produce big layer cakes, and pies made with pecans, bananas and citrus. Light, fluffy biscuits are served hot and well buttered, and grits (ground corn cooked to a porridge-like consistency) are a passion among Southerners, as are refreshing mint julep cocktails.

Louisiana's legendary cuisine is influenced by colonial French and Spanish cultures, Afro-Caribbean cooking and Choctaw Indian traditions. Cajun food, found in the bayou country, marries native spices such as sassafras and chili peppers with provincial French cooking. Creole food is more urban, and centered on New Orleans, where dishes such as shrimp remoulade, crabmeat ravigote, crawfish étouffée and beignets are ubiquitous.

The Southwest: Chili, Steak & Smokin' Hot Salsa

Two ethnic groups define Southwestern food culture: the Spanish and Mexicans, who controlled territories from Texas to California until well into the 19th century. While there is little actual Spanish food today, the Spanish brought cattle to Mexico, which the Mexicans adapted to their own corn- and chili-based gastronomy. The result is tacos, tortillas, enchiladas, burritos and chimichangas filled with everything from chopped meat and poultry to beans. Don't leave New Mexico without trying a bowl of spicy green-chili stew. Steaks and barbecue are always favorites on Southwestern menus, and beer is the drink of choice for dinner and a night out.

Pacific Northwest: Salmon & Starbucks

The cuisine of this region draws on the traditions of the local Native Americans, whose diets traditionally centered on game, seafood – especially salmon – and foraged mushrooms, fruits and berries. Seattle spawned the modern international coffeehouse craze with Starbucks, while the beers and wines from both Washington and Oregon are of an international standard, especially the Pinot Noirs and Rieslings.

California: Farm-to-Table Restaurants & Taquerías

Owing to its vastness and variety of microclimates, California is truly the US' cornucopia for fruits and vegetables. The state's natural resources are overwhelming: wild salmon, Dungeness crab and oysters; robust farm produce year-round; and artisanal products such as cheese, bread, olive oil, wine and chocolate. Starting in the 1970s and '80s, star chefs such as Alice Waters and Wolfgang Puck pioneered 'California cuisine' by incorporating the best local ingredients into simple yet delectable preparations. The influx of Asian immigrants, especially after the Vietnam War, enriched the state's urban food cultures with Chinatowns, Koreatowns and Japantowns, along with huge enclaves of Mexican Americans who maintain their own culinary traditions across the state. Don't miss the massive burritos in San Francisco's Mission District and the fish tacos in San Diego.

Vegetarian & Vegan Dining

Some of the most highly regarded US restaurants cater to vegetarians and vegans. Exclusively vegetarian and vegan restaurants abound in major US cities, though not always in small towns and rural areas away from the coasts. Eateries that have a good selection of vegetarian options are noted in our reviews using the vegetarian icon (🖉). Browse restaurants online at www.happycow.net.

Beer & Wine

Americans have a staggering range of choices when it comes to beverages. A booming microbrewery industry has brought finely crafted beers to every corner of the country. The US wine industry continues to produce first-rate vintages – and it's not just Californian vineyards garnering all the awards.

Craft & Local Beer

Craft beer production is rising meteorically, accounting for 11% of the domestic market. There are more than 1800 craft breweries across the USA, with Vermont and Oregon boasting the most per capita. In recent years it has become possible to 'drink local' all over the country.

Wine

US wines have made an even more dramatic impact: the nation is the world's fourth-largest wine producer, behind Italy, France and Spain. Today almost 90% of US wine comes from California, and Oregon, Washington and New York wines have achieved international status. Wine isn't cheap in the US, as it's considered a luxury rather than a staple – go ahead and blame the Puritans for that. But it's possible to procure a perfectly drinkable bottle of American wine at a liquor or wine shop for under $12.

Baseball game at Yankee Stadium (p83), New York City

Sports

What really draws Americans together – sometimes slathered in blue body paint or with foam-rubber cheese wedges atop their heads – is sports. It provides an important social glue, so whether a person is conservative or liberal, married or single, Mormon or pagan, chances are that come Monday at the office they'll be chatting about the weekend performance of their favorite team.

Seasons

The fun and games go on all year long. In spring and summer there's a baseball game nearly every day. In fall and winter, a weekend or Monday night doesn't feel right without a football game on, and through the long days and nights of winter, there's plenty of basketball to keep the adrenaline going.

Baseball

Despite high salaries and steroid rumors dogging its biggest stars, baseball remains America's favorite pastime. It may not command the same TV viewership (and subsequent advertising dollars) as football, but baseball teams have 162 games over a season, versus 16 for football.

Football game

Besides, baseball isn't to be experienced on TV – it's all about the live version: being at the ballpark on a sunny day, sitting in the bleachers with a beer and hot dog and indulging in the seventh-inning stretch, when the entire park erupts in a communal sing-along of 'Take Me Out to the Ballgame.' The final play-offs, held every October, still deliver excitement and unexpected champions. The New York Yankees, Boston Red Sox and Chicago Cubs continue to be the favorite teams, even when they're abysmal (the Cubs haven't won a World Series in over 100 years).

Tickets are relatively inexpensive – seats average about $15 at most stadiums – and are easy to get for most games. Minor-league baseball games cost half as much, and can be even more fun, with lots of audience participation, stray chickens and dogs running across the field and wild throws from the pitcher's mound. For more information, go to www.minorleaguebaseball.com.

Football

Football is big, physical and rolling in dough. With the shortest season and least number of games of any of the major sports, every match takes on the emotion of an epic battle, where the results matter and an unfortunate injury can deal a lethal blow to a team's play-off chances.

Football's also the toughest because it's played in fall and winter in all manner of rain, sleet and snow. Some of history's most memorable matches have occurred at below-freezing temperatures. Green Bay Packers fans are in a class by themselves when it comes to severe weather. Their stadium in Wisconsin, known as Lambeau Field, was the site of

★ **The Best Places to See a Pro Game**
Fenway Park, Boston
Wrigley Field, Chicago
Dodger Stadium, Los Angeles
Yankee Stadium, NYC
Sun Life Stadium, Miami
Nationals Park, Washington, DC

Fenway Park (p107), Boston

JARED WICKERHAM / GETTY IMAGES ©

the infamous Ice Bowl, a 1967 championship game against the Dallas Cowboys where the temperature plummeted to 13°F below zero – mind you, that was with a wind-chill factor of -48°F.

Different teams have dominated different decades: the Pittsburgh Steelers in the 1970s, the San Francisco 49ers in the 1980s, the Cowboys in the 1990s and the New England Patriots in the 2000s. The pro league's official website (www.nfl.com) is packed with information. Tickets are expensive and hard to get, which is why many fans congregate in bars to watch televised games instead.

Even college and high-school football games enjoy an intense amount of pomp and circumstance, with cheerleaders, marching bands, mascots, songs and mandatory pre- and postgame rituals, especially 'tailgating' – a full-blown beer-and-barbecue feast that takes place over portable grills in parking lots where games are played.

The rabidly popular Super Bowl is pro football's championship match, held in late January or early February. The other 'bowl' games (such as the Rose Bowl and the Orange Bowl) are college football's title matches, held on and around New Year's Day.

Basketball

The teams bringing in the most fans these days include the Chicago Bulls (thanks to the lingering Michael Jordan effect), the Detroit Pistons (a rowdy crowd where riots have broken out), the Cleveland Cavaliers, the San Antonio Spurs and, last but not least, the Los Angeles Lakers, who won five championships between 2000 and 2010. Small-market teams such as Philadelphia and Portland have true-blue fans, and such cities can be great places to take in a game.

College-level basketball also draws millions of fans, especially every spring when March Madness rolls around. This series of college play-off games culminates in the Final Four, when the four remaining teams compete for a spot in the championship game. The games are widely televised, and bet upon – this is when Las Vegas bookies earn their keep – and their Cinderella stories and unexpected outcomes rival the pro league for excitement.

Car Racing

Nascar – officially, the National Association for Stock Car Auto Racing – has played an unusual role in US culture. It flew under the radar for years, mostly thrilling fans in the southeast, where it originated. Money started to flow in during the 1990s, and it burst onto the national scene in a big way in 2002.

The Sprint Cup is the top-tier tour, with the Daytona 500 being the year's biggest race, attracting more than 250,000 spectators.

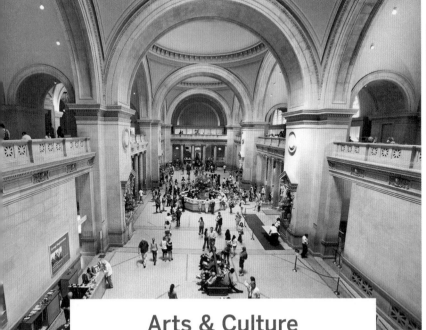

Metropolitan Museum of Art (p68), New York City

VISIONS OF OUR LAND / GETTY IMAGES ©

Arts & Culture

The US has always been a chaotic, democratic jumble of high and low cultures: Frank Lloyd Wright and Frank Sinatra, Georgia O'Keeffe and A Chorus Line, The Great Gatsby and Star Wars. Like so much else, America's arts are a pastiche, a crazy mix-and-match quilt of cultures and themes, of ideas borrowed and stolen to create something new, often leaving dramatic new paradigms along the way.

Music

No other US art has been as influential as popular music: blues, jazz, country, rock and roll, and hip-hop are the soundtrack of America's 20th century. The rest of the world has long returned the love, and American music today is a joyful, multicultural feast, a freewheeling blend of genres and styles. To witness it, head to the country's best live-music scenes, in New York City, Nashville, New Orleans, Memphis, Chicago and Austin.

The South is the mother of American music, most of which has roots in the frisson and interplay of black-white racial relations. Blues was the seminal sound, and nearly all subsequent American music has tapped this deep well. It developed out of the work songs of slaves, and black spiritual songs and their 'call-and-response' pattern, both of which were

Museum of Fine Arts (p105), Boston

LOU JONES / GETTY IMAGES ©

★ **The Best Art Museums**

Metropolitan Museum of Art (p68), NYC

Museum of Modern Art (p48), NYC

National Gallery of Art (p131), Washington, DC

Art Institute of Chicago (p160)

Museum of Fine Arts (p105), Boston

adaptations of African music. Famous musicians include Robert Johnson, Bessie Smith, Muddy Waters, BB King, John Lee Hooker and Buddy Guy.

The birthplace of jazz is New Orleans, where ex-slaves combined African-influenced rhythms with the reed, horn and string instruments of Creole musicians. This fertile cross-pollination has produced a steady stream of innovative sounds: ragtime, Dixieland jazz, big-band swing, bebop and numerous jazz fusions. Major artists include Duke Ellington, Louis Armstrong, Billie Holiday, John Coltrane, Miles Davis and Charles Mingus.

True fiddle-and-banjo country music developed in the Appalachian Mountains, the product of Scottish, Irish and English immigrants. In the Southwest, 'western' music was distinguished by steel guitars and larger bands. These styles merged into 'country-and-western' music in the 1920s, becoming centered on Nashville, TN, while bluegrass music mixed country with jazz and the blues. For the originals, listen to Bill Monroe, Hank Williams, Johnny Cash, Patsy Cline and Loretta Lynn.

Rock and roll, meanwhile, combined guitar-driven blues, rhythm and blues, and country-and-western music. Most say rock and roll was born when Elvis Presley started singing. From the 1950s, it evolved into the anthem for a nationwide social revolution in youth culture.

Finally, hip-hop emerged from 1970s New York, as DJs spun and mixed records, calling out rhymes with a microphone, to spur dance parties. Synonymous with urban street culture, it had become the defining rebel sound of American pop culture by the 1990s.

Film & TV

What would the US be without movies and TV? They are like the nation's mirror, where America checks its hair and profile before going out. That's fitting, as both mediums were essentially invented here.

Though France was developing similar technology, Thomas Edison is credited with creating the first motion pictures and the first movie studio, in New Jersey in the 1890s. Early films including *The Great Train Robbery* (1903) and *Birth of a Nation* (1915) introduced much of cinema's now-familiar language, such as the fade, close-up and flashback. In the 1920s, Hollywood established itself as the home of the film studios, and the rest, as they say, is history – very glamorous, celebrity-studded, Cinemascope-size history.

The first commercial TV set was introduced at the 1939 New York World's Fair. By the 1950s and 1960s, TV outshone the movies, nearly killing the film studios, and by the 1990s, the handful of original stations had multiplied into hundreds. For a long time, TV was looked down on as the doughy middle of US culture – the 'boob tube' – yet today many TV programs exhibit depth and storytelling that surpass that of cinema.

Literature

The greatest American novel remains *Huckleberry Finn* (1884), written by Samuel Clemens (aka Mark Twain), whose satirical humor and vernacular style came to define American letters.

After WWI, American novelists came into their own. They were revolutionary in style, and became often sharp critics of a newly industrialized, and later suburbanized, 20th-century American society. There are too many excellent, important writers to name, but a short list of those who are essential for understanding American literature include Ernest Hemingway (*The Sun Also Rises*, 1926), John Steinbeck (*The Grapes of Wrath*, 1939), William Faulkner (*The Sound and the Fury*, 1929), Zora Neale Hurston (*Their Eyes Were Watching God*, 1937), Flannery O'Connor (*Wise Blood*, 1952), Allen Ginsberg (*Howl*, 1956), Jack Kerouac (*On the Road*, 1957) and Toni Morrison (*The Bluest Eye*, 1970). Notable contemporary writers include Don DeLillo, Dave Eggers, Jonathan Lethem and Michael Chabon.

Visual Arts

Painting in the US did not draw much attention until the advent of abstract expressionism. Exposed to the shockwaves of European modernism in the early 20th century, America's artists found their voice after WWII. New York painters Franz Kline, Jackson Pollock and Mark Rothko pushed abstract expressionism to its extremes, throwing color and movement across epic canvases. In the 1960s, the US' other definitive style – pop art – developed in response to this: Jasper Johns, Robert Rauschenberg and Andy Warhol playfully blurred the line between art and commerce. Pop art co-opted media images, comics, advertising and product packaging in a self-conscious ironic wink that is now the media age America lives and breathes.

Minimalism followed, swinging back toward abstraction and emphasizing mixed media and installation art; major artists included Sol LeWitt, James Turrell, Richard Serra and Richard Tuttle. By the 1980s, civil rights, feminism and AIDS activism had made inroads in visual culture. Artists not only voiced political dissent through their work but embraced a range of once-marginalized media, from textiles and graffiti to video, sound and performance. To get the pulse of contemporary art in the US, check out works by artists like Jenny Holzer, Kara Walker, Chuck Close, Martin Puryear and Frank Stella.

Classic American Films

Western

High Noon (1952), Fred Zinnemann
The Searchers (1956), John Ford

Musical

42nd Street (1933), Lloyd Bacon
Singin' in the Rain (1952), Stanley Donen and Gene Kelly

Gangster

The Maltese Falcon (1941), John Huston
The Godfather trilogy (1972–90), Francis Ford Coppola
Goodfellas (1990), Martin Scorsese
Pulp Fiction (1994), Quentin Tarantino

Drama

Gone with the Wind (1939), Victor Fleming
Citizen Kane (1941), Orson Welles
Rear Window (1954), Alfred Hitchcock
Rocky (1976), John Avildsen

Comedy

The Gold Rush (1925), Charlie Chaplin
Some Like It Hot (1959), Billy Wilder
Dr Strangelove (1964), Stanley Kubrick
Annie Hall (1977), Woody Allen

FRANCESCO RICCARDO IACOMINO / GETTY IMAGES ©

Survival Guide

DIRECTORY A–Z   359

Accommodations..............359

Customs
Regulations 360

Climate.............................. 360

Discount Cards.................. 360

Food.................................. 360

Electricity 361

Gay & Lesbian Travellers 361

Health................................ 361

Insurance 362

Internet Access 362

Legal Matters 362

Money................................363

Opening Hours 364

Public Holidays 364

Safe Travel 365

Telephone...........................365

Time 366

Tourist Information 366

Travellers with
Disabilities......................... 366

Visas...................................367

Volunteering...................... 368

Women Travellers 368

TRANSPORT   369

Getting There
& Away................................369

Getting Around...................369

Directory A–Z

Accommodations

For all but the cheapest places and the slowest seasons, reservations are advised. In high-season tourist hot spots, hotels can book up months ahead. Many hotels offer specials on their websites. Online travel booking, bidding and comparison websites are another good way to find discounted hotel rates. Also check out Hotels.com, Hotwire (www.hotwire.com) and Booking.com. If you have a smartphone, each of these sites has a free app – which often are useful for finding great last-minute deals. The Hotel Tonight is another good app for booking rooms on the fly, and includes boutique hotels and historic properties.

House & Apartment Rentals

To rent a room, house or apartment from locals, visit **Airbnb** (www.airbnb.com), which has thousands of listings across the country.

B&Bs

In the USA, many B&Bs are high-end romantic retreats in restored historic homes run by personable, independent innkeepers who serve gourmet breakfasts. These B&Bs often take pains to evoke a theme – Victorian, rustic, Cape Cod and so on – and amenities range from comfortable to indulgent. Rates normally top $120, and the best run are $200 to $300. Some B&Bs have minimum-stay requirements, and most exclude young children.

European-style B&Bs also exist: these may be rooms in someone's home. These often welcome families.

B&Bs can close out of season and reservations are essential, especially for top-end places. To avoid surprises, always ask about bathrooms (whether shared or private). Recommended B&B agencies:

Bed & Breakfast Inns Online (www.bbonline.com)

BedandBreakfast.com (www.bedandbreakfast.com)

BnB Finder (www.bnbfinder.com)

Select Registry (www.selectregistry.com)

Hotels

Hotels in all categories typically include in-room telephones, cable TV, private bathrooms, wi-fi and a simple continental breakfast. Many midrange properties provide minibars, microwaves, hairdryers, internet access, air-conditioning and/or heating, swimming pools and writing desks, while top-end hotels add concierge services, fit-ness and business centers, spas, restaurants, bars and higher-end furnishings.

Even if hotels advertise that children 'sleep free,' cots or rollaway beds may cost extra. Always ask about the hotel's policy for telephone calls; all charge an exorbitant amount for long-distance and international calls, but some also charge for dialing local and toll-free numbers.

Motels

Motels have rooms that open onto a parking lot. They tend to cluster around interstate exits and on main routes into town. Motels can be good for discount lodging or when other options fall through. Note that breakfast is rarely included, and amenities might be a phone and TV (maybe with cable); most also have free wi-fi. Motels often have a few rooms with simple kitchenettes.

Book Your Stay Online

For more accommodation reviews by Lonely Planet authors, check out lonelyplanet.com/hotels. You'll find independent reviews, as well as recommendations on the best places to stay. Best of all, you can book online.

Customs Regulations

For a complete list of US customs regulations, visit the official portal for **US Customs & Border Protection** (www.cbp.gov).

Duty-free allowance per person is as follows:

○ 1L of liquor (provided you are at least 21 years old)

○ 100 cigars and 200 cigarettes (if you are at least 18 years old)

○ $200 worth of gifts and purchases ($800 if you're a returning US citizen)

○ If you arrive with $10,000 in US or foreign currency, it must be declared.

There are heavy penalties for attempting to import illegal drugs. Forbidden items include drug paraphernalia, lottery tickets, items with fake brand names, and most goods made in Iran, North Korea, Myanmar (Burma) and Sudan. Fruit, vegetables or other food or plant material must be declared or left in the arrival area bins.

Climate

New York City

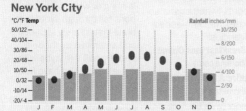

New Orleans

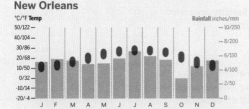

Los Angeles

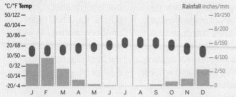

Discount Cards

The following passes can net you savings on museums, accommodations and some transport (including Amtrak):

International Student Identity Card (ISIC; www.isic.org) For international students.

Student Advantage Card (www.studentadvantage.com) For US and foreign travelers.

American Association of Retired Persons (AARP; www.aarp.org) For US travelers aged 50 and older.

Membership in the **American Automobile Association** (AAA; www.aaa.com) and reciprocal clubs in the UK, Australia and elsewhere can also earn discounts.

Food

See p348 for everything you need to know about food culture in the USA.

Eating Price Ranges

The following price ranges are used throughought this guide and refer to a main course. Tax (5% to 10%) and tip (generally 15% to 20%) are not included in price listings unless otherwise indicated.

$ less than $15
$$ $15–25
$$$ more than $25

Electricity

120V/60Hz

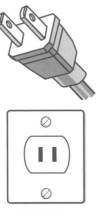

120V/60Hz

Resources

Advocate (www.advocate.com) Gay-oriented news website reports on business, politics, arts, entertainment and travel.

Gay & Lesbian National Help Center (☏888-843-4564; www.glnh.org; ☺1-9pm PST Mon-Fri, 9am-2pm PST Sat) A national hotline for counseling, information and referrals.

Gay Travel (www.gaytravel.com) Online guides to dozens of US destinations.

Purple Roofs (www.purpleroofs. com) Lists gay-owned and gay-friendly B&Bs and hotels.

Gay & Lesbian Travelers

Most major US cities have a visible, open LGBT community that's easy to connect with. Beaches and big cities are typically the most gay-friendly destinations.

Hot Spots

Manhattan has loads of great gay bars and clubs, especially in Hells Kitchen, Chelsea and the West Village. Other East Coast cities that flaunt it include Boston, Washington, DC and Provincetown on Cape Cod.

In Florida, Miami and the 'Conch Republic' of Key West support thriving gay communities. New Orleans has a lively gay scene.

San Francisco is probably the happiest gay city in America. There's also Chicago, Los Angeles and Las Vegas, where pretty much anything goes.

Attitudes

The level of acceptance varies nationwide. In some places, there is absolutely no tolerance whatsoever, and in others acceptance is predicated on LGBT people not 'flaunting' their sexual preference or identity. Bigotry still exists. In rural areas and conservative enclaves, it's unwise to be openly out, as violence and verbal abuse can sometimes occur. When in doubt, assume locals follow a 'don't ask, don't tell' policy. Same-sex marriage is now legally recognized by the federal government.

Health

The USA offers excellent health care. The problem is that, unless you have good insurance, it can be prohibitively expensive. It's essential to purchase travel health insurance if your regular policy doesn't cover you when you're abroad.

Bring any medications you may need in their original containers, clearly labeled. A signed, dated letter from your physician that describes all medical conditions and medications, including generic names, is also a good idea.

Availability & Cost of Health Care

In general, if you have a medical emergency the best bet is to go to the nearest hospital's emergency room.

If the problem isn't urgent, call a nearby hospital and ask for a referral to a local physician, which is usually cheaper than a trip to the emergency room.

Pharmacies are abundantly supplied, but you may find that some medications that are available over the counter in your home country (such as Ventolin, for asthma) require a prescription in the USA and, as always, if you don't have insurance to cover the cost of prescriptions, they can be shockingly expensive.

Insurance

No matter how long or short your trip, make sure you have adequate travel insurance, purchased before departure. At a minimum, you need coverage for medical emergencies and treatment, including hospital stays and an emergency flight home if necessary. Medical treatment in the USA is of the highest caliber, but the expense could bankrupt you.

You should also consider getting coverage for luggage theft or loss and trip cancellation. A comprehensive travel insurance policy that covers all these things can cost up to 10% of the total cost of your trip.

If you will be driving, it's essential that you have liability insurance. Car-rental agencies offer insurance that covers damage to the rental vehicle and separate liability insurance, which covers damage to people and other vehicles.

Worldwide travel insurance is available at www.lonelyplanet.com/travel-insurance. You can buy, extend and claim online anytime – even if you're already on the road.

Internet Access

Most hotels, guesthouses, hostels and motels have wi-fi (usually free, though luxury hotels are more likely to charge for access); ask when reserving.

Across the US, most cafés offer free wi-fi. Some cities have wi-fi-connected parks and plazas, and the public library is always a good standby.

If you're not from the US, remember that you will need an AC adapter for your laptop, plus a plug adapter for US sockets; both are available at larger electronics shops, such as Best Buy.

Legal Matters

In everyday matters, if you are stopped by the police, bear in mind there is no system of paying traffic or other fines on the spot. Attempting to pay a fine to an officer may result in a charge of bribery. For traffic offenses, the police officer or highway patroller will explain the options to you. There is usually a 30-day period to pay a fine.

If you are arrested, you have a legal right to an attorney, and you are allowed to remain silent. There is no legal reason to speak to a police officer if you don't wish to, but never walk away from an officer until given permission to do so. Anyone who is arrested is legally allowed to make one phone call. If you can't afford a lawyer, a public defender will be appointed to you free of charge. Foreign visitors who don't have a lawyer, friend or family member to help should call their embassy; the police will provide the number upon request.

As a matter of principle, the US legal system presumes a person innocent until proven guilty. Each state has its own civil and criminal laws, and what is legal in one state may be illegal in others.

Drinking

Bars and stores often ask for photo ID to prove you are of legal drinking age (ie 21 years or over). Being 'carded' is standard practice; don't take it personally. The sale of liquor is subject to local government regulations; in 'dry' counties, liquor sales are banned altogether.

Driving

In all states, driving under the influence of alcohol or

drugs is a serious offense, subject to stiff fines and even imprisonment.

Marijuana & Other Substances

The states have quite different laws regarding the use of marijuana, and what's legal in Colorado (and Washington, Oregon, Alaska and DC) may be illegal in other states (like Texas). Aside from Colorado and the other aforementioned states, 23 other states have either legalized medical marijuana or treat possession of small amounts of marijuana as a misdemeanor (generally punishable with a fine of around $100 or $200 for the first offense) – rather than a felony. In 23 other states, marijuana use is illegal. Thus, it's essential to know the local laws before lighting up.

Aside from marijuana, recreational drugs are prohibited by federal and state laws. Possession of any illicit drug, including cocaine, ecstasy, LSD, heroin and hashish, is a felony potentially punishable by a lengthy jail sentence. For foreigners, conviction of any drug offense is grounds for deportation.

Money

The currency is the US dollar. Most locals do not carry large amounts of cash for everyday use, relying instead on credit cards, ATMs and debit cards. Smaller businesses may refuse to accept bills larger than $20. Prices in our listings exclude taxes, unless otherwise noted.

ATMs

ATMs are available 24/7 at most banks, and in shopping centers, airports, grocery stores and convenience shops. Most ATMs charge a service fee of $2.50 or more per transaction and your home bank may impose additional charges. Withdrawing cash from an ATM using a credit card usually incurs a hefty fee; check with your credit-card company first.

For foreign visitors, ask your bank or credit-card company for exact information about using its cards in stateside ATMs. Before leaving home, notify your bank and credit-card providers of your upcoming travel plans. Otherwise, you may trigger fraud alerts with atypical spending patterns, which may result in your accounts being temporarily frozen.

Credit Cards

Major credit cards are almost universally accepted. In fact, it's almost impossible to rent a car or make phone reservations without one (some airlines require your credit-card billing address to be in the USA – a hassle if you're booking domestic flights once there). It's highly recommended that you carry at least one credit card, if only for emergencies. Visa and MasterCard are the most widely accepted.

Practicalities

Electricity AC 110V is standard; buy adapters to run most non-US electronics.

Newspapers & Magazines The *New York Times, Wall Street Journal* and *USA Today* are the national newspapers; *Time* and *Newsweek* are the mainstream news magazines.

Radio & TV National Public Radio (NPR) is at the lower end of the FM dial. The main TV broadcasting channels are ABC, CBS, NBC, FOX and PBS (public broadcasting); the major cable channels are CNN (news), ESPN (sports), HBO (movies) and the Weather Channel.

DVDs DVDs are coded for Region 1 (US and Canada only).

Weights & Measures Weights are measured in ounces (oz), pounds (lb) and tons; liquids in fluid ounces (fl oz), pints, quarts and gallons (gal); and distances in feet (ft), yards (yd) and miles (mi).

If your credit cards are lost or stolen, contact the issuing company immediately:

American Express (📞800-528-4800; www.american express.com)

Diners Club (📞800-234-6377; www.dinersclub.com)

Discover (📞800-347-2683; www.discover.com)

MasterCard (📞800-627-8372; www.mastercard.com)

Visa (📞800-847-2911; www.visa.com)

Money Changers

Banks are usually the best places to exchange foreign currencies. Most large city banks offer currency exchange, but banks in rural areas may not. Currency-exchange counters at the airport and in tourist centers typically have the worst rates; ask about fees and surcharges first. **Travelex** (📞516-300-1622; www.travelex.com) is a major currency-exchange company, but **American Express** (📞800-528-4800; www. americanexpress.com) travel offices may offer better rates.

Taxes

Sales tax varies by state and county, and ranges from 5% to 10%. Hotel taxes vary by city from about 10% to over 18% (in NYC).

Tipping

Tipping is *not* optional; only withhold tips in cases of outrageously bad service.

Airport & hotel porters $2 per bag, minimum per cart $5

Bartenders 15% to 20% per round, minimum per drink $1

Hotel maids $2 to $4 per night, left under the card provided

Restaurant servers 15% to 20%, unless a gratuity is already charged on the bill

Taxi drivers 10% to 15%, rounded up to the next dollar

Valet parking attendants At least $2 when handed back the keys

Traveler's Checks

Traveler's checks are becoming obsolete, except as a trustworthy backup. If you carry them, buy them in US dollars; local businesses may not cash them in a foreign currency. Keep a separate record of their numbers in case they are lost or stolen. American Express and Visa traveler's checks are the most widely accepted.

Opening Hours

Typical normal opening times are as follows:

Bars 5pm to midnight Sunday to Thursday, to 2am Friday and Saturday

Banks 8:30am to 4:30pm Monday to Thursday, to 5:30pm Friday (and possibly 9am to noon Saturday)

Nightclubs 10pm to 4am Thursday to Saturday

Post offices 9am to 5pm Monday to Friday

Shopping malls 9am to 9pm

Stores 9am to 6pm Monday to Saturday, noon to 5pm Sunday

Supermarkets 8am to 8pm, some open 24 hours

Public Holidays

On the following national public holidays, banks, schools and government offices (including post offices) are closed, and transportation, museums and other services operate on a Sunday schedule. Holidays falling on a weekend are usually observed the following Monday.

New Year's Day January 1

Martin Luther King Jr Day Third Monday in January

Presidents' Day Third Monday in February

Memorial Day Last Monday in May

Independence Day July 4

Labor Day First Monday in September

Columbus Day Second Monday in October

Veterans' Day November 11

Thanksgiving Fourth Thursday in November

Christmas Day December 25

During spring break, high school and college students get a week off from school, and they can overrun beach towns and resorts. This occurs throughout March and April. For students of all ages, summer vacation runs from June to August.

Safe Travel

Despite its list of dangers – violent crime, riots, earthquakes, tornadoes – the USA is actually a pretty safe country to visit. The greatest danger for travelers is posed by car accidents (buckle up – it's the law).

Crime

For the traveler it's not violent crime but petty theft that is the biggest concern. When possible, withdraw money from ATMs during the day, or at night in well-lit, busy areas. When driving, don't pick up hitchhikers, and lock valuables in the trunk of your car before arriving at your destination. In hotels, secure valuables in room or hotel safes.

Scams

Pack your street smarts. In big cities, don't forget that expensive electronics, watches and designer items sold on the cheap from

---

Government Travel Advice

Australia (www.smart traveller.gov.au)

Canada (www.voyage. gc.ca)

New Zealand (www. safetravel.govt.nz)

UK (www.gov.uk/ foreign-travel-advice)

---

sidewalk tables are either fakes or stolen.

Natural Disasters

The **US Department of Health & Human Services** (www.phe.gov) has preparedness advice, news and information on natural disasters such as hurricanes and earthquakes.

Telephone

Online phone directories include www.411.com and www.yellowpages.com.

Cell Phones

In the USA cell phones use GSM 1900 or CDMA 800, operating on different frequencies from other systems around the world. The only foreign phones that will work in the USA are GSM tri- or quad-band models. If you have one of these phones, check with your service provider about using it in the USA. Ask if roaming charges apply, as these will turn even local US calls into pricey international calls.

It might be cheaper to buy a compatible prepaid SIM card for the USA, like those sold by AT&T, which you can insert into your international cell phone to get a local phone number and voicemail. **Telestial** (www.telestial.com) offers these services, as well as cell-phone rentals.

If you don't have a compatible phone, you can buy inexpensive, no-contract (prepaid) phones with a local number and a set number of minutes, which can be topped up at will. Virgin Mobile, T-Mobile, AT&T and other providers offer phones starting at $10, with a package of minutes starting around $40 for 400 minutes. Electronics stores such as Radio Shack and Best Buy sell these phones.

Huge swathes of rural America, including many national parks and recreation areas, don't pick up a signal. Check your provider's coverage map.

Dialing Codes

All phone numbers within the USA consist of a three-digit area code followed by a seven-digit local number. In most places, you will need to dial the entire 10-digit number even for a local call.

If you are calling long distance, dial 1 plus the area code plus the phone number.

Toll-free numbers begin with 800, 888, 877 and 866, and when dialing are preceded by 1. Most can only be used within the USA.

○ 1 is the international country code for the USA if calling from abroad (the same as Canada, but international rates apply between the two countries).

○ Dial 011 to make an international call from the USA (followed by country code, area code and phone number).

○ Dial ☎00 for assistance making international calls.

○ Dial ☎411 for directory assistance nationwide.

○ ☎800-555-1212 is directory assistance for toll-free numbers.

Pay Phones

Local calls at pay phones that work (listen for a dial tone before inserting coins) cost 35¢ to 50¢ for the first few minutes; talking longer costs more. It's usually cheaper to use a prepaid phone card or the access line of a major carrier like AT&T (☎800-321-0288).

Phone Cards

A prepaid phone card is a good solution for travelers on a budget. Phone cards are easy to find in larger towns and cities, where they are sold at newsstands, convenience stores, super-

markets and major retailers. Be sure to read the fine print, as many cards contain hidden charges such as 'activation fees' or per-call 'connection fees' in addition to the rates. AT&T sells a reliable phone card that is widely available in the USA.

Time

The USA uses Daylight Saving Time (DST). On the second Sunday in March, clocks are set one hour ahead ('spring forward'). Then, on the first Sunday of November, clocks are turned back one hour ('fall back'). But Arizona (except the Navajo Nation), Hawaii and much of Indiana don't follow DST.

The US date system is written as month/day/year. Thus, 8 June 2015 becomes 6/8/15.

Time Zones

The Continental USA has four time zones:

○ EST Eastern (GMT -5 hours): NYC, New England and Atlanta

○ CST Central (GMT -6 hours): Chicago, New Orleans and Houston

○ MST Mountain (GMT -7 hours): Denver, Santa Fe, Phoenix

○ PST Pacific (GMT -8 hours): Seattle, San Francisco, Las Vegas

Most of Alaska is one hour behind Pacific time (GMT -9), while Hawaii is two hours behind Pacific time.

So if it's 9pm in New York, it's 8pm in Chicago, 7pm in Denver, 6pm in Los Angeles, 4pm in Anchorage and 3pm in Honolulu.

Tourist Information

The official tourism website of the USA is www.discover-america.com. It has links to every US state and territory tourism office and website, plus loads of ideas for itinerary planning.

Travelers with Disabilities

If you have a physical disability, the USA can be an accommodating place. The Americans with Disabilities Act (ADA) requires that all public buildings, private buildings built after 1993 (including hotels, restaurants, theaters and museums) and public transit be wheelchair accessible. However, call ahead to confirm what is available. Some local tourist offices publish detailed accessibility guides.

Telephone companies offer relay operators, available via teletypewriter (TTY) numbers, for the hearing

Smoking

As of 2015, 30 states, the District of Columbia and many municipalities across the US were entirely smoke-free in restaurants, bars and workplaces. You may still encounter smoky lobbies in chain hotels and budget-minded inns, but most other accommodations are smoke-free. For more on smoking, see www.cdc.gov.

impaired. Most banks provide ATM instructions in Braille and via earphone jacks for hearing-impaired customers. All major airlines, Greyhound buses and Amtrak trains will assist travelers with disabilities; just describe your needs when making reservations at least 48 hours in advance. Service animals (guide dogs) are allowed to accompany passengers, but bring documentation.

Some car-rental agencies, such as Budget and Hertz, offer hand-controlled vehicles and vans with wheelchair lifts at no extra charge, but you must reserve them well in advance. **Wheelchair Getaways** (📞800-642-2042; www.wheelchairgetaways. com) rents accessible vans throughout the USA. In many cities and towns, public buses are accessible to wheelchair riders and will 'kneel' if you are unable to use the steps; just let the driver know that you need the lift or ramp.

Most cities have taxi companies with at least one accessible van, though you'll have to call ahead. Cities with underground transport have elevators for passengers needing assistance.

Many national and some state parks and recreation areas have wheelchair-accessible paved, graded dirt or boardwalk trails. US citizens and permanent residents with permanent disabilities are entitled to a free 'America the Beautiful' Access Pass. Go online

(www.nps.gov/findapark/ passes.htm) for details.

Some helpful resources for travelers with disabilities include:

Disabled Sports USA (📞301-217-0960; www.disabledsports usa.org) Offers sport, adventure and recreation programs for those with disabilities.

Flying Wheels Travel (📞612-381-1622; www.flyingwheels travel.com) A full-service travel agency, highly recommended for those with mobility issues or chronic illness.

Mobility International USA (📞541-343-1284; www.miusa. org) Advises disabled travelers on mobility issues and runs educational international exchange programs.

Visas

Be warned that all of the following information is highly subject to change. US entry requirements keep evolving as national security regulations change. All travelers should double-check current visa and passport regulations *before* coming to the USA.

The **US State Department** (www.travel.state.gov) maintains the most comprehensive visa information, providing downloadable forms, lists of US consulates abroad and even visa wait times calculated by country.

Visa Applications

Apart from most Canadian citizens and those entering under the Visa Waiver Program (p368), all foreign visitors will need to obtain a visa from a US consulate or embassy abroad. Most applicants must schedule a personal interview, to which you must bring all your documentation and proof of fee payment. Wait times for interviews vary, but afterward, barring problems, visa issuance takes from a few days to a few weeks.

○ Your passport must be valid for at least six months after the end of your intended stay in the USA. You'll need a recent photo (2in by 2in), and you must pay a nonrefundable $160 processing fee, plus in a few cases an additional visa issuance reciprocity fee. You'll also need to fill out the online DS-160 nonimmigrant visa electronic application.

○ Visa applicants are required to show documents of financial stability (or evidence that a US resident will provide financial support), a round-trip or onward ticket and 'binding obligations' that will ensure their return home, such as family ties, a home or a job. Because of these requirements, those planning to travel through other countries before arriving in the USA are generally better off applying for a US visa while they are still in their home country, rather than while on the road.

Visa Waiver Program

Currently under the Visa Waiver Program (VWP), citizens of the following countries may enter the USA without a visa for stays of 90 days or fewer: Andorra, Australia, Austria, Belgium, Brunei, Chile, Czech Republic, Denmark, Estonia, Finland, France, Germany, Greece, Hungary, Iceland, Ireland, Italy, Japan, Latvia, Liechtenstein, Lithuania, Luxembourg, Malta, Monaco, the Netherlands, New Zealand, Norway, Portugal, San Marino, Singapore, Slovakia, Slovenia, South Korea, Spain, Sweden, Switzerland, Taiwan and the UK.

If you are a citizen of a VWP country, you do not need a visa *only if* you have a passport that meets current US standards *and* you have gotten approval from the Electronic System for Travel Authorization (ESTA) in advance. Register online with the Department of Homeland Security at https://esta.cbp.dhs.gov/esta at least 72 hours before arrival; once travel authorization is approved, your registration is valid for two years. The fee, payable online, is $14.

Visitors from VWP countries must still produce at the port of entry all the same evidence as for a non-immigrant visa application. They must demonstrate that their trip is for 90 days or less, and that they have a round-trip or onward ticket, adequate funds to cover the trip and binding obligations abroad.

In addition, the same 'grounds for exclusion and deportation' apply, except that you will have no opportunity to appeal or apply for an exemption. If you are denied under the Visa Waiver Program at a US point of entry, you will have to use your onward or return ticket on the next available flight.

○ The most common visa is a nonimmigrant visitor's visa, type B-1 for business purposes, B-2 for tourism or visiting friends and relatives. A visitor's visa is good for multiple entries over one or five years, and specifically prohibits the visitor from taking paid employment in the USA. The validity period depends on what country you are from. The actual length of time you'll be allowed to stay in the USA is determined by US immigration at the port of entry.

○ If you're coming to the USA to work or study, you will need a different type of visa, and the company or institution to which you are going should make the arrangements.

○ Other categories of nonimmigrant visas include an F-1 visa for students attending a course at a recognized institution; an H-1, H-2 or H-3 visa for temporary employment; and a J-1 visa for exchange visitors in approved programs.

Volunteering

Lonely Planet's *Volunteer: A Traveller's Guide to Making a Difference Around the World* provides useful information about volunteering.

Women Travelers

Women traveling alone or in groups should not expect to encounter any particular problems in the USA. However, normal precautions should be taken, such as avoiding dimly lit streets or rough neighborhoods, and advising someone of where you are going if you plan to hike alone.

If you are in immediate danger, call ☎911. If you have been assaulted, consider also calling the **National Sexual Assault Hotline** (☎800-656-4673; www.rainn.org).

The community website www.journeywoman.com facilitates women exchanging travel tips, and has links to other helpful resources. **Planned Parenthood** (☎800-230-7526; www.plannedparenthood.org) offers referrals to women's health clinics throughout the country.

Transport

Getting There & Away

Flights and tours can be booked online at www.lonelyplanet.com/booking.

Entering the USA

If you are flying to the US, the first airport that you land in is where you must go through immigration and customs, even if you are continuing on the flight to another destination. Upon arrival, all international visitors must register with the Department of Homeland Security's Office of Biometric Identity Management program, which entails having your fingerprints scanned and a digital photo taken.

Once you go through immigration, you collect your baggage and pass through customs. If you have nothing to declare, you'll probably clear customs without a baggage search, but don't assume this. If you are continuing on the same plane or connecting to another one, it is your responsibility to get your bags to the right place. There are usually airline representatives just

outside the customs area who can help you.

If you are a single parent, grandparent or guardian traveling with anyone under 18 years, carry proof of legal custody or a notarized letter from the nonaccompanying parent(s) authorizing the trip. This isn't required, but the USA is concerned with thwarting child abduction, and not having authorizing papers could cause delays or even result in being denied admittance to the country.

Airports

The USA has more than 375 domestic airports, but only a baker's dozen are the main international gateways. Many other airports are called 'international' but may have only a few flights from other countries – typically Mexico or Canada. Even travel to an international gateway sometimes requires a connection in another gateway city (eg London–Los Angeles flights may involve transferring in Houston).

Some international gateway airports in the USA are:

Logan International Airport (BOS; Boston; www.massport.com/logan-airport)

O'Hare International Airport (ORD; Chicago; www.ohare.com)

Los Angeles International Airport (LAX; Map p263; www.lawa.org/lax; 1 World Way)

Miami International Airport (MIA; Map p181; ☎305-876-7000; www.miami-airport.com; 2100 NW 42nd Ave)

John F Kennedy International Airport (JFK; New York; www.panynj.gov)

San Francisco International Airport (SFO; www.flysfo.com; S McDonnell Rd)

Getting Around

Air

When time is tight, book a flight. The domestic air system is extensive and reliable. Flying is usually more expensive than traveling by bus, train or car, but it's the way to go when you're in a hurry.

Main 'hub' airports in the USA include all international gateways plus many other large cities. Most cities and towns have a local or county airport, but you usually have to travel via a hub airport to reach them.

Airlines in the USA

Overall, air travel in the USA is very safe (much safer than driving out on the nation's highways); for comprehensive details by carrier, check out Airsafe.com.

The main domestic carriers that offer nationwide services are:

American Airlines (☎800-433-7300; www.aa.com) Nationwide service.

Delta Air Lines (☎800-221-1212; www.delta.com) Nationwide service.

Climate Change & Travel

Every form of transport that relies on carbon-based fuel generates CO2, the main cause of human-induced climate change. Modern travel is dependent on aeroplanes, which might use less fuel per kilometre per person than most cars but travel much greater distances. The altitude at which aircraft emit gases (including CO2) and particles also contributes to their climate change impact. Many websites offer 'carbon calculators' that allow people to estimate the carbon emissions generated by their journey and, for those who wish to do so, to offset the impact of the greenhouse gases emitted with contributions to portfolios of climate-friendly initiatives throughout the world. Lonely Planet offsets the carbon footprint of all staff and author travel.

United Airlines (☎800-864-8331; www.united.com) Nationwide service.

US Airways (☎800-428-4322; www.usairways.com) Nationwide service with hubs in Charlotte and Philadelphia.

Air Passes

International travelers who plan on doing a lot of flying might consider buying a North American air pass. Passes are normally available only to non-North American citizens, and they must be purchased in conjunction with an international ticket. Conditions and cost structures can be complicated, but all passes include a certain number of domestic flights (from two to 10) that typically must be used within a 60-day period. Often you must plan your itinerary in advance, but sometimes dates (and even destinations) can be left open. Talk with a travel agent to determine if an air pass will save you money.

Two of the biggest airline networks offering air passes are **Star Alliance** (www.staralliance.com) and **One World** (www.oneworld.com).

Bicycle

Regional bicycle touring is popular, though note that bicycles are often not permitted on freeways. Cyclists must follow the same rules of the road as automobiles, but don't expect drivers to respect your right of way. **Better World Club** (www.betterworldclub.com) offers a bicycle roadside assistance program.

For advice, and lists of local bike clubs and repair shops, browse the website of the **League of American Bicyclists** (www.bikeleague.org). If you're bringing your own bike to the USA, call around to check oversize luggage prices and restrictions. Amtrak trains and Greyhound buses will transport bikes within the USA, sometimes charging extra.

It's not hard to buy a bike once you're here and resell it before you leave. Every city and town has bike shops; if you prefer a cheaper, used bicycle, try the free classified ads at **Craigslist** (http://craigslist.org).

Long-term bike rentals are also easy to find. Rates run from $100 per week and up, and a credit-card authorization for several hundred dollars is usually necessary as a security deposit.

Bus

To save money, travel by bus, particularly between major towns and cities. As a rule, buses are reliable, clean-ish and comfortable, with air-conditioning, barely reclining seats, lavatories and no smoking.

Greyhound (☎800-231-2222, international customer service 214-849-8100; www.greyhound.com) is the major long-distance bus company, with routes throughout the USA and Canada. Routes generally trace major highways and stop at larger population centers. To reach country towns on rural roads, you may need to transfer to local or county bus systems; Greyhound can usually provide their contact information. Greyhound often has excellent online fares – web-only deals will net you substantial discounts over buying at a ticket counter.

Competing with Greyhound are the 75-plus franchises of **Trailways** (☎703-691-3052; www.trailways.com). Trailways may not be as useful as Greyhound for long trips, but fares can be competitive. Long-distance bus lines that offer decent fares and free wi-fi (that doesn't always work) include **Megabus** (☏877-462-6342; www.megabus.com) and **BoltBus** (www.boltbus.com); both operate routes primarily in the Northeast and Midwest.

Most baggage has to be checked in; label it loudly and clearly to avoid it getting lost. Larger items, including skis, surfboards and bicycles, can be transported, but there may be an extra charge. Call to check.

Many bus stations are clean and safe, but some are in dodgy areas; if you arrive in the evening, it's worth spending the money on a taxi. Some towns have just a flag stop. If you are boarding at one of these, pay the driver with exact change.

Costs

For lower fares on Greyhound, purchase tickets at least seven days in advance (purchasing 14 days in advance will save even more). Round-trips are also cheaper than two one-way fares. Special promotional fares are regularly offered on Greyhound's website.

Reservations

Tickets for some Trailways and other buses can only be purchased immediately prior to departure. Greyhound, Megabus and BoltBus tickets can be bought on-line. You can print all tickets at home or in the case of Megabus or BoltBus, simply show ticket receipts through an email on a smartphone. Greyhound also allows customers to pick up tickets at the terminal using 'Will Call' service.

Seating is normally first-come, first-served. Greyhound recommends arriving an hour before departure to get a seat.

Car & Motorcycle

For maximum flexibility and convenience, and to explore rural America and its wide open spaces, a car is essential. Although gas prices are high, you can often score fairly inexpensive rentals (NYC excluded), with rates as low as $20 per day.

Automobile Associations

The **American Automobile Association** (AAA; www.aaa.com) has reciprocal membership agreements with several international auto clubs (check with AAA and bring your membership card from home). For its members, AAA offers travel insurance, tour books, diagnostic centers for used-car buyers and a wide-ranging network of regional offices.

A more eco friendly alternative, the **Better World Club** (☏866-238-1137; www.betterworldclub.com) donates 1% of revenue to assist environmental cleanup, and offers ecologically sensitive choices for every service it provides.

With these organizations, the primary member benefit is 24-hour emergency roadside assistance anywhere in the USA. Both also offer trip planning, free travel maps, travel-agency services, car insurance and a range of travel discounts (eg on hotels, car rentals, attractions).

Driver's License

Foreign visitors can legally drive a car in the USA for up to 12 months using their home driver's license. However, an International Driving Permit (IDP) will have more credibility with US traffic police, especially

Bus Fares

Here are some sample standard one-way adult fares and trip times on Greyhound:

Service	Price ($)	Duration (hr)
Chicago–New Orleans	96-164	24
Los Angeles–San Francisco	35-71	8
New York–Chicago	70-138	18
New York–San Francisco	250-330	72
Washington, DC–Miami	87-170	25

if your home license doesn't have a photo or isn't in English. Your automobile association at home can issue an IDP, valid for one year, for a small fee. Always carry your home license together with the IDP.

To ride a motorcycle in the USA, you will need either a valid US state motorcycle license or an IDP specially endorsed for motorcycles.

Insurance

Don't put the key into the ignition if you don't have insurance, which is legally required. You risk financial ruin and legal consequences if there's an accident. If you already have auto insurance, or if you buy travel insurance that covers car rentals, make sure your policy has adequate liability coverage for where you will be driving; be aware that states specify different minimum levels of coverage.

Car-rental companies will provide liability insurance, but most charge extra. Rental companies almost never include collision-damage insurance for the vehicle. Instead, they offer an optional Collision Damage Waiver (CDW) or Loss Damage Waiver (LDW), usually with an initial deductible cost of between $100 and $500. For an extra premium, you can usually get this deductible covered as well. Paying extra for some or all of this insurance increases the cost of a rental car by as much as $30 a day.

Many credit cards offer free collision-damage coverage for rental cars, if you rent for 15 days or less and charge the total rental to your card. This is a good way to avoid paying extra fees to the rental company, but note that if there's an accident, sometimes you must pay the car-rental company first and then seek reimbursement from the credit-card company. There may be exceptions that are not covered, too, such as 'exotic' rentals (eg 4WD Jeeps, convertibles). Check your credit-card policy.

Rental

Most rental companies require that you have a major credit card, be at least 25 years old and have a valid driver's license. Some major national companies may rent to drivers between the ages of 21 and 24 for an additional charge of around $25 per day. Those under 21 years are usually not permitted to rent at all.

The average daily rate for a small car ranges from around $30 to $75, or $200 to $500 per week.

Road Conditions & Hazards

For nationwide traffic and road-closure information, click to www.fhwa.dot.gov/trafficinfo/index.htm.

In places where winter driving is an issue, many cars are fitted with steel-studded snow tires; snow chains can sometimes

be required in mountain areas. Driving off road, or on dirt roads, is often forbidden by car-rental companies, and it can be very dangerous in wet weather.

In deserts and range country, livestock sometimes graze next to unfenced roads. These areas are signed as 'Open Range' or with the silhouette of a steer. Where deer and other wild animals frequently appear roadside, you'll see signs with the silhouette of a leaping deer. Take these signs seriously, particularly at dusk and dawn.

Road Rules

In the USA, cars drive on the right-hand side of the road. The use of seat belts and child safety seats is required in every state. Most car-rental agencies rent child safety seats for around $13 per day, but you must reserve them when booking. In some states, motorcyclists are required to wear helmets.

On interstate highways, the speed limit is sometimes raised to 75mph. Unless otherwise posted, the speed limit is generally 55mph or 65mph on highways, 25mph to 35mph in cities and towns, and as low as 15mph in school zones (strictly enforced during school hours). It's forbidden to pass a school bus when its lights are flashing.

Unless signs prohibit it, you may turn right at a red light after first coming to a full stop – note that turning right on red is illegal in NYC. At four-way stop signs, cars should proceed in order of arrival; when two cars arrive simultaneously, the one on the right has the right of way. When in doubt, just politely wave the other driver ahead. When emergency vehicles (ie police, fire or ambulance) approach from either direction, pull over safely and get out of the way.

In many states, it is illegal to talk on a handheld cellphone while driving; use a hands-free device instead.

The maximum legal blood-alcohol concentration for drivers is 0.08%. Penalties are very severe for driving under the influence of alcohol and/or drugs (DUI). Police can give roadside sobriety checks to assess if you've been drinking or using drugs. If you fail, they'll require you to take a breath test, urine test or blood test to determine the level of alcohol or drugs in your body. Refusing to be tested is treated the same as if you'd taken the test and failed.

In some states it is illegal to carry 'open containers' of alcohol in a vehicle, even if they are empty.

Local Transportation

Except in large US cities, public transportation is rarely the most convenient option for travelers, and coverage can be sparse to outlying towns and suburbs. However, it is usually cheap, safe and reliable. In addition,

more than half the states in the nation have adopted ☏511 as an all-purpose local-transportation help line.

Airport Shuttles

Shuttle buses provide inexpensive and convenient transport to/from airports in most cities. Most are 12-seat vans; some have regular routes and stops (which include the main hotels) and some pick up and deliver passengers 'door to door' in their service area. Costs range from $15 to $30 per person.

Bicycle

Some cities are more amenable to bicycles than others, but most have at least a few dedicated bike lanes and paths, and bikes can usually be carried on public transportation.

Bus

Most cities and larger towns have dependable local bus systems, though they are often designed for commuters and provide limited service in the evening and on weekends. Costs range from free to between $1 and $3 per ride.

Subway & Train

The largest systems are in New York, Chicago, Boston, Philadelphia, Washington, DC, Chicago, Los Angeles and the San Francisco Bay Area. Other cities may have small, one- or two-line rail

systems that mainly serve downtown.

Taxi

Taxis are metered, with flag-fall charges of around $2.50 to start, plus $2 to $3 per mile. They charge extra for waiting and handling baggage, and drivers expect a 10% to 15% tip. Taxis cruise the busiest areas in large cities; otherwise, it's easiest to phone and order one.

Tours

Hundreds of companies offer all kinds of organized tours of the USA; most focus on either cities or regions.

Backroads (☏800-462-2848, 510-527-1555; www.backroads. com) Designs a range of active, multisport and outdoor-oriented trips for all abilities and budgets.

Gray Line (☏800-472-9546; www.grayline.com) For those short on time, Gray Line offers a comprehensive range of standard sightseeing tours across the country.

Green Tortoise (☏800-867-8647, 415-956-7500; www. greentortoise.com) Offering budget adventures for independent travelers, Green Tortoise is famous for its sleeping-bunk buses. Most trips leave from San Francisco, traipsing through the West and nationwide.

Road Scholar (☏800-454-5768; www.roadscholar.org) For those aged 50 and older, this venerable nonprofit offers 'learning adventures' in all 50 states.

Train

Amtrak (☎800-872-7245; www.amtrak.com) has an extensive rail system throughout the USA, with Amtrak's Thruway buses providing connections to and from the rail network to some smaller centers and national parks. Compared with other modes of travel, trains are rarely the quickest, cheapest, timeliest or most convenient option, but they turn the journey into a relaxing, social and scenic all-American experience.

Amtrak has several long-distance lines traversing the nation east to west, and even more running north to south. These connect all of America's biggest cities and many of its smaller ones. Long-distance services (on named trains) mostly operate daily on these routes, but some run only three to five days per week. See Amtrak's website for detailed route maps.

Commuter trains provide faster, more frequent services on shorter routes, especially the northeast corridor from Boston, MA, to Washington, DC. Amtrak's high-speed Acela Express trains are the most expensive, and rail passes are not valid on these trains. Other commuter rail lines include those serving the Lake Michigan shoreline near Chicago, IL, major cities on the West Coast and the Miami, FL, area.

Classes & Costs

Amtrak fares vary according to the type of train and seating; on long-distance lines, you can travel in coach seats (reserved or unreserved), business class, or 1st class, which includes all sleeping compartments. Sleeping cars include simple bunks (called 'roomettes'), bedrooms with en-suite facilities and suites sleeping four with two bathrooms. Sleeping-car rates include meals in the dining car, which offers everyone sit-down meal service (pricey if not included). Food service on commuter lines, when it exists, consists of sandwich and snack bars. Bringing your own food and drink is recommended on all trains.

Various one-way, round-trip and touring fares are available from Amtrak, with discounts of 15% for seniors aged 62 and over and for students with a 'Student Advantage' card ($23) or an International Student Identity Card (ISIC), and 50% discounts for children aged two to 15 when accompanied by a paying adult. AAA members get 10% off. Web-only 'Weekly Specials' offer deep discounts on certain undersold routes.

Generally, the earlier you book, the lower the price. To get many of the standard discounts, you need to reserve at least three days in advance. If you want to take an Acela Express or Metroliner train, avoid peak commute times and aim for weekends.

Amtrak Vacations (☎800-268-7252; www.amtrak vacations.com) offers vacation packages that include car rental, hotels, tours and attractions. Air-Rail packages let you travel by train in one direction, then return by plane the other way.

Reservations

Reservations can be made any time from 11 months in advance up to the day of departure. Space on most trains is limited, and certain routes can be crowded, especially during summer and holiday periods, so it's a good idea to book as

Train Fares

Sample standard, one-way, adult coach-class fares and trip times on Amtrak's long-distance routes:

Service	Price ($)	Duration (hr)
Chicago–New Orleans	127	20
Los Angeles–San Antonio	182	29
New York–Chicago	104	19
New York–Los Angeles	357	68
Seattle–Oakland	163	23
Washington, DC–Miami	140	23

far in advance as you can; this also gives you the best chance of fare discounts.

Train Passes

Amtrak's USA Rail Pass offers coach-class travel for 15 ($460), 30 ($690) or 45 ($900) days, with travel limited to eight, 12 or 18 one-way 'segments,' respectively. A segment is *not* the same as a one-way trip. If reaching your destination requires riding more than one train (for example, getting from New York to Miami with a transfer in Washington, DC), that one-way trip will actually use two segments of your pass.

Present your pass at an Amtrak office to pick up your ticket(s) for each trip. Reservations should be made by phone (call ☎800-872-7245, or 215-856-7953 from outside the USA) as far in advance as possible. Each segment of the journey must be booked. At some rural stations, trains will only stop if there's a reservation. Tickets are not for specific seats, but a conductor on board may allocate you a seat. Business-class, 1st-class and sleeper accommodations cost extra and must be reserved separately.

All Aboard!

Who doesn't enjoy the steamy puff and whistle of a mighty locomotive as glorious scenery streams by? Dozens of historic narrow-gauge railroads still operate today as attractions, rather than as transportation. Most trains only run in the warmer months, and they can be extremely popular – so book ahead.

Some of the best routes are:

Cumbres & Toltec Scenic Railroad Depot (☎888-286-2737; www.cumbrestoltec.com; 5234 Hwy 285, Antonito; adult/child from $89/49; 👫) A living, moving museum from Chama, NM, into Colorado's Rocky Mountains.

Great Smoky Mountain Railroad (☎800-872-4681; www.gsmr.com; 226 Everett St, Bryson City; Nantahala Gorge trip adult/child 2-12yr from $55/31) Rides from Bryson City, NC, through the Great Smoky Mountains.

Mount Hood Railroad (☎800-872-4661; www.mthoodrr.com; 110 Railroad Ave) Winds through the scenic Columbia River Gorge outside Portland, OR.

Skunk Train (☎707-964-6371; www.skunktrain.com; foot of Laurel St; adult/child 2-12yr $60/34; 👫👪) Runs between Fort Bragg, CA, on the coast and Willits further inland, passing through redwoods.

Also worth riding are the vintage steam and diesel locomotives of Arizona's **Grand Canyon Railway** (☎reservations 800-843-8724; www.thetrain.com; Railway Depot, 233 N Grand Canyon Blvd; round-trip adult/child from $65/25; 👫), New York State's **Delaware & Ulster Rail Line** (☎845-586-3877; www.durr.org; 43510 Hwy 28, Arkville; adult/child $18/12; ⊙Sat & Sun Jun-Nov, additional trips Thu & Fri Jul-Sep; 👫) and Colorado's **Pikes Peak Cog Railway**.

All travel must be completed within 180 days of purchasing your pass. Passes are not valid on the Acela Express, Auto Train, Thruway motorcoach connections or the Canadian portion of Amtrak routes operated jointly with Via Rail Canada. Fares can double if you don't buy them at least three or four days in advance.

Behind the Scenes

Acknowledgements

Climate map data adapted from Peel MC, Finlayson BL & McMahon TA (2007) 'Updated World Map of the Koppen-Geiger Climate Classification', *Hydrology and Earth System Sciences*, 11, 163344.

Illustrations pp42–3, 134–5 by Javier Martinez Zarracina; pp298–9 by Michael Weldon.

This Book

This book was curated by Karla Zimmerman and researched and written by Amy C Balfour, Sandra Bao, Sara Benson, Adam Karlin, Becky Ohlsen, Zora O'Neill, Kevin Raub, Brendan Sainsbury, Regis St Louis, Ryan Ver Berkmoes, Mara Vorhees and Greg Ward. This guidebook was commissioned in Lonely Planet's Melbourne office, and produced by the following:

Destination Editor Dora Whitaker
Series Designer Campbell McKenzie
Cartographic Series Designer Wayne Murphy
Associate Product Director Liz Heynes
Product Editors Kate Mathews, Katie O'Connell, Luna Soo
Senior Cartographers Corey Hutchison, Anthony Phelan
Book Designers Cam Ashley, Mazzy Prinsep
Assisting Editor Anne Mulvaney
Cartographers Julie Dodkins, Gabriel Lindquist
Cover Researcher Naomi Parker
Thanks to Sasha Baskett, Sarah Billington, Andrew Bigger, Katie Coffee, Daniel Corbett, Ruth Cosgrove, Ryan Evans, James Hardy, Anna Harris, Victoria Harrison, Indra Kilfoyle, Georgina Leslie, Dan Moore, Jenna Myers, Darren O'Connell, Kirsten Rawlings, Diana Saengkham, Dianne Schallmeiner, Ellie Simpson, Lyahna Spencer, John Taufa, Angela Tinson, Lauren Wellicome, Amanda Williamson, Juan Winata

Send Us Your Feedback

We love to hear from travelers – your comments keep us on our toes and help make our books better. Our well-traveled team reads every word on what you loved or loathed about this book. Although we cannot reply individually to postal submissions, we always guarantee that your feedback goes straight to the appropriate authors, in time for the next edition. Each person who sends us information is thanked in the next edition, the most useful submissions are rewarded with a selection of digital PDF chapters.

Visit lonelyplanet.com/contact to submit your updates and suggestions or to ask for help. Our award-winning website also features inspirational travel stories, news and discussions.

Note: We may edit, reproduce and incorporate your comments in Lonely Planet products such as guidebooks, websites and digital products, so let us know if you don't want your comments reproduced or your name acknowledged. For a copy of our privacy policy visit lonelyplanet.com/privacy.

A – Z
Index

A

Acadia National Park 92-5
accommodations 359
activities, *see individual activities*
Affordable Care Act 337
air travel 369-70
airports 33, 369
Alcatraz 296-9
amusement parks
Carousel Gardens Amusement Park 223
Discovery Cove 209
Disneyland 276
Disney's Hollywood Studios 206
Pacific Park 264
Universal Orlando Resort 208
Walt Disney World 12, 201-11, **203**
Wizarding World of Harry Potter 209
aquariums
Aquarium of the Americas 226
Aquarium of the Bay 305
Aquarium of the Pacific 276
California Academy of Sciences 309
Mirage (Las Vegas) 239
New England Aquarium 101
Santa Monica Pier Aquarium 265
Shedd Aquarium 165
Aquinnah Cliffs 114
architects
Gehry, Frank 159, 273, 274
Herzog & de Meuron 193, 309
Piano, Renzo 309
Wright, Frank Lloyd 68, 165, 169, 173
architecture 24, 165, *see also* historic buildings, notable buildings
art deco 186-9
New York City 54-5
area codes 33, 365-6
Arlington National Cemetery 145
art 196
Art Basel 28
Art Deco Historic District 186-7
art galleries & museums 356
Art Institute of Chicago 161-2
Frick Collection 68
Guggenheim Museum 68
Institute of Contemporary Art 104
Los Angeles County Museum of Art 276
Metropolitan Museum of Art 68
MoMA PS1 49
Museum of Arts & Design 64
Museum of Fine Arts 105
Museum of Modern Art (MoMA) 48-9
National Gallery of Art 131
New Orleans Museum of Art 227
Ogden Museum of Southern Art 226
Pérez Art Museum Miami 193
Phillips Collection 141
Portland Museum of Art 122
Provincetown Art Association & Museum 114
Reynolds Center for American Art & Portraiture 140
Art Institute of Chicago 161-2
arts 355-7
ATMs 363

B

Bar Harbor 125
Barataria Preserve 229
baseball 83, 352-3
basketball 83, 354
beaches
Chicago 170
Martha's Vineyard 117
Miami Beach 193
Nantucket 116
Orange County 286
beer 351
Beverly Hills 276-7
bighorn sheep 253
boat tours, *see also* cruises
Boston 106
Chicago 170
Everglades 185
New England 113, 114, 119, 124
books 29, 357
Boothbay Harbor 124-5
Boston 96-111, **98, 102-3**
children, travel with 101
itineraries 98-9, **98**
travel to/from 110
travel within 111
Boyd Woods Audubon Sanctuary 91
breweries 119
Broadway 52-3
Brooklyn 80
Brooklyn Bridge 46-7
Burlington 118-20
bus travel 370-1, 373
business hours 33, 364

C

cable cars 294-5
cabs 373
Cadillac Mountain 94-5
California condors 253
Cambridge 105-6
Cape Cod 112-15

Cape Cod National Seashore 113
Capitol 136-7
Capitol Hill 136-9
car rental 372
car travel 371-3
Carnegie Hall 73
casinos 239
cathedrals, *see* churches & cathedrals
cell phones 365
cemeteries 145, 225, 267
Central Park 38-43, **42-3**
Chatham 113
Chicago 10, 154-77, **157**, **166-7**
　children, travel with 170
　itineraries 162, **162**
　travel to/from 177
　travel within 177
Chicago Blues Festival 27
Chicago Cultural Center 163, 164
children, travel with 30-1, 305
　Boston 101
　Chicago 170
　Los Angeles 276
　Miami 195
　New Orleans 223
　New York City 59
　Washington, DC 146
Chinatown 302-3, 309-10
Chrysler Building 55
churches & cathedrals
　Mission Dolores 308
　St Louis Cathedral 222-3
　Trinity Church 105
　Washington National Cathedral 144
Cinco de Mayo 27
climate 26-8, 32, 360
Cloud Gate 158
Coastal Maine 121-5
Colorado River 254

Columbus, Christopher 339
condors 253
Connecticut 91
costs 33
credit cards 363-4
Crown Fountain 159
cruises 122, 124, 125, *see also* boat tours
cycling 150, 370, 373
　Acadia National Park 94-5
　Cape Cod Rail Trail 109
　Chicago 170
　Grand Canyon National Park 253
　Los Angeles 265, 277
　Miami 196
　New Orleans 228
　Washington, DC 144-5

D

dangers, *see* safety
disabilities, travelers with 366-7
Dolby Theatre 266-7
drinking 362
drinks 351
driver's licenses 371-2
driving 371-3
driving tours 117, 118
drugs 363
DVDs 363

E

electricity 361, 363
elk 253
Ellis Island 45
emergency services 33
Empire State Building 55, 64
environmental issues 337
Epcot 205
events, *see* festivals & events
Everglades National Park 182-5

F

fall foliage 90-1
family travel, *see* children, travel with
Faneuil Hall 99, 101
Fenway Park 107
Ferry Building 300
festivals 26-8, 36, 91
　Mardi Gras 216-19
films 29, 356-7
Flagstaff 257-9
food 24, 76, 174, 348-51, 360
football 83, 353
Franconia Notch 121
Freedom Trail 96-9, **98**
Fremont Street Experience 241

G

galleries, *see* art galleries & museums
gay marriage 336
Gay Pride 27
gay rights 336
gay travelers 361
　GLBT History Museum 308-9
　Los Angeles 283
　San Francisco 310
Glacier Point 324-5
Golden Gate Bridge 292-3
Golden Gate Park 309
Grafton 90
Granary Burying Ground 96-7, 98
Grand Canyon National Park 15, 247-59, **249**
　travel to/from 248, 253, 255, 257
　travel within 255, 257
Grand Central Terminal 55
Great Barrington 91
Griffith Observatory 270
Griffith Park 268-9

H

Haight & Ashbury 309
Half Dome 326-7
Halloween 28
Harvard University 106
health 361-2
healthcare 337
High Line 50-1
hiking
  Acadia National Park 94-5
  Glacier Point 324-5
  Grand Canyon National Park 250-9
  Half Dome 326-7
  Los Angeles 277
  Mt Washington 121
  Yosemite National Park 332
historic buildings 342
  Coit Tower 304
  Empire State Building 64
  Faneuil Hall 99, 101
  Presidio Officers' Club 305
  Rockefeller Center 64
  Shelburne Museum 118
  Vizcaya Museum & Gardens 195
  Willie Dixon's Blues Heaven 165
historic sights 24, 340
history 338-47
  Civil Rights movement 345
  Civil War 341-2
  Declaration of Independence 341
  Great Depression 344
  Industrial Revolution 343
  Revolutionary War 340-1
  September 11 347
  WWII 344-5
holidays 364
Hollywood 266-7
Hollywood sign 270-1
Hyannis 112-13
Hyde Park 173

I

immigration 369
Independence Day 28
insurance
  travel 362
  vehicle 372
internet access 362
internet resources 33
itineraries 2-3, 18-23, 272-5, **19**, **21**, **23**, *see also individual locations*

J

Jazz Fest 27
John F Kennedy Hyannis Museum 113
John F Kennedy National Historic Site 106
John F Kennedy Presidential Library & Museum 106

K

kayaking 123, 185
Kennedy, John F 106, 113, 346
Kent Falls State Park 91
King, Martin Luther 345-6

L

La Brea Tar Pits 276
Lake Waramaug 91
Lake Willoughby 90
Las Vegas 14, 235-45, **237**
  travel to/from 236, 245
  travel within 245
legal matters 362-3
lesbian travelers 361
  GLBT History Museum 308-9
  Los Angeles 283
  San Francisco 310
Library of Congress 137, 138
lighthouses 122, 314
Lincoln Center 65
literature 357

Lollapalooza 28
Los Angeles 16, 261-87, **263**, **275**, **278**
  children, travel with 276
  itineraries 263, 272-3, **272**
  travel to/from 262, 286
  travel within 286
Lowell Observatory 258

M

magazines 363
Magic Kingdom 205
Mardi Gras 26, 216-19
marijuana 363
Marin County 314
Maritime National Historical Park 305
markets
  New Orleans 225
  New York City 63, 72
  San Francisco 300-1
  Washington, DC 138, 149
Martha's Vineyard 117-18
Massachusetts 91
measures 363
medical services 361-2
Miami 10, 179-99, **181**, **192**
  children, travel with 195
  itineraries 188-9, **188**
  travel to/from 180, 199
  travel within 199
Millennium Park 158-9, 162
mobile phones 365
MoMA PS1 49
money 33, 360, 363-4
money changers 364
monkeys 195
monuments & statues
  Bunker Hill Monument 97, 99
  Lincoln Memorial 131
  Martin Luther King Jr Memorial 133
  National WWII Memorial 133

monuments & statues
continued
Vietnam Veterans
Memorial 133
Washington Monument 131
Monument Valley 257
motorcycle travel 371-3
Mount Vernon 150
movie studios 267
Mt Greylock State Reservation
91
Mt Mansfield 90
Mt Washington 121
Mt Washington Valley 120-1
Muir Woods National
Monument 314
mule deer 253
mule rides 253
Muscle Beach 272
Museum of Modern Art
(MoMA) 48-9
museums 25, *see also* art
galleries & museums
American Museum of Natural
History 65
Beat Museum 304-5
Boston Tea Party Ships &
Museum 101
California Academy of
Sciences 309
California Science
Center 275-6
Chicago Children's
Museum 170
Chicago History Museum 169
Children's Creativity
Museum 305
de Young Museum 309
Ernest Hemingway
Museum 169
Exploratorium 304
Field Museum of Natural
History 165
Getty Center 276-7

GLBT History Museum 308-9
Grammy Museum 274
Isabella Stewart Gardner
Museum 105
Japanese American National
Museum 274
John F Kennedy Hyannis
Museum 113
John F Kennedy Presidential
Library & Museum 106
La Plaza de Cultura y
Artes 274
Louisiana Children's
Museum 223
Lowe Art Museum 196
Lower East Side Tenement
Museum 62
Miami Children's Museum 195
Mob Museum 240
Museum of Science &
Industry 173
National Air & Space
Museum 131
National Atomic Testing
Museum 240
National Museum of
African American History &
Culture 132
National Museum of American
History 132
National Museum of Natural
History 132
National Museum of the
American Indian 133
National September 11
Memorial Museum 58
National WWII Museum 225-6
Natural History Museum of
Los Angeles 275
Newseum 141
Page Museum & La Brea Tar
Pits 276
Shelburne Museum 118
Smithsonian Institution 141
United States Holocaust
Memorial Museum 133

Vizcaya Museum &
Gardens 195
Wolfsonian-FIU 193
music 29, 107, 355-6
festivals 27, 28

N

Nantucket 115-16
Nascar 354
National Archives 140
National Cherry Blossom
Festival 26
National Mall 130-5, **134-5**
national parks, *see also* parks
& gardens
Acadia National Park 92-5
Everglades National Park
182-5
Grand Canyon National Park
15, 247-59, **249**
Yosemite National Park 17,
321-33, **323**
natural disasters 365
New England 8, 87-125, **89**
travel to/from 88
New Hampshire 120-1
New Orleans 13, 213-33, **215**,
224
children, travel with 223
travel to/from 214
newspapers 363
New York City 6, 35-85, **36**,
60-1, **66-7**, **74**, **85**
itineraries 37, 54-5, 56-7,
54, **56**
travel to/from 84
travel within 84
New York Film Festival 28
nightlife 25
Nixon, Richard 346
notable buildings
Binoculars Building 273
California Academy of
Sciences 309

Chicago Cultural Center 164
de Young Museum 309
Ford's Theatre 140-1
Frank Lloyd Wright Home &
    Studio 169
Guggenheim Museum 68
Oak Park 169
Pérez Art Museum Miami 193
Pritzker Pavilion 159
Robie House 173
Sewell-Belmont House 139
Vizcaya Museum & Gardens
    195
Walt Disney Concert Hall 274
Willis Tower 164

O

Oak Park 169
Obama, Barack 347
observatories
    360° Chicago 168
    Griffith Observatory 270
    Lowell Observatory 258
    One World Observatory 58
opening hours 33, 364
Orange County 286
Orlando 201-11, **203**
    travel to/from 202

P

parks & gardens 25, see also
    national parks
    Barataria Preserve 229
    Boston Common 98, 100
    Central Park 38-43, **42-3**
    City Park 227
    Crescent Park 225
    Crissy Field 305
    Dumbarton Oaks 141
    Ernest Coe Visitor
        Center 184-5
    Exposition Park 274-5
    Flamingo Visitor Center 185
    Golden Gate Park 309

Griffith Park 268-9
Jean Lafitte National
    Historical Park &
    Preserve 229
Lincoln Park 168-9
Maggie Daley Park 164
Máximo Gómez Park 194
Millennium Park 158-9, 162
Minute Man National Historic
    Park 105
Monument Valley Navajo
    Tribal Park 257
Public Garden 104
Rincon Park 301
Shark Valley 185
Vizcaya Museum &
    Gardens 195
Parks, Rosa 345
passports 367-8, 369
Paul, Alice 139
Paul Revere House 97, 99
pay phones 366
performing arts 73
performing arts venues
    Adrienne Arsht Center for the
        Performing Arts 196
    Kennedy Center 146
    Lincoln Center 65
    Pritzker Pavilion 159
phone cards 366
planetariums 65, 165, 270
planning 32-3, 37
    calendar of events 26-8
    children, travel with 30-1
    itineraries 2-3, 18-23
    travel seasons 32
Portland (Maine) 121-4
Pritzker Pavilion 159
Provincetown 113-15
public holidays 364
public transportation 373

Q

Queens 64

R

radio 363
rafting 254
Reagan, Ronald 346
Revere, Paul 97
road rules 372
rock climbing 330-1, 332
Rockefeller Center 54, 64
Route 66 257

S

safety 365
sailing 119
Salem 112
same-sex marriages 336
San Francisco 17, 289-319, **291**,
    306-7, **319**
    children, travel with 305
    itineraries 291
    travel to/from 290, 318
    travel within 318
Santa Monica 264-5, 277
Santa Monica Pier 264-5
Sausalito 314
senior travelers 360
September 11 58
sequoia trees 333
skating 277
Smithsonian Institution 141
smoking 366
Sonoma Valley 318
sports 83, 352-4
sports venues 354
    Fenway Park 107
    Nationals Park 146
    Wrigley Field 169
Squantz Pond 91
St Charles Avenue Streetcar
    220-1
Statue of Liberty 44-5
statues, see monuments &
    statues
subway 373

Supreme Court 137, 139
surfing 277, 286
swimming 113, 195, 277

T

taxes 364
taxis 373
TCL Chinese Theatre 266
telephone services 365-6
television 356
terrorism 347
Thanksgiving 28
theaters 52-3, 266, 271, *see also* performing arts veues
theme parks, *see* amuseument parks
The Strip 238-9
time 366
Times Square 63-4
tourist information 366
tours 373, *see also* boat tours, walking tours
  Boston 106
  celebrity-spotting 280
  Chicago 170
  Freedom Trail 97, 106
  Grand Canyon National Park 253
  New Orleans 228
  New York City 69
  San Francisco 309-10
  Washington, DC 145
  wildlife watching 114
  Yosemite National Park 332
train journeys 375
  Conway Scenic Railroad 120
  Griffith Park Southern Railroad 271
  Mt Washington Cog Railway 121
train travel 373, 374-5
travel to/from USA 369
travel within USA 369-75

traveler's checks 364
Tribeca Film Festival 36
Tuolumne Meadows 331
TV 363

U

Universal Orlando Resort 208
USS Constitution 99

V

vacations 364
vegan travelers 351
vegetarian travelers 351
vehicle rental 372
Venice Beach 272-3
Venice Boardwalk 272
Vermont 90, 118-20
Village Halloween Parade 36
Visa Waiver Program 368
visas 367-8
visual arts 357
volunteering 368
voodoo 226

W

walking tours
  Chicago 162-3, **162**
  Freedom Trail 98-9, **98**
  Miami 188-9, **188**
  New York City 54-7, **54**, **56**
  Venice Beach 272-3, **272**
  Washington, DC 138-9, **139**
Walt Disney Concert Hall 274
Walt Disney World 12, 201-11, **203**
  travel to/from 202
  travel within 207
Washington, DC 9, 127-53, **129**, **142-3**
  children, travel with 146
  itineraries 129, 138-9, **139**
  travel to/from 128, 153
  travel within 153

waterfalls 328-9
Wawona 333
weather 26-8, 32, 360
websites, *see* internet resources
weddings 244
weights 363
West Cornwall 91
whale-watching 114, 125
White House 140
wi-fi 362
wildlife-watching 331
  Everglades National Park 185
  Grand Canyon National Park 253
  Miami 195
  Monomoy National Wildlife Refuge 113
wine 351
wineries 318
Wizarding World of Harry Potter 209
women travelers 368
WWII 344-5

Y

Yosemite National Park 17, 321-33, **323**
  travel to/from 322
Yosemite Valley 330
Yosemite Valley Waterfalls 328-9
Yosemite Village 331-3

Z

ziplining 241
zoos
  Audubon Zoological Gardens 227
  Disney's Animal Kingdom 204-5
  Lincoln Park Zoo 169
  Miami 195
  National Zoo (Washington, DC) 144